Lloyd J. Ogilvie General Editor

THE PREACHER'S COMMENTARY

ACTS

Lloyd J. Ogilvie

THOMAS NELSON PUBLISHERS
Nashville

THE PREACHER'S COMMENTARY SERIES, Volume 28: *Acts.* Copyright ©
1983 by Word, Inc.

Published in Nashville, Tennessee, by Thomas Nelson, Inc.

Library of Congress Cataloging In Publication Data

The preacher's commentary (originally The communicator's commentary)

    Includes bibliographical references.
    Contents: v. 28. Acts/Lloyd J. Ogilvie
    I. Ogilvie, Lloyd John. II. Lloyd J. Ogilivie.
BS2341.2.C65   225.7'7   81–71764
ISBN 0-7852-4811-0   AACR2

Printed in the United States of America
  3 4 5 6 — 08 07 06

CONTENTS

EDITOR'S PREFACE

God has called all of His people to be communicators. Everyone who is in Christ is called into ministry. As ministers of "the manifold grace of God," all of us—clergy and laity—are commissioned with the challenge to communicate our faith to individuals and groups, classes and congregations.

The Bible, God's Word, is the objective basis of the truth of His love and power that we seek to communicate. In response to the urgent, expressed needs of pastors, teachers, Bible study leaders, church school teachers, small group enablers, and individual Christians, the Preacher's Commentary is offered as a penetrating search of the Scriptures to enable vital personal and practical communication of the abundant life.

Many current commentaries and Bible study guides provide only some aspects of a communicator's needs. Some offer in-depth scholarship but no application to daily life. Others are so popular in approach that biblical roots are left unexplained. Few offer compelling illustrations that open windows for the reader to see the exciting application for today's struggles. And most of all, seldom have the expositors given the valuable outlines of passages so needed to help the preacher or teacher in his or her busy life to prepare for communicating the Word to congregations or classes.

This Preacher's Commentary series brings all of these elements together. The authors are scholar-preachers and teachers outstanding in their ability to make the Scriptures come alive for individuals and groups. They are noted for bringing together excellence in biblical scholarship, knowledge of the original Greek and Hebrew, sensitivity to people's needs, vivid illustrative material from biblical, classical, and contemporary sources, and lucid communication by the use of clear outlines of thought. Each has been selected to contribute to this series because of his Spirit-empowered ability to help people live in the skins of biblical characters and provide a "you-are-there" intensity to the drama of

5

events of the Bible which have so much to say about our relationships and responsibilities today.

The design for the Preacher's Commentary gives the reader an overall outline of each book of the Bible. Following the introduction, which reveals the author's approach and salient background on the book, each chapter of the commentary provides the Scripture to be exposited. The New King James Bible has been chosen for the Preacher's Commentary because it combines with integrity the beauty of language, underlying Greek textual basis, and thought-flow of the 1611 King James Version, while replacing obsolete verb forms and other archaisms with their everyday contemporary counterparts for greater readability. Reverence for God is preserved in the capitalization of all pronouns referring to the Father, Son, or Holy Spirit. Readers who are more comfortable with another translation can readily find the parallel passage by means of the chapter and verse reference at the end of each passage being exposited. The paragraphs of exposition combine fresh insights to the Scripture, application, rich illustrative material, and innovative ways of utilizing the vibrant truth for his or her own life and for the challenge of communicating it with vigor and vitality.

It has been gratifying to me as Editor of this series to receive enthusiastic progress reports from each contributor. As they worked, all were gripped with new truths from the Scripture—God-given insights into passages, previously not written in the literature of biblical explanation. A prime objective of this series is for each user to find the same awareness: that God speaks with newness through the Scriptures when we approach them with a ready mind and a willingness to communicate what He has given; that God delights to give communicators of His Word "I-never-saw-that-in-that-verse-before" intellectual insights so that our listeners and readers can have "I-never-realized-all-that-was-in-that-verse" spiritual experiences.

The thrust of the commentary series unequivocally affirms that God speaks through the Scriptures today to engender faith, enable adventuresome living of the abundant life, and establish the basis of obedient discipleship. The Bible, the unique Word of God, is unlimited in its resource for Christians in communicating our hope to others. It is our weapon in the battle for truth, the guide for ministry, and the irresistible force for introducing others to God. In the New Testament we meet the divine Lord and Savior whom we seek to communicate to others. What He said and did as God with us has been faithfully recorded under the inspiration of the Spirit of God. The cosmic implications of the Gospels are lived out in Acts and spelled out in the Epistles. They have stood the test of time because the eternal Communicator, God Himself, communicates through them to those who would be communicators of grace. His essential nature is exposed, the plan of salvation is explained, and the gospel for all of life, now and for eternity is proclaimed.

A biblically rooted communication of the gospel holds in unity and oneness what divergent movements have wrought asunder. This commentary series courageously presents personal faith, caring for individuals, and social responsibility as essential, inseparable dimensions of biblical Christianity. It seeks to present the quadrilateral gospel in its fullness which calls us to unreserved commitment to Christ, unrestricted self-esteem in His grace, unqualified love for others in personal evangelism, and undying efforts to work for justice and righteousness in a sick and suffering world.

A growing renaissance in the church today is being led by clergy and laity who are biblically rooted, Christ-centered, and Holy Spirit-empowered. They have dared to listen to people's most urgent questions and deepest needs and then to God as He speaks through the Bible. Biblical preaching is the secret of growing churches. Bible study classes and small groups are equipping the laity for ministry in the world. Dynamic Christians are finding that daily study of God's Word allows the Spirit to do in them what He wishes to communicate through them to others. These days are the most exciting time since Pentecost. The Preacher's Commentary is offered to be a primary resource of new life for this renaissance.

—LLOYD J. OGILVIE

Publisher's Note

Acts, a pivotal volume in the *Preacher's Commentary* series, was written by Lloyd Ogilvie, during his tenure as Senior Pastor of the First Presbyterian Church of Hollywood, California—a church noted for more than half a century as a center for biblical preaching and exposition.

Through his preaching and his books, Lloyd Ogilvie has firmly established and distinguished himself as a bold and lucid interpreter and communicator of biblical truth. From 1995 to 2003 he served as chaplain of the U.S. Senate. Now he is back in Southern California, continuing to pursue his lifelong calling of speaking, teaching, and writing.

Because of his long history of study and work on the Book of Acts, the one request we, the Publishers, made during the planning stages for the commentary was that Lloyd Ogilvie, in addition to his duties as General Editor, do the writing on this particular volume. Through his masterful treatment, the pages of this volume mirror the beginnings of Christianity in an alive and vivid style. The reader is taken into the story, not as a spectator, but as an on-the-spot participant—drawn into the scenes with rare sensitivity. The drama powerfully unfolds from the return of the risen Christ in the Holy Spirit through the rapid-fire movement into the centers of influence and culture in Asia and parts of Europe.

Here is a superb combination of exegesis and contemporary application as we view the movement of the Holy Spirit in the lives of early Christians. Echoing the theme of the apostles and early church leaders, Lloyd Ogilvie urges that Christians of our time remain *open to being open* to all that God through the Holy Spirit has for us.

The detailed outline contained in this commentary will enable Bible students, teachers, and ministers in personal study and in teaching and preaching. And the scholarly and spiritual tone of the commentary itself under the skillful interpretation and illumination of Lloyd Ogilvie will speak with warmth and understanding to the hearts as well as the heads of readers. A careful study of the twenty-eight chapters of Acts will better enable us to live out a twenty-ninth chapter in our time.

INTRODUCTION

This commentary on Acts is written by a communicator for communicators. From start to finish it is meant to be a dialogue between us who share the high calling of communicating the Word of God through expository preaching and teaching. Thirty years of preparing biblical messages for congregations and classes has sharpened my perception of the needs of Christian communicators committed to excellence. Conversations with clergy and laity over the years have confirmed my understanding of what we need to help us in our preparation. What is written here is in response to those expressed needs.

Whenever we prepare to preach or teach we need a rich blend of inspiration, information, and application. We long for in-depth expository scholarship, vivid background material, incisive illustrations to spark our own creativity, and an author's own witness to enrich our own experience in preparation for our own communication. Too often we have to search for these qualities in a multiplicity of commentaries, word study books, theological works, and encyclopedias of the collected preaching and teaching of communicators of previous generations. Over the years, I have longed to read an expositor who talks to me as a communicator, sharing his insight and methods as he works his way through a book of Scripture. This longing gave birth to the idea for the format of this commentary on Acts. I have tried to take seriously what I have needed in my own preparation and at the same time talk over texts and passages of Acts with you as if we were studying together, seeking to help each other be at our maximum in the sermon or class for which we were preparing.

I have spent thirty years seeking to grow in being an effective communicator through preaching and teaching the Bible. A prolonged study retreat is spent each summer outlining the text, title, theme, and development of the sermons and lectures to be given in the following program year. The equivalent of two days' research and writing of a manuscript is spent in the final week before preaching and teaching any message. During those long hours of study I work with the verse or passage at hand in the original language, then read the works of admired and trusted expositors of the ages, and finally begin the rigorous search for illustrations from classical and contemporary literature. At last, I am ready to sit back and recall parables from life which have come out of my own experience of what I have observed or heard around me. Only then am I ready to outline and subsequently to write the message in long hand. The typing is a further revision and the memorization a final polishing. And because I believe the Lord is as much a source of power in preparation as in delivery, I depend on prayer to enable a companionship with Him through the whole process. "Lord, what do you want me to say? What is the thing you want to say to my people? Speak to me so I may speak!"

Apart from the sublime communion with the Lord, the arduous hours of preparation can be lonely. I long for expositors whom I read to tell me what a truth means to him or her. I quest for a sense of shared adventure with the authors I read, wishing they would combine with scholarship their own experience of a text or passage. In short, I want to be prepared as a person, not just as a preacher or teacher. I want something to happen to me so it can happen through me. Sensing you may have the same desire, I have tried to make this commentary a pilgrimage which we take together in our preparation to communicate the adventure of the Book of Acts.

One of my favorite quotes about Christian communication comes from Bishop Quayle, an American Methodist bishop. I found it in Paul Sangster's biography of his father, W. F. Sangster. What he said applies equally to preaching, teaching, or sharing our faith one to one with individuals. "Preaching is the art of making a sermon and delivering it. Why no, that is not preaching. Preaching is the art of making a preacher, and delivering that. Preaching is the outrush of soul in speech. Therefore the elemental business in preaching is not with preaching but with the preacher. It is no trouble to preach, but a vast trouble to construct a preacher. What then, in the light of this, is the task of a preacher? Mainly this, the amassing of a great soul so as to have something worthwhile to give—the sermon is the preacher up to date."

That is never more true than for a preacher or teacher who sets out to exposit the Book of Acts in a series of messages or classes. Acts is a biography of the Holy Spirit, the risen Christ, from the time immediately following the Resurrection through the birth and growth of the infant church. It is not a historical account of a one-time, never-to-be-repeated effluence of the Spirit, but a stirring benchmark of the irreducible maximum for Christianity in any age. What happened then, can and is happening today. Acts cannot be studied without the honest question, "Why is this power, vitality, excitement, and joy so seldom evident in our lives and churches today?" This commentary is written with the unquenchable conviction that we are living in the most exciting days since Pentecost, in which the Book of Acts is both our charter and challenge.

There is a great hunger in people today to receive the indwelling power of the Holy Spirit, experience His guidance, live in the resources of His gifts, and know the intellectual and physical resiliency He provides. But coupled with this desire for supernatural power is a confusion about who He is and how we can become riverbeds for the flow of His unlimited power. Acts provides the most creative vehicle for communicating the dynamic resources of the Holy Spirit.

A MASTER COMMUNICATOR TELLS THE STORY

The authorship of Acts, with rare exception, is attributed to Luke the physician and missionary companion of Paul. The reference to Theophilus as recipient of both the Gospel bearing Luke's name and Acts makes any discussion of the authorship of Acts inseparable from the authorship of the Gospel. It is obvious that the Gospel and Acts were written as a two-part treatise to a Greek official about the incarnate life and ministry of Jesus Christ and what He continued to do after the Resurrection. Careful study of the medical terms used in both the Gospel and Acts strongly suggest the authorship of a physician. As far as we know there was only one physician who was an intimate companion of Paul. The "we" and "us" references in Acts 16:10 and from 20:6 to the end of chapter 28 indicate that the same man wrote the rest of the personal pronouns throughout the rest of Acts. All ancient Greek manuscripts credit the Gospel to Luke in the title. It follows that the companion manuscript of Acts was also written by him. Early writers like Irenaeus, Clement of Alexandria, Tertullian, and others assert the Lukan authorship of the Gospel. The same style is undeniably evident in both the Gospel and Acts. Therefore, we accept the traditional view that Luke the physician was the author of Acts.

Luke was a master chronicler of the continuing ministry of the risen and glorified Christ in the power of the Holy Spirit. He communicates what he has to say by telling stories that reveal profound truth. The Acts of the Apostles could more accurately be entitled The Acts of the Holy Spirit. Acts is His story. Rather than giving us a theological dissertation on the Holy Spirit, Luke tells the exciting story of who He is and what He does. In this way we are irresistibly drawn into an unfolding drama about real people in whom the Holy Spirit took up residence. The birth and growth of the church, the new Israel and the new creation, is the story line of the dramatist's word portrait of the Lord's strategy for human history. With remarkable skill, we are invited to live in the skins of real people with hopes and hurts like ours, and to discover with them the adventure of truly abundant living.

Teaching and preaching Acts gives us as communicators an opportunity to learn how to communicate the power of life in the Spirit. Luke shows us how to do this by telling the stories of real people. Everyone enjoys a gripping story. It provides the vehicle to expose truth in an enjoyable way. A study of Acts is a basic course in communication. I will comment on that throughout our exposition.

DATE AND SOURCES OF ACTS

The abrupt ending of Acts indicates that Luke probably wrote it during the first of two of Paul's imprisonments in Rome. I date that around A.D. 63. If Luke had written later, Acts would likely have included accounts of Paul's missionary activity after his release from prison in Rome and his second arrest, imprisonment, and death.

Major portions of Acts from the time Luke joined Paul at Troas were written from Luke's firsthand observations. Chapters 8 to 28 indicate the personal records and reminiscences of Paul himself. The first seven chapters of Acts draw mainly on the experience and memory of Peter. Paul's contact with Peter in Jerusalem and Antioch would have supplied these accounts. Barnabas, Paul's companion in the first missionary journey, would have been a reliable source of information. In addition many scholars attest to the existence of a written document giving the exact details of Pentecost and the early stages in the growth of the church. The vivid detail of what happened reads as if Luke had access to a carefully written document chronicling the events. So Luke, an accurate historian, careful physician, and firsthand witness, combined what he had experienced, plus Paul's account, Barnabas's and Peter's records, oral tradition, and under the direct inspiration of the Holy Spirit, wrote Acts. His literary skill is evident, and his personal conviction and experience are undeniable.

ACTS IN PREACHING AND TEACHING

I have divided Acts into sections to provide an outline of a series of messages or teaching themes. This is so that you can utilize the exposition, research, and illustrative application in your own development of a series of sermons or classes on Acts. For the communicator who wishes to select one passage from Acts for a separate presentation, it is my hope that each chapter stands on its own. Those who wish to do a prolonged series will find that the twenty-one chapters will guide a comprehensive study of Acts. Preaching or teaching through Acts not only provides us with an opportunity to focus on the Holy Spirit, but also gives us historical context to appreciate more fully the other books of the New Testament. You will be given the historical background and circumstances of the writing of many of the Pauline Epistles.

THE ADVENTURE AHEAD OF US

This is not a commentary on others' commentaries. References to other scholars will be utilized not to support an interpretation, but to clarify further the meaning of the text. My prayer is that your own experience of the Holy Spirit will be deepened and that you will discover the delight of being part of an authentic renewal with your listeners. They are longing to live beyond the limitations of human wisdom and strength.

Jesus promised, "Most assuredly, I say to you, he who believes in Me, the works that I do he will do also; and greater works than these he will do because I go to My Father" (John 14:12). But He came back! After the Ascension and glorification, He returned in the Holy Spirit to make the promise a reality in and through His disciples. He continued His ministry and continues in us today. That's the breathlessly moving story Luke has to tell. It is the most important message you and I are privileged to communicate. Acts is happening today and we have been elected to be part of the new chapter being written in our time.

I want to express my gratitude to my assistant, Jeri Gonzalez, for her typing of the manuscript for publication and for her enthusiasm for this effort to communicate the power of the Holy Spirit for our time.

—LLOYD J. OGILVIE

An Outline of Acts

CHAPTER ONE—BETWEEN THE LIGHTNING AND THE THUNDER

ACTS 1:1–3

Scripture Outline

Theophilus and Us (1:1)

Whom Do You Expect? (1:2)

The Strategy of the Holy Spirit (1:3)

When I was a boy in the Middle West, the summer months were punctuated by thunderstorms. I was fascinated by the amount of time which elapsed between the lightning and the thunder. My friends and I would count the seconds between the brilliant flashes of light which pierced the gray sky and the turbulent rumble of the thunder caused by the heating and expansion of the air along the line of the lightning flash. We would argue as lads about which we liked best—the lightning or the thunder. I supported a case for thunder without lightning. One day my father overheard us. "Son," he said, "you can't have the thunder without the lightning."

The first chapter of Acts is the account of what happened between the lightning of the Incarnation of Christ and the thunder of Pentecost. The two cannot be separated. The birth, life, ministry, message, death, Resurrection, Ascension, and the return of the Lord in the infilling, infusing power of the Holy Spirit are all part of the cosmic atonement and the birth of the new Israel, the church. What took place during the fifty-day interval between the Passover events of Crucifixion, Resurrection, and the empowering of Pentecost is as critical for us as it was for the disciples and followers of Jesus. What He said and did during that crucial period solidified what had been, and raised expectation for what was to come. The same preparation for power must happen in us. We need to understand who the Holy Spirit is, what we can expect when He takes up residence in our minds and hearts, and what we can do to open the riverbed of our personalities for His flow.

THEOPHILUS AND US

1:1 The former account I made, O Theophilus, of all that Jesus began both to do and teach,

—Acts 1:1

The first three verses of chapter 1 of Acts give us the prologue. Luke states his purpose and establishes his central theme. Acts is a continuation of an account of Jesus' life from birth to the Ascension. Luke and Acts overlap and Acts, chapter 1, is like a recapitulation of the concluding verses of the Gospel account, but with greater detail and insight. The story line is established.

The key word is *"began."* The *"former account,"* the Gospel of Luke, is the compelling story of the Incarnation. *"All that Jesus began both to do and teach"*: that puts the three years of Jesus' ministry and passion into the perspective of the first act of an unfolding drama. It also puts us into the center of the stage with our Lord. We can know Him with greater intimacy than the disciples did during the three years of His ministry. What He began, He continues. That's good news to Theophilus . . . and to us! Immanuel, God with us, of the Gospel of Luke is Immanuel, God with us still, of the Book of Acts.

Theophilus means God-lover or God-beloved. In the salutation of Luke's Gospel, he is referred to as "most excellent Theophilus," indicating that he was a personage of high rank in government. The fact that Luke drops the title of honor in the opening of Acts may indicate a growth of friendship during the interval between the first and second letters. Luke's purpose in writing both letters is stated clearly in Luke 1:3–4 and gives us a clue to Theophilus and why Luke wanted to give him this account: "It seemed good to me also, having had perfect understanding of all things from the very first, to write to you an orderly account, most excellent Theophilus, that you may know the certainty of those things in which you have been instructed." The Greek word for "instructed" is *katēchēthēs,* meaning to sound down, to instruct. The official was a catechumen, one being instructed. The Revised Standard Version translates the word "informed." Some scholars suggest that Theophilus was an official of government who had been informed of the political dangers of Christianity and needed Luke's intelligence about the true nature of the facts. That's to miss the impact of Luke-Acts as dynamic teaching for a new Christian who needed sound instruction in the faith. The style of Luke-Acts is not an argument against false information, but forceful teaching to a receptive learner. Luke wanted Theophilus to understand the full story of what Jesus began to do and teach, as well as what He was continuing to do. He desired this "lover of God" to experience the fullness of what God in Christ had done and could do in his life. The same is true for us.

This puts into perspective our efforts to communicate what the Lord has to say through our exposition of Acts in teaching or preaching today. We stand with Luke as ready learners of his communication technique under the guidance of the Holy Spirit. He has an exciting story to tell. It is not only the account of what Jesus continued to do, but also what He is continuing to do in Luke himself. Luke tells each event with the personal intensity of reliving it in his own mind and heart. One of the most important truths I have discovered about communicating the gospel is that nothing can happen through us which is not happening to us in a fresh way. The Lord has taught me to live in a passage of Scripture for a long time before I seek to communicate its meaning to any group or congregation. That makes possible a "this is what it means to me—I can't wait to share it with you" impact.

In a time of study in Edinburgh, Scotland, I had the privilege of prolonged times with two men who have taught me the adventure of living in a passage. Both James S. Stewart and Thomas F. Torrance are brilliant communicators. When I was a student years ago, both had a strong impact on my life and have been personal friends through the years. Dr. Stewart is one of the great preachers of our time, and Dr. Torrance one of the most profound theological thinkers today. Each time I have visited with these men, they have pressed me on in the quest for excellence in communicating. I am always impressed by their enthusiasm over some portion of Scripture that has been the focus of their recent study. They are gripped by it personally. As they talk about it, I am caught up in their excitement about the truth they've discovered afresh. Even the discussion of a Greek verb or a theological concept is shared with verve and gusto for what it means to them and to the church today. The result is that I am blessed spiritually and intellectually as a person.

The people with whom we communicate the gospel have every right to expect the same thing from us. And they will, if we put ourselves into each passage and allow the truth to "get at us" so that we can get through to people about its essential meaning and its application to life now.

But also, here at the beginning of Acts, we are called to live in the skin of Theophilus. The best way to do that is to allow the Holy Spirit to speak through Luke's picturesque pen. We too are catechumen, learners, all of our lives. And however many times we go through Acts, the beloved physician catechizes us in the power of the Holy Spirit for today. I have read Acts hundreds of times in my own devotional time, studied it in the Greek, and written and spoken about it for twenty years, but still feel I have only begun to grasp what it means to my life as a contemporary Theophilus, one both beloved by God and a lover of God.

That enables profound empathy when I want to share the treasure of Acts with the Theophiluses with whom I am given the opportunity to share. So much of the church today is where Theophilus was when he was the first to read the stirring account of Acts. We have been instructed in the things Jesus did, but know far too little about what He continues to do today as indwelling Spirit and engendering power. The Theophiluses of our time are more ready and open than we realize. Our challenge is to help people know both halves of their "rebirthright"—abiding in Christ and Christ abiding in them. The task of presenting Christ to people who don't know Him is to present both so they don't have to spend years of their Christian lives in defeating self-effort without power. And since so few Christians seem to know and claim the joy of a Spirit-filled life, we are called to understand and experience it to the fullest so that we can share the open secret with them. There is no more impelling way than through an exposition of Acts. And the Spirit has made them ready!

We can be sure of several things about the Theophiluses with whom we communicate today. They would not be interested or responsive to what Jesus did and continues to do if His Spirit had not first been at work in them. People are not naturally drawn to the gospel until the Spirit creates the desire and draws them. Our wills are in bondage to willful self-centeredness until they are liberated by the Spirit. As communicators, we get into the strenuous bind of feeling we have to convince and cajole people into believing or receiving the power of the Spirit. Success or failure in helping people is not decided only by our methods or techniques of communication. When there is a positive response from an individual with whom we are counseling or class we are teaching or a great throng to which we are preaching, it is because the Holy Spirit has set people free to hear and to want to accept truth we've presented. When we are effective, all the glory goes to Him!

We are living in a time when the Spirit is releasing Theophiluses to respond in great numbers. He is doing His miraculous work in their minds, emotions, and wills—especially their wills. Our inherited, fallen nature includes a will that has been diverted from its intended function of being the servant of thought. The will was given to us to be the implementer of our thoughts. Instead it has become the impediment. What was meant to be a servant becomes the master. The thought that we can run our own lives has triggered our wills imperiously to accomplish our independence from God or anyone else. Often, the will takes more than the assignment from the mind; it takes charge of thought and actually begins to control what we are able to think. It becomes a fullback without a coach and tries to call the plays. The mess we get into is the willful determination to be in charge. The will becomes so strong it controls our capacity to hear about God's love and respond. The condition is called sin.

But the exciting Good News is that Jesus Christ came into the world to be and do something to liberate us from that condition. He was the mediator and reconciling grace of God. He revealed both God and what we were meant to be. As the God-man in history in whom divine and human natures blended perfectly, He was completely obedient in the midst of disobedience. "Thy will be done" was His constant prayer and purpose. And then He went to the Cross, not just because He loved people, but because He knew that in His death the sin of willfulness would be forgiven *and* healed. As Jesus of Nazareth, He could expose what willing God's will was intended to be; but it was as the crucified Savior that He atoned for what willfulness had created in people's minds. Through His death, the healing power of God is released to liberate us from the confused condition of thinking that we are in charge of our lives.

Now as Christ *continues* His ministry, He invades our belligerent wills and creates a willingness to be made willing to consider the truth of His love for us. Through His gift, the will allows the possibility for our minds to entertain the thought of our great need for love and forgiveness. That usually happens through some crisis of difficulty, or challenge of an opportunity we cannot handle. The thought that we are loved and that the Lord wants to help us, becomes a comfort, growing into a dominant thought, more powerful than the will to resist. As this Spirit of the Lord continues to impinge on our consciousness, we become increasingly open to use our hearing for listening to what He has to say through people's communication about Him. And when the Bible, the Word of God, is the basis of what they share, what He inspired to be written penetrates to the core of our minds and heals the cleavage of thought and will. We have been made capable of hearing the Good News of the gospel through a gracious gift of the Spirit. We think love and feel loved. And we are ready for that to be congealed into the greatest miracle of life: Our wills become the activating agent of implementing a response of love and commitment of our lives. Theophilus is on the way! And the Lord did it.

So, as communicators, we can present what Christ means to us and has done to and through us with the sure confidence that He is actively preparing the recipients, creating a desire, and impacting our words about His Word in their lives. All of these things He does so that what He did in the Incarnation and in His continuing ministry in the Holy Spirit will be what He continues to do today. We need to know Whom we can expect to prepare us for power and then release it.

WHOM DO YOU EXPECT?

² until the day in which He was taken up, after He through the Holy Spirit had given commandments to the apostles whom He had chosen,

—*Acts 1:2*

The major thing that Jesus did between the lightning of the Incarnation and the thunder of Pentecost was to be sure His disciples understood how He would continue His ministry with them. Luke tells us *"He through the Holy Spirit had given commandments."* This second verse can be rendered that Jesus taught His disciples about, or concerning, the Holy Spirit. He wanted them to know that after His Ascension He would be back. The Holy Spirit would be His continuing, present-tense ministry among them. They needed to know that the same Lord who had lived and died and been raised up for them would be the source of their power to live the abundant life He had promised them. He had told them that they would never be alone. He would come to them and never leave them.

I believe that the same things He taught them in the last days of His ministry before the Crucifixion were the themes on which

He dwelt before the Ascension. He had promised that He would make His home in them, that they were to abide in Him and He would abide in them, and whatever they asked in His name would be released for their continuing discipleship. The crucial thing was that He had revealed and personified the character and attributes of the Spirit for them. But now their relationship with Him would be radically different. He would not only be with them, but He would live *in* them! The power they would receive would not be something but Someone: Himself. The eternal Word through whom God created the universe (John 1:1), who had dwelt among them and whom they had beheld in glory full of grace and truth (John 1:14), would be in them.

And that is He Whom we can expect! Not a separate scepter, but Immanuel, God with us. Christianity is a relationship with the living Christ. Over and over again, throughout His ministry, Jesus boldly used the powerful "I AM" to declare who He was. The same words spoken to Moses at the burning bush were used twenty-three times by the Master: I am the bread of life, the light of the world, the resurrection and the life, and all the rest. I AM in Hebrew stands for the name of God, YHWH, derived from the verb *hāyāh,* "to be." In Exodus 3:14 the Hebrew verb is in the future tense meaning, "I will be who I will be." When that verse was translated into the Greek version of the Old Testament, called the Septuagint, the present tense is used. *Égō eimí,* I AM. The verb is used when Jesus said, "Most assuredly, I say to you, before Abraham was, I AM" (John 8:58). There was never any lack of clarity or directness. Jesus said, "I and My Father are one" (John 10:30). And He promised, "Behold, I am with you always" (Matt. 28:20). And He has been faithful to His word.

The reason it is so important to understand Whom Jesus teaches us we can expect in our needs is that there is great lack of clarity about the Holy Spirit today. Some of the people who believe the most in the Holy Spirit's power often end up being a cause of great confusion about Him. They speak of the Holy Spirit with esoteric exclusivism as if they have something (or Someone) different from or in addition to Christ. Others, especially Christians who are coming alive to the reality and availability of the Spirit, refer to It, and not always with a capital I.

My wife and I are part of a fellowship group which meets together regularly to study the Bible, pray, and support each other in the adventure of contemporary discipleship. When we went through Acts, many in the group had a difficult time at first referring to the Holy Spirit with the pronouns "Him" and "His." The often-repeated reminder to each other was, "Mind your pronouns!" And "mind" picked up the implication of more than "watch out for"; the admonition became a challenge to think clearly. The Holy Spirit is not an "it" separated from Him, the living Christ.

The early church alternatively used the designations "Spirit of Jesus," "Holy Spirit," "the Lord." Paul's benediction included the statement of his faith: the love of God, the grace of the Lord Jesus, and the communion of the Holy Spirit. Some trinitarian formulations in history have ended up with three Gods rather than an awe- and wonder-filled affirmation of how the one God is our Father whom we know because of what He revealed of His forgiving, loving heart in Christ, and whose presence we experience through His Spirit with us. He is sovereign Lord of all creation, redeeming Savior in the Incarnation, and indwelling power for our transformation. "God was in Christ reconciling the world to Himself" (2 Cor. 5:19) is Paul's clarification of the Atonement. His statement in Romans 8 reveals God's continuing reconciliation in us. "But you are not in the flesh but in the Spirit, if indeed the Spirit of God dwells in you. Now if anyone does not have the Spirit of Christ, he is not His. And if Christ is in you, the body is dead because of sin, but the Spirit is life because of righteousness. But if the Spirit of Him who raised Jesus from the dead dwells in you, He who raised Christ from the dead will also give life to your mortal bodies through His Spirit who dwells in you" (Rom. 8:9–11).

Three different Spirits? No. The eternal Spirit who brooded over the waters at creation broods over the turbulent sea in our hearts and produces a new creation. His Spirit convinces us of His unmerited favor toward us, of His love in the Cross, and of His power to raise us out of the grave of our old selves. God's divine Logos, His Word, is Christ, His active Spirit in creation and recreation. And so we can say that the Holy Spirit is none other than the eternal Christ, the immanent and intimate approach to us in the present tense. And He is the sublime communicator from whom all our communication of Him flows. He excavates a place for Himself in us, shows us how empty we are, communicates His limitless acceptance through His Cross, gives us the gift of faith to respond, and then fills our emptiness with Himself.

Our own in-depth experience of the Book of Acts is dependent on that kind of clarity. And so is our communication of Acts' message to others. Then we can focus our exposition in the sublime purpose expressed by Paul when he told of his reason for wanting to visit the Christians at Rome: "But I know that when I come to you, I shall come in the fullness of the blessing of the gospel of Christ" (Rom. 15:29). Nothing is left out. He would bring them Christ and His gospel for all of life's exigencies. The blessing would be the offer of abundant life now and eternal life forever. But the apostle would come in the fullness—the fullness of the living, reigning Christ: "For in Him dwells all the fullness of the Godhead bodily" (Col. 2:9). That's what we have to share to fill the emptiness of people today! John Henry Jowett was on the mark: "We get no deeper into Christ than we allow Him to get into us."

THE STRATEGY OF THE HOLY SPIRIT

[3] to whom He also presented Himself alive after His suffering by many infallible proofs, being seen by them during forty days and speaking of the things pertaining to the kingdom of God.

—*Acts 1:3*

The power Jesus Christ offers us in His Spirit is a surging, rushing, relentless river of new life. The riverbed in history that directs the flow is the strategy of the kingdom of God. The risen Christ coupled His teaching about the kingdom with His promise to return in power. It is not surprising that He continued to teach what had been the central focus of His life, message, and ministry. He began His ministry declaring that the kingdom was at hand. The establishment of it in people's minds and hearts was His daily purpose. For Jesus, the kingdom meant the absolute reign and rule of God. Being born again was declared the qualification of entering it. He made that abundantly clear to Nicodemus (John 3:1–8). Only by beginning life all over, with a complete surrender, could anyone experience the promise that the kingdom of the Lord's reign and rule would be within him or her. There was no need to look for it to come elsewhere until it began in the depths of a person's intellect, emotion, and will.

"The kingdom of God does not come with observation; nor will they say, 'See here!' or 'See there!' For indeed, the kingdom of God is within you" (Luke 17:20–21). Other versions translate the word "within" as "among" or "in the midst." The alternatives are possible in the Greek. Once the Lord reigns supreme in a person, a whole new agenda is given. Jesus said we were to seek first the kingdom and then everything else that we *need* would be provided. We offer the Lord no place if it is second place. The natural result of putting the

Lord at the center of our wills is that the kingdom's priorities become our goals. The kingdom is then both among and in the midst of us. It is first within, then between us and others, and then in all our affairs. Nothing can be omitted from its sweeping inclusiveness. It is the Lord's strategy for life.

So many Christians are involved in a furtive search for guidance. The kingdom gives us a sure guide for all of life. When we put the Lord's will first, people and their needs follow in close second. And when we begin to care deeply for people, our society looms before us as a focus of our obedience, and social justice becomes our third priority. Anything which dehumanizes or debilitates people is now our call to action. We can be sure that the Lord's guidance will begin with those top three items in His strategy.

Jesus wanted His disciples prepared for Pentecost. Unless they had the kingdom as the basis of their life plan, the power soon to come upon them would not be used for the purpose intended. He had to be sure that they understood what had been the theme of His parables and one of the essential reasons for His death and Resurrection. He had come to call a kingdom people—reconciled, forgiven people in whom He could live. Opening ourselves completely to the sovereign reign and rule of the Lord is an essential prelude to Pentecost.

Recently, a man in my church came to talk to me about how to receive the power of the Holy Spirit. He had observed the deep joy and contagious love in some people who openly identified its only source as the Spirit's indwelling, artesian power. He wanted what they had. I asked him if he knew the secret of their abundance. He did not. Knowing some of them, I knew that the floodgate was in their unreserved commitment to the Lord's first-place sovereignty in their lives. The man thought that spiritual power came through having the right "experiences." I affirmed that receiving the Spirit's power was preceded by a surrender of our wills and then all our relationships and responsibilities. We took an incisive inventory, including attitudes, prejudices, broken relationships, and then looked at his marriage, money, job, and plans for the future. He discovered that he was running his own life and not attempting anything big or adventuresome enough to need the Spirit's power. That shocked and stunned him. But the same Spirit for whom he longed was at work, and He helped him through the painful process. The first thing it required was checking those decisions about time and money which precluded any availability to consider doing the Lord's will. I am happy to say that his preparation for Pentecost worked. He did receive what he was looking for—and so much more. A freedom to live a daring life of adventure in the kingdom. The King's power is for the kingdom people!

The prologue of Acts has set before us Luke's purpose and plan. We have met Theophilus, to whom he wrote, and the Holy Spirit, about whom he wrote. It has given us an opportunity to think clearly about who the Holy Spirit is and the basic qualifications for being filled with His power. We have stressed that Acts is the account of what the risen Christ continued to do through His Spirit.

I have discovered that devoting a separate class session or sermon message to the prologue helps us as leaders to do for our listeners what Luke has done for us. The concept of Acts being Christ's continuing ministry through the Spirit must be clarified in order for people to appreciate what follows. And adequate time must be spent to clear the ground of tangled underbrush of confused thinking about the Holy Spirit. Once we have done this by living in Theophilus's skin, we can help our people realize that Pentecost, and the birth of the church, was the pivotal event for which the Incarnation, the Cross, and the Resurrection were preparation. That radical shift of focus does not diminish the Atonement and the empty tomb in the slightest, but instead, maximizes their meaning as part of one act of reconciliation and the birth of a new humanity.

A good way to be sure we have come to grips with that is to ask: if we had to forgo the celebration of Christmas, Good Friday, Easter, or Pentecost, which one would seem least crucial? Many Christians, because of the congregational and cultural emphasis of the first three, would probably say, "Well, if I must choose, I can do without Pentecost." Not so! Without Pentecost the other three would not be celebrated at all. Just as the resurrection vindicated Jesus' death on the Cross, so too His indwelling in His followers gave them the power to believe what He had done and tell the world about it. Actually, there could not have been Good Friday without the advent of Christ we celebrate at Christmas, and Good Friday would have been a meaningless martyrdom without the victory of Easter. But Pentecost engenders the gift of faith by which we can know that Christ's birth, death, and Resurrection were for us! Christ was not finished when He arose from the dead, or ascended to be glorified with reigning power. He came back to give the greatest gift of all—His own Spirit to live in us. With that awesome thought we press on to experience further preparation for Pentecost—this time in the skins of the disciples.

CHAPTER TWO—THE PURPOSE OF THE POWER OF PENTECOST

ACTS 1:4–26

Scripture Outline

I am always amazed at the ineptness as well as the impatience of the disciples during this period between the lightning and the thunder. Their attitudes make me a bit more patient with myself—and others.

Jesus' continued teaching of the kingdom and His return in the power of the Holy Spirit brings a strange reaction, *a non sequitur* with what has been promised. Actually, it exposed the disciples' inner agenda. They were looking back hoping for the reestablishment of a previous glory, while Jesus was looking forward to an even more glorious future. When the disciples blurted out their long suppressed question, it exposed where they were: *"Lord, will You at this time restore the kingdom to Israel?"*

It's good for any of us as communicators to know where our people are. Sometimes it is very disappointing, whether we are trying to share the faith with an individual or a group. But great communication is not thinking that because we say a truth, it is heard. Effectiveness is being secure enough to draw out people's perception of what we've said. Jesus was very astute at doing this. He always followed a truth with an action, and often with the secret that hearing and doing are inseparable in learning. His teaching on the kingdom and the power to live it confronted the disciples with just how dependent they were to be. They completely bypassed His promise that it was about to happen in them by the power of the Holy Spirit. Instead they exposed how little they had been listening—both during His ministry and now during this special time of preparation for Pentecost. Note the way they throw all responsibility back on the Lord, and show that they are reluctant to stride into His auspicious vision for the future. "Will *You* at this time *restore . . . ?*"

BUT WHEN, LORD, WHEN?

4 And being assembled together with them, He commanded them not to depart from Jerusalem, but to wait for the Promise of the Father, "which," He said, "you have heard from Me; 5 for John truly baptized with water, but you shall be baptized with the Holy Spirit not many days from now."
6 Therefore, when they had come together, they asked Him, saying, "Lord, will You at this time restore the kingdom to Israel?"
—Acts 1:4–6

That astounding response of lugubriousness about the future was based on a strong bedrock of presuppositions the disciples had labored with all through Jesus' ministry. Even the events of the Cross and Resurrection had been mortared into that foundation of their preconceived thinking.

Some background will help us understand. The idea of God being King of Israel goes back to the early history of the Exodus. He was considered greater than any pagan gods or rulers on earth. "The Lord shall reign forever and ever" (Ex. 15:18). The people of Israel were secure that this kingdom on earth was His chosen people. The Davidic kingdom was the closest they had come to God's kingdom in their history. When that kingdom was divided and when Israel eventually lost its political power and independence, the kingdom of God was envisioned in the future when they would return to that time of David's glory. That's why there were so many questions asked by Israel's leaders about whether Jesus was the true son of David. The Messiah was expected to return Israel to the grandeur of international power and political freedom. His peace was understood to be the result of victory over other nations and the supremacy of God's people as a theocracy. God reigning over Israel and Israel a military leader of the world were the vision and hope.

34

Judas was more open in his expression of his presuppositions than the other disciples. While James and John were arguing about who would sit on the Lord's right or left hand when as their Messiah He came into His full power, Judas—whom I believe careful study reveals to have been an insurrectionist—was planning to force the Master's hand. The reason he disclosed where Jesus was praying in Gethsemane was to get the Sanhedrin to mount a task force to try to arrest Him. I am persuaded that Judas's fondest hope and expectation was that Jesus would call down the legions of heaven and begin the revolt which would be the first phase of Israel's emergence again as a leader of the world.

His scheme didn't work. He had pinned his dreams on a very different kind of Messiah than the one Jesus came to be. The betrayer had not read the prophets very well. Jesus was Israel's suffering servant, not the insurrectionist's ploy. James and John wanted to know who would be greatest; Judas wanted political victory. But the other disciples were no clearer in their expectations. Jesus had explained the nature of His kingdom for three years. And yet they joined with the crowds in singing "Hosanna! Blessed is He who comes in the name of the LORD! Blessed is the kingdom of our father David that comes in the name of the Lord! Hosanna in the highest!" (Mark 11:9–10). The problem was that the idea of the highest they expected was far too low.

Now we can empathize more readily with the difference between Jesus' anticipation for the future and that of the disciples. Their question shows that even Jesus' teaching about His return in the power of the Spirit was twisted into the framework of their idea of the kingdom. They still were not on His agenda but wanting Him to meet theirs. And they were very religious about it!

A woman said to me, "I really wish we'd stick to the simple gospel rather than all this talk about commitment and our ministry as members!" I could hardly believe what I had heard. I felt led to reply with a question couched in a bit of humor. "Which pages of the Bible do you want to tear out?" She didn't catch the humor, nor the challenge. Her idea of the church was a place of comfort and reassurance. And beneath that was a conception of a cultural brand of Christianity which calls for little personal involvement or consecration. The frightening thing was that after we'd talked she thought she had convinced me of her nonbiblical point of view! Because I had taken time with her she became my loyal supporter, but she heard little more of what I was saying in expositions from the Scripture about surrendering our wills, inviting Christ to live in us, and becoming obedient disciples in sharing our faith and working for justice. Now she had one more grid over her carefully protected, strong-willed ego. She became a part of the cheering section, but was stuck on dead-center spiritually.

There was nothing to do but put her on the top of my prayer list. She was using her brand of religion to oppose God. She was verbally supportive but this was her best defense against hearing what her pastors were saying and the direction the elders of the Session were leading her church. It took a crisis in her personal life with her son to force her to realize that she was not able to communicate the "simple gospel" she had cherished so long. When pious phrases and simplistic, guilt-producing admonition didn't help, the Lord began to crack the hard shell around her mind. The difficulties finally led to her own commitment and a new life of both abiding in Christ, and allowing Him to abide in her. Then she was given a whole new set of priorities conditioned by the kingdom and not her cultural religion.

The experience taught me again to take no one for granted and to realize that inside heads nodding in approval or displaying signs of comprehension there may be steel-trapped brains with the doors tightly closed. The encouraging thing is that the Spirit can and does open those doors!

The disciples were beginning to have that experience as they contemplated what Jesus was saying between the Resurrection and Ascension. At least now they saw the issues and could confess their panic and fear. Their question expressed both in an inept way. In substance they were saying, "We appreciate all you did in the Cross and Resurrection, and what you've been saying about the kingdom and power is fine, but is it going to move toward our agenda? We became your disciples because we thought you were to restore the kingdom to Israel. Now, we are reluctant to press you, Lord, but are you going to do it or not?"

The Lord's response tore the epaulets off the uniform of their authority to control the battle plan as well as the purpose and goal of the envisioned nature of victory. It was like corporals demanding accountability from the Commander-in-Chief. The Lord relieved them of that assumed authority and told them of a new conquest in which they were to be field marshals—if they would dare to trust the battle plan and the timing to the Sovereign of the universe. Not a bad offer!

INFLOW AND OUTFLOW

⁷ And He said to them, "It is not for you to know times or seasons which the Father has put in His own authority. ⁸ But

you shall receive power when the Holy Spirit has come upon you; and you shall be witnesses to Me in Jerusalem, and in all Judea and Samaria, and to the end of the earth."

—*Acts 1:7–8*

Jesus' response is filled with a precaution and a prescription for spiritual power. He tells them what is not their business and what is. The secret of guidance in the Lord's will and the power to do it is revealed: *"It is not for you to know times or seasons which the Father has put in His own authority"* (v. 7). F. F. Bruce translates the Greek of that as, "It does not belong to you to know," i.e., "It is not your concern." What is not within the purvey of our responsibility is knowledge of the times or seasons. The Greek words are *chrónos* and *kairós*. *Chrónos* denotes a space of time or duration of time. *Kairós* is event-oriented time. For example, *chrónos* would be used to describe the length of time of the germination, sprouting, cultivating, and growth of a field of grain; *kairós* would be used for the actual time of harvesting. The time spent working on a degree would be *chrónos* and *kairós* would be the time of the awarding of the degree. W. E. Vine is helpful here. He says, "Broadly speaking, chronos expresses the duration of a period, kairos stresses it as marked by certain features . . . chronos marks quantity, kairos quality."[2]

The point for the disciples—and us—is that both kinds of time are under the control and planning of the Lord's strategy. How long we must wait and what will be given at the end of the wait is up to Him. Jesus already had given clear guidance on Whom and what to expect. He reacted strongly to the demand to know the exact *kairós* time. He knew that the new kingdom people had to be those who could wait for the Lord's best, and on His time schedule. He always is on time, and in time—never late, never early. The *chrónos* waiting duration is for us, not for Him. We must be made ready.

We've all chaffed under the impatience of waiting times. We want everything yesterday. We ruminate over our problems and finally pray about them and expect an immediate answer. The Lord waits until we are able to appropriate the answer.

What I sense Jesus is saying to the disciples and to us in His response, is that the power of His Spirit will be entrusted to people who can accept His authority over timing. Now, I know that from my experience, but just recently, however, I faced a crisis of financial needs for the maintenance and expansion of my church's television ministry. I experienced both a *chrónos* and a *kairós*. Decisions had to be made about production costs and air time. I told the Lord that the *kairós* time was at the end of the month. I was willing to wait out the *chrónos*. How's that for telling the Lord to meet your time schedule? In the waiting time I watched Him do so much more than I had anticipated and solved the problem in three weeks instead of four. He knew something I didn't. If the *kairós* solution had come in four weeks, I would have missed a crucial opportunity He opened up in that last week of the month I had set, and I could not have responded if He had waited for the date I had set.

But there are situations and relationships which come to mind in which I have had to wait way beyond the time that I thought was best. In these situations I wanted expedience and not excellence. When the answers did come, much later than *I* scheduled, they were so much better than I had expected. If I had received the answer earlier, it would have been all wrong. The Lord knows what He's doing. . . and when!

Oswald Chambers puts this into perspective. We are in danger of forgetting that we cannot do what God can do and that God will not do what we can do. It is in the *chrónos* that we do what we can do; the propitious intervention to do what only He can do will be done on His timing and by His power.

That's where the inflow and outgo of the gift of Pentecost is so crucial. The Lord's Spirit is given for a very special purpose. Jesus now makes that clear: *"You shall receive power . . . you shall be witnesses to Me. . ."* (v. 8). The power, *dúnamis*, would be given specifically for being witnesses, *mátures*. Power here means supernatural power of the quality revealed in Jesus' own life. Why do we need that kind of power? Look at His own awesome promise in John 14:12–14. "Most assuredly, I say to you, he who believes in Me, the works that I do he will do also; and greater works than these he will do, because I go to My Father. And whatever you ask in My name, that I will do, that the Father may be glorified in the Son. If you ask anything in My name, I will do it." He clearly tells us that He will continue to do what He did in His Palestinian ministry. That means love without limits; primary concern for people; communication of truth; healing of minds, emotions and bodies; and foot-washing practical service.

And there's something greater we will be able to do than He did as Jesus of Nazareth! What is this greater work? Certainly He meant that living in His people, His movement would spread to the corners of the earth. But also, prior to Pentecost, He could not present Himself and His finished work of redemption through the Cross and the Resurrection. That would become the purpose and passion of His followers through the generations. There are very few examples in two thousand years of Christian history of people becoming Christians with no direct or indirect influence from witnesses in whom the Savior communicated His love. Surely, many have made their initial commitment to Christ alone with their Bibles. But prior to that was the influence of individuals or the church, however misguided or inept they might have been. Augustine was alone when he gave his life to the pursuing Savior, but his mother, Monica, was praying!

The effluence of the Spirit is given for effectiveness in being a witness. We do that in all the ways Jesus' challenge implies and in the special calling to be communicators of grace, to introduce people to Christ, to help them realize the secret of His indwelling power to live a new life, and to stand with them as they grow. "Witness" in the basic Greek, *mártus,* means one who avows what he has seen, heard, or knows. Our word "martyr" comes from the same root, denoting someone who bears testimony for another person, or some cause, with his death. That has happened to many Christians through the years. We must be ready and willing to pay that ultimate cost, but we should not miss the more applicable usage for our lives. We are to die to ourselves and our control of our privacy and schedules and become available to share by life and action what Christ means to us and can mean to others.

The dynamic power of the Holy Spirit will be given in constant flow as long as we are engaged in communicating. We are to be conduits or channels, not reservoirs or holding tanks. A flowing river purifies itself; a swamp has inlets but no outflow. The Dead Sea is used often as an example. Fish can live only around the closest reaches of the inflow from the Jordan. But since there is no outflow to the sea, they would die a few yards away. Our lives become dull and dreary as Christians if all we do is take in inspiration from study of the Bible, worship and preaching, and an endless round of classes taught by stirring teachers where application is not mandated. The Holy Spirit's power is given for witness!

Here are some good questions to ask ourselves and others in preparation for our first Pentecost or for a flow of its continuing power. Who has the Lord put on our agenda to love and introduce to Him? Who now is alive forever because we cared about him or her and were used as the Lord's spiritual obstetrician? Who in our lives may have missed both the abundant and eternal life because of our silence? Are we willing to be made willing for the basic, undeniable calling of every Christian?

The Lord's power will not be squandered on us for long if we refuse to be channels of His grace as witnesses. And where? ". . . *Jerusalem, and in all Judea and Samaria, and to the end of the earth"* (v. 8). Not only the extent, but the quality of the Lord's movement is implied. Jerusalem for the disciples would not be easy, with conflict over Jesus' death and Resurrection. To announce that Jesus is alive would not win a popularity contest with the Sanhedrin. Judea, somewhat easier. But Samaria? the area filled with half-breeds who had been the subject of hundreds of years of prejudice ever since the return from the Exile? Yes, Samaria too. And to the ends of the earth. The Spirit of Christ would reach all nations.

For us the focus of our mission is at home in life's most intimate relationships where people really know us. And it has a focus at work and in the community where the consistency of our life and witness can be observed. But also it means our nation and the world. Most of all, it includes wherever we are or are sent. But don't wait for a call to be a missionary or a clergyperson. Start with the people at hand, and, wherever life leads, there will be people waiting whose lives are being prepared mysteriously for the serendipity of meeting the Savior or growing in Him because He arranged for us to be in the right place at just the right time.

Here is one possible outline to use in presenting this text either separately or as a part of an overall exposition of the whole chapter. A Christ-filled witness is marked by his or her:

1. *Accountability* to Christ and people.
2. *Approachability* as a receptive, relaxed, responsive human being.
3. *Adaptability* in presenting the essential message for particular needs.
4. *Accountability* in taking responsibility for following through.

OUR ASSURANCE FROM CHRIST'S ASCENSION

9 Now when He had spoken these things, while they watched, He was taken up, and a cloud received Him out of their sight. 10 And while they looked steadfastly toward heaven as He went up, behold, two men stood by them in white apparel, 11 who also said, "Men of Galilee, why do you stand gazing up into heaven? This same Jesus, who was taken up

from you into heaven, will so come in like manner as you saw
Him go into heaven."

—Acts 1:9–11

A further preparation for the power of Pentecost was the
Lord's Ascension. This essential doctrine, which is a part of the
Apostle's Creed, makes an excellent springboard for the communicator from at least two vantage points. The first is the event
itself and what happened to Jesus through it. The second is the
response of the disciples and what happened to them because of
it. Both are related to the descending of the divine to the human
so that the human could be ascended to the divine. Put another
way, in the sagacity of the church fathers, "Christ became what
we are in order to make us what He is."

First consider what the Ascension meant to Jesus. It was His
ascent to heaven for glorification. The first part of the mighty
work of the divine Word was completed. A small band of people
were ready to receive the transformation of His Spirit in them. He
had lived and died and risen from the dead for the birth of a new
creation. Now the Lord's ministry, which had been limited to the
body of Jesus of Nazareth, was home with the triumphant company of heaven. His return would be with reigning power, ubiq-
uity, and omniscience. His Spirit would be the master strategist of
the movement of His people. In order to return as indwelling
power in His chosen, called, and redeemed followers, He had to
leave them as the self-limited Jesus who had taken on our humanity. As the glorified Christ He commanded all power in heaven
and earth which He had promised would be released in prayer in
His name. The Christ in the man Jesus, "the power of God and the
wisdom of God" (1 Cor. 1:24), was liberated from the confines of
locality to make His followers like Him.

And what did that mean for His followers? They could never
disassociate what He had been for them as Friend, Companion,
Master, Lord, and crucified and risen Savior. Just as our conception
of what Christ is like will forever be focused in His incarnate life, the
Gospels will be always our source of how he calls and ministers to us.
In times of failure we will feel His gentle touch and hear, "Neither
do I condemn you; go in peace." In sickness we will pray and envi-
sion ourselves as one to whom He says, "Rise and walk." In times
of doubt He will come to us as He came to Thomas and offer to do
whatever is necessary to get us moving forward again. When, like
Peter, we are filled with self-incrimination, He will come to give us

forgiveness for our denials—both of Him and ourselves—and give us new self-esteem rooted in His recall to the ministry of feeding His sheep. He will appear on our Emmaus road so that the banked fires of our hearts can be set ablaze again.

But just as our visualization of how Christ ministered is rooted in the ministry of Jesus of Nazareth, it is multiplied by His ascended glory to equal the sum of infinite, ever-present, engendering and enabling power. We can sing with John Greenleaf Whittier,

> Warm, sweet, tender, even yet
> A present help is He;
> And faith has still its Olivet,
> And love its Galilee.[3]

But we also join our voices with Edward Perronet,

> All hail the pow'r of Jesus' name!
> Let angels prostrate fall;
> Bring forth the royal diadem,
> And crown Him Lord of all!
>
> O that with yonder sacred throng
> We at His feet may fall!
> We'll join the everlasting song,
> And crown Him Lord of all![4]

The disciples were soon to be released at Pentecost to join the everlasting song. But in the meantime, a spiritual principle was being imparted: Jesus Christ went in order to return. For His followers, life in Him would know that alternation in their relationship with Him. Just as He left them as Master and Friend in order to return as reigning, glorified Christ, so too there would be other times when He would leave, however much they had become accustomed to in their knowledge of Him, to return in a new and deeper way. The same is true for us. These withdrawals are to draw us on to the next stage of growth. It isn't that He literally leaves us, for He promised that He would be with us always, but He brings closure to a phase of our pilgrimage in order to open new depth in our relationship with Him. It seems that we have lost Him; it is only that He's down the road calling us to a new dimension of the adventure of knowing Him more profoundly. The transition sometimes seems to break our hearts. But hearts aren't made of frail glass; they are more like clay on the Potter's wheel. And our Potter has a magnificent design to follow: His own nature! It would have been sad to leave the disciples where they were as people, looking up as their beloved Master left them!

What shall we say in our communication of this passage about the two men in white apparel who gave comfort and a sense of expectation in the grief the disciples were experiencing? Who they were is explained by their attire. Obviously, they were messengers from heaven sent to cushion the shock of Jesus' departure and to turn the disciples' attention to the future. We are so earth-bound and limited in our perception of the spiritual world that our minds may well picture this scene as nothing more than a church pageant peopled by angelic characters. But these angels were what the disciples needed in those days before the infilling of Pentecost. It's unnecessary to get bogged down in describing the angels; Luke has said all that he needed to say. The crucial issue is what the messengers of heaven said. It was the final clarification of Whom they were to expect. *"This same Jesus, who was taken up from you into heaven, will so come in like manner as you saw Him go into heaven"* (v. 11).

That's our message out of this passage. The disciples were told clearly that the One who would return would be the same Lord whom they had seen leave them. The word for "manner" is significant. In Greek it is *trópos,* meaning fashion, character, way of life. How would Christ return in the power of the Spirit that would be in the same *trópos?* I believe it meant the way Christ left, that is, unexpectedly, surprisingly, as His own decision, and in His own way. His return in the Spirit at Pentecost would be the same way. None of the disciples would be stage manager of the event to give His cue. The time and *manner* would be of His choosing. And that, as we shall see, was more than the disciples dared imagine as they stood there watching Him ascend. G. Campbell Morgan's descriptive words add to our understanding: "He was received up—that is, onto a higher level of life; the life that is higher than the merely material, and manifest, and localized, and limited."[5]

TWO THINGS WE CAN DO TO BE READY FOR PENTECOST

[12] Then they returned to Jerusalem from the mount called Olivet, which is near Jerusalem, a Sabbath day's journey.
[13] And when they had entered, they went up into the upper

room where they were staying: Peter, James, John, and Andrew; Philip and Thomas; Bartholomew and Matthew; James the son of Alphaeus and Simon the Zealot; and Judas the son of James. [14] These all continued with one accord in prayer and supplication, with the women and Mary the mother of Jesus, and with His brothers.

—Acts 1:12–14

There are two things we can do to be ready for the power of Pentecost. Both were taking place as the disciples left Mount Olivet and made their way to the Upper Room, a room above a street in Jerusalem, now hallowed for them by the experience there of the Last Supper and the post-Resurrection appearances of Jesus.

Luke carefully tells us that it was a Sabbath day's journey from Mount Olivet to the Upper Room. Based on Exodus 16:29, amplified by Numbers 34:5, a Hebrew's movements on the Sabbath were limited in the *Mishna* to what was called in the Hebrew term, the *têhüm bra-Sabbath,* or the limit of the Sabbath. It was required that he go no further than 2,000 cubits or 6 furlongs. A cubit is about 18 inches while a furlong equals 220 yards. There are 1,760 yards in a mile, so the distance was about three-quarters of a mile, or 1,320 cubits. Luke's reference to this tells us what the distance of the Upper Room was from Mount Olivet, that it was probably the Sabbath, and that these were faithful Jews who kept the regulations of their religion. Why else would a careful historian like Luke make the reference, other than to tell us these things?

As the disciples walked this distance, we may strongly suppose that they questioned, "What does all this mean? What are we to do now? The Master has promised us the kingdom. It will be different from what we expected. And He has assured us that He will come again. What can we do to be prepared for His return? It is the Sabbath. We dare not be seen in the temple, for surely we will be arrested. Let's pass the word and gather all the Lord's followers, tell them what the Master has told us, and wait for His return together!"

And that's exactly what they did. Again Luke is a thorough chronicler in telling us who was among those who gathered for prayer—the eleven disciples, now minus Judas Iscariot. The women referred to must have been those who went to the tomb on the Resurrection morning—according to Luke's Gospel, "Mary Magdalene, Joanna,

Mary the mother of James, and the other women who were with them" (Luke 24:10). Also in the Upper Room were Jesus' mother and His brothers. That would have included James, to whom the Lord had appeared, who was to assume a very crucial role in the post-Pentecost organization of the church. In verse 15 we are told that there were 120 in all, probably including people like Nicodemus and Joseph of Arimathea.

That sets the stage for the two things that must have been central in their preparation. The two are part of one experience. We know they prayed, and I think they had a profound time of reconciling relationships. There had been competition among the disciples and there must have been the residue of criticism of each other. Peter had denied the Lord, Thomas had doubted, and James and John had wrangled over who was greatest and what position they would have in Jesus' kingdom. Also, there were bad feelings between Jesus' family and the disciples. His mother and brothers had tried to dissuade Jesus, and had come to take Him home to Nazareth on at least one occasion. From the Cross, Jesus had assigned John the responsibility of His mother, and we are sure John was sorting out what that would mean in the light of the challenges Jesus had given them on Olivet before departing.

Then, added to that mix were the people whom Jesus had healed from sins that no good Jew could tolerate. Had the disciples ever worked through their real feelings about a person like Mary Magdalene? With Jesus' absence, they were confronted by the fact that their relationship always had been cushioned with His gracious acceptance. Did they feel as He did? And what about the Pharisee Nicodemus? Was he really one of them? He was a member of the Sanhedrin and yet had not been able to stop the excruciating thing the Jewish leaders had done to the Lord. The Pharisee had shown his loyalty by asking for the body of Jesus and assisted in His burial. But could he be trusted? And what about rich Joseph of Arimathea? He provided the tomb in the garden outside the city wall. But with all that Jesus had said about the rich and the responsibility for the poor, was his presence a genuine concern? If he had provided the tomb, probably as a secret admirer and follower of the Lord, was he really to be accepted among the inner band of loyal followers?

A strange mixture of humanity was gathered there in the Upper Room. Each had his or her reason for being there—the knowledge of what Jesus had meant to each of them. But what were they to each other except people who had a common loyalty to Jesus? And He was gone! They now had to sit and wait . . . look each other in the eye . . . open their hearts to one another . . . share their loneliness, their grief over Jesus' absence, and their wonderment about the future. Here were rich and poor, people of high social status, and reclaimed people whose lives would never have touched each other apart from Jesus. And the family and disciples had little upon which to build a relationship. Had there been hostility among Jesus' brothers resulting from the feelings that Jesus had spent His time with a motley band of fishermen, a tax collector, and a zealot—with no time for His own family? And had the disciples resented the filial protectiveness of Jesus' family? Surely. Put yourself into this drama of human relationship. It resembled what you would find in a group of people gathered for a funeral who had no basis for relating other than through the deceased. You've been to strained gatherings like that, haven't you? We all have.

But a common grief can open strangers to one another. It can begin to build relationships. And it can put conflicts between friends into perspective. Mutual need can break through the fabric of hurting memories of what we have said or done to each other.

And yet, it is a shared hope that really galvanizes people. Jesus said that He would be back. All was not lost! The frail thread of anticipation in each of the people in that Upper Room was woven into a strong bond of oneness. I believe differences were confessed, hurts were shared, and reconciliation was started. What was about to happen to them would be the only lasting basis of true relationship, but the immensity of Jesus' promise before He left forced them to get ready by being open to one another. *"These all continued with one accord in prayer and supplication . . ."* (v. 14).

Prayer brings unity. We can't seek the loving heart of the Lord for long without recognizing the needs of and our relationships with the sisters and brothers with whom we pray. Surely Jesus' followers, huddled together in prayer, remembered that He had assured them that wherever two or more are gathered together in His name, He would be there among them. We wonder what they prayed about. I think it was the disciples' report on what Jesus promised in those last hours before His Ascension: they should not depart from Jerusalem but wait for the promised baptism of the Holy Spirit and the power He was to give them. A sublime reason for a prayer meeting in any age!

That brings us back to ourselves as communicators and the people whose lives we want to impact with our communication. Our need for the indwelling power of the Holy Spirit makes prolonged prayer and getting right with ourselves and others more than elements of good preparation; they are a necessity! We can't determine how or when the Lord will bless us with an initial endowment of power and daily replenishment. But the two things left for us to do are to pray for the Holy Spirit and to be sure there is nothing in our relationships blocking the full acceptance of the blessing.

Through the years, I have repeatedly seen it happen to individuals, marriages, and groups. In the parables of the importune friend asking for bread at midnight and a father's response to a son's request for food leads to the unequivocal assurance that God is unreserved in His offer of the Holy Spirit. "How much more will your heavenly Father give the Holy Spirit to those who ask Him!" (Luke 11:5–13). And yet, so many Christians live less than the abundant life personally and struggle with a lack of power in their relationships and in their churches and groups. Some have never prayed to be filled with the Holy Spirit. Others have, and their prayer seems unanswered. Why? There is something unconfessed in them or between them and others. Or there is a block of unwillingness to let go of their own imperious control. And, there may need to be radical surgery of attitudes, unhealed memories, or unguided plans for the future which have never had the Lord's blessing or direction.

I could fill this book with illustrations of this one point. This account, briefly told, is an example of all the rest. In a church where I served some years ago, I saw the Session of Elders of the church transformed by the power of the Holy Spirit at a retreat. After planning the church's program for the next year and fretting over finances, one elder said, "I think we are trying to do this all on our human steam. And it's not working. I think we need to get right with the Lord and each other before we go any further!" That opened us all up to an honest time of confrontation, healing, and reconciliation.

It happened in a very creative way. I felt led to call for silence and a quiet time of reflection. "Is there anything in any of us as persons blocking the flow of power? With whom in the group do you need to seek forgiveness or express it?" I asked. After a prolonged time, I suggested that we take a long walk with the person with whom each of us felt we needed a closer relationship. Later, when we gathered for the next meeting, the group was entirely different. In a Communion service we asked for the Holy Spirit to fill us with power both as individuals and as a group of leaders. We were blessed . . . and so was the future ministry and mission of the church. The same thing is offered for marriages, friendships, and people with whom we work.

I also remember a teammate on a staff with whom I had a pleasant, but strained, relationship. There was some problem I couldn't identify. Things had been great, and then one day a distance developed. On a staff retreat it all came out. He related that more than a year before he had shared a concern about one of his children. We had prayed together as a staff for the man's need. Then several weeks later from the pulpit, I shared an illustration from my own life about one of my own children, and what the Lord was teaching the two of us as we were both growing up in a situation of conflict of wills. My beloved fellow-pastor did not catch the first part of the account in which I said it was my own story. What he did hear was my application about clergy and their children which was more confession than admonition. He felt I had used the privately shared need in his life as an illustration.

It helped little for me to explain. The hurt was there. And I had to take responsibility for the impression I'd created. Where the blame lies is not the issue in blocked relationships; but clearing away the impediment *is* the issue. When I asked for and received forgiveness for what I had inadvertently done to cause the pain, we were both able to be channels of the Spirit's flow to each other and the rest of the staff.

I've known the same kind of cleaning out of the blockage in my spiritual and emotional plumbing repeatedly. And a fresh Pentecost follows. So often we are reluctant to assume responsibility for our preparation for Pentecost. The Lord wants to bless us with His Spirit. Prayer and reconciled relationships with ourselves and the people of our lives are the place to begin and then begin again and again all through our Christian adventure.

THE QUALIFICATIONS OF AN ADVENTURER

15 And in those days Peter stood up in the midst of the disciples (altogether the number of names was about a hundred and twenty), and said, 16 "Men and brethren, this Scripture had to be fulfilled, which the Holy Spirit spoke before by the mouth of David concerning Judas, who became a guide to those who arrested Jesus; 17 for he was numbered with us and obtained a part in this ministry."

18 (Now this man purchased a field with the wages of iniquity; and falling headlong, he burst open in the middle

and all his entrails gushed out. [19] And it became known to all those dwelling in Jerusalem; so that field is called in their own language, *Akel Dama*, that is, Field of Blood.)

[20] "For it is written in the Book of Psalms:

'*Let his dwelling place be desolate,*
And let no one live in it';

and,

'*Let another take his office.*'

[21] "Therefore, of these men who have accompanied us all the time that the Lord Jesus went in and out among us,

[22] beginning from the baptism of John to that day when He was taken up from us, one of these must become a witness with us of His resurrection."

[23] And they proposed two: Joseph called Barsabas, who was surnamed Justus, and Matthias. [24] And they prayed and said, "You, O Lord, who know the hearts of all, show which of these two You have chosen [25] to take part in this ministry and apostleship from which Judas by transgression fell, that he might go to his own place." [26] And they cast their lots, and the lot fell on Matthias. And he was numbered with the eleven apostles.

—Acts 1:15–26

One final aspect of our preparation for Pentecost is given us in the account of the election of Judas's replacement. Luke relates it in great detail. In giving an extensive review of Peter's explanation of the need for the replacement, perhaps Luke was bringing Theophilus up to speed on Judas's betrayal. I think he also had something else in mind. Remember that Luke had been Paul's loyal companion both in missionary journeys and in the apostle's imprisonment. Paul had been both teacher and cherished friend. Through Paul's encounter with the resurrected Christ on the Damascus Road, he had become first a disciple and then an apostle recognized among the official twelve. Knowing that, and also the strange lack of any further reference to the one elected in the Upper Room before Pentecost, we conjecture that perhaps Luke is pointing out that the apostles, prior to the gift of the Holy Spirit, were precipitous in replacing Judas when the Lord already was planning ahead for a Pharisee named Saul of Tarsus to fill that position.

Also, we wonder if Luke was pointing out that casting lots, used all through the Old Testament, was a poor substitute for the guidance of the Holy Spirit, who became the source of wisdom and discernment for such decisions after Pentecost. He certainly did not relate the account of the election to clarify how Spirit-guided decisions should be made. In the Old Testament the objects used in casting lots were small pieces of wood or stone which were numbered or inscribed with the names of those from whom the choice was being made. They were put into a container or garment and shaken together, after which they were cast out. The lot which fell out first was deemed to be a clear sign of the person to be chosen. That's essentially what the 120 followers of Jesus in the Upper Room did to elect the one who would join the eleven in leading the future of the Master's movement! That sounds crude to us, and it was, in comparison to the inner guidance the Holy Spirit gives to individuals and groups in making decisions and choices.

But there's something more in this section which draws our consideration of the first chapter of Acts to a close. The essential qualifications of both candidates for apostleship, and for the gift of Pentecost, were that they had to have been thoroughly familiar with Jesus' Palestinian ministry, *"all the time that the Lord Jesus went in and out among us"* (v. 21), and *"witness with us of His resurrection"* (v. 22).

For us today, our preparation for Pentecost and being sent as apostles *(apóstolos: apó,* "from," combined with *stéllō,* "to send") is Christ's life, message, death, and Resurrection for us. We cannot slip around the Incarnation to get to Pentecost! When we know that the abundant life Jesus proclaimed is our deepest longing, when we really believe His atoning death was for us and would have been necessary if each of us had been the only person alive in Jerusalem on that Friday, and when we know that He is alive through the miracle of the Resurrection and is our living contemporary—we are ready to receive the unlimited power of His Spirit.

What happened to Matthias? We are not told. He never is mentioned again. Did he defect or drop out? Probably not. I believe we would have been told if that happened, and Luke's thoroughness would have included that data. What we do know is that the position was filled by Paul. There is no need to be down on Matthias. He responded to a call. He was ready with his knowledge of Christ and an open mind and heart to receive His Spirit. He was there at Pentecost—that's all that matters. Whether his ministry afterward received the recognition of history is unimportant. The same is true for us. Once we have experienced what Christ said and did for us in His death and Resurrection and then returned to continue to do, titles, or history's recognition, or even the accolades of people today become unimportant.

What I've tried to do in this second chapter is to give the salient elements of the preparation for Pentecost. I have done that at some length because the rest of Acts is heightened by the clear understanding of Whom we are to expect at Pentecost, what He does to get us ready, and what we can do to prepare ourselves to receive Him. Those three headings could well be the outline for a message on these verses of Acts 1 or a series of messages leading up to Pentecost Sunday.

Now on to Pentecost. Both the lightning and the thunder are for us!

NOTES

1. F. F. Bruce, *The Acts of the Apostles* (Grand Rapids: Eerdmans, 1951, repr. 1968), p. 70.

2. W. E. Vine, *An Expository Dictionary of New Testament Words* (London: Marshall Morgan Scott; repr. 1981), pp. 137–39.

3. "We May Not Climb the Heavenly Steeps," John Greenleaf Whittier, 1866.

4. "All Hail the Power of Jesus' Name," Edward Perronet, 1779.

5. G. Campbell Morgan, *The Acts of the Apostles* (Old Tappan, N.J.: Fleming H. Revell Co., 1924), p. 22.

CHAPTER THREE—THE MIRACLE OF PENTECOST

ACTS 2:1–47

Scripture Outline

Waiting on the Edge of a Miracle (2:1)

The Dynamics of the Miracle (2:2–4)

The Miracle of Communication (2:5–11)

The Miracle of Preaching (2:12–39)

The Miracle of the Church (2:40–47)

WAITING ON THE EDGE OF A MIRACLE

2:1 When the Day of Pentecost had fully come, they were all with one accord in one place.

—Acts 2:1

A few years ago, I had an experience which radically changed my life as a communicator. I want to share it with you as an introduction to my exposition of Acts, chapter 2. The experience gave me a sense of urgency in explaining the miracle of Pentecost as the secret to meeting the deepest longings in the church today.

The Lord led me into a ministry of listening—to people and then to Him in preparation for preaching, writing, and teaching. This is how it happened. Early one summer, in preparation for my study leave, I asked my congregation to tell me their deepest needs. I distributed cards in the worship service for several Sundays on which my people were asked to write their needs in living out their faith. I was astonished by the enthusiasm with which people responded. "Thanks for asking!" was expressed on many of the cards. And on all of them were listed the frustrations my people were experiencing in daily living. The needs were much more urgent and profound than I had perceived.

I took the cards with me for my prolonged time of preparation of the sermons for the next fall, winter, and spring. Each expression of need was reread repeatedly as I studied the Scriptures, listening to what the Lord had to say in response in His Word. Again and again, the plea of these church members was for power to live their faith. In countless different ways, people asked for a deeper understanding of the Holy Spirit and an experience of His transforming strength for their feelings of spiritual inadequacy and impotence. Many put it bluntly: what really happened at Pentecost; can it happen today?

The following year, my church began a television ministry. In preparation, I did a national survey of the most urgent questions the American people were asking. I should not have been surprised that the same note was sounded. People inside and outside the church wanted to know about the Holy Spirit.

As our syndication of the program spread across the nation and people began to write me, I hit on still another method of enlisting their expression of need. I had an opportunity to speak at a conference where each preacher was asked to give the sermon he would preach if he had only one last message to give. It was a very exciting conference. As I preached, I thought, "What if my television viewers had an opportunity to tell me the one message they most need to hear?" I wrote thousands of letters asking for people's response. Again the Lord pressed my listening heart to the spiritual pulsebeat of people today. The response was overwhelming: requests came tumbling in by the mailbag full. In a multiplicity of ways, the plea was for power. One person's expression capsulizes them all: "Please give a message on how to live the abundant life. I'm tired of the struggle and strain! How do I find the freedom and joy of being a Christian?"

You can imagine that my exposition of the Scripture was intensified by daring to listen to people. There's nothing more foolish than the answer to an unasked question, and nothing more powerful than an exposition from Scripture that is the Lord's answer to the urgent questions people really are asking.

What I hear from people today is an agnosticism about the Holy Spirit. Not disbelief, but an aching, "I just don't know"—and a longing to understand who He is and how to live in the flow of His power.

Listening to the expression of these needs, questions, and yearnings has put me in touch with where people are. The greatest longing in the church today, stated both directly and indirectly, is the quest for something more than dull religion. People are in need of the intimacy, inspiration, and impelling power of the Holy Spirit. Answering that cry is the key to church renewal and prophetic preaching and teaching. It is impossible to live the Christian life without the indwelling Spirit. Courageous discipleship in the crisis of society cannot be accomplished without the guidance and enabling energy of supernatural power. The church today, like the disciples in the Upper Room, is waiting on the edge of a miracle.

Pentecost was a miracle. I have used the word "miracle" carefully. By it I mean the intervention of supernatural power in keeping with a higher spiritual law which supersedes the laws of human nature. Our laws are the statements of how things usually work. Observation and experience of human potential are articulated into maxims about the physical and intellectual capabilities we possess. Environment, conditioning, and training are said to shape our personalities irrevocably. Our talents and intellectual abilities are believed to define the limits of our performance. It is a miracle when a personality is transformed, or a person is able to think and act beyond the limitations of his or her capacities. A higher power, exercising a higher law, has multiplied the human potential. The word "impossible" no longer has its restricting confinement. The impossible happens. The miracle of a changed personality results with supernatural gifts of intellect, emotional freedom, and a conviction that all things are possible. That's the miracle of Pentecost. One hundred and twenty frightened, impotent, self-centered, willful, and discouraged men and women were transformed into new creatures. They were infused with supernatural power—intellectually, emotionally, volitionally, and physically. In Greek, the words "miracle" and "power" come from the same root.

This higher spiritual law had been explained by Jesus long before Pentecost. The One through whom all things were created, the eternal Logos, had come to recreate humankind. He clearly revealed the higher law of transformation in His life and message. He asserted, "God is Spirit, and those who worship Him must worship in spirit and truth" (John 4:24). God is Spirit, *pneûma,* and we are created spiritual beings, *pneumatikós.* We were created for Spirit-to-spirit union and communication. Our spirit can be infused and empowered by His Spirit. Jesus went on to say, "But the hour is coming, and now is, when the true worshipers will worship the Father in spirit and truth; for the Father is seeking such to worship Him" (John 4:23). The Greek word for "worshipers" here is *proskunētaI,* from *proskuneó,* to bow the knee, to prostrate oneself in total openness. That willing receptivity would be the result of the Lord seeking us. Our desire is the manifestation of His far greater desire to invade the spirit of men and women with His own Spirit. When this happens, a miracle takes place. Our spirit is the port of entry for the divine Spirit. When He enters a human being, the mind is transformed, the computer of the brain is given new data, the will is released from bondage, and the nervous system becomes the channel of supernatural energy. That's what happened at Pentecost, beginning a new age of spiritual renaissance. The higher spiritual law Jesus had explained was manifested: God's Spirit engendered in the spirits of people produced a potential beyond human limitations. What Jesus incarnated and promised was given to His followers.

The greatest need in the church today is for contemporary Pentecost. When we listen to people intently, we can respond incisively. The need in people today matches the mood of Jesus' followers waiting in the Upper Room. An empathetic exposition of Acts 2:1 gives us an opportunity to tell people we have heard their plea for power. Interpreting and dramatizing the condition of the waiting disciples is a vivid way of touching the raw nerves in people inside and outside the church today.

The final hours before Pentecost were filled with the anxious frustration of the impossibility of living Christ's message and emulating His life. How could this happen without Him? Though He had said clearly that He would come and make His home in them, they had not realized what He meant. They were limited by the preposition "with"; He would shift that to the awesome, mysterious preposition of the abundant life. They were to be women and men "in" Christ and He would dwell "in" them! The encouraging preposition of true Christianity would be "in." And until it happened, the disciples waited on the edge of a miracle, history's greatest miracle—the transformation of human personality and the beginning of a new humanity. It is on this same edge of expectation that we will find so many of our people. Our task as communicators is to join them and be ready for the miracle of a supernatural endowment of power today.

THE DYNAMICS OF THE MIRACLE

² And suddenly there came a sound from heaven, as of a rushing mighty wind, and it filled the whole house where they were sitting. ³ Then there appeared to them divided tongues, as of fire, and one sat upon each of them. ⁴ And they were all

filled with the Holy Spirit and began to speak with other tongues, as the Spirit gave them utterance.

—Acts 2:2–4

The dynamics of Pentecost were wind, fire, and praise. Picture the disciples expectantly seated, waiting, praying. Suddenly a wind began to stir in the room, gently at first; then it grew stronger. The followers of Jesus looked up from their prayers. Now the wind was rushing with a rumble like thunder.

The Hebrew word for spirit and wind is *ruach*. The pronunciation of the word depicts its meaning. Its first and last letters are gutturals, and the word rumbles from the larynx and ends with a breathy sound as the last bit of the word is enunciated with air from the throat. The wind had been an emblem of the Spirit for the Hebrew people through the generations. When the Lord spoke to Ezekiel in the valley of the dry bones, He told the prophet to "prophesy to the breath, prophesy, son of man, and say to the breath, 'Thus says the Lord God: "Come from the four winds, O breath, and breathe on these slain, that they may live"'" (Ezek. 37:9). The dry bones symbolized the defeated, dejected people of Israel in exile in Ezekiel's day. They needed the Spirit for life to come into them again. Jesus used the image of the wind for the Spirit when He said to Nicodemus, "Do not marvel that I said to you, 'You must be born again.' The wind blows where it wishes, and you hear the sound of it, but cannot tell where it comes from and where it goes. So is everyone who is born of the Spirit" (John 3:7–8).

Now in the Upper Room the wind was blowing, rushing with irresistible force. Surely Nicodemus was among those who heard and saw the undeniable evidence of the wind. The Lord gave outward signs of His presence in tangible ways so they would understand. He communicated in a way that would be identified immediately. And what wind does when it rushes, so too the Holy Spirit was doing in their souls: blowing out cobwebs of fear and the layered dust of uncertainty. The presence of the wind outwardly was soon an inward rushing of new thought, emotion, and will. The Lord's people were being stirred up, quickened, brought back to life because He had come.

The second dynamic was equally an outward sign of what was happening within. John the Baptist's prophecy was being enacted. Luke had recorded it in his Gospel: "I indeed baptize you with water; but One mightier than I is coming, whose sandal strap I am not worthy to loose. He will baptize you with the Holy Spirit and fire" (Luke 3:16). Fire and the Spirit of God are as synonymous as wind and Spirit in the Old Testament. With the prophetic zeal of an Old Testament prophet, John explained what this new fire from heaven would do: "His winnowing fan is in His hand, and He will thoroughly clean out His threshing floor, and gather the wheat into His barn; but the chaff He will burn with unquenchable fire" (Luke 3:17).

What sounds like a fierce purging is also a great promise. The Spirit's fire burns out the chaff in those who have survived the winnowing fan's test. The wheat of the Lord have chaff in their minds and hearts which the Spirit burns away. Luke also quoted Jesus about fire in his Gospel account: "I came to send fire on the earth, and how I wish it were already kindled!" (Luke 12:49). The statement was given in the context of His judgment. The gift of His Spirit is that also. He burns out anything in us which could cripple us in His service. His Spirit is given for the continuation of His ministry.

We hear and sing a great deal about the peace and comfort of the Holy Spirit, but how our words have drifted from their original meaning! Peace is what He gives after reconciliation and a surrendered will. The word *eirēnē* means harmonious relationships between God and us and, also, between us and others. The chaff of anything which separates us from God or any other person is burned away with the baptism of the Holy Spirit. And comfort means much more than the refortification of our anxious hearts. *Paráklēsis* is a combination of *pará*, "beside," and *kaléō*, "to call to one's side." But it also means to exhort. When the Spirit comes into us, He is Companion and Friend in life's challenges, but loves us so much that He burns away what will debilitate us or prevent us from fully becoming the persons we were meant to be.

But the fire of the Holy Spirit does so much more than burn away; He refines and galvanizes. The dross is burned off and the pure metal is left. What a great promise! We don't have to stay the way we are. My experience of this is expressed in what I have called a character transplant. The indwelling Lord makes us like Himself. He's only begun with me. I'm not what I used to be, nor all that I'm going to be. And that leads to the further implication of the effect of the fire of the Holy Spirit.

He kindles enthusiasm, warmth, spontaneity. Just as the wind of the Spirit engendered new thought, so too, the fire of the Spirit set the followers of Jesus aflame with emotional intensity. The visual evidence of the fire above the heads of the people was another outward sign that became an inner reality. The Spirit never bypasses our humanity; He transforms it and then flows through it. The miracle of Pentecost was that the followers of Jesus became capable of warm, inclusive love. Each in his or her own uniqueness became free of the limits of the categories of personality. I believe the extrovert was deepened and the introvert released. They were free to love each other, and, as we shall see, they were given an unquenchable love for people in the world.

We all need the fire of the Spirit to convince us of the fact that we are loved unqualifiedly and released to love unreservedly. The undeniable test that we have been baptized with the fire of the Holy Spirit is a new and deeper capacity to love. Love is both thought and felt. The quality of love given by the Holy Spirit is first conceived in the mind, then formulated into transformed thought in the cerebral cortex of the brain and then triggered in the part of the nervous system that controls the emotional responses. Love is not something we feel only; the feeling is the result of an ordered process in our inner mind and brain. The reaction may take place in less than a split second, but the process of receiving, perception, and willing precedes the feeling of being loved or feeling love.

It is fascinating to note that nowhere in the Gospels do we read that the disciples expressed love for Jesus or each other. At no point do they say, "We love you, Lord." And yet Jesus constantly told them of His and the Father's love for them.

Even when pressed with the direct question in John 21, Peter sidestepped Jesus' use of the word "love" and responded that the Lord knew he was His friend. Twice Jesus asked, "Do you love me?" and each time Peter responded with an affirmation of his friendship. The third time Jesus used Peter's word for friendship. And once again Peter protested his loyalty and affection. The miracle of the Pentecost fire later produced the ability to love the Lord and others.

A look at the two words for love used in the Greek New Testament is very revealing and leads to the point I want to make. *Agapáō* is the verb form of the noun *agápē*. It means giving, forgiving, unqualified love expressed in consistent, constant, unreserved self-giving. It is not dependent on the adequacy or performance of the recipient. This word is used to describe God's nature (1 John 4:8, 16); His love for the world (John 3:16); His love of His Son (John 17:26), and to those who believe in Christ (John 14:21); and the attitude He wants His people to have toward one another and the world.

59

This is the Greek for the word Jesus used when He asked, "Simon, do you love Me?" The word used in the Greek New Testament for Simon's response is *philéō;* a word of tender affection. That was the best he could offer. Not bad for openers, but if Christ had wanted to know about his friendship, He would have asked him that. John carefully made a definite distinction when he told this story about Peter.

Even though there are three times that Jesus used the verb translated by the Greek *philéō* (John 5:20, 16:27, and 20:2) for the Father, believers, and the disciple John, the rest of His message and expressions of love are rendered as *agapáō in* the Greek. These three were tender expressions of friendship affection, *philéō,* in the context of many other prior affirmations of His *agápē.*

The point of this sortie into the Greek words for love, with a particular focus on John 21 and the example of Peter, is to emphasize the fact that prior to the experience of Pentecost and the infilling of the Spirit, the disciples were incapable of profound love. The closest we have is Peter's verbal expression of friendship and he had to be asked outright for that. Prior to Pentecost, he struggled to express *philéō* admiration and loyalty, and failed often even at that.[1]

The quality of *agapáō* for God or others is impossible without the Spirit's fire of love burning in us. *Agapáō* was perfectly revealed and expressed by Christ in His life, message, and atoning death. That love came into the disciples when they were filled with the Holy Spirit. *Agápē* is a fruit of the Spirit (Gal. 5:22).

This is crucial to communicate to people in our exposition. So many are troubled about the inability to express either of the two qualities of love. Their problem of impatience with people, difficulties in forgiving and forgetting, and reluctance to give themselves away freely to others, is a constant contradiction to their faith in Christ as their Savior. Many feel defeated and frustrated. The tender friendship of *philéō* comes with real effort and *agapáō* hardly at all. The shocking discovery is that Christ's quality of love is inseparable from Him. He is *agápē* and *agápē* cannot be fully experienced apart from His Spirit residing in us.

A friend of mine put it this way. "I experienced Christ's unqualified love when I accepted His death for me. But I struggled all the time trying to love people. His Spirit gave me a feeling of being loved; my problem still was loving. Christ was out there somewhere—an example—but I had no power to express what I'd experienced in hearing about the gospel. I guess I had enough to live forever, but I sure wasn't living abundantly. Then I heard about the indwelling Spirit of Christ. Some Christian friends at work whom I meet with over lunch once a week told me the difference that made in their lives. They prayed for me, and since then I've been freer than I've ever been. It's as if all my experience as a Christian up to this point was like a low-burning pilot light without the burner going. It wasn't anything I did that set me on fire, except to ask. The great difference is in my relationships—especially with my wife and kids. There's no more of that 'I'll love you if you do what I want' stuff. The judgmental attitudes I had since I was a kid seemed to have changed completely. I can feel what people are feeling, what they are going through, and I want to do everything I can to help. What a difference! How'd I miss that all these years?" The Pentecost miracle of the Spirit's fire has been injected into this man. It's happening today!

The third manifestation of the Holy Spirit was for the 120 *and* the crowds that had gathered in Jerusalem for the celebration of Pentecost. The followers of Jesus were filled with the Holy Spirit for praise and proclamation. The two go together. The Spirit releases us to praise, and that praise becomes very effective proclamation. It was the sound of the rushing wind that brought the crowds to the area of the Upper Room. Then it was the quality of praise that made them want to know what was happening. Following that, Peter had a ready audience for an compelling proclamation of the true nature of what was happening, and how the pilgrims gathered in Jerusalem could participate with them. The followers of the Lord were given unction for utterance; they experienced the communion of the Holy Spirit for communication. The Spirit and His gifts are for ministry.

Luke tells us that the people in the Upper Room were *"filled with the Holy Spirit"* (v. 4). The word "filled" is *eplērōsen.* The use here in the Greek is that of a definite act at a specific time in the past, *eplēsthēsan,* in the passive voice. The Spirit had filled the room; now He filled the ready disciples and followers whose preparation had made room for Him. The Greek means that they were filled to the full, or made full. The result was that they were Spirit-filled, as a vessel is filled.

What does this mean? The best way to explain is to consider the human vessel which was filled. As human beings they had minds, brains, wills, emotions, and physical bodies. To be filled to the full, as the Greek implies, means that the Spirit invaded every facet, function, and facility of their nature. The entry was through their spirits, the conscious self. Then the tissues of their brains were engendered with the Spirit, which made possible an emotional response, and their bodies were energized, producing a physical radiance and energetic movements. Their minds were captured by the truth of the Spirit, their brains thought it out, and their nervous system channeled it, with every part of the body responding in unity and oneness. All that they were was infused by the all-powerful Spirit of the Lord. Praise was the undeniable evidence.

One of the manifestations of this was that they *"began to speak with other tongues, as the Spirit gave them utterance"* (v. 4) Galileans whose language was Aramaic were able to speak in Latin, Greek, and all other languages represented by the people gathered from around the then-known world.

THE MIRACLE OF COMMUNICATION

5 And there were dwelling in Jerusalem Jews, devout men, from every nation under heaven. 6 And when this sound occurred, the multitude came together, and were confused, because everyone heard them speak in his own language.
7 Then they were all amazed and marveled, saying to one another, "Look, are not all these who speak Galileans? 8 And how is it that we hear, each in our own language in which we were born? 9 Parthians and Medes and Elamites, those dwelling in Mesopotamia, Judea and Cappadocia, Pontus and Asia,
10 Phrygia and Pamphylia, Egypt and the parts of Libya adjoining Cyrene, visitors from Rome, both Jews and proselytes,
11 Cretans and Arabs—we hear them speaking in our own tongues the wonderful works of God."

—*Acts 2:5–11*

When we understand the complicated mechanism of articulation through the system of the brain, we begin to see what a phenomenal thing happened to the Lord's people. The cerebral cortex of the brain sends a signal to the Brochas speech center where words are formulated. This area lies on the lateral side of the dominant brain. With the aid of the motor cortex on both sides of the brain, messages are sent deep into the brain where the medulla lies. Here two cranial nerves, the twelfth, which controls the tongue, and the seventh, which controls the mouth, are stimulated into action. At the same time, the cerebral motor cortex takes over voluntary control of respiration from the medulla oblungata, where the involuntary respiratory center usually controls respiration. Signals are sent down the phrenic nerve to the diaphragm and to the thoracic nerves to cause the person to exhale on command. The combination of all this produces speech. That we can think and then express our thoughts in words in our own language is evidence of the wonder of our creation.

But what about "other" tongues? Luke tells us that the praise of the Spirit-filled believers was spoken in the languages of the people gathered in Jerusalem. This is an indication of how completely "filled" and under the influence of the Spirit they were. The magnificent mechanism of speech was utilized by Him to enable the believers to think and articulate in languages they had not learned previously.

It is important to distinguish between "other" tongues and the gift of tongues. On Pentecost, for the 120 to speak in the languages of the different nationalities was a miracle for the communication of what was happening to them. Later in the development of the fellowship of the church, the Holy Spirit gave a gift of utterance which was not a specific language. Rather, words and sounds were given by the Spirit to release the believers for praise beyond the capacity of expression in the words of their own languages, and for prophesies to the church. When the gift was used in the assembly of believers, the Spirit also gave the gift of interpretation so that the words spoken could be interpreted for the edification of the church. This is extranatural, in that a person cannot produce the gift, but can be a cooperative agent for it to happen. This is a legitimate New Testament gift which is given by the Spirit to a believer for praise in his own prayers, as well as in the church when instruction of its proper use is given and the gift of interpretation is also utilized.

The "other" tongues of Pentecost and the gift of tongues that was later provided to believers have this in common: they both required a Spirit-filled yieldedness for the speech system of the brain to function. It is helpful to think of what happened on Pentecost as a miracle and what later happened to believers as a gift. We will have more to say about the gift of tongues as we do an exposition of subsequent passages in Acts where the gift was evidenced. Now we must keep our train of thought focused on Luke's account of what happened at Pentecost.

The followers of the Master were ecstatic with praise. The *ruach* wind had stimulated their minds and the fire had kindled their emotions. They both thought and felt uncontainable adoration. The evidence of the filling of the Holy Spirit is a freedom from self-concern and to Spirit-consciousness. We are released to praise God with unfettered joy and gratitude. The motivation for this in the Upper Room was based on several definite things. The believers felt blessed and cherished as the Lord's beloved. He had been faithful to His promise to return to them. He was not only resurrected from the dead, He was with and in them. The rushing wind communicated His power. The fire set their minds and hearts ablaze.

Remember the finest things which have ever happened to you and multiply them a million times and you begin to know what happened in the Upper Room. Think of a human relationship in which you felt freed, cared about, and helped in a specific need. Or remember the time when you first experienced the love of the Lord in hearing the awesome truth of the gospel. Further, consider a time when you prayed in an impossible situation and had a specific intervention which was so spectacular that you knew that only the Lord could have done it.

With those identifying illustrations, get into the skins of the disciples at Pentecost and allow your imagination to capture all that they thought, experienced, and felt. It must have been like the Lord's walking on the water to them on the turbulent Sea of Galilee, but so much more. It was Easter morning with the news that Jesus was alive, but so much greater. All those were external observations of the Lord's power. Pentecost was the invasion of their total being by the same Lord. No wonder their praise was ecstatic, their enthusiasm knew no limits, and their inspiration was so contagious.

A word about praise as the secret of the liberated life is poignant application of this section of Acts. There is a power in praise that needs to be discovered by the people to whom we communicate. Praising the Lord for what He has done frees us to receive what He will do. But also, praise is the ultimate level of human relinquishment to the Spirit of the Lord. When we praise Him for problems or unresolved tensions, we release them to Him in an unreserved way that frees us from the grip of anxiety. I have learned that the turning point in excruciating difficulties came when I praised the Lord for them. He has something to show me and wants to do for me that I would not be able to receive if life were smooth and easy.

The point is that when we seek to communicate what happened in the praise of Pentecost, at least half of the people who hear us will not feel like praising the Lord. The impact of the passage will skim over their heads and hearts with a kind of evasion that says, "Well, that was fine for them, but they weren't going through what I'm enduring." Pentecost praise will elude them because they think they have no praise to match the essence of the passage. But they have! That is, if we open the way for them. The disciples were not a jolly, carefree band of believers before Pentecost. They had personal problems, relational difficulties, and a hostile world to face without much confidence that they would have the courage to grapple with them. We are not told that praise was a part of their prayers before Pentecost, but are told repeatedly that it was a never-ceasing note of their prayers afterward. And we live today as recipients of the secret they discovered. The same Holy Spirit who produced unfettered praise in them is the source of our ability to praise in difficult times. He knows that the blessings He wants to give cannot be received until we praise in advance of a resolution. Praising enables endurance, pertinacity, fortitude—and an openness to the future.

Praising is also an irresistible, magnetic attraction for communicating our faith to others. A praising Christian will have no limit of opportunities to talk to others about Christ. Robert Louis Stevenson said, "Show me your praises and I will think more of your prayers."

The praise of the newly filled believers was what caused the crowd to gather that day in Jerusalem. It was not just that they heard in their own language, but *what* they heard that was so astonishing. Like a homing instinct that inherently knows the way to a destination, the desire to praise lies deep within every human being, and the praise the crowd heard for what the Lord was doing touched a resounding chord within them. When we see authentic praise, we are drawn mysteriously, irrevocably. That is why it is sin to use the capacity for praise for the wrong subject or object.

In the miracle of communication at Pentecost, the effusion of other tongues was coupled with the gift of hearing. It was as much a miracle that those pilgrims heard as it was that the disciples spoke in languages they did not know. And the same Spirit who gave the power to the disciples gave the pilgrims the capacity to hear. Both miracles take place when you and I seek to communicate the gospel. Our spiritual gift of lucidness is multiplied by the Spirit's gift of elucidation in the hearer. Pentecost is not just a date on the calendar but a revelation of the hearing capacity the Spirit gives to our listeners.

THE MIRACLE OF PREACHING

[12] So they were all amazed and perplexed, saying to one another, "Whatever could this mean?"

¹³ Others mocking said, "They are full of new wine."

¹⁴ But Peter, standing up with the eleven, raised his voice and said to them, "Men of Judea and all who dwell in Jerusalem, let this be known to you, and heed my words. ¹⁵ For these are not drunk, as you suppose, since it is only the third hour of the day. ¹⁶ But this is what was spoken by the prophet Joel:

¹⁷ 'And it shall come to pass in the last days, says God,
That I will pour out of My Spirit on all flesh;
Your sons and your daughters shall prophesy,
Your young men shall see visions,
Your old men shall dream dreams.
¹⁸ And on My menservants and on My maidservants
I will pour out My Spirit in those days;
And they shall prophesy.
¹⁹ I will show wonders in heaven above
And signs in the earth beneath:
Blood and fire and vapor of smoke.
²⁰ The sun shall be turned into darkness,
And the moon into blood,
Before the coming of the great and awesome day of the
LORD.
²¹ And it shall come to pass
That whoever calls on the name of the LORD
Shall be saved.'

²² "Men of Israel, hear these words: Jesus of Nazareth, a Man attested by God to you by miracles, wonders, and signs which God did through Him in your midst, as you yourselves also know— ²³ Him, being delivered by the determined purpose and foreknowledge of God, you have taken by lawless hands, have crucified, and put to death; ²⁴ whom God raised up, having loosed the pains of death, because it was not possible that He should be held by it. ²⁵ For David says concerning Him:

'I foresaw the LORD always before my face,
For He is at my right hand, that I may not be shaken.
²⁶ Therefore my heart rejoiced, and my tongue was glad;
Moreover my flesh also will rest in hope.
²⁷ For You will not leave my soul in Hades,
Nor will You allow Your Holy One to see corruption.
²⁸ You have made known to me the ways of life;
You will make me full of joy in Your presence.'

²⁹ "Men and brethren, let me speak freely to you of the patriarch David, that he is both dead and buried, and his tomb is

with us to this day. [30] Therefore, being a prophet, and knowing that God had sworn with an oath to him that of the fruit of his body, according to the flesh, He would raise up the Christ to sit on his throne, [31] he, foreseeing this, spoke concerning the resurrection of the Christ, that His soul was not left in Hades, nor did His flesh see corruption. [32] This Jesus God has raised up, of which we are all witnesses. [33] Therefore being exalted to the right hand of God, and having received from the Father the promise of the Holy Spirit, He poured out this which you now see and hear.

[34] "For David did not ascend into the heavens, but he says himself:

'The LORD said to my Lord,

"Sit at My right hand,

[35] Till I make Your enemies Your footstool."'

[36] "Therefore let all the house of Israel know assuredly that God has made this Jesus, whom you crucified, both Lord and Christ."

[37] Now when they heard this, they were cut to the heart, and said to Peter and the rest of the apostles, "Men and brethren, what shall we do?"

[38] Then Peter said to them, "Repent, and let every one of you be baptized in the name of Jesus Christ for the remission of sins; and you shall receive the gift of the Holy Spirit. [39] For the promise is to you and to your children, and to all who are afar off, as many as the Lord our God will call."

—Acts 2:12–39

A careless, scoffing comment prompted the first Christian sermon. Some of the people who heard the praise of the believers asked, *"What does this mean?"* But not all. Others mocked, saying, *"They are full of new wine."* That got Peter on his feet! He had to explain the absurdity of that criticism: *"For these are not drunk, as you suppose, since it is only the third hour of the day."* The third hour of the day was about 9:00 A.M., calculated from the time of sunrise. Josephus, the Jewish historian, tells us that the first meal of the day was not until the fourth hour, and on the Sabbath, a larger meal was served at the sixth hour, around noon. Peter's responses in our language and custom today would be, "What do you mean? We haven't even had breakfast yet and lunch won't be for three hours!" The Jews of that time made morning sacrifices before the first meal and wine was consumed only at the main meal. The criticism was out of line and Peter wanted those who had made it to know how absurd it was.

Not the best topic paragraph for an opening of a sermon! And yet, it started Peter preaching about what really happened. I once heard a pastor open a sermon to his congregation explaining the renewal of the Holy Spirit in many of his people: "Some of you are concerned about what's happening in your church, and I want to show you how it is solidly biblical and sane." Real communication took place because he first took the objections seriously and then launched into a thoroughly biblical message on the validity of what was happening and why every member should be involved. When I complimented him on his exposition, he said, "I'm very thankful for the objections—they gave me a chance to explain and exhort."

Once Peter started, he was caught up by the Spirit's power. A further miracle of Pentecost resulted: the miracle of preaching. You may wonder why I call preaching a miracle; we've all heard plenty of it that didn't seem very miraculous to us! But preaching of a biblical text with the power of the Spirit, to people whom He has prepared, seldom lacks for miraculous result: conviction, faith, and changed lives. Authentic preaching is really prophecy—not foretelling, but forthtelling. It is done with boldness, courage, and urgency. And it's not only done in hand-carved pulpits with colored hangings for the right season of the Christian year. Preaching is certainly a special calling, but its main purpose is to proclaim the gospel in an impelling way so that every member can be prophetic in sharing the faith.

Peter explained that the gift of the Holy Spirit had produced the prophetic praise the crowds had observed the believers forthtelling. It was exactly what the prophet Joel had predicted, based on what the Lord had told him: *"I will pour out My Spirit in those days; and they shall prophesy"* (Acts 2:18; Joel 2:29). Having established the Scriptural basis for what was happening, Peter went on to utilize and exemplify the very gift that was being given. He had bigger things to do than defensively explain away the sobriety of Jesus' followers!

The first Christian sermon was Christ-centered. Peter preached Christ, His incarnate life, death, Crucifixion, Resurrection and immanent presence. And the apostle did it in 569 words! He explained God's offer of Himself in Christ; what people did to refuse it; what God did in spite of the refusal; and what could happen now to those who would respond.

The basic thrust is a clear declaration that life in Christ is God's will for His people and all creation. This is unequivocally and convincingly stated right from the beginning. It was God who

68

was manifested in the Man Jesus. He did the miracles, wonders, and signs through Him. Peter could preach with such obvious courage because he was convinced that the Messiah's life, death, and Resurrection were the manifestation of God's immutable, irrevocable will for the salvation of the world. The preacher's authenticity reverberated from that authority.

Note verse 23. Don't miss the strong word behind the English word "purpose." Jesus was *"delivered by the determined purpose and foreknowledge of God. . . ."* The Greek word used here, *boulê*, is the stronger of two words used in the New Testament for the will of God. The other, *thélēma*, means desire. *Boulê* is God's irrevocable will which will be done with or without our cooperation or response. *Thélēma* expresses His desires for us which do call for our response and acceptance as a part of the freedom He's given us.

What Peter is saying to the crowds in Jerusalem is that God's will for the Atonement and reconciliation could not have been stopped or altered by them. It was God's plan and He did it. Those who crucified Jesus thought they were the imperious deciders of His destiny, but God's greater will was being done through it all. We wonder if any from the Sanhedrin were listening to Peter that day. What he said about God's will in the Atonement stripped away their arrogance. They thought they had judged Jesus and put Him to death. Jesus was God's judgment on the world. The Suffering Savior's death was God's will for the judgment and Atonement of sin.

But it was also God's grace. And to that point Peter presses on to put the Atonement and Resurrection into historical perspective. The one through whom God had predestined to save the world had been spoken of by David in Psalms 16 and 110. This is Peter's second source of authority for his Hebrew listeners. And this is climaxed in his own and the other disciples' experience. The Messiah was raised up, exalted, and with the authority of the Father, He poured out His power on the 120 in the Upper Room. And God has done it all. He was in Christ in the Incarnation and in Him in His continuing ministry in the world.

"When they heard this, they were cut to the heart. . ." (v. 37). What does *this* imply? What appeal of Peter's prophetic preaching cut to the core of their consciousness? The clear declaration of who Christ is as the will of God for them. They were not trifling with a Galilean carpenter, but God!

No wonder they cried out, *"What shall we do?"* Peter was ready with an answer and the first Christian invitation to a congregation: *"Repent, and let every one of you be baptized in the name of Jesus Christ for the remission of sins; and you shall receive the gift of the Holy Spirit"* (v. 38). In a way, all three were gifts of the Holy Spirit working in the people who heard Peter.

The word "repent," *metanoéō,* is a two-part word—*metá,* "after," and *néō,* "to perceive," from *noûs,* "the mind." To repent means to change one's mind, to perceive after a mind-changing truth or understanding. Peter wanted them to change their minds about Christ and to see their own desperate need for Him as Lord and Christ of their lives.

The call to be baptized must have been shocking to them. Baptism was used for initiation into Judaism or a radical reconsecration of one who needed forgiveness for sin. It was the latter that Peter obviously implied. Their sins were both spiritual and moral. The word for sin, *hamartía,* means to miss the mark, and it also is used to describe separation from God. The sins we perform are the result of this separation from the sovereignty and guidance of God. The thrust of Peter's challenge is, "You've missed God's offer of salvation in Christ; you are separated from Him, and you are missing the purpose for which you were born and made a part of God's chosen people. What can you do about that? Change your mind! Turn around. Admit your separation from the Lord. Confess the dissoluteness of the direction of your life!"

The call to be baptized in Jesus' name is also bold. "Name" means power and authority. Jesus Christ has that authority through His Cross and Resurrection. As incarnate Christ He said, "Your sins are forgiven." And as exalted, glorified, reigning Lord of all, He has the power to convince the repentant changed mind that it is accomplished. Through the Holy Spirit He liberates people to both repent and confess their sins. He clears the way for Himself, creating the desire and the response. Receiving His Spirit, we find that being filled is the natural result. He prepares a place for Himself and then moves in. It may seem that the decision to receive the Holy Spirit is our choice, but behind that choice is His infused desire, making us willing to receive. Looking back we say, "It was all the Lord from the start to finish. He set me free to want what He wanted to give!"

In verse 23, we looked at the word "purpose" *(boulê).* Let us look at another place in the New Testament where *boulê* is used for God's will. "Who has resisted His will?" (Rom. 9:19). Who wants to? It is the eternal Word of God who made us and who is remaking us!

After a sermon like Peter had preached, we are not surprised that 3,000 souls were added to the 120 to become part of the church that was born that day. Our task as communicators is to claim that same authority, preach and teach with that same conviction, and invite a response, knowing that the same Spirit who helps us prepare and is at work as we speak, will enable a response.

An invitation for people's response in evangelistic meetings is expected and easily given. But I am convinced that some method for an invitation should be worked out for the regular worship services in our congregations. Sometimes it is effective to have a place where people can go to meet with trained officers or members. In my church in Hollywood, the following invitation was printed in the bulletin:

"The pastors and elders will be in the front of the sanctuary to meet with those who desire to receive Christ as Savior and Lord, those who wish to renew their relationship with Him, those who want to unite with the church, and those who need prayer for specific needs." At the end of the services I go to the center of the chancel steps and extend the invitation personally. A Sunday seldom goes by without people coming forward to accept their election and calling to be new persons in Christ, or to receive prayer for some challenge or opportunity of living in Him.

People are more ready than we dare to assume. And why not? The Holy Spirit is at work!

THE MIRACLE OF THE CHURCH

[40] And with many other words he testified and exhorted them, saying, "Be saved from this perverse generation."
[41] Then those who gladly received his word were baptized; and that day about three thousand souls were added to them.
[42] And they continued steadfastly in the apostles' doctrine and fellowship, in the breaking of bread, and in prayers. [43] Then fear came upon every soul, and many wonders and signs were done through the apostles. [44] Now all who believed were together, and had all things in common, [45] and sold their possessions and goods, and divided them among all, as anyone had need.

[46] So continuing daily with one accord in the temple, and breaking bread from house to house, they ate their food with gladness and simplicity of heart, [47] praising God and having favor with all the people. And the Lord added to the church daily those who were being saved.

—Acts 2:40–47

The final miracle of the Holy Spirit on that day of Pentecost was the birth of the church. You may wonder why I call that a miracle. It is because I know human nature. Next to the transformation of persons, the second greatest miracle is oneness with others who have been transformed.

The best of human relationships, apart from the Holy Spirit, are based on the barter of mutual needs, interests, causes, or fears. We do not naturally live in close, harmonious, giving, and forgiving relationships. Unless there is something we need either to get or provide, we are not drawn into either friendship or partnership. Without the Holy Spirit, we use people or are used by them depending on our dominance-subservience personality quotient. Loneliness drives people into one place, but that does not mean that they are *together*, really. We are fundamentally selfish.

But when the living Christ sets us free we are able to participate in His external purpose for His people: that they become one—one with Him and one with each other. My definition of the church is: the fellowship of those given by Christ to be to each other what He has been to them, so that together they can be to the world a demonstration of the new humanity He died and lives to make possible. When He performs the miracle of His love in us, it is then that a character transformation begins which makes it possible for us to love unselfishly. The church as it was meant to be is made up of those people.

In this passage we witness the beginning of that miracle. The reasons the new humanity was born are given us to behold with wonderment and reflection. What happened to cause the loss of this unblemished authenticity in the fellowship of so many churches today?

The first quality of the church was that it was made up of 3,120 people who had come to a sure knowledge of salvation through Christ's death and Resurrection, and had received His living presence in His Spirit. Regretfully, arguing theology or judging who was an inside-outsider or an outside-insider came later. But those newly filled believers on Pentecost night were sure of who they were because they were sure of Christ. Let's not give up the example of the irreducible maximum of a church made up of thoroughly convinced, soundly converted, and Holy Spirit-filled believers. The Lord hasn't given up. Nor should we.

The second quality of the newly born church was that they had an objective basis for the subjective experience of being together. What had happened was thoroughly rooted in Scripture.

The completed Bible is that for us today. A Christ-centered church is also a biblical church. The Lord guides His people in the study and preaching of the Word.

Third, the Pentecost church was one which had all things in common. In our benedictions we speak of the communion of the Holy Spirit. The word "communion," *koinōnía*, means having in common. It also means fellowship. There is no true fellowship without Christ's Spirit in us and between us. He is what we have in common. And that is greater than anything or anyone else. He draws us into oneness and loves each of us through each other. Sharing what we have is a natural result of this communion. The newly born believers were together and they shared their possessions and goods. They had been liberated to live for Christ and each other. There was none of the defensive clutching of their own wealth which is so evident in churches today.

A pastor friend of mine serves a small church in a rural community. During the stewardship drive one fall, he went to the local banker and asked for an estimate of the net worth of all of his members. The amount was astonishing. He announced to the congregation the figure and told them what a tithe of that would do for the mission of that church. The people were both amazed and disturbed. How did the pastor know? The exposure of the resources they were holding back was a telling example of how far we have drifted from the infant church on that Pentecost night. The gift of the Holy Spirit made the new believers free to give away what they had to each other.

The fourth quality flows out of that. Life together in the early church is described as breaking of bread and prayers. In order for people to be galvanized into oneness in Christ, it takes time to be together to listen to each other, care, and be *for* each other. Prayer together becomes the time of communication with the Lord in which we are replenished by His Spirit in order to continue unselfish and nonmanipulative concern and caring for each other.

Praise is the fifth quality of the infant church. They had *"gladness and simplicity of heart, praising God"* (v. 46–47). Praise had been an outward sign of the indwelling of the Spirit when He filled them. It continued to be as He lived in them and in their fellowship. They could not praise enough for all that had happened.

The final quality, I believe, was the natural outgrowth of that praise. People were attracted to their joy and wanted to know the source of it. Evangelism was not based on elaborate handbooks or slick brochures. People wanted to be with those contagious, praising Christians and have what the Spirit had given them.

Here Acts 2 comes to a close, yet this chapter really is only beginning, for what happened on Pentecost is what the Lord wants for every Christian and congregation. Everything led up to Pentecost—the Virgin Birth, the Master's ministry, the Cross, the empty tomb. Without Pentecost there would have been no church. Somewhere in someone's obscure history, a Galilean carpenter might have been mentioned or perhaps the record of the visit of the Messiah to the planet Earth. But it took Pentecost to perform the miracle of the transformation of human personality. Pentecost could not have happened without Calvary and the empty tomb, but if it had not happened, we would not have known what Christ did for us.

When the all-powerful Spirit of the creation power of the Lord sets about the work of recreation, a new creature is made possible. Nothing less is what began at Pentecost. No observable law of human personality was contradicted; a higher law was demonstrated. The human spirit can be enabled by the divine Spirit to know unqualified love. It can be thus enabled to receive unlimited wisdom to maximize the thought of the mind about the purpose and potential of life. And it can thus realize supernatural power through the brain's releasing of energy and healing through the nervous system to the body. The attributes of the Spirit become the abilities of the human spirit; the character of the divine Person becomes the characteristics of the human personality. The life Christ lived can become both model and might. When the eternal Logos comes within us, we are freed not just to live our lives for Him, but to live as recipients and communicators of His life. What happened to Gideon, in a much more sublime and lasting way happens to us. The accurate translation of the Hebrew, "The Spirit of the Lord came upon Gideon," (Judg. 6:34) is, "The Spirit of the Lord clothed Himself with Gideon." In the Upper Room the Lord clothed Himself with 120 ready, eager followers. Then he added 3,000 more. And today, He is clothing Himself with you and me.

NOTE

1. Archbishop William Temple's exposition of John 21 is very helpful in his *Gospel of John*.

CHAPTER FOUR—PENTECOST FAITH FOR THE NEEDS OF PEOPLE

ACTS 3:1–26

Scripture Outline

What Happened? (3:1–10)

Why Did It Happen (3:11–16)

Can It Happen Today? (3:17–26)

Thirty minutes after Pentecost, the apostles knew more about Jesus Christ than they had known from three years of following Him as His disciples. The effluence of Pentecost had given them a new capacity they had not experienced before. The infilling of the Spirit had given them the gift of faith. Prior to Pentecost they had felt dependence and loyalty, but they had no faith. They had witnessed Christ's death with anguish and His resurrection with wonderment, but didn't really understand the cosmic or personal meaning of it all until the gift of faith was mysteriously birthed within them. The apostles were not born again until that joyous Pentecost morning. Conversion was not possible until then.

Now everything began to make sense. The scattered pieces of the puzzle in their minds suddenly all fit together, and what they had heard during the three previous years echoed in their souls. What they were experiencing was the abundant life Jesus had talked about. This is what He meant by their abiding in Him and He in them. For the first time they understood Calvary and the empty tomb. Their minds were flooded with an understanding of why Christ had gone to the Cross and what the Resurrection meant, not only for the vindication of the Master, but for the victorious life it now made possible for them. They had come alive and would live forever. They knew it was all true . . . for them!

But that's not all. This new capacity to believe in what Christ had done for them began to grow into an expectant confidence in what He could do through them. The primary faith they were given by the Spirit for their salvation became a powerful faith to believe that nothing was impossible.

In those early weeks after Pentecost, the apostles had little time to write an analysis of what was happening. Later Peter wrote of it as being "partakers of the divine nature" (2 Pet. 1:4). John called it the "anointing . . . received from Him [that] abides in you" (1 John 2:27). And Paul described it as "Christ in you, the hope of glory" (Col. 1:27). Through the reflection of their focus we can understand what was taking place. What we see manifested right from the beginning, and all through the Book of Acts, is what Paul called the fruit of the Spirit and the gifts of the Spirit. In Galatians 5:22–23 he lists the character traits of people in whom the Spirit lives: "Love, joy, peace, longsuffering, kindness, goodness, faithfulness, gentleness, self-control." The character of Jesus Christ transplanted! In 1 Corinthians 12 and 13 Paul lists the gifts of the Spirit. They are the grace gifts, *chárismata*—endowments graciously given producing a charisma previously unexperienced. Specifically, they are love, wisdom, knowledge, faith, healings, working of miracles, discerning the spirits, the power of praise in tongues, and the gift of interpretation. Under the guidance of the Holy Spirit, and by careful observation of the authentic experience of being filled with Him, the church clarified for itself and all ages the undeniable evidence of an empowered life.

In Acts 3 we see the manifestation of three of the gifts of the Spirit: faith, gifts of healing, and working of miracles. The three belong together. The latter two are really part of the first. Closely intertwined, they equal a daring faith given to the Spirit-filled believers for ministry to people. The need before us brings forth the gift from the Spirit within us. And Christ in us continues to do through us what He did as Jesus of Nazareth. The same power which dwelt in Him is ours. And it's for the healing of the lame of the world—in body, mind, and spirit. The power of Pentecost faith is for people in need. It is for our joy, but never our private enjoyment. Rather, it is so that the things Jesus did for people, we can do.

In this third chapter of Acts, the focus is on the remedial faith which grows out of the reconciling faith of salvation. The chapter is divided into two sections, 3:1–10 and 3:11–26. The first deals with the healing of the lame man by Peter and John; the second with Peter's exposition of what happened. To put it another way, which is helpful in communicating to others the rich treasure of this chapter, it is the exposure of the gift of faith, and the explanation of its source. A helpful outline which I plan to follow in this chapter is represented by three questions: (1) What happened? (2) Why did it happen, and (3) How can it happen today? The empathizing bridge to the real meaning of this passage for ourselves and others is to identify what paralysis of body, mind, or spirit we may have, or may be crippling the people around us. Then we can appreciate and appropriate the gift of healing faith for ourselves and them.

Actually identify the paralysis you are feeling right now. Think of the ways people you love are disabled in personality or relationships as well as their bodies. Now let's live in the passage.

WHAT HAPPENED?

> 3:1 Now Peter and John went up together to the temple at the hour of prayer, the ninth hour. ² And a certain man lame from his mother's womb was carried, whom they laid daily at the gate of the temple which is called Beautiful, to ask alms from those who entered the temple; ³ who, seeing Peter and John about to go into the temple, asked for alms. ⁴ And fixing his eyes on him, with John, Peter said, "Look at us." ⁵ So he gave them his attention, expecting to receive something from them. ⁶ Then Peter said, "Silver and gold I do not have, but what I do have I give you: In the name of Jesus Christ of Nazareth, rise up and walk." ⁷ And he took him by the right hand and lifted him up, and immediately his feet and ankle bones received strength. ⁸ So he, leaping up, stood and walked and entered the temple with them—walking, leaping, and praising God. ⁹ And all the people saw him walking and praising God. ¹⁰ Then they knew that it was he who sat begging alms at the Beautiful Gate of the temple; and they were filled with wonder and amazement at what had happened to him.
> —Acts 3:1–10

Peter and John are on the way to the temple for afternoon prayers. Josephus tells us in his *Antiquities* that the stated times for worship were the early morning for prayers, and again at the ninth hour, or 3:00 P.M., and the evening oblation at sunset when the sacrifices were offered in keeping with Exodus 23:39. The two disciples made their way from the Upper Room area of the city into the temple. Luke tells us that at the Beautiful Gate they met a man lame from birth. There has been lengthy discussion through the years about which gate this was. Some have suggested the Shusan Gate which led into the court of the Gentiles called the Golden Gate. But most New Testament scholars identify the Beautiful Gate with the Corinthian Gate which led from the Court of the Gentiles to the Court of the Women. In volume 5 of his *Wars,* Josephus describes the Corinthian Gate in great detail. It was made of Corinthian bronze. Its doors were forty cubits high and the gate itself, fifty cubits high. Says Josephus, "It was adorned after a most costly manner having much richer and thicker plates of gold and silver." Other sources tell us that it was cast with the symbol of a vine, signifying Israel's cherished confidence of being the vine of God in the vineyard of history. In the sunshine, the polished bronze, gold, and silver shone with spectacular beauty. I believe that it was just outside this gate, on the side of the Court of the Gentiles, that the lame man was carried each day to beg for alms.

When he saw Peter and John approach the gate, his attention was attracted to them immediately. Their radiant countenance was like the gate itself. And what was about to happen would be a fulfillment of Jesus' declaration, "I am the vine, you are the branches" (John 15:5). The fruit that He said His followers would produce was about to be harvested in the life of a crippled man whose paralysis was symbolic of the humanity Christ had come, and then returned in the Spirit, to liberate.

We are pleased especially that Luke, a physician, was the one who described the event. Medical Greek terms diagnose the lame man's condition and his cure. W. K. Hobart shows the use of the same terms in *Hippocrates.* "The words used to describe the seat of the lameness tend to show that the writer was acquainted with medical phraseology, and had investigated the nature of the disease under which the man suffered." The paralytic's congenital difficulty was centered in his feet. He was lame, *chōlós,* with paralysis in the base or heels of his feet in the socket of the ankle. The bones were out of place from birth and he was not able to walk. His only livelihood was the merciful alms of people on their way in or out of worship in the temple. I have watched beggars in cities all over the world. They have a highly developed sense of who will respond. While walking down a street one day, I spied a beggar at the end of the block. I noticed that his eyes darted from person to person as they passed by him, and he called out for a gift from only certain people. He could tell which ones were likely to stop. I felt pity for the man long before he saw me. Just to test out my theory, I purposely looked away as I passed him, fully intending to return and follow Jesus' admonition to "give to those who ask you." But all this thought about my experiment affected me enough to alert the beggar's heightened sense of a good prospect. He called for my attention and a gift, to which I responded with an extra measure for helping me with my experiment.

A very professional woman beggar in Edinburgh, Scotland, stopped me on George Street while I was there writing this commentary. She had a well-rehearsed story of why she needed a shilling. It was carefully told in the thickest of burrs. I responded reluctantly because of the polished, oft-told tale of woe. But, I saw her often on my walks between periods of writing. She stopped me a second time and then looked at me more carefully. "Auch, I've 'done' you before. On your way!"

The lame man at the gate in Jerusalem must have known Peter and John and observed their joyous faces. He knew with a beggar's skill that they would be good marks. He asked for alms. The form of the Greek verb, *ērōta*, inchoative imperfect, indicates that it was a reiterated appeal which he had chanted for years, but began to repeat especially for Peter and John.

The apostles stopped and looked at him intently. They fixed their eyes on him. The text means they stopped, looked at the man, and really thought about him and what he was asking. That's significant, for they saw a pitiful beggar seated helplessly next to the magnificence of the bronze, silver, and gold of the Corinthian gate. What a contrast of the splendid and squalid!

The two apostles said a curious thing: *"Look at us"* (v. 4). Why did they have to get his attention after he had gotten theirs? The reason was that he kept on calling out to others while he had two good prospects in hand. If he had a response from them, he didn't want to miss any other possibilities in the meantime. But Peter and John cared about the man. Their request for his full attention expressed their deep feelings of compassion, and it quickened the man's expectation.

And it quickened something else. The Spirit-filled disciples sensed a stirring within them. What would Jesus have done in that situation? Healed the man! Could they? Dare they try? Faith that it would happen surged in them as they came eye to eye with the lame man. The gift of faith was given.

Peter spoke amazing words, which I think he accompanied with a gesture toward the silver and gold of the gate: *"Silver and gold I do not have, but what I do have I give you: In the name of*

Jesus Christ of Nazareth, rise up and walk" (v. 6). What he offered was more valuable than all the silver and gold of that gate. But the man could not respond to the words. It was when Peter took him by his right hand that the miracle began to happen. Luke's careful attention to detail in saying it was Peter's right hand is an interesting exposure of his intimate knowledge of him and the fact that he was right-handed. In such an important move as Peter made, the motor reflex of his brain would be to use his dominant hand. As he grasped the man he followed Jesus' usual practice of actually making contact with touch in the healing of a person. When Peter lifted up the man and spoke the name of Jesus, divine, healing energy flowed to the sockets of his ankles. A joining together, an articulation, took place, linking what had been out of connection. The gift of faith was now being released in the gift of healing. The Lord was continuing to heal through His grace-gifted apostles!

The word *exallómenos,* "leaping up," from *hállomai,* is an ancient medical term for the socketing of the heel and ankle. The process, which would have taken corrective surgery and months of prolonged healing and learning to walk, took place in a split second.

Picture the previously lame man with newfound strength in his ankles, walking, leaping. And he did something else which indicates a Hebrew religious background. He praised God. Imagine in your mind's eye how he took those first cautious steps, then tried walking, and finally leaped about in uncontainable gratitude to God. It would be difficult for an energetic expositor who is teaching or preaching this passage not to impress on his listeners the wonder of it all by actually demonstrating those movements of stepping, walking, and leaping. It might be a "look-at-us" attention-arrester for the really salient thing which needs to be said next in the exposition.

Before moving on, however, I'd like to share an illustrative aside on movements in the pulpit. While I was serving the First Presbyterian Church of Bethlehem, Pennsylvania, I preached a message on the inseparability of faith and works called, "The Two-Legged Gospel," in which I tried to clarify that to walk or run with the Master takes personal faith and social responsibility. In the first five minutes, standing on my right leg, I preached hard about faith. Because it was an enclosed pulpit, the people did not see that I was on one leg. As I neared the end of that, my balance on one leg was lost and I fell toward the left, catching myself with a quick grasp on the pulpit side. The same was repeated on the left leg until I again lost my balance. Then I spent the last ten minutes explaining why we must stand, walk, and run with Christ on both legs of the gospel. If I had done something like that every Sunday in the years as pastor, it would have become anticipatable showmanship. It is interesting—anytime I return to Bethlehem, someone reminds me of that sermon. Years of rhetoric about wholesome discipleship got focused in a carefully selected physical movement.

The important thing, however, is that preaching be combined with signs of the Lord's power at work in the lives of people. The early church discovered through experience that the Lord had called them to preach, teach, and heal in His name. When the Spirit of the Lord is given full reign in a congregation, there will be healings of people's spiritual, psychological, and physical needs. When we preach and teach Christ and pray for people's needs, miracles do happen. And the greatest miracle, as we have said at length earlier, is the transformation of a person from self-centeredness to Christ-centeredness and then to a person-centric ministry. When emotionally troubled people receive the healing of the Holy Spirit through loving counseling and prayer, both the congregation and the community sit up to take notice. And He continues to heal physical illness, not only through the practice of skilled medical professionals, but through the direct prayer for healing of those who claim His gifts of faith, healing, and working of miracles. For that to be more the expected than the rare exception today, we need to press on to why the lame man was healed.

WHY DID IT HAPPEN?

[11] Now as the lame man who was healed held on to Peter and John, all the people ran together to them in the porch which is called Solomon's, greatly amazed. [12] So when Peter saw it, he responded to the people: "Men of Israel, why do you marvel at this? Or why look so intently at us, as though by our own power or godliness we had made this man walk? [13] The God of Abraham, Isaac, and Jacob, the God of our fathers, glorified His Servant Jesus, whom you delivered up and denied in the presence of Pilate, when he was determined to let Him go. [14] But you denied the Holy One and the Just, and asked for a murderer to be granted to you, [15] and killed the Prince of life, whom God raised from the dead, of which we are witnesses.

16 And His name, through faith in His name, has made this man strong, whom you see and know. Yes, the faith which comes through Him has given him this perfect soundness in the presence of you all.

—Acts 3:11–16

What happened to the lame man drew the attention of the worshipers at the temple. They knew him, having seen him in his customary place, perhaps for years. The Lord had had three purposes in the healing. First, He loved that lame man and released His healing power out of His heart of compassion and concern. Second, He wanted to alert the people, particularly the leaders of Israel, that the movement He had begun as Jesus of Nazareth was continuing through His disciples in whom He was living. During the Incarnation, Jesus had healed people out of sheer love for them, but also as a sign of His authority and power as the Messiah. The healing of the lame man was an undeniable, further sign that He was alive. Once again, He had Jerusalem's attention. The rushing wind of Pentecost a few days before was the talk of the city. The wind was still blowing. But now the Lord had chosen, called, and convinced people who had become like wind tunnels through whom His force was focused. And they were the third purpose for the healing miracle. They, most of all, needed to know that He had meant it when He said, "Until now you have asked nothing in My name. Ask and you will receive, that your joy may be full" (John 16:24).

The gifts of the Lord's Spirit were being manifested, in a confirmation of Pentecost. The church had discovered that the power and passion of the wind and fire was given to them for a needy, paralyzed world. That's why a forceful exposition of Acts 3 is so important to us today. We tend to want to linger with the excitement of the effluence. Some Christians never get to Pentecost; others have never moved on to use what they have received in ministry to people. How very sensitive Luke was to follow the dynamics of Pentecost with an example of the purpose of that power.

Peter's sermon to the *"greatly amazed"* crowd was really an exposition of a miracle. He seized the opportunity and went straight to the vital need. The people needed to know that neither he nor John had healed the lame man. He pointed away from the two of them to the One who had done it. *"Why look so intently at us, as though by our own power or godliness we had made this*

82

man walk?" Notice that he picked out the two qualities among the Jews which were the greatest source of pride—moral impeccability and religious diligence. Could either of these have healed this man? That's powerful communication. He affirmed the best that they had accomplished as religious people and went beyond it to talk about a whole new dimension of life, and a neglected and rejected one at that! Peter had experienced the gifts of faith and healing; now he was being given the gifts of wisdom, knowledge, and discernment.

He was given the power to make clear that no human piety or perfection had made possible the miracle. Then with wisdom, the deep understanding of the mysteries of the Lord, he went on to explain who had done the miracle with refined Christology only the Spirit could have empowered. He used five illuminating divine names to get to the place where he could talk about what faith exercised in the name of Jesus had done. They serve as a basis of clear communication of Christology for us. Acts 3:12–16 is worthy of a message or class in itself. Let's consider these five names as points of clarification.

Peter began with the basics. (1) *"The God of Abraham, Isaac, and Jacob"* was the source behind what had happened. The Lord God of Israel had come in the life of Jesus of Nazareth. (2) *"His Servant"* is taken directly from Isaiah 52:13 in the passages about the sin-bearing servant (also note 42:1–9, 49:1–13, 52:1–12). The uses of this sacred name of the Messiah with Jesus' name left little doubt of what Peter believed Jesus had come to be and do. *"His Servant Jesus"* established the preacher's conviction. This is the same One whom Israel denied. (3) He was truly *"the Holy One."* The term was used for the majesty, glory, and purity of God. The Redeemer God is the Holy One of Israel in Isaiah 31:1, 41:14, and 43:14. Peter is growing in boldness as he adds (4) *"the Just,"* again, a term used for God to assert the perfect congruity between His nature and His acts. "Righteous One" is used in the Revised Standard Version. The Greek word *dikaíos* is used for both "the Just" and "the Righteous One." The gift of wisdom and knowledge is flowing through Peter as he nears the climax of his impelling Christology. (5) Christ is also *"the Prince of life."* This glorious name is also translated as Author of life, Pioneer of life, and Guide of life. The creative power of God, the divine Logos, the Word of life, is the same One who came in the Messiah Jesus. The Greek word *archēgós* is used. It means author, the one who is the instigator, who takes a lead, but most of all, who is the first occasion of anything—the uncreated Creator, the unmoved Mover, the uncaused Cause. It was through Christ that all things were made! (John 1:3). And Christ was not only the cause of salvation through the Cross; He became our salvation.

This display of spiritual wisdom must have stunned Peter's listeners that day there on Solomon's porch of the temple area. It was all in preparation for his final thrust in verse 16, *"And His name, through faith in His name, has made this man strong, whom you see and know. Yes, the faith which comes through Him has given him this perfect soundness in the presence of you all."*

Faith in the name! That's the secret of the lame man's healing. And it is the secret of unlocking all power in heaven and earth. The name, as we have observed, meant the authority and power of a person which could be called forth by another who was given that right. The phrase "in the name of Caesar," when used by an official, meant that the power of the emperor and all his kingdom could be brought to bear on that particular situation. "In the name of the king," in more recent history, implies by the authority and imperial power of that king. But there is something deeper here for us. In Hebrew, *šēm*, translated "name," was used as a sacred synonym for God. In order not to break the third commandment, and because no Hebrew spoke the name Yahweh, "Name" became the acceptable designation of God.

The Spirit had given Peter the gift of faith in the divine Savior. His name was synonymous with His presence and His power. His use of faith in his explanation that day meant acceptance of who Christ was, what He had done in the Atonement on Calvary, and that He was the risen, present Lord. That acceptance also meant complete trust and commitment by will to do His will. There is no record of Peter using the word "faith" before that day, not even in his message on Pentecost morning. It was a new word which he had heard in Christ's teaching, but which now had been given to him as a gift by His Spirit. Note how he stresses the essential, crucial role of faith. *"Through faith in His name. . . . Yes, the faith which comes through Him. . . ."* The name is the power of Jesus Christ, and faith in Him opens us and any person or situation needing healing to that power!

CAN IT HAPPEN TODAY?

[17] "Yet now, brethren, I know that you did it in ignorance, as did also your rulers. [18] But those things which God foretold by the mouth of all His prophets, that the Christ would suffer,

He has thus fulfilled. [19] Repent therefore and be converted, that your sins may be blotted out, so that times of refreshing may come from the presence of the Lord, [20] and that He may send Jesus Christ, who was preached to you before, [21] whom heaven must receive until the times of restoration of all things, which God has spoken by the mouth of all His holy prophets since the world began. [22] For Moses truly said to the fathers, 'The LORD your God will raise up for you a Prophet like me from your brethren. Him you shall hear in all things, whatever He says to you. [23] And it shall be that every soul who will not hear that Prophet shall be utterly destroyed from among the people.'
[24] Yes, and all the prophets, from Samuel and those who follow, as many as have spoken, have also foretold these days. [25] You are sons of the prophets, and of the covenant which God made with our fathers, saying to Abraham, 'And in your seed all the families of the earth shall be blessed.' [26] To you first, God, having raised up His Servant Jesus, sent Him to bless you, in turning away every one of you from your iniquities."

—Acts 3:17–26

Once again, as in his first sermon, Peter faithfully draws the net. There is sensitive compassion in gracious acceptance of the people's ignorance. But that does not lessen the need for a response now. We sense Peter's longing for the people to be given the same gift of faith he has received. There is warning and clarification of the danger of one more refusal. And the apostle ends with a reminder of how much the Lord wants to bless them.

What does all this mean for us today? Can it still happen? Acts 3 is not a description of a one-time, never-to-be-repeated period in the Holy Spirit's activity in the world. The great, debilitating delusion is that the gifts of faith, healing, and working of miracles ended with the apostolic age. Not so! The Lord is the same. The needs of people are not essentially different. What He did through His Spirit, living in people just like you and me, He wants to do today.

I want to draw our consideration to a close with several statements that summarize what Acts 3 teaches us and to ask a question about each.

1. Faith is not a humanly initiated capacity. It is utterly futile and guilt-producing to tell ourselves or anyone else that what we need is faith or more faith. We can't produce it! Faith is a response to Christ's love revealed on the Cross and in the Resurrection. Faith comes by

hearing that sublime truth. When our minds are invaded with the assurance of His forgiveness and acceptance, He gives the gift to respond. That response is expressed in the elements of faith—acceptance, surrender of our lives, a commitment of all that we have and are to serve Him as Lord of our lives, and an openness and willingness to be filled with His Spirit. Are we alive in the abundant life with the confidence of eternal life because of that faith?

2. The Holy Spirit who gave us the gift of faith to believe the gospel also gives us a gift of applied faith for the specific needs and challenges of life. Paul speaks of it as being revealed "from faith to faith" (Rom. 1:17)—from one level of faith to a greater level . . . from some to more . . . from what Christ did for us to what He is ready to do for us. It is the confidence that nothing is impossible for the Lord. Has our being filled with the Spirit given us this bold quality of faith?

3. The Spirit of the resurrected Lord is the healing power of the world. There is no healing that takes place apart from Him, even though often He is neither acknowledged nor thanked by the majority of people today. That healing power is available to Christians today through the Spirit's gift of healing for the physical, emotional, personal, interpersonal needs of our lives and the people for whom He guides us to pray. First we are to pray in order to know what to ask and then to ask it with the gift of confident faith. Have you ever asked for the gift of healing?

4. The advanced gift of faith gives us the courage to pray in the name of Jesus. That clarifies what is in keeping with all we know of what He said, did, and does. Unless a prayer request glorifies Him, His name cannot be used nor His power released. But once the rightness is established, we are given the release of His Spirit to ask for and expect what through the facility of imagination He has pictured for us as the focus of our prayers of intercession and supplication. Have we discovered the power of the name?

The result of saying "Yes!" to these questions will be the quality of boldness Luke describes in Acts 4. It is to that birthright blessing that we press on with eager anticipation!

NOTE

1.   W. K. Hobart, *The Medical Language of St. Luke* (Dublin, 1884), p. 34.

CHAPTER FIVE—THE GIFT OF BOLDNESS
ACTS 4:1–31

Scripture Outline

The Boldness of the Resurrection (4:1–4)

The Boldness of the Holy Spirit (4:5–8)

The Boldness of the Name (4:9–11)

The Boldness of Jesus Only (4:12)

The Boldness of the Transformed Life (4:13–14)

The Boldness of Responding to Opposition (4:15–22)

The Boldness of Prayer (4:23–31)

An undeniable sign of the indwelling power of the Holy Spirit is boldness. It's the inner delight of a liberated person expressed in daring. In the midst of human impotence and the timidity of institutionalized religion, the great need is for boldness in loving, forgiving, speaking the truth in love, and obedience to the strategy of God revealed to us in prayer.

Boldness is the key to an exposition and vivid communication of Acts 4:1–31. The fulcrum verse of the section is verse 13: *"Now when they saw the boldness of Peter and John, and perceived that they were uneducated and untrained men, they marveled. And they realized that they had been with Jesus."* The word "boldness" is *parrēsía*, "telling all" *(pan-rēsia).* It means the conviction, communication, and character of an adventuresome life based on undeniable truth and experience. Boldness arrests attention, compelling people to listen. It combines the emphasis of "I know this is true because it's happened to me," with a "thus saith the Lord" clarity. It is rooted in Scripture and personal communion with the

Lord. There is no apology or solicitous equivocation. True boldness, which comes from "being with Jesus" is winsome because we know that He has won the battle with death, Satan, and the world (John 6:20).

The apostles had a holy boldness. They were possessed by a great affection, a passion motivated by their experience of Jesus, His Resurrection, and His return in power in the Holy Spirit. Someone, not just something, had happened to them both before and after Pentecost. They were the new creation, God's new breed, filled with the excitement of the promise Jesus had made them: "Most assuredly, I say to you, he who believes in Me, the works that I do he will do also; and greater works than these he will do, because I go to My Father. And whatever you ask in My name, that I will do, that the Father may be glorified in the Son" (John 14:12–13). The greater works of quantity, not quality, were being done. Christ was unloosed on the world. The apostles were filled with His Spirit; thousands had responded to their preaching of the gospel; a lame man had been healed; and nothing was impossible now.

In this section of our exposition, we will consider the source and substance, the motive and nature, of authentic boldness. The passage falls into a natural sequence for very exciting Bible study, preaching, and teaching.

THE BOLDNESS OF THE RESURRECTION

4:1 Now as they spoke to the people, the priests, the captain of the temple, and the Sadducees came upon them,
2 being greatly disturbed that they taught the people and preached in Jesus the resurrection from the dead. 3 And they laid hands on them, and put *them* in custody until the next day, for it was already evening. 4 However, many of those who heard the word believed; and the number of the men came to be about five thousand.

—*Acts 4:1–4*

The motive of the boldness of the apostles was the Resurrection— Christ's and their own. They were the Easter people for whom Christ's Resurrection was the central fact of history and the focus of their faith in a living Lord. The experience of the empty tomb, now maximized by the power of the Holy Spirit, gave them a mission and a message. The Resurrection had enabled regeneration in them. Their character was being transformed by the same power that raised Jesus from the dead. The more they focused on the victory of the empty tomb, their experience of the resurrected Lord, and the fire of His Spirit burning within them, the more they sensed a new freedom from self-centeredness, competitiveness, pride, and defensiveness. What had happened to them, they wanted to happen through them to everyone.

That was the verve and vitality of their bold preaching. The Resurrection was recapitulated in them. What Paul later organized into theological clarity in Romans 6 was unstudied, irrepressible dynamic in their lives: they had died to themselves and had been raised to a death-defying, life-affirming, everything's-possible, contagious faith.

Christ's Resurrection is the source of triumphant disillusionment. The true meaning of disillusionment is to set free of illusions. Think of the false illusions about God, life now and forever, death and the power of Satan, that Christ's Resurrection smashes! The worst that man can do is only a prelude to the best that God has to offer. Rebellious humanity thought it had shrieked the final word at Calvary, only to find that God had had the last word on Easter morning. The illusion that death had the ultimate power over life was exposed as false. The Resurrection made death a helpless comma in eternal life and put an exclamation point in every event of daily living. Christ's hope-filled assertion to Martha became the charter of a bold people: "I am the Resurrection and the life. He who believes in Me, though he may die, he shall live. And whoever lives and believes in Me shall never die. Do you believe this?" (John 11:25–26). The apostles remembered and believed.

A famous heart surgeon sat in the Easter service of my church. He had been attending services for a long time but had never made a commitment to Christ. As the Scripture was read about the Resurrection, he was given the gift of faith to believe. "This is true, this is really true!" he whispered to his wife. A few days later, he gave his life to Christ and received the indwelling power of the Holy Spirit. He has grown rapidly in his new life. An immense intellect, he has found that his skill, training, and learning have been multiplied by the Spirit's power. Miraculous things are happening in his practice. Recently he made an outstanding gift to our church's medical ministry in Japan as part of a special missions fund drive. The challenge was to trust God for extra monies He would channel through faithful givers for the mission work. A month later, he received a royalty check for the amount of his pledge. His textbook on cardiovascular surgery had been translated into Japanese! A long succession of interventions by the Holy Spirit has made him a bold spokesman for Christ. Nothing can stop him now—the things he's seen and heard are undeniable.

Note that the apostles *"taught the people and preached in Jesus the resurrection from the dead"* (v. 2). That implies that they preached Christ's Resurrection, the resurrection from the dead for those who believed in Him, and the joy of resurrection living filled with interventions of the uplifting power of God for life's problems and perplexities. Christ's Resurrection, plus our regeneration, equals release from fear and frustration. No wonder the number of those who believed *"came to be about five thousand"* (v. 4).

It also explains why *"the priests, the captain of the temple, and the Sadducees came upon them, being greatly disturbed"* (v. 1). The word for "disturbed" is *diaponoúmenoi*, the present passive particle of *diaponéō*, meaning that they were worked up with indignation and annoyance. Why this strong reaction?

Some background is helpful. The leaders were from the Sanhedrin, the highest ruling body of the Jews. It was made up of seventy leaders plus the high priest, who served as president. There were three groups and two parties represented in the seventy. The rulers were the chief priests of the temple. Each was appointed to represent one of the twenty-four courses of priests who served on a weekly rotation in the temple to perform the sacrifices and maintain the purity and propriety of worship. The elders were the tribal or family heads of the nation. The scribes were the experts in the Law and the oral tradition, the accumulated implications of the Law for practice in daily life.

The two religious parties in the Sanhedrin were the Pharisees and the Sadducees. The Pharisees were vigilant, nationalistic leaders who were committed to the preservation of the Law, the traditions of the people, and the minute detail of the regulations of their religion. They abhorred foreign domination, admitted the possibility of spirits, accepted the idea of resurrection, and awaited the coming of the Messiah, but only according to their carefully defined presuppositions. Most of them had come from the trade class and were known for impeccable legalism.

The Sadducees were the landed gentry. They controlled the wealth, owned most of the land, and wielded immense power. Collaboration with foreign conquerors was accepted as a necessity for the maintenance of their material advantages. Therefore, they wanted peace at any price, and the price had become exorbitantly high under Roman domination. They wanted no disturbance of the balance of power, the détente they had carefully worked out with Rome. As the wealthy aristocracy, they held control of the purse strings and kept them tightly closed around their holdings. Theologically, they were often in direct conflict with the Pharisees. For example, they did not believe in resurrection, a life beyond the grave, or the spirit realm of either angels or devils. They did not live in anxious expectation of the messianic kingdom—for very specific political reasons. The turbulence and conflict that would bring would surely threaten their financial security. F. J. Foakes-Jackson underlines the fear: "To the Jew of this time, it meant imminent world catastrophe, in which the powers of the earth would be destroyed and a new order miraculously set up." For the Sadducees, resurrection and revolution were synonymous. Both spelled disturbance for those who desperately wanted to keep things as they were.

Now we can see why the Pharisees opposed Jesus for theological reasons and why the Sadducees abhorred the early Christians for political and economic reasons. It was the Sadducean party which precipitated the conflict with the apostles. Luke is pointed in his inclusion of the Sadducees as part of the group which *"came upon"* (v. 1) Peter and John. The Greek reads *epéstēsan autoîs,* or "burst upon them suddenly and expressed a hostile attitude of anger." They were alarmed because of the preaching of resurrection through Jesus, the miracle they had performed in His name, and the assurance of the immediacy and intensity of the Holy Spirit.

This presses us to ask: who are the Sadducees today? Or, more personally, what are the things we must protect and defend which make the bold living and sharing of the victorious life in Christ difficult for us? And what of the local congregation? Luke has given us a convicting comparison between the defensive blandness of the officialdom and the boldness of the church alive with the resurrection hope and power. After the healing of the lame man at the Beautiful Gate, the crowds gathered on Solomon's portico to hear Peter forcefully preach that the miracle had been done in the name of Jesus. The message was unmistakable: Christ, whom the Jews had crucified, had been resurrected and was alive with them through the Holy Spirit, continuing His miraculous ministry through the apostles.

When word of that reached the Sadducees, they quickly gathered the temple police, who were stationed to keep law and order, and the chief priests, who wanted no disturbance of the sacrifices of the temple. The Sadducees instigated the arrest and had Peter and John put in custody overnight. We wonder why they didn't call the Sanhedrin together immediately for a trial. Of course, it was evening, and Jewish law forbade a trial after sundown. But surely what they really wanted was to use the night hours for gathering their forces and making sure their party represented a majority to tip off the balance of power with the Pharisees. The Sadducees had cooperated with the Pharisees, the chief priest, and the high priest in sealing the decision for the death of Jesus; now some clever levering pressure had to be put on the Pharisees to get their compliance to silence these bold witnesses to the Resurrection. We can only imagine the maneuvering that went on that night.

THE BOLDNESS OF THE HOLY SPIRIT

5 And it came to pass, on the next day, that their rulers, elders, and scribes, 6 as well as Annas the high priest, Caiaphas, John, and Alexander, and as many as were of the family of the high priest, were gathered together at Jerusalem. 7 And when they had set them in the midst, they asked, "By what power or by what name have you done this?"

8 Then Peter, filled with the Holy Spirit, said to them, "Rulers of the people and elders of Israel:

—*Acts 4:5–8*

Imagine the awesome confrontation. Here were two Galilean fishermen face to face with the most powerful authority figures in Israel—enough to freeze anyone with fear. Picture the array of scowling, angry, and hostile leaders robed in dignity, seated in a semicircle in their auspicious chamber. Empathize with what the apostles must have felt as they stood in the center, all eyes fixed negatively on them and the lame beggar they had healed. Feel the conflicting emotions which surged within them as they looked into the faces of the very people who had condemned their beloved Lord to death less than two months before. Did they have frightening flashbacks to that anguishing Passover night? When we get inside the skins of Peter and John, we begin to capture the turbulent thoughts and feelings they experienced.

The drama of the scene intensifies as we feel the rage and consternation of Annas and Caiaphas. They had assumed that they had dealt with Jesus and His followers once and for all when they had manipulated the Sanhedrin and checkmated Pilate to assure the Galilean's Crucifixion. Not so! Here were two of the Crucified's disciples who were claiming that He was alive, preaching the

Resurrection through Him, and performing miracles in His name. If Jesus the Rabbi who claimed to be the Messiah had been dangerous, a movement of His followers preaching His living presence was fraught with the potential of revolution. All of the fear and hatred Annas and his family had felt for Jesus was now focused in hurricane force on Peter and John. What was behind this alarm? Why had Annas and Caiaphas acted so imperiously to destroy Jesus and now moved so swiftly to check the rising popularity of His followers?

Again, background is helpful. Annas was the infamous power behind the ecclesiastical throne in Jerusalem. He had been high priest from A.D. 6–14. Five of his sons, and now Caiaphas, his son-in-law, had followed him in the powerful office. Before the Roman occupation, a high priest had held office for life, but by this time an appointment was made each year by the Roman governor. It went to the highest bidder and one who was willing to be a collusive collaborator with Rome. Annas had used his immense wealth to assure the continuance of his nepotistic dynasty. The plot thickens as we discover how he amassed his fortune. The "Bazaars of Annas," as they were called, in the Court of the Gentiles of the temple, sold sacrificial animals at extortionist prices. Only these animals were accepted by the inspectors who were appointed by Annas or the members of his family in office. Tragic exploitation resulted and Annas's fortune grew. The common people hated the high-priestly family. It would not have taken much to ignite an insurrection. Jesus' growing popularity had had to be checked, of course. His preaching and miracles, culminating in the raising of Lazarus from the dead, had instigated the plot of Annas and Caiaphas against Him. But it was the cleansing of the temple of the profitable money-changing and bazaars that sealed His death. Uncalculable time and energy had been expended by the high priest to assure the Crucifixion. Imagine the fiendish delight of the archmanipulators on the Sabbath day after Calvary! Jesus was sealed in His tomb forever. News of the Resurrection had reached them, which they squelched with rumors that someone had stolen the body of Jesus. They were finished with Him forever. . . or so they thought.

Now we can understand the precipitous action against Peter and John. Something had to be done immediately before the people rallied behind them.

Note the mingled caution and consternation expressed when Caiaphas (surely it was he!) led the questioning of the apostles. He knew all too well the answer to his incriminating question, *"By what power or by what name have you done this?"* (v. 7). Jewish law stipulated that a prisoner be asked no question which would incriminate him. This was painfully reminiscent of the mockery of justice violated by Annas and then Caiaphas in the trial of Jesus.

It's against this backdrop that we can appreciate the boldness of Peter and John. Their lives were at stake. Only the Holy Spirit could give them the courage they displayed.

Then Peter, *"filled with the Holy Spirit,"* responded. This alone can explain Peter's daring capacity to speak in that frightening situation. The Spirit took possession of his mind, saturated his emotions, compelled his will, and energized his body. In Acts, there is a difference between being "full of the Holy Spirit" and being "filled with the Holy Spirit." The first begins when we surrender our lives and open ourselves to be both containers and transmitters of the living Spirit of God. The second is given for special need for witness or ministry. Luke tells us that when he was before the Sanhedrin, Peter was "filled." The past aorist passive participle, *plēstheis,* "filled," indicates an act performed upon Peter, rather than a continuing state. He should not have been surprised. Jesus had promised that: "Now when they bring you to the synagogues and magistrates and authorities, do not worry about how or what you should answer, or what you should say. For the Holy Spirit will teach you in that very hour what you ought to say" (Luke 12:11–12). The need before Peter brought forth the power the Holy Spirit infused in him.

The Holy Spirit is both sanctifier and strengthener. He brings to our remembrance what Christ did and said, gives us the gift of faith to believe, and enables us to grow in Christlike character. But it is by the special "filling" of the Holy Spirit that we are given the substance for our boldness. He equips us for a unique situation, pressing problem, difficult challenge, or dangerous extremity. Peter and John's boldness before the Sanhedrin gives us the assurance that we will be given the wisdom, discernment, knowledge, and power to be faithful and obedient in any circumstance or relationship. The anointing of the Holy Spirit will more than match the danger or opportunity. The unlimited resources of God through His own Spirit will be given! We will be filled with the Holy Spirit.

Johannes Weiss put it clearly. He says that the early Christians had "a tempestuous enthusiasm, an overwhelming intensity of feeling, an immediate awareness of the presence of God, an inconquerable sense of power, and an irresistible control over the will and inner spirit and even the physical conditions of other men—these are the ineradicable features of historic early Christianity."[1]

But that presses a question. What are we attempting which could not be accomplished without the Holy Spirit? What is there about our lives that demands an explanation? We will be "filled with the Holy Spirit" when we dare to do what could never be accomplished on our strength and insight.

THE BOLDNESS OF THE NAME

[9] If we this day are judged for a good deed done to a helpless man, by what means he has been made well, [10] let it be known to you all, and to all the people of Israel, that by the name of Jesus Christ of Nazareth, whom you crucified, whom God raised from the dead, by Him this man stands here before you whole. [11] This is the 'stone which was rejected by you builders, which has become the chief cornerstone.'
—*Acts 4:9–11*

The name of Jesus was the secret of the boldness of the apostles. The Lord had promised that He would be with them and whatever they asked in His name would be given them. As we have seen, it was in the name of the Lord Jesus that they had healed the lame man who now stood with them before the Sanhedrin as living testimony. And yet, it was with a supercilious, mocking tone that the high priest had asked by what name they had performed the miracle, implying that it had been by some magical formula or incantation of an exorcist. Peter's response was more than the Sanhedrin had bargained for.

At that time, the word "name" meant the nature, personality, authority, and power of a person. The name was the counterpart of its bearer: his character and essence. In Hebrew, the name of God was synonymous with His presence. Second Samuel 7:13 speaks of the name of God dwelling in His sanctuary. Jeremiah quotes God as swearing by His name. The biblical name of God denotes His attributes. Jesus came in the name of the Lord and sent His disciples out to preach and heal in His name. To speak or act in the name of another was to invoke his presence and power.

Note that when Jesus healed or did a miracle, He did not do it by God's name. He was the name! Immanuel, God with us. The authority and power which was in Him was now delegated and entrusted to the apostles and the church. By His name—His presence—they were empowered to do what He had done during His messianic ministry. As He had said to the man by the Pool of Bethesda, "Rise, take up your bed and walk" (John 5:8), so too in His power the apostles had said to the beggar, "In the name of Jesus Christ of Nazareth, rise up and walk" (Acts 3:6). It had worked just as Jesus had promised. The power of the living Christ was at work through them. The actual manifestation of healing quickened their faith. That explains the boldness before the Sanhedrin. Personal experiences of the power of the name working through us make us unafraid, ready-for-anything people.

Now Peter begins to soar in his lucid, impelling witness. He wants no mistake as to what name healed the lame man. It was Jesus of Nazareth, the same Jesus whom the Sanhedrin crucified. Peter actually accused the leaders of the death of Jesus. Bold. Then he went on to make very clear that this Jesus was none other than the Messiah. He quoted Psalm 118:22, "The stone which the builders rejected has become the chief cornerstone," and Isaiah 28:16, "Therefore thus says the Lord God: 'Behold, I lay in Zion a stone for a foundation, a tried stone, a precious cornerstone, a sure foundation; whoever believes will not act hastily.'" The apostle felt the impact of the objective standard of Scripture as he spoke— another vital source of boldness for the believer. Jesus Christ was the fulfillment of the prophets of old. He was the foundation stone or the keystone at the top of the corner, binding the walls together where they meet. Both meanings are intended by Peter. The point for us is that when we are founded on Scripture, on more than our own subjective ideas, feelings, or experience, we are able to speak with unfettered audacity. The apostle had the testimony of the objective standard of the Old Testament containing the prophecies about the Messiah. Throughout the preaching of Acts and the teaching of the epistles, there is always a fresh explosion of excitement and enthusiasm when ancient Scripture is identified with the historical event of the Incarnation.

I know this to be true in my own life. My life is spent studying the Scriptures and in working with people. The two can never be separated. Boldness in loving, enabling, and helping people discover the triumphant adequacy of Christ is empowered by daily inspiration in the Word of God. The power of the name flashes like lightning and thunders on every page.

As I mentioned earlier, sometime ago I did a survey of the deepest needs in the American people in preparation for a twenty-six week television series. I wanted to speak to the raw nerves in people. When my inventory of thousands of people was completed, I was not surprised to find that anxiety, fear, loneliness, frustration, discouragement, and lack of self-esteem headed the list.

Then I did a comprehensive study of the message of Jesus to find His healing strength to help people turn their struggles into stepping stones. I had not seen it before, but I found that each one of the "I Am" statements in John's Gospel and Revelation powerfully spoke to each one of those struggles.

The pulsebeat of my studies quickened when I rediscovered that the same words that God spoke to Moses at the burning bush are used by Christ when He said "I Am" in declaring He was the living God incarnate, the Messiah. As mentioned in chapter 1, in Hebrew, God's words to Moses are, "I will be that I will be," the implication being that God is "He who will make things happen." The verb *hāyāh*, "to be," when rendered in the third person, masculine, in future tense, and spelled with consonants only, stands in the Old Testament for the divine name Yahweh. When in the translation of this Exodus passage in the Greek Septuagint, the verb "to be" was put in the present tense, *Egō eimí*, the meaning was that Yahweh is the One who causes things to happen *now*. When Jesus said "I Am" in exposing His identity and intention, He made the bold claim to be none other than Yahweh, the pre-existent Lord of all creation, God with us to save us from our sins and make us whole.

In that light, the "I Am" self-affirmations leap off the pages of Scripture. "Before Abraham was, I am," "I am, have no fear," "I am the bread of life," "I am the way, the truth and the life," "I am the vine," "I am the resurrection and the life," and all the others—provide us with the only reliable source of our salvation and the healing of our personalities. I felt a new boldness in proclaiming Christ's power for the deepest needs of people, an authority inseparably related to Jesus' own promises recorded in His claim to be God with us, for us, and in us!

The powerful name of Jesus is available to us today. My own congregation is discovering that power in Jesus' name unlocks the resources of God. In the name of Christ, we have access to the heart of God and an assurance of His availability in the immanence and intimacy of the Holy Spirit.

A few years ago, we began prayer and healing services in our congregation. At the conclusion of each service, people came forward to kneel for prayers of the elders of the church. After the need is explained, the elder intercedes for the person in the name of Jesus, asking for the healing of the physical, spiritual, emotional, interpersonal need in God's timing and plan. The personal prayer ends with the elder saying, "In the name of Jesus, claim your healing, rise, and go in peace." An exciting stream of miracles, healings, reconciliations, revelations of guidance, and new power convinces us that the "I Am," Yahweh, in our midst is the liberating name above all names!

But it's time for an accountability check in our exposition of this section of Acts. Why is there so little evidence of the utilization of the power of the name in contemporary Christianity? Why do we wring our hands at the immensity of untouched human need in churches today? Here's an inventory that will help:

1. Do we believe that Jesus was who He said He was?

2. Did He do the miraculous works of God recorded in the Gospels?

3. Do we accept that what He did as Jesus of Nazareth He continued to do through the apostles and the early church?

4. Is He ready and willing to do the same today in the new chapter of Acts being written in our time?

5. Are we open to the possibility that this can be an age of miracles if we dare to believe and pray adventuresomely in Jesus' name?

6. What is it in me, or in my church, which has blighted our boldness with the blandness of expecting little and settling for it?

This presses us on to the next verse in our exposition. Peter goes on to express an exclusivity which actually resulted in a contagious inclusiveness.

THE BOLDNESS OF JESUS ONLY

12 Nor is there salvation in any other, for there is no other name under heaven given among men by which we must be saved."

—*Acts 4:12*

An impelling boldness is the result of the conviction not just that Jesus saves but only Jesus saves. The key word in this verse is "salvation," *sōtēría*, the free gift of deliverance from sin. It actually means healing and health, wholeness and oneness. The magnificent word stands for everything Jesus Christ came to be and do for us. Through

His life, death and Resurrection, we are reconciled to God. The Cross was a one-time, never-to-be-repeated sacrifice for the sins of the whole world. When we accept His atoning death for our sin, we are forgiven and set free of guilt and self-condemnation. We are born again, beginning life anew as a loved and forgiven new creature. When we let God love us, a new creation begins, the past is forgiven and healed, the future is open to amazing possibilities of freedom and joy. We come alive—now and forever. The Holy Spirit comes to live in us and the healing process of making us whole people begins. We can dare to be ourselves as loved unreservedly by God. His grace—unlimited favor and acceptance—makes us graciously affirming and loving. We cannot contain the ecstasy and delight we feel. Others are blessed with an unqualified acceptance. A lively hope springs up within us. Problems are only the prelude to fresh discoveries of the Spirit's potential. The aching needs in our hungry hearts are fed by a daily, moment-by-moment companionship with the Holy Spirit. Layer by layer, He penetrates into our psyches, reorienting and reconstituting us around the mind of Christ, His wisdom, disposition, and intuition. The will to destroy is replaced by the will to live the abundant life and share it with others. No other religion or cult can promise that!

Recently a young man came to me with the old shibboleth that all religions are but alternative paths to the same God. In response, I asked him to do an extensive study of the historic and contemporary religions of the world, along with some of the cults growing in popularity today. His assignment was to write out what each believed about the essential nature of God, the plan of salvation, the result in the personal experience of the believer, the meaning of death and eternal life, and the accountable lifestyle manifested in the world. When the man completed his work a month later, he exclaimed, "I am astounded! There is an immense difference. I'll never make that simplistic statement again. When I really grappled with what salvation means and compared what other religions offer, I decided that I want to be a Christian. Christ is not an answer; He is *the* answer!" He became a Christian that afternoon by surrendering his life to Christ, accepting the forgiveness of a gracious Lord, and inviting Him to make His home in him. He's on the way! But the best is still to be as the adventure unfolds.

The reason for the growing demise of institutional Christianity in America is that we have lost the "Christ-only" verve. We need Peter's boldness to preach and teach, and then model with our living, that there is no other way. In the apostle's stupendous statement, he brushed aside nationalism, the sacrificial system of ancient Israel, and the compulsive complex of rules and regulations of religion. Christ is all or not at all. He alone can save us.

This verse was spoken to the religious leaders of Israel. Religious pride and self-justifying defensiveness had become a substitute for God and a personal relationship with Him. The same is true today. The great challenge of our time is to introduce religious people to Christ and a saving experience of His love. One of the remarkable things of our time is the number of church people who are discovering the reality of what they've heard for years. A fresh experience of God's grace, the transformation of human personality and a Holy Spirit-empowered life is the aching need in churches today. This verse should be explained with vigor and gusto from pulpits and in Bible classes, in personal witness and in caring relationships. Those who have experienced its promise will rejoice; those who have never discovered the profound experience of salvation it offers will respond. Last year I preached from this text and over a hundred people responded. Half of them were church members of long standing!

THE BOLDNESS OF THE TRANSFORMED LIFE

13 Now when they saw the boldness of Peter and John, and perceived that they were uneducated and untrained men, they marveled. And they realized that they had been with Jesus. 14 And seeing the man who had been healed standing with them, they could say nothing against it.

—Acts 4:13–14

There had to be some explanation! Peter and John were uneducated and untrained men. They had not been trained in the professional rabbinical schools of Hillel or Shammai. Where did they get their wisdom and lucid speech? Note the progression of the dawning comprehension of the Sanhedrin. They *saw* the boldness of Peter and John, *perceived* that they were laymen, *marveled* at what they were able to say and do, and *realized* they had been with Jesus. A remarkable compliment!

The same can be true for us. A Christ-captivated life enables us to live an extraordinary life. We are not limited to the confines of our own intellect or talent. The secret is Christ in us. Paul discovered that and communicated the wonder of the transferred life when he wrote to the Colossians about the mystery hidden for ages but now manifested in Christ's people: *Christ in you, the hope of glory* (Col. 1:27). Glory is manifestation. Christ manifests Himself in us and transforms us into His own image. The secret of the Christian life is not only that we have been *with* Jesus but that He *is* in us! There should be daily amazement—first in us and then in others—at what we are able to discern, dare, and do. Christ in us is the inner source of wisdom beyond human sagacity, discernment beyond comprehension, love beyond our cautious affection, truth beyond our experience. The deeper we grow in Christ, the more people will be forced to wonder.

But most telling of all, there will be changed lives around us because of Christ in us. The apostles had the lame man as evidence that Christ had used them as agents of healing. And yet, the greatest miracle is in the conversion and transformation of a person with whom we have shared the love of Christ. When we give ourselves away in caring, costly relationships of affirmation and encouragement with those who do not know Christ, He uses us to model His power and introduce them to Him. People will live forever because of the Lord's ministry to them through us.

And Christ will get the glory. We can enjoy being a channel of His grace. All the compliments and adulation go to Him. Our reward is a boldness in knowing who we are, whose we are, and for what we were born. People will see. . . be sure of that. They will wonder what has happened to us; they will marvel at what has happened around us; and then finally, they will realize what is happening in us. Jesus. There can be no other explanation!

THE BOLDNESS FROM OPPOSITION

[15] But when they had commanded them to go aside out of the council, they conferred among themselves, [16] saying, "What shall we do to these men? For, indeed, that a notable miracle has been done through them is evident to all who dwell in Jerusalem, and we cannot deny it. [17] But so that it spreads no further among the people, let us severely threaten them, that from now on they speak to no man in this name."

[18] So they called them and commanded them not to speak at all nor teach in the name of Jesus. [19] But Peter and John answered and said to them, "Whether it is right in the sight of God to listen to you more than to God, you judge. [20] For we cannot but speak the things which we have seen and heard." [21] So when they had further threatened them, they let

them go, finding no way of punishing them, because of the people, since they all glorified God for what had been done. ²² For the man was over forty years old on whom this miracle of healing had been performed.

—Acts 4:15–22

Opposition crystallizes boldness. Difficulties deepen our determination. Conflict forces us to clarify the irreducible maximum of what we believe.

The ruling of the Sanhedrin was a gift of God! Startling? Perhaps. But look at it this way: the prohibition against speaking and teaching in the name of Jesus solidified the apostles and the church in courageous witness in a way that could never have happened without opposition. Peter and John had to decide whether to be obedient to God or to the Sanhedrin. Now they could understand existentially what Jesus had meant when He had challenged them to seek first the kingdom of God and put Him first before family, friends, recognition, or popularity. I know of no truly bold person who has not experienced the sharp razor's edge of that decision. When we know who we are and what we are to do because of prolonged time in prayer, we can play to the right audience. Pressure comes in our lives when we equivocate and try to please everyone. Our insecurity often makes life a popularity contest and we must win people's approval at all costs. The cost is always exorbitant.

We live in a time when strong convictions about anything are suspect. Our need to be liked drains our pertinacity. C. S. Lewis says about a character in one of his novels: "Mark liked to be liked. There was a good deal of spaniel in him." There may be a good deal of solicitious spaniel in all of us. But when the issues are focused, we are forced to discover the real center of our security in Christ.

Praise God for opposition! Lives are not changed without it, parishes are not renewed without its pain, and we do not become the toughened disciples we were meant to be without its honing discipline.

The opposition of the Sanhedrin has given us a motto for courageous living. We would be less without it. Peter and John's response to the threats of the frightened high priest should be memorized and kept ready for life's tight places where we are tempted to give in or give up: *"Whether it is right in the sight of God to listen to you more than to God, you judge. For we cannot but speak the things which we have seen and heard"* (vv. 19, 20). The impact has echoed through the ages. Martyrs, gallant saints under persecution, and hassled reformers have said with Luther, "Here I stand; I can do no other!"

Don't miss the fact that it was what the apostles had *seen and heard* that prompted their statement. That encompassed their life with Jesus, His death for them, the Resurrection, Pentecost, and a miracle done through them. Nothing less for us! We have all that—and more.

Someone asked why a certain pastor never talked about what was happening to him when he preached. The response was telling: "Perhaps it's because so little is happening to him!"

The Lord wants to amaze us so that we can amaze the world. Wherever we are in our growth in Christ, there's a next step to take today. We all have problems that ache for solutions. Difficult people populate everyone's life. Some of us need healing. The Lord is going to break through! He will meet our needs beyond our wildest expectation. All so that our gratitude can be expressed by speaking *"the things which we have seen and heard."*

THE BOLDNESS OF PRAYER

23 And being let go, they went to their own companions and reported all that the chief priests and elders had said to them. 24 So when they heard that, they raised their voice to God with one accord and said: "Lord, You are God, who made heaven and earth and the sea, and all that is in them, 25 who by the mouth of Your servant David have said:
'Why did the nations rage,
And the people plot vain things?
26 *The kings of the earth took their stand,*
And the rulers were gathered together
Against the LORD and against His Christ.'
27 "For truly against Your holy Servant Jesus, whom You anointed, both Herod and Pontius Pilate, with the Gentiles and the people of Israel, were gathered together 28 to do whatever Your hand and Your purpose determined before to be done. 29 Now, Lord, look on their threats, and grant to Your servants that with all boldness they may speak Your word, 30 by stretching out Your hand to heal, and that signs and wonders may be done through the name of Your holy Servant Jesus."

³¹ And when they had prayed, the place where they were assembled together was shaken; and they were all filled with the Holy Spirit, and they spoke the word of God with boldness.

—Acts 4:23–31

We are amazed by the response of the church to Peter and John's report of the threats of the Sanhedrin. They had narrowly escaped imprisonment and physical punishment—even death, if the chief priest could have found a way. The church did not respond with fear, anxiety, or desire for safety. Instead they went to prayer. Their prayer time is a model of prayer for sustained boldness. In this portion of our exposition, we want to study this prayer and underline the convictions it expressed.

1. *The undergirding conviction of the absolute sovereignty of God.* Much can be discerned about people in the way they address God in their prayers. *"Lord, You are God, who made heaven and earth and the sea, and all that is in them . . ."* (v. 24). The Greek word for "Lord" here is different from the one used elsewhere in the New Testament to express a believer's reverence. Here it is *déspota*, meaning "despot," or in the implication for the Christians, "absolute ruler, final sovereign, master." The faith of the church was that the Lord was in charge of all things. He was creator and sustainer of all. Nothing happens without His knowledge, and He can use all things for His purposes and glory. That led to the second conviction.

2. *Opposition and threats.* What they had endured had happened to the Lord's people through the ages. They could not put their trust in people. Their experience was not unlike that of David long before. His question in Psalm 2:1–2, repeated from memory in their prayer, gave profound comfort (vv. 25–26). The church was in good company! God's faithful people have always been in trouble. It was the acid test that they were obeying God rather than men. We wonder if Jesus' words about persecution stirred within them as they prayed. He had called persecution for righteousness' sake "blessed."

3. *The assurance of God's overruling.* We can take anything if we know that God is in charge and will intervene. The next section of the prayer dealt with what had happened to Jesus. God had allowed the Cross for the sins of the world and followed it with the victory of the Resurrection. Thus the church could pray, *"For truly against Your*

holy Servant Jesus, whom You anointed, both Herod and Pontius Pilate, with the Gentiles and the people of Israel, were gathered together to do whatever Your hand and Your purpose determined before to be done" (vv. 27–28). Jesus was not alone. God was in Christ, reconciling the world to Himself. The central source of the courage of the early church was that if God could overrule the worst that man had done and give His best, He could use anything that happened to them. He is able to bring good out of evil! There's a purpose to everything if we trust Him. He wastes nothing. There is an ultimate strategy. We can never drift beyond His intervening, overruling care.

William Cowper caught the wonder of this in his poem, "God Moves in a Mysterious Way," which is now a great hymn of the church.

Judge not the Lord by feeble sense
But trust Him for His grace;
Behind a frowning providence
He hides a shining face.

4. *The final conviction of the church's prayer* was that God would confirm the witness of the church with a continuation of signs and wonders. They expected miracles to attend their preaching! That's why they prayed for more boldness and more manifestations of the Holy Spirit's power, for further visible proof that God had heard their prayer for courage. Amazing. They prayed for the Lord to continue the healings which had caused such consternation and trouble. The spectacular events spread across the pages of Acts can all be traced back to praying like that.

It forces us to evaluate our prayers. When have we asked for boldness and for signs and wonders to be performed through us? The Lord is more ready to give both than we are to ask.

The Lord's answer to the prayer of the church is what we can dare to anticipate. The room where they were assembled was shaken—an outward indication of the Lord's presence in the Holy Spirit. *"And they were all filled with the Holy Spirit, and they spoke the word of God with boldness"* (v. 31). Exactly what they prayed for. Again, Luke uses the word *"filled,"* this time in the aorist passive indicative to show that on this occasion a special filling occurred and boldness resulted. Boldness is the outer sign of the possession of the Holy Spirit's anointing.

We need to picture ourselves as bold people. How would we act; what would we say; what would we dare? Perhaps it's an act of love which we've resisted doing, or an opportunity to share our faith which has been neglected because of embarrassment or timidity. Or perhaps it's forgiveness we need to express, or taking a stand and speaking forthrightly what we believe. Most of all, it's following the Lord's guidance with faithfulness and obedience, regardless of cost. Ask for a special infilling of the Holy Spirit. He's faithful. He will give us power to act and speak with boldness.

NOTE

1. *Earliest Christianity: A.D. 30–150,* 2 vols. (New York: Harper and Row, 1959), 1:42–43.

CHAPTER SIX—LIBERATED FOR LOYALTY

ACTS 4:32—5:16

Scripture Outline

Commitment is Spelled L–O–Y–A–L–T–Y (4:32–35)

Barnabas, the Loyal Encourager (4:36–37)

The Great Holdout (5:1–11)

Signs and Wonders (5:12–16)

Recently a pastor asked me to pray for his church. I asked him to share with me what he felt was the greatest need for which I should pray. His response was immediate and direct, indicating he'd hoped I would ask. "We are an evangelical church, but our members have no deep relationships with each other," he said. "They just don't take any responsibility for each other. I guess they think that's what I'm paid to do. There's no mutual support or encouragement. Pray that I can communicate that they belong to each other as well as Christ."

I have prayed for the man and his church ever since. But his analysis of his church has rumbled about in my mind. I've heard the same plea from clergy, church officers, and members hundreds of times. In addition to a willingness to pray for their churches, I also recommend forceful preaching and teaching of the passage from Acts which is the focus of this chapter. Acts 4:32—5:16 is a very effective vehicle for communicating what the Holy Spirit wants to enable a congregation to be before He can guide it on to all that He intends it to do in the world.

In the previous chapter, we considered the gift of boldness that the Holy Spirit gave the disciples for their witness. Now we turn our attention to the blessing He helped them be to each other. The courage the disciples displayed beyond the fellowship was dependent on the quality of life they experienced in that fellowship.

Acts 4:32—5:16 fits together as a unit. It's one of those passages that has a cause-and-effect progression of thought. I find that in Scripture portions like this, a brief statement of the effect, especially if it touches the deep needs or hopes of people, heightens the exposition of the causes. In a very stirring way Luke describes the effectiveness of the church. There were signs and wonders done among the people of Jerusalem. Power was being released through them. Changed lives, reconciliations, healings, and joy were the evidence of the church alive with the Holy Spirit. The church was growing and dynamic. Would you like to be a part of a church like that? The church was a vital movement. That's the effect. What was the cause? Now we are ready to go back to the beginning of the passage for the answer.

Luke tells us about an essential ingredient of a great church: an unlimited commitment to Christ and each other which is expressed in unrestrained loyalty. Not only to the Lord, but one another! The beloved physician gives us a moving, narrative description of this ingredient and then provides two illustrations, one to show what loyalty really is, and the other to alarm us as to what happens when it is lacking. The first is very positive and the second is equally negative. Luke is generous in his praise of Barnabas as demonstrating loyalty, and then is honest with us about Ananias and Sapphira as an example of the denial of it.

COMMITMENT IS SPELLED L-O-Y-A-L-T-Y

32 Now the multitude of those who believed were of one heart and one soul; neither did anyone say that any of the things he possessed was his own, but they had all things in common. 33 And with great power the apostles gave witness to the resurrection of the Lord Jesus. And great grace was upon them all. 34 Nor was there anyone among them who lacked; for all who were possessors of lands or houses sold them, and brought the proceeds of the things that were sold, 35 and laid them at the apostles' feet; and they distributed to each as anyone had need.

—*Acts 4:32–35*

In Acts 5:11, Luke uses the word "church" for the first time. This passage (4:32–35) is an excellent description of what the word meant to him. The Greek word used in 5:11 was *ekklēsía*. Its original meaning was an assembly called together. *Ek* means "from" or "out of"; *klēsis* is rooted in *kaléō*, "to call." In Luke's time the word was used for a body of citizens called together to discuss the affairs of a local community or the state. In the Septuagint, the Greek translation of the Old Testament, *ekklēsía* is the word selected to translate the Hebrew word for an assembly of the people of Israel. Simply stated, it means "called out and called together." Originally, for the followers of Christ it meant an assembly of believers gathered together for prayer and fellowship. The idea developed of their being called out by the Lord, called into oneness in Him, and called into the world to serve.

Again, we remember that Luke's tutor in the faith was Paul. We sense that when Luke uses the word "church" it carries the full implications of the apostle's teaching. For Paul, the favorite phrase was "the body of Christ." His letters to the Ephesians and Corinthians express the powerful image. "The church, which is His body, the fullness of Him who fills all in all" (Eph. 1:22–23). This is explained vividly in 1 Corinthians 12. "For as the body is one and has many members, but all the members of that one body, being many, are one body, so also is Christ. For by one Spirit we were all baptized into one body—whether Jews or Greeks, whether slaves or free—and have all been made to drink into one Spirit. . . . Now you are the body of Christ, and members individually" (1 Cor. 12:12–13, 27).

Paul goes on to explain the interdependence of the members of a body as an example of how Christians are to be mutually dependent on each other. And Luke, his faithful friend and companion, describes the birth and growth of the church as Christ's body. We are called to be Christ's people, called to communion with Him and each other, and together as the church to be the divine agent for the continuing ministry of His Spirit today. The expression "body life," used often today, expresses the quality of the ingredients of how Christ lives and ministers through the parts of the body equipped with the gifts of His Spirit.

There are four things that were part of the loyalty of the members of the body to one another. They were of one heart, one soul, one blessing, all rooted in one great conviction. The heart, *kardía*, is used by Luke in the Hebrew sense of reason, emotions, and will. It stood for a person's entire mental and emotional activity. Why did Luke add soul? The *psuché* is the life spirit in a person which can be touched and quickened and then filled by the Holy Spirit. In essence what Luke is saying is that the early Christians had their minds, emotions, and wills open to each other, and Spirit in each enabled oneness with the others.

The one thing about which they were one heart and soul was the resurrected Christ who lived in them. That prompted them to know that all that they had and were belonged to Him. No one said that what *"he possessed was his own, but they had all things in common"* (4:32). That's a shocker for "what's mine is mine—one stewardship sermon a year" Christians today. And yet, sharing our material blessings may be the least of our difficulties with the passage. These early Christians had *"all"* things in common. To be of one mind is to have the mind of Christ in common—not our ideas about Him, or even our carefully polished theology, but our heart and soul. That means our inner selves—our thinking, willing, feeling. We can be supportive of each other only if we know what's going on inside each other. And the handle of the door to our lives is on the inside. We must want to be known. One of the finest gifts we can give the churches of which we are a part is our openness to talk about what we are thinking *and* feeling. It's then that our intellectual difficulties in growing in the faith can be given the insight and experience of others who have struggled with the same doubts. How we are feeling about ourselves, other people, and life in general affects everything we do and are.

For example, the Session of my church has discovered that a time of Bible study, sharing, and prayer not only shortens meetings, but makes them open to the Spirit's guidance of decisions. The sharing is a crucial part of this time. Bible study refocuses us around the Spirit of Christ present with us, and that opens us to share both difficulties and victories which have happened to us between meetings. The questions "How are you feeling really—what do you bring to this meeting—how can we help?" often clear away frustrations, fears, and tensions which would render us incapable of either knowing or doing the mind of Christ unless they were shared and cleansed. The same is true for the joy of answered prayer. Christ blesses each of us for each other in the fellowship. The good things which have happened to us, if they are not shared, will become a block also. The issue is one of being Christ's friend and befriending one another. And how foolish it would be to be with a really good friend and not allow him or her to share the burden or the blessing.

Congregations which are becoming infectiously alive have some strategy for members being together in smaller, more informal gatherings where the Scriptures can be studied, needs and gratitudes shared, and prayer for one another offered. Prayer and Bible study groups enable this; so do classes which, in addition to being taught, share their mutual adventure in the new life.

It is out of really knowing what's happening in each other's lives that we know when and how to help in a specific or tangible way. I am gratified by how the Book of Acts' "all things in common" is working in some of the small groups in our congregation in Hollywood. People are helped through times of unemployment, economic crunch, and physical needs as well as problems in relationships, emotional stresses, and physical problems which need prayers for healing. So many people who are on the move in a growing, adventuresome faith are part of this quality of sharing. A good example is in the area of singles ministry where supportive groups, divorce recovery workshops, and prayer groups provide an opportunity for mutual support. A group for aspiring entertainment people also provides help to artists for whom disappointment and unfulfilled dreams can diminish their effectiveness when an opportunity to perform does come. I think also of a group of women leaders in the community who meet consistently to support each other in effective ministry in the community. Businessmen in various parts of the city function in this same way.

These people are of one heart and one soul caring about each other because of the conviction that Christ is risen, indwelling, and has called them to be a miniature *ekklēsía.* The groups of which I am a part personally, as an individual, and with my wife as a couple, strengthen my conviction that what Luke is talking about in the early church after Pentecost can happen today. I would not want to face the challenges and opportunities, along with the pressures and problems I know, without the help I receive as a person, a husband, and a fellow struggler-adventurer with the others.

But all this would not be possible without the assurance of loyalty. We all need a handful of people who are loyal to us and to whom we are loyal because of Christ's unswerving loyalty to us. He is for us; He will not leave or forsake us when we succeed or fail. When He lives in our "heart and soul," to repeat Luke's words, He enables His own loyalty within us—first to Him and then to people. We will open up our inner heart and share only when we have an assurance of loyalty which keeps confidences and supports us under the fire of criticism from others. Luke's example of that kind of person is Barnabas.

BARNABAS, THE LOYAL ENCOURAGER

[36] And Joses, who was also named Barnabas by the apostles (which is translated Son of Encouragement), a Levite of the country of Cyprus, [37] having land, sold it, and brought the money and laid it at the apostles' feet.

—*Acts 4:36–37*

III

In two brief verses we are introduced to one of the most admirable personalities of the New Testament. If all we had to enable us to know this man's character were these two verses, we'd still have enough to stand in admiration and then desire to be like him.

We are told that his name was Joses, or Joseph as it is rendered in the RSV, and that he was a Levite from Cyprus. The Levites were descendants of the tribe of Levi who assisted and served the priesthood in the sanctuary, distributed the tithes to the needy, and taught and interpreted the verdicts of the law.[1] Joses' home was in Cyprus where there was a strong colony of Jews. But the Cypriot had strong ties in Jerusalem because of members of his father's family who lived there. John Mark was his cousin. Tradition has it that the Upper Room, where Jesus celebrated the Passover and where the 120 celebrated His return in the Power of the Holy Spirit, was located in Mark's home. I believe that the Upper Room also became the central meeting place of the apostles after Pentecost. If Joses was not there at the time of Pentecost, which I suspect he was, he was in Jerusalem soon afterward. He was introduced to Christ by the apostles, received His indwelling presence, and committed all that he had to the Lord's work. His experience of Christ's love motivated him to sell his land, presumably in Cyprus, and give all the proceeds of the sale to the apostles for the support and work of the early church's mission.

That, along with the magnanimity of spirit the Holy Spirit developed within him, prompted the apostles to give him a new name. Just as God had given a new name to people in the Old Testament which was recognition of His blessing and the person's potential with His power, as in the case of Abram made Abraham, so too Jesus has given new names in promise of a new nature, as with vacillating Simon Bar-Jonah, who was called Peter, the rock. The situation was different with Joses. Not just his potential, but what he performed, awarded him a new name. And he certainly lived up to it all through the rest of his adventuresome life.

The apostles, who spoke Aramaic, named him Barnabas. The name is power-packed, having the meaning "son of prophecy," from *bar*, "son of," combined with *nebū'ā*, "prophecy." Some scholars have given it a slightly different emphasis, "son of refreshment." In Luke's Greek, however, we have the reflection not just of translation into another language, but the intimate personal observation by the physician of Joses of Cyprus. In a powerful parenthesis, Luke uses *huiòs paraklēseōs*, which can be rendered "son of consolation, exhortation, or encouragement." It is exciting to understand that the same basic word was used to translate Jesus' Aramaic promise of the ministry of the Holy Spirit: "And I will pray the Father, and He will give you another Helper, that He may abide with you forever— the Spirit of truth, whom the world cannot receive, because it neither sees Him nor knows Him; but you know Him, for He dwells with you and will be in you. I will not leave you orphans; I will come to you" (John 14:16–18). In this case the Greek word for "Helper," or as it is in the RSV, "Counselor," *parákletos,* means one who is called to one's side to help who strengthens and helps us to stand. Joses had clearly displayed inherent inclination toward being that kind of person. But a clear understanding of the potent words Luke uses indicates that what was evident in Joses was an endowment of the Holy Spirit. The Spirit of the Lord had distinguished Himself in Joses! The King James Version of Luke's parenthesis about him uses "son of consolation" and the American Standard Version, "son of encouragement." The same meaning is implied. Joses, now Barnabas, became all of the various emphases. His life became like that of Jesus who lived in him.

We will meet Barnabas often as we move through Acts, but this brief synopsis of his ministry may be helpful. Whenever we meet him on the pages of the New Testament, he is helping, encouraging, affirming, uplifting, and untiring in claiming the best for people. He was Paul's missionary companion; he believed in Mark when he became a missionary drop-out; and he served the needs of people to the end of his life. His ministry with Paul, his affirmation of the young man Mark, his faithfulness when Paul was imprisoned, and his consistency in helping new Christians are an indication that his life was consistent with his name. And it was the *Parákletos,* the Holy Spirit in him, who enabled him to be an outstanding *huiòs parakléseōs,* a son of comfort and courage. Only the indwelling Lord could produce an affirmer and encourager like Barnabas. And it all was focused in his stable loyalty to the Lord, to his friends, and to new believers. What would we do without the Barnabases? And with the *Parakletos* in us, can't we go beyond just emulating Barnabas, and become the Lord's own unique miracle of an encourager? Whatever our name is now, it can be loyal encourager.

The true nature of the life of the body of Christ is the fellowship of the daughters and sons of encouragement. We are called to stand with each other, helping each other to learn from the difficulties and to rejoice fully in the delights of life. We are called out, and called into, a loyal assembly of believers, an *ekklēsía,* to be liberators and maximizers for each other.

Perhaps Luke had heard Paul dictate Ephesians 4, which I sense the beloved physician had in mind when he described the body life of the early church. It is a charter and guide for a challenging Order of Saint Barnabas in any congregation today.

> I, therefore, the prisoner of the Lord, beseech you to walk worthy of the calling with which you were called, with all lowliness and gentleness, with longsuffering, bearing with one another in love, endeavoring to keep the unity of the Spirit in the bond of peace.
>
> And do not grieve the Holy Spirit of God, by whom you were sealed for the day of redemption. Let all bitterness, wrath, anger, clamor, and evil speaking be put away from you, with all malice. And be kind to one another, tenderhearted, forgiving one another, even as God in Christ forgave you (Eph. 4:1–3, 30–32).

I have a Barnabas Club in my life made up of people whose basic purpose for being together consistently is to encourage me in my ministry and to be supportive of each other in attempts to be channels of the Holy Spirit. It is exciting to see a group of people adopt these words of Paul to the Ephesians and Luke's example of them in Acts and allow the Holy Spirit to guide them in living them. But no church is made up of all Barnabases. Sadly, Christianity still has its Ananiases and Sapphiras. They are examples of:

THE GREAT HOLDOUT

> **5:1** But a certain man named Ananias, with Sapphira his wife, sold a possession. [2] And he kept back part of the proceeds, his wife also being aware of it, and brought a certain part and laid it at the apostles' feet. [3] But Peter said, "Ananias, why has Satan filled your heart to lie to the Holy Spirit and keep back part of the price of the land for yourself? [4] While it remained, was it not your own? And after it was sold, was it not in your own control? Why have you conceived this thing in your heart? You have not lied to men but to God."
>
> [5] Then Ananias, hearing these words, fell down and breathed his last. So great fear came upon all those who heard these things. [6] And the young men arose and wrapped him up, carried him out, and buried him.

⁷ Now it was about three hours later when his wife came in, not knowing what had happened. ⁸ And Peter answered her, "Tell me whether you sold the land for so much?"

She said, "Yes, for so much."

⁹ Then Peter said to her, "How is it that you have agreed together to test the Spirit of the Lord? Look, the feet of those who have buried your husband are at the door, and they will carry you out." ¹⁰ Then immediately she fell down at his feet and breathed her last. And the young men came in and found her dead, and carrying her out, buried her by her husband. ¹¹ So great fear came upon all the church and upon all who heard these things.

—Acts 5:1–11

The names Ananias and Sapphira were as much a contradiction of their old nature as Barnabas's was an affirmation of his new nature. The Hebrew form of Ananias means "Yahweh is gracious," and Sapphira means "beautiful." There was nothing gracious about what Ananias did nor anything beautiful about Sapphira's collusive cooperation in the swindled pretense of loyalty to the Lord and the body. They had heard only half of the call of the *ekklēsía*. Surely they had heard Christ's call to faith in Him, but they had not heard the call to loyalty to His people. So what's so wrong in what they did? Any stewardship chairperson would like a gift such as they offered.

The problem was that they *pretended* to give all the proceeds of the sale of the property. No one had said that they had to give anything. But the spirit of giving to the One who had given all for the believers was very strong. No one said that what he or she had was his or her own. Except Ananias and Sapphira! The deception was the sin.

And Peter knew. It was written on their faces. Their grand protestation about giving all the proceeds of the sale of property was an effort to hide the fact that they were holding some of it back. We advertise what we are hiding. The careful eye of one who has been adept at that can see it in others, and Peter had been an expert at that before the Holy Spirit had filled him. But also notice the evidence that Peter had another one of the gifts of the Spirit we talked about in chapter 3—the power to discern the spirits, mentioned by Paul in 1 Corinthians 12:10. This Spirit-given capacity to see what was really motivating a person enabled Peter to see that, in this case, it was Satan, and not the Holy Spirit to whom Ananias and Sapphira were devoting their loyalty. That kind of spiritual dishonesty gave him grave concern for the fellowship. Ananias and Sapphira were not lying to the church, but to God!

But in fact, we can't lie to God. He knows everything anyhow. The dangerous thing is pretending with the fellowship of believers. God is never deceived. His heart breaks over what we do with the gift of life, but we can't fool Him. Because He has given us freedom, we can block His best for us. And that hurts the fellowship of the church most of all. The dishonesty of duality spreads like cancer. When we are not real and authentic with others, it is difficult for them to be genuine with us. Spiritual superficiality sets in. The great holdout becomes a hold-up!

The difficulty in local churches today is not the keeping back of part of the proceeds of a sale of property, it is the holding back of part of ourselves. It had been a positive blessing for Ananias and Sapphira to sell that property. As a result of their sharp dealing they had something to give. This is the key for what this means to us. The Lord has been blessing us in more than what we are; He has made a very special, never-to-be-repeated miracle of human personality in each of us. To hold back ourselves and what the Lord is doing in us is the greatest act of disloyalty—to God and to others. Paul talked about "the dispensation of the grace of God which was given to me for you" (Eph. 3:2).

To withhold any portion of ourselves from people around us is to deny the gift given to us for them. And the congregation in its worship, study, and deep fellowship is where we were meant to have all things in common—especially the person inside us whom the Lord recreated to be shared with others. And when we do, we have opportunities to really care about others. What He has done in us is exactly what someone else needs to hear.

We are stunned by Luke's account of the cardiac arrest both Ananias and Sapphira suffered when confronted. Peter did not cause it; they brought it on themselves. The fear of exposure was so drastic, their nervous systems could not take it. My own suspicion is that, having been exposed, Ananias and Sapphira found their lifelong patterns of being closed people made it impossible to confess their sin and make a new start. I think they really wanted to die as a way out. Their bodies complied!

But we must not miss the point for us. We die spiritually each time we withhold love or forgiveness or sensitive caring. And why not live? Now and forever!

Luke tells us that what happened to Ananias and Sapphira brought great fear on the church. Awe and wonder are implied.

The members of the body saw the wondrous things the Holy Spirit could do with a willing Joses now named Barnabas, and with Ananias, a man who missed the meaning of his own name and refused to allow the Lord to be gracious. Loyalty and the lack of it were both visibly, then frighteningly, exposed. The Lord who had battled the forces of evil and won was not about to give up the infant church to Satan's ploy of spiritual pretense. The Lord's movement was pressing on! There was a sick and suffering world that needed the gospel from a church free of any holdouts.

SIGNS AND WONDERS

[12] And through the hands of the apostles many signs and wonders were done among the people. And they were all with one accord in Solomon's Porch. [13] Yet none of the rest dared join them, but the people esteemed them highly. [14] And believers were increasingly added to the Lord, multitudes of both men and women, [15] so that they brought the sick out into the streets and laid them on beds and couches, that at least the shadow of Peter passing by might fall on some of them. [16] Also a multitude gathered from the surrounding cities to Jerusalem, bringing sick people and those who were tormented by unclean spirits, and they were all healed.
—*Acts 5:12–16*

The church which resulted from being of one mind and soul with loyal commitment to the risen Christ and loyalty to each other, had undeniable miracles.

1. *It was a supernatural church.* Signs and wonders were done. Signs, *sēmeîa*, were an outward evidence of the inner working of the power of the Lord in a person or situation. It tells us the Spirit is at hand. And wonders, *térata*, were signs which caused one to be gripped by awe. Something beyond human ability was involved in the healings and transformed lives which were occurring as a result of Christ's Spirit in the apostles. This prompts us to ask, "What is happening in our churches which could be explained only by the presence of His Spirit at work?" That leads to my favorite question of church leaders at conferences: "What are you attempting which could not be done without the power of the Holy Spirit?"

2. *It was a respected and growing church.* Verses 13 and 14 seem to be a contradiction. The first says that people did not dare to join the

church and verse 14 says that believers were added increasingly. The key to the difference is *"the rest"* of verse 13 and *"believers"* of verse 14. What had happened to Ananias and Sapphira had put the cost of commitment to Christ and loyalty to the fellowship at a high price, and the opportunists were not able to raise that kind of spiritual capital. The church really stood for something in those days! It was preaching Christ boldly rather than begging for new members in order to raise the budget or build a building.

But the real reason for the growth was that authentic believers were being born. That was the Lord's doing! Only His Spirit can convict, convince, and confirm His love in a person. Luke is pointing to the Lord in verse 13, not just the excellent sermons or even the healing ministry of the apostles.

Something more must be said about what that means for church growth today. The churches which are growing are those that: are authoritative, not authoritarian in preaching the Bible; are an example, not just an explanation of the new birth; are living, not legislating the Spirit-filled life; are gracious and not grim in their quality of inclusive fellowship; and are loyal, not lax in their members' commitment to each other. A church like that will not have to look for new members but rather will have to look for ways of effectively assimilating all whom the Lord calls to Himself and then calls into their fellowship.

3. *It was a healing church.* People are ill today. They need Christ's healing hand on their hearts, minds, and bodies. There's a difference between sermons on healing and providing opportunities for people to receive prayer for Christ's healing. Prayers for healing can be offered at the end of every service, at special services offered on a consistent basis, in small groups, and in one-to-one contact. Luke tells us that the sick were laid in Peter's path so that at least his shadow would fall on them. But people need more than the shadow of our busy lives. They need personal contact; they need to be listened to; and they need the physical contact of touch. The gentle laying on of hands is prescribed in James 5:14. "Is anyone among you sick? Let him call for the elders of the church, and let them pray over him, anointing him with oil in the name of the Lord." But not just the elders have that power. The hand is indicative of the imparting of power, i.e., the hand of the Lord. And He will use our gentle touch as a physical sign of His spiritual hand. And there will be wonders, be sure of that!

A supernatural church, a respected growing church, a healing church. That three-point thrust makes us want the same things for our churches today. And all three were based in the authentic, Spirit-filled *ekklēsía* of people called to the Lord and then called to loyalty to the members of His body.

NOTE

1. See Deut. 10:8; 17:9–11; Num. 3:5–9; 18:3–20; 2 Chr. 31:11–19; 17:9–11; 35:10–14; Jer. 32:7 ff. (land holders).

CHAPTER SEVEN—THIS IS THE LIFE
ACTS 5:17–42

Scripture Outline

Liberated for the Life (5:17–21)

On Trial for Life (5:22–33)

The Amazing Surprises of the Life (5:34–42)

The Old Course at the auspicious and dignified St. Andrews Golf Course in St. Andrews, Scotland, is not only one of the most beautiful golf courses in the world, it is frustratingly difficult. For a weekend golfer from the United States to shoot under 90 is a great accomplishment. But the scenery along the cragged coastline of northern Scotland is compensation for the humiliating over-par scores on the holes.

It's not easy to get on the course. The stately starter is not exactly out soliciting tourists to play. In fact, there are times when they must stand in line for hours to get into a foursome to play. When I asked the towering, dignified starter if I could get a game, he scowled and asked, "What month do you want to play?" I sheepishly responded that I had that day in mind. Gruffly he asked my name. "Ogilvie," I responded with hat-in-hand obsequiousness, and I began to spell my name for him. "There'll be no need to spell your name," the awesome Scot implied, a smile invading his imperious face. "If you're an Ogilvie, as you say, there'll be no difficulty in yer playin' today. Know the Ogilvies well. Had a couple of them in my regiment in the war." A long conversation about the Ogilvies he had known ensued with gusto. My Highland clan name had won the day.

Coming anywhere near winning on the course was another thing! I was given three other old Scots gentlemen in plus-fours (knickers) to play with and started off nervously. On one of the more difficult holes I surprised myself and my reserved partners by shooting a one under par. I could hardly contain my excitement. So I didn't. I threw my putter in the air and, filled with the delight of the surroundings and my unbelievable score at *that* hole, shouted a broad American accent, "Wow, this is the life!"

One of my fearsome foursome looked up from his interrupted putt and commented warmly, "It is rather grand, isn't it? Tuck that one in your memory for when not just golf, but life, gets tedious."

Taking his advice, I tucked the memory in the cherished picture book of my mind. Not only that, I later also wrote down the man's comment in my sermon illustration book that goes with me wherever I am. What he had said was true. Life gets both tedious and tiresome at times. And when it does, we need good memories of what the Lord has done for us in bigger and more crucial things than a golf game on a historic course. The times when we've said, "This is the Life!" with a capital "L," when we knew that we were blessed to be part of eternal life and the abundant life in Christ, come back from the careful cataloging of our memories. We are sustained and strengthened in times when difficulties hit. Then in those times we are able to say much more profoundly, "This is the Life!," with quiet gratitude for the Lord's indwelling steadying Spirit.

The apostles needed to experience that quality when they were arrested once again and put in prison. The memory of the days of supernatural ministry in the Spirit, described in our exposition in the previous chapter, gave the apostles courage in the prison. What happened to them was a reaffirmation of their call to be communicators and of what their central message should continue to be.

Acts 5:17–42 is focused on *The Life.* An exposition of it is especially exciting and helpful when done in the context of Christ's "I Am" statement "I am . . . the life" (John 11:25) and His assurance "I have come that they may have life, and that they may have it more abundantly" (John 10:10). Using Life as a sublime synonym for Christ's indwelling Spirit, this passage from Acts falls into three headings: Liberated for the Life, On Trial for the Life, and The Surprises of the Life.

LIBERATED FOR THE LIFE

[17] Then the high priest rose up, and all those who were with him (which is the sect of the Sadducees), and they were

filled with indignation, [18] and laid their hands on the apostles and put them in the common prison. [19] But at night an angel of the Lord opened the prison doors and brought them out, and said, [20] "Go, stand in the temple and speak to the people all the words of this life."

[21] And when they heard that, they entered the temple early in the morning and taught. But the high priest and those with him came and called the council together, with all the elders of the children of Israel, and sent to the prison to have them brought.

—*Acts 5:17–21*

The words of the angel were a recall to the communication of *the* message of the early church. The apostles were told that they were being released miraculously for a specific purpose—the only purpose of a Christian communicator. We can imagine the reconfirmation the angel's words were to the apostles. They had been on target with a singular, unswerving emphasis on Christ and the abundant life in Him. Christ the Life had empowered their preaching and brought tremendous results. Now the heavenly messenger said, in substance, "*You* have been on the mark. Don't change. It's working. Now I am setting you free of this prison so you can get back to communicating Life!"

The different translations of this compelling command are helpful and very interesting. We quoted the New King James Bible above. It is exactly the same in this verse as the regular King James. The New English Bible translates it, "Go, take your place in the temple and speak to the people about this new life and all that it means." J. B. Phillips's translation is direct and forthright, "Go . . . and tell the people all about this new life." All these and other contemporary paraphrases catch the incisiveness and the urgency of this recall to active service. Go to where the people are. Offer them the only gift that will give them life now and forever. Don't water it down in the slightest. There's no need to veer off into side issues. Life in Christ and His life in people is the only hope . . . and the only power!

And that's specifically what the apostles did, and precisely what every communicator of the many-splendored gift of Life Himself is called and recalled to do. Our message is, *"This is the life!"*

Christ the Life is the center of the center. The word "life" is used thirty-six times in the New Testament. It is a synonym for the Lord Himself. The apostle John, who was among those released from the prison that day, was to know difficulties and imprisonment again, but the Lord of Life sustained him. Nearing the conclusion of his long life of ministry in the power of the Lord, he wrote, "In Him was life, and the life was the light of men," and, "That which was from the beginning, which we have heard, which we have seen with our eyes, which we have looked upon, and our hands have handled, concerning the Word of life—the life was manifested, and we have seen, and bear witness, and declare to you that eternal life which was with the Father and was manifested to us—" (John 1:4 and 1 John 1:1–2).

The word "life" also summarizes Jesus' ministry and message. His "I Am" statements include His assertion to be God's bread from heaven to feed the deepest needs for life: "I am the bread of life" (John 6:35). He had come from God's heart to reveal divine life but also human life as it had been intended. Then He went to Calvary to prepare an eternal place for us. His authority to do that? "I am the way, the truth, and the life" (John 14:6).

Further, life is used to symbolize the new quality of existence that comes to us when we receive the Life as our Lord and Savior and indwelling King. "Therefore, if anyone is in Christ, he is a new creation; old things have passed away; behold, all things have become new" (2 Cor. 5:17). The secret of that is stated in Colossians 1:27, "Christ in you, the hope of glory." And that glory begins *now!* Joy, peace, hope, freedom.

And last, the word "life" is used to summarize all that happens between and among those in whom Christ lives. When we speak of "our life together," we employ the word "life" to define what happens when two people or a group are in a place with some level of communication as persons. When we say a party had life, we mean that something happened that gave it zest and vitality. Or when we say that the life of a church is dynamic or inspiring, we are trying to put into words a spiritual something that occurs. Actually, it's not something, but "Someone." When my wife says, "Well, one thing you can say, our life has never been dull or boring!" what she means is that Christ is the most interesting Person in the world and having Him as the basis of marriage and family, work and fun, is an adventure. I agree with her!

This section of Acts gives us two great keys to a vital ministry of communicating with people. People are interested in life and desperately want to maximize the years of their living, however stifled that desire can become by the pressures of living. People

THIS IS THE LIFE!

have an inherent life-wish in their psyches. Christ appeals to that and then shows people what real living is all about.

A word about the prisons from which He releases us to go tell *all the words of this life.* There are those prisons of our own making—reserve, fear of being criticized, lack of daring courage. Secondary loyalties to people and positions can keep us from pulling out all the stops. So can anxiety about failure. But by far the most tightly locked prison in which many communicators live is their own lack of freedom in living the abundant lives themselves. There's a direct ratio between fresh discoveries of new life in Christ and vital communication of it. There is no prison worse than sameness. The best gift we can give the people to whom we are sent to tell all about life is to concentrate on being all that life entails in our own study of Scripture and our abandonment of the safe and secure for the adventure of a Spirit-filled life. We won't be able to control what happens to and around us. But the Spirit will be in control. *What's* your prison? Security? A job? The success of the past? Or *who* is your security? Anyone holding you back? Friend, spouse, church board? The Spirit wants to set us free!

ON TRIAL FOR LIFE

22 But when the officers came and did not find them in the prison, they returned and reported, 23 saying, "Indeed we found the prison shut securely, and the guards standing outside before the doors; but when we opened them, we found no one inside!" 24 Now when the high priest, the captain of the temple, and the chief priests heard these things, they wondered what the outcome would be. 25 So one came and told them, saying, "Look, the men whom you put in prison are standing in the temple and teaching the people!"

26 Then the captain went with the officers and brought them without violence, for they feared the people, lest they should be stoned. 27 And when they had brought them, they set them before the council. And the high priest asked them, 28 saying, "Did we not strictly command you not to teach in this name? And look, you have filled Jerusalem with your doctrine, and intend to bring this Man's blood on us!"

29 But Peter and the other apostles answered and said: "We ought to obey God rather than men. 30 The God of our fathers raised up Jesus whom you murdered by hanging on a tree. 31 Him God has exalted to His right hand to be Prince and Savior, to give repentance to Israel and forgiveness of sins.

³² And we are His witnesses to these things, and so also is the Holy Spirit whom God has given to those who obey Him."

³³ When they heard this, they were furious and plotted to kill them.

—*Acts 5:22–33*

The guards could not explain what happened. They were confounded. The members of the Sanhedrin expressed further consternation. What was happening? They could not silence the apostles or keep them in prison. What could they do? The apostles' popularity among the people precluded the possibility of doing what they had done to Jesus of Nazareth. The leaders were cornered and they knew it. There was nothing to do at that point but bring the apostles back before them for a further threatening and warning. When they did that, Peter made a further speech, emphasizing the same three points he had used before: (1) he and the apostles must obey God and not men—including the Sanhedrin; (2) Jesus Christ is God's Messiah and He's alive! and (3) He is living in us.

The rage of the Sadducees and Pharisees burned so furiously at hearing those things again that their previous caution about killing the two men was abandoned. The word "furious" actually means they were "torn asunder" or "sawn apart" in their anger. They *"took counsel,"* that is, with resoluteness of will, they were determined to do it. The disciples were in trouble. And for the right reason!

That's the implication of this passage for us. Most of us get into trouble—some not often, others all the time. But is it for the right reason? Often our lack of prayer for guidance or our reluctance to be willing to be made willing to do the Lord's will gets us into all sorts of skirmishes which are not a part of the real battle we were meant to fight. Our determination sends us off in directions the Lord has not guided. Or we fuss with people over minor issues and end up with a trail of broken relationships. And then too, those areas of our personalities which have not been surrendered to the Spirit's character-transplant, make us less than effective communicators. The problem arises when we want to point to Jesus and the gospel as an explanation of why we get into trouble! It is a sign of Christian maturity that we can discern the difference between the trouble we caused out of willfulness or insensitivity or stubbornness, and what has been the result of courageous living of life in Christ and telling all about this new life. Here's a good way to take an inventory: are there soul-sized,

Christ-centered, Spirit-guided issues involved in our reason for being in trouble?

THE AMAZING SURPRISES OF THE LIFE

34 Then one in the council stood up, a Pharisee named Gamaliel, a teacher of the law held in respect by all the people, and commanded them to put the apostles outside for a little while. 35 And he said to them: "Men of Israel, take heed to yourselves what you intend to do regarding these men. 36 For some time ago Theudas rose up, claiming to be somebody. A number of men, about four hundred, joined him. He was slain, and all who obeyed him were scattered and came to nothing. 37 After this man, Judas of Galilee rose up in the days of the census, and drew away many people after him. He also perished, and all who obeyed him were dispersed. 38 And now I say to you, keep away from these men and let them alone; for if this plan or this work is of men, it will come to nothing; 39 but if it is of God, you cannot overthrow it—lest you even be found to fight against God."

40 And they agreed with him, and when they had called for the apostles and beaten them, they commanded that they should not speak in the name of Jesus, and let them go. 41 So they departed from the presence of the council, rejoicing that they were counted worthy to suffer shame for His name. 42 And daily in the temple, and in every house, they did not cease teaching and preaching Jesus as the Christ.

—Acts 5:34–42

When obedience to the Lord is the real cause of our trouble as a result of communicating life, we can expect the serendipities, the unexpected surprises of His Spirit. That's what happened that day before the Sanhedrin. Who would have suspected or imagined that they would be dissuaded from the decision to kill the apostles by a Pharisee from among them, and by the greatest teacher of Israel at the time—Gamaliel? He was the grandson of the famous Hebrew scholar, Hillel, and was head of a school for the training of the conservative segment of the Jewish religion called Pharisaism. The movement had begun to recall Israel back to strict nationalism, to protect the law from being polluted by secularism, and to preserve the strictest of moral resoluteness.

Gamaliel was a wise man. His counsel to the Sanhedrin was to calm down, wait and see. He drew the enraged attention of his fellow Pharisees and the Sadduccees back to the real issue. He reminded them of an insurrectionist named Theudas who raised an army of four hundred and a great deal of confusion. But he was slain in a riot and his movement came to nothing. That led Gamaliel to his point: *"And now I say to you, keep away from these men and let them alone; for if this plan or this work is of men, it will come to nothing; but if it is of God, you cannot overthrow it—lest you even be found to fight against God"* (5:38–39). Very wise counsel! For the Sanhedrin. . . and for us. There are times when certain people and causes are so obviously a contradiction to the Word of God that we know they are not of Him. There are other times when they may be great truths packaged in new methods with which we are not familiar. Wait. If they are of God we can't stop them. If not, they will not succeed anyhow!

Gamaliel's sensitivity to what was happening, and the possible dangers of blocking what God might be doing, won the day. The apostles were released with one more warning. The brilliant Pharisee had saved the church! Without the apostles, the movement of new life would have faded out. The Lord had work for them to finish. Later when their part was completed and leadership was passed on to others, they faced their deaths with the same obedience and courage displayed on that day. But the crucial thing is that the Lord stepped in and saved them from sure death at the hands of the Sanhedrin. Gamaliel was used without knowing it. Or did he know? Surely in his wisdom and training he saw and felt the authenticity of these men.

The Lord of life intervenes to help us. Always on time! Never late. And out of gracious love and care He even intervenes in troubles in our lives that have little to do with His cause—troubles we have brought onto ourselves. He loves us that much. That too is part of the Life we have to communicate.

CHAPTER EIGHT—THE TURNING POINT
ACTS 6:1—8:3

Scripture Outline

The Potential in Every Problem (6:1–7)

A Crown to Live a Name (6:8–15)

If I Had Only One Last Sermon to Preach (7:1–37)

Stiff Necks and Hard Hearts (7:38–53)

The Seed of the Church (7:54—8:3)

Luke is a skilled dramatist. Like a sensitive playwright, he prepares us well for the entrance of his key characters. He knows human nature, that we like to sense when something really crucial is about to take place. The suspense and intrigue carries us along with anticipation. As the story line unfolds, we feel that the author has let us in on intimate details with subtle intimations. By the time an important character walks to center stage, we can't wait to observe him and hear what he has to say.

That's exactly what I sense Luke doing in Acts 6:1—8:3. He got us ready for the return of Jesus Christ in the power of the Holy Spirit at Pentecost. Then, as he described the acts of the Holy Spirit in the new humanity, the church, he revealed the birth of a movement. All along we sensed that movement was to change the course of history. Now in these two transitional chapters, Luke builds our anticipation for the person who will head that movement beyond being a sect of Judaism—the apostle Paul. So that we may fully appreciate the carefully orchestrated series of events which led to Paul's conversion, Luke carefully introduces us to the person who dramatically influenced Paul's life.

His name was Stephen. Without Stephen there might not have been an apostle Paul, a break with Judaism, nor world-wide

Christianity. Stephen is the personification of the transition Luke wants us to feel.

You may have been surprised by the large segment of Acts I selected for this chapter of our exposition. This has been done purposely from years of experience of teaching and preaching Acts to large and small groups. I have found that in the challenge of bringing along our listeners and fellow-adventurers in the unfolding drama, there is a danger of getting bogged down at this point. We need to understand that everything Luke says and describes in this transition has a deeper meaning. He sees what the Spirit did to arrange seemingly unrelated events and circumstances to accomplish His purpose, and at the end of this section, Luke exposes what He's been doing. It is a classic understatement that provides us with an exclamation of excitement, "Aha. Now I see what was happening!" A short terse sentence focuses it all: *"Now Saul was consenting to his death"* (8:1). As we shall see, Saul did more than consent. He arranged it. But behind that arrangement, Someone else had plans for him!

In that light we turn with new eyes of appreciation to look at Stephen. Acts 6:1–7 brings him on stage, Acts 6:8–15 gives us a chance to observe his Spirit-filled character, Acts 7:1–53 provides an analysis of his beliefs, Acts 7:54–60 shows us the faith with which he died, and Acts 8:1–3 reveals what the Holy Spirit was doing through it all. Each segment is built on the one before it and draws us on to the concluding purpose.

THE POTENTIAL IN EVERY PROBLEM

6:1 Now in those days, when the number of the disciples was multiplying, there arose a complaint against the Hebrews by the Hellenists, because their widows were neglected in the daily distribution. **2** Then the twelve summoned the multitude of the disciples and said, "It is not desirable that we should leave the word of God and serve tables. **3** Therefore, brethren, seek out from among you seven men of good reputation, full of the Holy Spirit and wisdom, whom we may appoint over this business; **4** but we will give ourselves continually to prayer and to the ministry of the word."

5 And the saying pleased the whole multitude. And they chose Stephen, a man full of faith and the Holy Spirit, and Philip, Prochorus, Nicanor, Timon, Parmenas, and Nicolas, a proselyte from Antioch, **6** whom they set before the apostles; and when they had prayed, they laid hands on them.

⁷ Then the word of God spread, and the number of the disciples multiplied greatly in Jerusalem, and a great many of the priests were obedient to the faith.

—Acts 6:1–7

Out of the insignificant can come the infinitely important things the Holy Spirit is trying to teach us and is using for a greater strategy. The organization of the early church was not laid out for the apostles by the Holy Spirit. They simply were in the flow of His power; and when a problem arose, they did what seemed guided by Him. This section of this transitional chapter of Acts tells us that we should be open to the Spirit's guidance in the mundane. He may be using it as a step onward to something magnificent.

Let's look at the problem and the potential hidden in it. Two different groups of people responded to the Holy's Spirit's ministry through the proclamation of the gospel by the apostles. The Palestinian Jews were one of these groups. Descendants of the exiled Jews who returned from Babylonia to rebuild Jerusalem under the leadership of Nehemiah and Ezra, they were intensely nationalistic, vigilant in the observance of the law and the traditions of the Jewish religion. They spoke either Hebrew or a form of the ancient language called Aramaic.

Those in the other group were called Hellenists. The word refers to Greek-speaking Jews, or more accurately, Jews living in the Greek-speaking world around the Mediterranean who maintained their religion through the synagogues in their own cities. Some were descendants of the Dispersion, Jews who did not return to Palestine after the Exile and who were scattered around in various nations and cities. Others were part of the large number of Jewish merchants drawn away from Palestine for economic and business enterprises.

The passion of every Jew was to return to Jerusalem to worship in the temple, particularly during the time of the Passover through the Feast of Pentecost. These Jews were part of the crowd that observed what happened when the Holy Spirit filled the disciples on Pentecost morning. The saying of the dispersed Jews, "This year in Jerusalem," expressed their longing to return to Jerusalem, the Holy City. Many of them remained in the city long after a return visit, and some became permanent citizens. But they did not lose their Greek cultural background, and thus were never fully accepted by the Palestinian Jews.

A tension between these two groups had grown up through the years. When both Palestinian and Hellenistic Jews responded to the gospel, they were drawn into a close relationship that could not otherwise have been possible. But the prejudices persisted even after they became followers of the Lord. In the account of this squabble, Luke allows us an honest look at an age-old problem. Just as happened in the infant church in Jerusalem, we often bring our prejudices into the new life in Christ and into our attitudes in the church. We sometimes have the illusion that the only solution to twenty-first-century problems in the church is to get back to the peace and unity of the early days when the church was all that the Lord intended. But Luke helps us see that our task is to live in our time with the Lord of all time. And the only way to do that is to look for the potential hidden in our problem.

It is a comfort, however, to know that everything was not perfect. The Hellenist converts felt that the Palestinian converts were given preference in the distribution of the offerings that had been collected from the members of the church in expression of their "all things in common" sharing. The Hellenists believed that what they had put into the common offering was not being equally distributed among their widows and people in need.

There is a tendency in human nature, even after conversion, to split the fellowship into factions with different emphases. What the Lord has brought together we put asunder, and the budget often is the focus of the wrangle. Think of the examples of that today: local programs versus world missions; caring for our own needy within the congregation versus caring for those in the community; the local congregation versus the denominational organization. Or consider the rifts between the pietists and social activists, the evangelicals and the traditional church people, the high church advocates and the low, the Protestants and the Roman Catholics, the charismatics and the people who believe that most of the gifts were for apostolic times, the traditional church musicians and the advocates of contemporary gospel music, the intellectuals and the relationalists. I have called these differences the tyranny of the either/or. It is bringing to the gospel our previous conditioning and wanting it all our way in affirmation of previous experience of loyalties. We often miss the potent formula of authentic Christianity: the both/and.

I am impressed with the lack of defensiveness among the apostles as, with the Holy Spirit's guidance, they confronted the problem headon. If the Hellenists were disturbed about a seeming inequality, put Hellenists in charge of the distribution! Ingenious? Yes. But more than that: guided and wise.

The qualifications of the Hellenists to be selected are very significant. They were to be *"from among you"* (6:3). Not just Greek-speaking Jews, but people who were involved in the church because of conversion and transformation in the new life. The second qualification is an expression of that. They should be *"men of good reputation"* (v. 3). The New King James uses "reputation" instead of "report" as in the old King James. The word in Greek is *marturouménous,* from *mártus,* meaning witness. The word has two uses—it can mean a person of whom a good witness is given and also a person who is good in witnessing. Certainly the apostles wanted people of impeccable character, but that character should be a witness to Christ in them and activate involvement in communicating His love to others. And the ultimate qualification was that they be *"full of the Holy Spirit."* This was to be exemplified in all dimensions of their lives—intellectual, emotional, volitional. The test would be in the gift of wisdom. The evidence of the Spirit's indwelling would be the gift to penetrate the deep mysteries of God and apply them in guidance for daily life.

These qualities should be the basis of leadership in the church today for clergy and laity, elders, deacons, and trustees. So often our temptation is to bypass these criteria and select people with natural abilities or training in an area. Important as these are, without the maximizing power of the Spirit, they can stand in the way of spiritual leadership of the church. It is perilous to lead a church on human training and conditioning alone.

I think of a trustee of a church I served some years ago. He was a financial wizard who had had a distinguished career in the business world. However, he had drifted into church membership without a commitment of his will to Christ. He seldom prayed, and he depended on his own strength to get on top and stay there in the competitive commercial world. It had been thought by the membership that he would bring dignity, acumen, *and* a big pledge if he were elected as a trustee. He was elected and was named head of an important finance committee. I inherited him when I arrived as a new pastor. He was ill-equipped spiritually to make the crucial decisions about the distribution of funds. His cultural background, political prejudices, attitudes toward the poor, and vision for the future of the church's mission were an immovable roadblock to progress in the church.

I am thankful that is not the end of the story. The Bible study and prayer time before the monthly meeting, objected to at first, became the Spirit's tool in reaching the man. Before long, he came to see me. He confessed he did not know the same Christ I was talking about in our meetings. But his interest was piqued. That conversation led to many others and one day, he committed his immense intellectual and personal abilities to Christ. He invited the Lord to live in him and began a consistent program of daily Bible reading and prayer. The difference was apparent to him and to everyone else.

It was exciting to observe that as he began to share his own faith with others, his concern for the evangelism and mission program of the church was transformed. He became the advocate of tithing and mission-giving. One comment he made has lingered in my mind through the years. "What unsettles me are those years when I decided things on my own before I knew the Lord!" His natural talents and training were not set aside. Instead they were maximized by the indwelling Lord for His plans and purposes for the church.

The qualifications for leadership in the church of Christ have not changed since the first century. We can do church work without them but not the real work of the church.

Luke names the men who were selected to be deacons. Note that all were Hellenists, as their names clearly indicate. And the selection was not done by casting lots as with Matthias before Pentecost, but through the guidance of the Spirit. Those Spirit-filled men, who were known for their witness and wisdom, were brought to the apostles and consecrated with the laying on of hands. Peace and unity returned to the young church, and the central work of sharing the good news was continued with a particular sign of blessing. Luke tells us that *a great many of the priests were obedient to the faith"* (6:7). That means that a very significant segment of Israel's leadership was being affected. It also accounts for the alarm of the Pharisees over the influence of the disciples—and one Pharisee in particular. Luke is getting us ready!

The impact of this section of the sixth chapter for us today, in addition to helping us get our thinking straight about the basic requirements of church leadership, is to get us to see how every problem has in it the seeds of a greater potential we could miss if we had not gone through the problem. The apostles were hindered by trying to do everything. They were probably troubled by that more than the Hellenists! But when they faced the problem nondefensively, the Holy Spirit provided a solution which brought a strategy of expansion out of a squabble. From the time of their selection and consecration by the apostles, the deacons did so much more than wait on tables, important as that was. We read of their preaching and teaching, witnessing and converting people; and we see that two of them, Stephen and Philip, were the cutting edge of breaking barriers and moving to new frontiers. Problems are the prelude to new discoveries if we simply ask the Holy Spirit to help us.

To the church and to history, the problem of the Hellenists gave Stephen, and through his witness, the apostle Paul. We move on eagerly to see what happened.

A CROWN TO LIVE A NAME

8 And Stephen, full of faith and power, did great wonders and signs among the people. 9 Then there arose some from what is called the Synagogue of the Freedmen (Cyrenians, Alexandrians, and those from Cilicia and Asia), disputing with Stephen. 10 And they were not able to resist the wisdom and the Spirit by which he spoke. 11 Then they secretly induced men to say, "We have heard him speak blasphemous words against Moses and God." 12 And they stirred up the people, the elders, and the scribes; and they came upon him, seized him, and brought him to the council. 13 They also set up false witnesses who said, "This man does not cease to speak blasphemous words against this holy place and the law; 14 for we have heard him say that this Jesus of Nazareth will destroy this place and change the customs which Moses delivered to us." 15 And all who sat in the council, looking steadfastly at him, saw his face as the face of an angel.

—*Acts 6:8–15*

Stephen's name in Greek means "crown." This crown could be one of regal power or a crown used as a symbol of triumph in the Greek games. Stephen's mother and father did not know when they gave him that name that he would become a disciple of One who wore a crown of thorns. Through Him the deacon won a far greater crown than his given name intended.

Luke's admiration for Stephen's character and radiance is evident in the terms he carefully chooses to paint a word portrait of the deacon. In verses 5 and 8, he tells us that Stephen is full of faith, the Holy Spirit, and power. Note that the word "faith" is used twice in the New King James in describing Stephen. The footnote in the biblical text of this translation alerts us to the fact that "faith" in verse 8 was actually "grace" in the original Greek text. *Plērēs cháritos kaì dunámeōs* is the wording in Greek, translated, "full of grace and power." F. F. Bruce suggests that Luke may have employed the word "grace" in its pre-Christian usage as "charm," or charisma. My opinion is that Luke hardly would have used such a potent word as grace without its deeper Christian implication of the unlimited love, favor, and acceptance of the Lord. Perhaps he had both in mind. He introduces a man in Christ and in whom Christ lived. He had experienced the grace of the Atonement, had responded with the gift of faith, and had the power to do wonders and signs. But Luke's use of the word "grace" in verse 8, after he had told us already that Stephen was a man full of faith and the Holy Spirit in verse 5, indicates an emphasis.

The grace of the Lord had produced an identifiable grace, *cháris,* a charisma, about Stephen. This distinguishes the unique way he manifested the Holy Spirit. Luke tells us that he had the same power to do signs and wonders as Peter and the apostles, but he was also a person especially radiant with grace and an impelling and infectious graciousness about his witness. That impression is woven all through Luke's account of what happened to Stephen. He was a man full of faith in Christ's death and Resurrection for him, full of daring belief that all things were possible through Him. In a continuing experience of that unmerited favor and acceptance, his countenance was filled with the gracious disposition of Christ, and miraculous supernatural things happened to people who heard him teach. A person like Stephen, crowned with faith, grace, and power, becomes a magnet to people in need. He also becomes a moving target of opposition.

That opposition came with hurricane force from the Synagogue of the Freedmen, a special synagogue in Jerusalem made up of Hellenistic Jews from Alexandria, Cyrenia, Cilicia, and Asia. It was natural that Stephen, a Hellenist himself, would choose that synagogue as a natural place to witness. These were his people with a common background in Greek thought, culture, and a more intellectual, philosophic approach to the Jewish religion. It was the custom in that synagogue in Jerusalem to have debates over religious issues. Stephen went there to tell the good news of Jesus Christ as Messiah, crucified Savior, risen Lord, and indwelling Spirit. That caused more than a pleasant exchange of ideas! But his listeners found the grace-filled Stephen difficult to resist. Luke tells us that *"they were not able to resist the wisdom and the Spirit by which he spoke"* (v. 10).

Obviously all the human endowments and special gifts of the Spirit were working at full power. Stephen's gifts of charisma and wisdom were the most irresistible. The intellectual Jews to whom he spoke could not help being impressed.

A strange, intriguing twist takes place in Luke's account of what happened. Verse 9 introduces the incident, verse 10 tells us of Stephen's communicating so effectively that these Jews to whom he spoke could not resist his wisdom and the Spirit's power moving through him; then suddenly verse 11 tells us that they, the same people, induced others to accuse him of blasphemy. Something is between the lines here.

Not "something" at all—there was someone between those lines. At one moment all the people are impressed, and the next moment they are arch-opponents. Who would have been in the Synagogue of the Freedman who knew how to incite people to devise a plot with accusations, witnesses, and a fully documented case against Stephen? Who knew the codes for arrest and had the power to make one? Who but the head of the Sanhedrin's gestapo—Saul of Tarsus!

Saul was undoubtedly a member of the synagogue. He was a Hellenistic Jew and, as a brilliant Pharisee, the style and life of the synagogue would have suited him. He must have been there, watching, listening, waiting. His task was to purge Jerusalem of the followers of Jesus of Nazareth. And charismatic Stephen was his target. The involvement of Hellenistic Jews in this movement of following a "dead Galilean" was particularly abhorrent to him. With the authority of the head of the secret police task force to destroy Jesus' followers, Saul arrested Stephen and had him arraigned before the Sanhedrin. He had everything planned perfectly: the false witnesses with a charge of blasphemy, a charge suited for the death penalty Saul desired, an enraged Sanhedrin thirsty for blood.

The disturbing thing for Saul of Tarsus was the response given to this magnetic man. The Sadducees and the Pharisees all sat looking steadfastly at him, transfixed as if they were looking at the face of an angel. Something would have to be done about that. Get him to start preaching! He will come soon enough to his convictions about Jesus. And when the Sanhedrin hears from him the same words that enraged them from Peter, the officials would confirm the penalty Saul had asked for.

Who but an eyewitness could have relayed what happened that day? Who could have told Luke? Who but Saul of Tarsus?

IF I HAD ONLY ONE LAST SERMON TO PREACH

7:1 Then the high priest said, "Are these things so?"

[2] And he said, "Brethren and fathers, listen: The God of glory appeared to our father Abraham when he was in Mesopotamia, before he dwelt in Haran, [3] and said to him, 'Get out of your country and from your relatives, and come to a land that I will show you.' [4] Then he came out of the land of the Chaldeans and dwelt in Haran. And from there, when his father was dead, He moved him to this land in which you now dwell. [5] And God gave him no inheritance in it, not even enough to set his foot on. But even when Abraham had no child, He promised to give it to him for a possession, and to his descendants after him. [6] But God spoke in this way: that his descendants would dwell in a foreign land, and that they would bring them into bondage and oppress them four hundred years. [7] 'And the nation to whom they will be in bondage I will judge,' said God, 'and after that they shall come out and serve Me in this place.' [8] Then He gave him the covenant of circumcision; and so Abraham begot Isaac and circumcised him on the eighth day; and Isaac begot Jacob, and Jacob begot the twelve patriarchs.

[9] "And the patriarchs, becoming envious, sold Joseph into Egypt. But God was with him [10] and delivered him out of all his troubles, and gave him favor and wisdom in the presence of Pharaoh, king of Egypt; and he made him governor over Egypt and all his house. [11] Now a famine and great trouble came over all the land of Egypt and Canaan, and our fathers found no sustenance. [12] But when Jacob heard that there was grain in Egypt, he sent out our fathers first. [13] And the second time Joseph was made known to his brothers, and Joseph's family became known to the Pharaoh. [14] Then Joseph sent and called his father Jacob and all his relatives to him, seventy-five people. [15] So Jacob went down to Egypt; and he died, he and our fathers. [16] And they were carried back to Shechem and laid in the tomb that Abraham bought for a sum of money from the sons of Hamor, the father of Shechem.

[17] "But when the time of the promise drew near which God had sworn to Abraham, the people grew and multiplied in Egypt [18] till another king arose who did not know Joseph. [19] This man dealt treacherously with our people, and oppressed

our forefathers, making them expose their babies, so that they might not live. 20 At this time Moses was born, and was well pleasing to God; and he was brought up in his father's house for three months. 21 But when he was set out, Pharaoh's daughter took him away and brought him up as her own son. 22 And Moses was learned in all the wisdom of the Egyptians, and was mighty in words and deeds.

23 "Now when he was forty years old, it came into his heart to visit his brethren, the children of Israel. 24 And seeing one of them suffer wrong, he defended and avenged him who was oppressed, and struck down the Egyptian. 25 For he supposed that his brethren would have understood that God would deliver them by his hand, but they did not understand. 26 And the next day he appeared to two of them as they were fighting, and tried to reconcile them, saying, 'Men, you are brethren; why do you wrong one another?' 27 But he who did his neighbor wrong pushed him away, saying, 'Who made you a ruler and a judge over us? 28 Do you want to kill me as you did the Egyptian yesterday?' 29 Then, at this saying, Moses fled and became a dweller in the land of Midian, where he had two sons.

30 "And when forty years had passed, an Angel of the Lord appeared to him in a flame of fire in a bush, in the wilderness of Mount Sinai. 31 When Moses saw it, he marveled at the sight; and as he drew near to observe, the voice of the Lord came to him, 32 saying, 'I am the God of your fathers— the God of Abraham, the God of Isaac, and the God of Jacob.' And Moses trembled and dared not look. 33 'Then the LORD said to him, "Take your sandals off your feet, for the place where you stand is holy ground. 34 I have surely seen the oppression of My people who are in Egypt; I have heard their groaning and have come down to deliver them. And now come, I will send you to Egypt."'

35 "This Moses whom they rejected, saying, 'Who made you a ruler and a judge?' is the one God sent to be a ruler and a deliverer by the hand of the Angel who appeared to him in the bush. 36 He brought them out, after he had shown wonders and signs in the land of Egypt, and in the Red Sea, and in the wilderness forty years.

37 "This is that Moses who said to the children of Israel, 'The LORD your God will raise up for you a Prophet like me from your brethren. Him you shall hear.'

—Acts 7:1–37

Richard Baxter said, "I preach as a dying man to dying men and women as if never to preach again." Who can be sure he or she will have another chance? And think of the people to whom we've preached, who in the following week, were killed in an accident, or had a heart attack, or left for the hospital never to return. But most of all, think of those who, by the Holy Spirit's timing, were there giving the gospel one last chance!

This past spring, I was in Israel leading a tour. While we were at the Sea of Galilee, we had two opportunities to sail on the Sea. One of them was a study and prayer time on the way to Capernaum. The second was a twilight sail arranged by the hotel especially for our group. Some vacationing Israelis did not know that it was a chartered craft and came aboard for the sail. When we were under way they realized that they were on a boat with Americans, all of whom were Christians, and that worship was planned as a part of the event. They looked as if they wanted to abandon ship!

There was nowhere to go except to sit out the service of singing and preaching. I felt led to change the talk I'd prepared and instead preached on Abraham and Isaac. I noted the flush of relief on their faces. They laughed and cried with the rest of us as we made our way through the preparation for Isaac, his birth, and the sacrifice. When I explained the deeper meaning of the ram as the substitute for the sacrifice of Isaac, we were ready for the move from what happened on Mount Moriah to Calvary. If I had started with Calvary, we would have lost them before the end of the introduction.

Did Stephen know what would happen to him? We do not know. What we do know is that he preached with an incisive power as if he knew intuitively that he might never have another chance. Certainly he must have known he probably would never again have that kind of opportunity to speak to the highest leaders of Israel.

We wonder about the approach Stephen took when he was given the opportunity to speak. It would appear that he took an inordinately long period of the precious time recounting the history of Israel and telling at great length about personalities of the Old Testament about whom the Sadducees and Pharisees had heard thousands of times since they were old enough to understand. But had they understood? Did they have any idea of the deeper meaning, the purpose, the fulfillment, and culmination in the Messiah? Stephen carefully selected the events he retold, each one to build to the one point he wanted to make.

But Stephen was doing something else. The Sanhedrin was obviously agitated and filled with anger. How could he sway them except to calm them down with what they had in common? He also wanted to establish his credentials as a faithful Hebrew scholar who knew his faith. Further, he wanted to show the faithfulness and goodness of God all through Israel's history, leading up to the gracious and forgiving gift of His Son. And don't miss the way Stephen showed how God's chosen people had repeatedly resisted Yahweh's overtures of grace. We feel the deacon gripped by the Spirit as he picks up pace and power. He has prepared his audience well for the laser thrust of truth the Spirit is guiding him to preach.

STIFF NECKS AND HARD HEARTS

38 "This is he who was in the congregation in the wilderness with the Angel who spoke to him on Mount Sinai, and with our fathers, the one who received the living oracles to give to us, 39 whom our fathers would not obey, but rejected. And in their hearts they turned back to Egypt, 40 saying to Aaron, 'Make us gods to go before us; as for this Moses who brought us out of the land of Egypt, we do not know what has become of him.' 41 And they made a calf in those days, offered sacrifices to the idol, and rejoiced in the works of their own hands. 42 Then God turned and gave them up to worship the host of heaven, as it is written in the book of the Prophets:

'Did you offer Me slaughtered animals and sacrifices during forty years in the wilderness,

O house of Israel?

43 *You also took up the tabernacle of Moloch,*

And the star of your god Remphan,

Images which you made to worship;

And I will carry you away beyond Babylon.'

44 "Our fathers had the tabernacle of witness in the wilderness, as He appointed, instructing Moses to make it according to the pattern that he had seen, 45 which our fathers, having received it in turn, also brought with Joshua into the land possessed by the Gentiles, whom God drove out before the face of our fathers until the days of David, 46 who found favor before God and asked to find a dwelling for the God of Jacob. 47 But Solomon built Him a house.

48 "However, the Most High does not dwell in temples made with hands, as the prophet says:

49 *'Heaven is My throne,*

And earth is My footstool.
What house will you build for Me? says the LORD,
Or what is the place of My rest?
50 *Has My hand not made all these things?'*
51 "You stiff-necked and uncircumcised in heart and ears!
You always resist the Holy Spirit; as your fathers did, so do
you. 52 Which of the prophets did your fathers not persecute?
And they killed those who foretold the coming of the Just
One, of whom you now have become the betrayers and mur-
derers, 53 who have received the law by the direction of angels
and have not kept it."

—*Acts 7:38–53*

Stephen has made no exposition except by inference thus far.
Now we see him more as preacher than chronicler. We see the direct
correlation between the sins of the people in the wilderness and resistance of the leaders to whom he was speaking. He shifts tenses from
the past to the present and changes pronouns from "they" and
"them" to "you." He exposes the false worship of the temple when
God does not dwell in temples made with hands. Then he makes his
direct confrontation: The leaders of Israel are like their fathers of old.
They have persecuted the prophets and killed any who foretold the
coming of the Just One. The term was clearly messianic, denoting the
advent of the Messiah. And they have betrayed and murdered Him.
They are stiff-necked and uncircumcised in heart and ears. Both
invective terms are from Jeremiah and Ezekiel and are frequently used
throughout the Old Testament (Jer. 4:4; 6:10; 9:26; Ezek. 44:7).

Do you see what Stephen has done? He has appealed to the
pride of a shared heritage of great personalities of sacred history
whom every Hebrew admired and wanted to emulate. When he
has them with him, he begins to show how rebellious Israel has
been to God's overtures of love. Most drastically, they have
resisted the predictions of the Messiah and murdered Him when
He came. All this is based on a common element in apostolic
preaching to the Hebrew people: there can be no forgiveness without acknowledgment of sins. The deed done to Jesus the Christ
had to be confessed. No wonder the Sadducees and Pharisees cried
out and gnashed their teeth.

THE SEED OF THE CHURCH

54 When they heard these things they were cut to the
heart, and they gnashed at him with their teeth. 55 But he,

being full of the Holy Spirit, gazed into heaven and saw the glory of God, and Jesus standing at the right hand of God, [56] and said, "Look! I see the heavens opened and the Son of Man standing at the right hand of God!"

[57] Then they cried out with a loud voice, stopped their ears, and ran at him with one accord; [58] and they cast him out of the city and stoned him. And the witnesses laid down their clothes at the feet of a young man named Saul. [59] And they stoned Stephen as he was calling on God and saying, "Lord Jesus, receive my spirit." [60] Then he knelt down and cried out with a loud voice, "Lord, do not charge them with this sin." And when he had said this, he fell asleep.

8:1 Now Saul was consenting to his death. At that time a great persecution arose against the church which was at Jerusalem; and they were all scattered throughout the regions of Judea and Samaria, except the apostles. [2] And devout men carried Stephen to his burial, and made great lamentation over him.

[3] As for Saul, he made havoc of the church, entering every house, and dragging off men and women, committing them to prison.

—Acts 7:54—8:3

The force of the Greek is that the members of the Sanhedrin wailed in erratic, wild, jeering shouts of anger and hostility. The descriptive phrase *"cut to the heart"* means that they were convicted. The raw nerve had not only been touched, it had been cut to the core. The shift of pronouns to the prophetic "you!" and the attack on the temple were more than they were willing to take. *"Gnashed at him with their teeth"* means that they ground their teeth at Stephen with a hissing sound, exposing them in a hateful screwing up of their mouths. Not a pretty picture. And in comparison, for Saul to observe, was the radiant face of Stephen. Peace, rectitude, resoluteness, joy.

Stephen's face was not set against the grim faces of the Sanhedrin but up toward the face of the Lord. And Stephen's face was magnificently shining because he never took his eyes off the face of His Lord.

Then the rage of the Sanhedrin, pent up so long in repeated trials and confrontations with the followers of Jesus, could be contained no longer. It was as if someone had given a prearranged signal and they all rushed in on Stephen. Mob violence instigated and manipulated by an expert: Saul.

It was no easy feat to arrange a death sentence and assure an execution and not become directly involved. But Saul was no ordinary man. His brilliance, fired by his hatred, worked it all out. Later, near the end of his life, he clearly stated that he added his vote to the Sanhedrin's death sentence. His task, however, was to assure Stephen's death while getting no blood on his own hands. After Stephen was beaten, the Jews were in a frenzy. They had to finish what they had started. Since no blood could be spilled in the temple precincts, they dragged the dazed and beaten Stephen outside the city wall for one of the most painful and prolonged methods of execution imaginable. He was pushed over the wall into the pit from which there was no escape from the hurling stones. A blow to the head with death-giving concussion would have been merciful. The crowd that day was not as accurate or precise in aim as an execution squad. Probably the vital death blow was a long time in coming.

And Saul stood by to make sure that everything measured up to the Deuteronomic code for stoning a blasphemer. The witnesses were the first ones to throw the stones. Luke tells us they stripped their outer garments for the task and laid their garments at Saul's feet. He watched as the first stones plummeted down on Stephen's body and then his face. How could it be that that face was still radiant? Who was this man anyhow? What was it that gave him that kind of courage?

Stephen's prayer as the death blow hit revealed to Saul Whom the martyr believed was his sustaining power. A chill must have run through the Pharisee's heart as he heard the name he had grown to hate so passionately: *"Lord Jesus, receive my spirit"* (7:59). And as Stephen was dying, he prayed for his executioners. Saul looked at his face one more time. It held the same peace in death as in living. That face was to haunt him until the day he met the One whose love and power it reflected. But in the meantime his hatred was mingled with one more emotion—fear. And that made him more determined and dangerous than ever!

Before we close this phase of Luke's unfolding drama, we need to pause and reflect on what Stephen's death did to the church.

First of all, it raised profound questions. What was the Lord doing? How could He allow this to happen to one so faithful as Stephen? Why didn't He stop it? Stephen was at the height of his power as a witness. Why snuff out so bright a flame? We've all asked these questions about tragedies and unexplainable reversals.

The questions about Stephen, however, can be answered only by the reflection of history. The Lord was not finished. Through

Stephen's death the sect of Judaism was forced to flee Jerusalem. The Christians were scattered, and their faith with them. They were to be part of the worldwide movement. They would never have left Jerusalem without the persecution and punishment inflicted on them. The death of Stephen ignited the fire of the pent-up hatred for the followers of Jesus. It exploded with fury. They had to leave. And their deployment in a dispersion throughout the cities of the Mediterranean basin planted the seed which would germinate until it was ready to sprout in indigenous churches.

The saying is true: the blood of the martyrs is the seed of the church. This is never more true than with the blood of the first martyr. Stephen, whose natural crown of human ability was crowned with gifts of the Lord's Spirit, then His crown of thorns, and finally the crown of glory, had lived a relatively short life. But he accomplished his purpose. Stephen was the turning point, and eventually the cause of the gnawing questions of Saul of Tarsus that only the Lord could answer.

CHAPTER NINE—COMMUNICATING WITH THE SPIRIT'S POWER

ACTS 8:4–40

Scripture Outline
   The Initial Blessing (8:4–13)
   The Full Blessing (8:14–17)
   Simony—Then and Now (8:18–25)
   South at High Noon (8:26–27a)
   How to Share Our Faith (8:27b–40)

Saul's plan had backfired. He had hoped that Stephen's execution would frighten the followers of Jesus into silence and subservience. Instead, it scattered the fire of the faith. A Jerusalem-based sect of Judaism was pressed out into the very areas of Judea and Samaria where the Lord said they would be witnesses.

Luke makes a rather matter-of-fact statement that one of the deacons by the name of Philip was sent by the apostles to Samaria to preach. That implies so much. The disciples had watched Jesus minister to some of the Samaritans and had kept their inner prejudices to themselves. But their real feelings had reflected the Jews' hatred of the Samaritans at the time. When the northern kingdom fell in 722 B.C., many of the Jews were killed and others were carried off to Assyria. A few were left and intermarried with the Assyrians who were brought in to repopulate the conquered land. Their offspring were known as Samaritans. When the exile ended, and the Jews of pure blood were called to return to Palestine, a deep hatred developed between them and those who were despised as half-breeds.

Eventually Mt. Gerizim became the Samaritan center of worship, while the Jews meanwhile had rebuilt the temple and restored Jerusalem to its place as Holy City. The Jews had no dealings with the Samaritans. Jesus passed through Samaria on his way back and forth from Galilee to Jerusalem. He ministered to some of them and used one as an example in his daring parable about a "good" Samaritan.

It is very significant that the time-worn prejudice was superseded by the apostles' sending Philip to preach to a Samaritan city. The expansion of the movement had begun.

What happened to Philip, recorded in Acts 8, is a powerful analysis of communication to others about what Christ means to us. Philip has much to teach us both from what he didn't do, and then from what he did.

THE INITIAL BLESSING

4 Therefore those who were scattered went everywhere preaching the word. 5 Then Philip went down to the city of Samaria and preached Christ to them. 6 And the multitudes with one accord heeded the things spoken by Philip, hearing and seeing the miracles which he did. 7 For unclean spirits, crying with a loud voice, came out of many who were possessed; and many who were paralyzed and lame were healed. 8 And there was great joy in that city.

9 But there was a certain man called Simon, who previously practiced sorcery in the city and astonished the people of Samaria, claiming that he was someone great, 10 to whom they all gave heed, from the least to the greatest, saying, "This man is the great power of God." 11 And they heeded him because he had astonished them with his sorceries for a long time. 12 But when they believed Philip as he preached the things concerning the kingdom of God and the name of Jesus Christ, both men and women were baptized. 13 Then Simon himself also believed; and when he was baptized he continued with Philip, and was amazed, seeing the miracles and signs which were done.

—Acts 8:4–13

Philip had a three-point message which brought about three great results. He preached Christ, the kingdom of God, and the name of Jesus Christ. This brought about conversion, new life in Christ, and miracles of healing and liberation from possession of evil spirits and sickness. It is fascinating to note how this met three of the four great needs of the people in the Samaritan city. These three are part of the quadripod on which the Christian life stands firmly. We will consider the fourth as Luke's account unfolds.

Preaching Christ is the basic purpose of any ministry. Spurgeon said, "We have a great need for Christ and a great Christ for our needs." And before him, reformer Zinzendorf said, "I have one passion only: It is He! It is He!" Philip would have agreed. He came to Samaria with only one passion and purpose: to preach Christ. That means making known, in a clear and incisive way, a Person we know. Preaching Christ is not preaching about Him; it is introducing a Friend who has changed our lives. But that means sharing how He has met our basic needs for now and forever. Every message we teach or preach ends up with the Man of Galilee, the Lamb of God, the resurrected Savior, the infilling Lord. What Christ said, what He did, and what He does are all part of preaching Jesus Christ. We all need clear direction for living, forgiveness of our sins, victory over death that invades our living and makes every problem a little death; and we need power to live the new life in Christ. Philip preached Christ!

The framework of his preaching was the kingdom of God, His reign and rule, as we discussed in the first chapter. Acceptance of Christ as our Savior will not last long unless He is made Lord of every facet and relationship of our lives. The kingdom must be within us through that surrender of our wills. We do not preach Christ in a vacuum. We call people into a personal relationship with Christ and then into a movement. People flounder without a kingdom call and purpose.

But Philip knew that introducing people to Christ without sharing the secret of Christian growth and victory is like recruiting and training a soldier and never giving him a weapon for the battle. The moment a person turns his life over to Christ, he or she is free of one set of problems and inherits another. He or she now must face living the new life in an evil world. For that we need the power of the name of Jesus. The third thing Philip preached was the liberating power of the name.

The people of Samaria were entangled in magic and sorcery, not unlike people today who are seeking shortcuts for meeting their needs. We all want a quick trip to wonderland. There is only one power to release us from possession of evil and magic—the name of Jesus! Once we accept Christ as Savior and Lord, we realize that a battle starts inside us. The possession of old habits, ways of thinking, modes of relating, values that dominate our lives—all need Christ's liberation and reconciliation around Him as the new center of our lives. The name of Jesus helps us. It is the one-word course in how to pray. All things are possible if we pray in the name of Jesus. But there are many things about which we will not pray if we pray in His name. When Philip preached the name, he shared the secret of unlocking the power of the Lord for specific situations. He also gave them the powerful tool against evil possession of their minds and behavior. The one thing Satan cannot abide is the name of Jesus. His name is our secret weapon for the battle with evil. We can sing, "His name is wonderful!" and "Jesus the name that charms our fears." Philip's preaching of the name enabled his ministry to set a city free.

Philip's three-point message provides a good test for any communicator to evaluate his or her ministry. Are people soundly converted, brought under the Lordship of Christ's kingdom goals, and liberated from the possession of the past? Our best preparation is to allow Him to reaffirm all three in our own lives each day so we can have something fresh to share.

That leads us to consider the fourth need the Samaritans had, which Philip did not meet. Peter and John had to come down to Samaria to finish what Philip had begun. The deacon had left out of his preaching the dimension so often left out today. We must consider why. Philip was one of the seven deacons who was "full of the Holy Spirit and wisdom." And yet he did not preach the Holy Spirit as part of his message. Why?

THE FULL BLESSING

14 Now when the apostles who were at Jerusalem heard that Samaria had received the word of God, they sent Peter and John to them, 15 who, when they had come down, prayed for them that they might receive the Holy Spirit. 16 For as yet He had fallen upon none of them. They had only been baptized in the name of the Lord Jesus. 17 Then they laid hands on them, and they received the Holy Spirit.

—Acts 8:14–17

We could fill a book with the reasons expositors of this passage have suggested to explain why Philip did not tell the Samaritans about the Holy Spirit. Some have suggested that he himself had not been baptized with the power. Others have reasoned that in his experience of the warmth and comfort of the Jerusalem church he had come to take the indwelling Spirit for granted. Still others postulate that though Philip was full of the Holy Spirit when elected a deacon, he had drifted from this essential of the faith. And others have said that praying for the filling of the Spirit was an apostolic prerogative. It's not really important that we decide why Philip omitted mention of the Holy Spirit from his preaching, but it *is* important that we recognize how debilitating it is to leave out this enabling dimension of the gospel.

Peter and John saw this immediately when they arrived. They knew that these people could not live the new life in Christ without His indwelling Spirit. They probably explained this to the people and they laid hands on them for the receiving of the Holy Spirit. Until that moment, they had the influence of the Spirit, for He gives the gift of faith, but they did not have the power to live the new life they had begun.

The danger in expositing this passage is that we are tempted to use it as a basis of a whole system of theology about the first and second blessing that asserts that conversion is the first blessing and the baptism of the Holy Spirit is the second. It seems to me that this interpretation leads to the idea that the Holy Spirit is separate from the risen Christ in whom we place our trust when we hear the gospel, and that conversion and the baptism of the Holy Spirit must always happen in two stages. Now, *always* is an almighty word that is dangerous to use. I believe there are people who received the filling of the Spirit at conversion. But I believe that is based on one very important fact—that they were told about the need for an infilling as a part of their introduction to Christ and the gospel. It is important, though, whatever our doctrinal position may be, that we not assume our particular experience to be the norm and then solidify that into an irrevocable tenet of our theology.

The great warning signal sounded by this passage on Philip is that when the baptism of the Holy Spirit is left out of our teaching and preaching, we will produce converted people who are born again but have no power. And since the indwelling of Christ in the Spirit is left out of so much preaching and teaching today, a generation of people now exists in many churches who feel that they must do their best on their own with prayer to a Lord "out there somewhere" in the hope that He will interrupt His other actions and come help them.

Then when a "Spirit-filled" Christian witnesses to them, they realize Who has been missing in their lives and, unless they were effectively instructed, they seem to think of the Holy Spirit as Someone different from the living, present Christ. An unfortunate outgrowth of this experience is that some people then become very critical of their churches and clergy for keeping the secret hidden with a once-a-year, vague Pentecost sermon about the Holy Spirit.

But clergy cannot share what they do not have. If our own training has not included sound teaching and experience in the theology of the Holy Spirit, we will not make it a part of the thrust of our teaching and preaching.

And yet, there is something else here that must be said. It is possible that the ministry of the indwelling Christ may have been clearly taught and that we have missed it because we were not listening or because life has not brought us to crises or challenges big enough to demand anything more than our own self-generated discipleship in following Jesus Christ.

That was my case. I was converted to Christ in my freshman year of college and began the adventure of following Christ. I was an evangelical who believed in the Bible and seldom missed a day of study and prayer. I witnessed, led people to as much of Christ as I knew, and worked hard to be faithful in seeking first the kingdom in all of life. I went through graduate school and postgraduate training under some very fine teachers. I've looked back at my carefully kept lecture notes and realize that teaching about the indwelling Christ was not lacking. I have pondered the question of how I missed it with James S. Stewart, who, I mentioned earlier, had been my New Testament professor. His response was, "Lloyd, you were not ready. Do not wonder why it did not happen then; allow yourself to be lost in wonder that it has happened now."

What caused me to be ready, finally, was a series of personal and professional crises in my own life. There is one word that describes those early days in my first full-time parish—struggle! I struggled to be adequate, to preach orthodox biblical sermons, to meet the needs of my people, and to build a church that was Christ-centered. As I have shared in other writings, I was confronted with my need in my inability to love people profoundly—especially my wife. Also confounding me was the look in the mirror given me by the people I had led to Christ. They were struggling to live the new life in Christ as converted, but unempowered people. I saw what was lacking in them and realized something had been lacking in the way they were led to Christ.

That sent me on a long search. It involved a study of the Scriptures and very long conversations with people in whom I observed authentic spiritual power. The Book of John, particularly chapters 14, 15, and 16, plus the Book of Acts, became the focus of my Bible study. One summer I took a month to do nothing but try to find the answer. The needs in my own life, the clear message about the abiding, indwelling Spirit of Christ, and most important, the Lord's indefatigable persistence in pressing me on, became the liberating combination. Finally one day I got on my knees and asked for the Spirit of the Lord to fill me. He did. I felt every part of my being invaded with the Spirit. I felt deeply loved as never before, intellectually equipped with the mind of Christ, and endowed with spiritual gifts which were so far beyond my talents that I marveled I had lived so long on my own strength. The struggle was gone! The real struggle had not been with people or circumstances but with the Lord whose blessings I was resisting.

The point of this personal sharing is to emphasize that it is possible to be a highly trained, theologically conservative, Bible-preaching clergyperson, and not have the full blessing the Spirit wants to give. Through the years, I have tried not to make a law out of my own experience by thinking everyone is either in the same need I was in, or that the Lord will deal with him or her in only the same way. Many of my friends received Christ and His indwelling Spirit at conversion. I am thankful for that. But it seemed that so many other friends, clergy and laity, had not. And they appear to be in the same struggle of self-propelled discipleship that characterized my earlier experience.

What I went through has made me very sensitive to how we communicate the fullness of all the blessing in our teaching and preaching. And since the indwelling power is so often missed, I take extra time with people when outlining the steps of salvation to be sure they understand that the Christian life cannot be lived without the power-dimension of the infilling of the Spirit.

The next section of Acts 8 helps us to be patient when we've tried to be faithful in communicating the full blessing and people want the power without a surrender of their wills. The historic problem of communicating the gospel is that people have a capacity to let down the moat bridge of their carefully castled minds and hearts and want to take Christ into their lives as one more trophy, but not as the Lord of the castle. He is given a side room as an honored guest, but they are still running the castle! The problem is called simony—and it has implications for more than our money and possessions.

SIMONY—THEN AND NOW

[18] And when Simon saw that through the laying on of the apostles' hands the Holy Spirit was given, he offered them

money, [19] saying, "Give me this power also, that anyone on whom I lay hands may receive the Holy Spirit."

[20] But Peter said to him, "Your money perish with you, because you thought that the gift of God could be purchased with money! [21] You have neither part nor portion in this matter, for your heart is not right in the sight of God. [22] Repent therefore of this your wickedness, and pray God if perhaps the thought of your heart may be forgiven you. [23] For I see that you are poisoned by bitterness and bound by iniquity."

[24] Then Simon answered and said, "Pray to the Lord for me, that none of the things which you have spoken may come upon me."

[25] So when they had testified and preached the word of the Lord, they returned to Jerusalem, preaching the gospel in many villages of the Samaritans.

—Acts 8:18–25

Simon is the patron of a spiritual malady called simony. The word "simony" traditionally means buying and selling offices within the church, and it denotes a common practice in the Middle Ages in which an office or bishopric could be purchased with money or influence. The origin of the word goes back to Simon the magician and sorcerer in the eighth chapter of Acts. The subtle implications of the sickness are still virulent, but not so much in the buying of offices in the church as in wanting the power of the Spirit for our own preconceived ideas and predetermined direction. My definition of simony is the desire to have the Life Christ promises without the surrender of all of life to Him who said, "I am the way, the truth, and the life" (John 14:6).

Luke exposes the basic problem that Simon of Samaria had, and he alerts us to the possibility of the same confusion today. In verse 9, he gives us the diagnosis of Simon's problem. He *"astonished the people of Samaria, claiming that he was someone great."* Note the difference in Simon's exclamation about Philip. *"This man is the great power of God"* (v. 10). We are tempted to say that Simon hoped for greatness and, when he saw it in Philip, he honestly recognized it and turned his followers over to Philip's teaching and leadership. Not so! Read the account further. When Peter and John laid hands on the people and they received the Holy Spirit, Simon wanted the power also to add to his bag of sorcerer's magic. Peter's reply implies that Simon offered the apostles money for the power of the Spirit: *"Your money perish with you, because you thought that the gift of God could be purchased with money!"* (v. 20). That's strong spiritual medicine for a false medicine man to take. Peter was testing his real motives. I've always imagined that there was a pause between that thrust and what Peter went on to say. I think he waited for repentance and the expression of wanting an authentic experience of the salvation which he had heard Philip preach so forcefully. When that was not forthcoming, Peter went on. *"You have neither part nor portion in this matter, for your heart is not right in the sight of God. Repent therefore of this your wickedness, and pray God if perhaps the thought of your heart may be forgiven you"* (vv. 21–22).

The implication for us and for the people around us is that, just as it is possible to have belief in Christ as Lord and Savior and not be filled with His Spirit, it is also possible to want His Spirit's power for our own self-controlled lives without repentance and total commitment to the Lord. Neither works.

Peter used a very potent word in confronting Simon with his spiritual imperiousness and desire to get and control the Spirit—"wickedness," *ponēría* in Greek, meaning compulsive determination to continue in a direction we know is wrong. It is sin which becomes so much the focus of the will that we no longer desire to change it and want God to approve it and bless us anyway. Another way of saying that is: we want the Lord on our own terms without surrender of our volitional determination to run our own lives. This is pointedly exemplified in Simon's response to Peter. He completely sidestepped the challenge to repent. He asked Peter to pray that none of the things with which he confronted him would happen, but he did not do the one thing which could prevent it—repent! Simon was still in charge of Simon, and he received neither the initial blessing Philip preached nor the fullness of the blessing Peter and John offered. He was left with the same old Simon and a city which no longer was impressed by his assertions of greatness. They had seen that and experienced it to the full. Who needed Simon or his magic after that? The account leaves us stunned. We can say no. But who wants to? We need all that Philip offered and that the apostles brought. We needn't try to have one without the other. Wholeness, fullness, is offered.

While we ponder that, Luke reminds us again that both conversion and the infilling of the Spirit is for ministry to others. The Lord gave Philip no time to sit about and luxuriate in what had happened in the Samaritan city or to condemn himself for not preaching the Holy Spirit as part of the plan of salvation. That's the way the Lord works. At the moment we want to sit back and think about how the

Lord is using us or to lacerate ourselves about our failures, He presses us on to another challenge that keeps our eyes on Him and His power, rather than on how well or poorly we've done in the previous assignment. He's got someone waiting whom He has prepared to be ready for what we have to say.

SOUTH AT HIGH NOON

[26] Now an angel of the Lord spoke to Philip, saying, "Arise and go toward the south along the road which goes down from Jerusalem to Gaza." This is desert. [27] So he arose and went.

—*Acts 8:26–27a*

Here is a dynamic gem of Scripture on guidance. Most people who ask, "How can I know God's will for my life?" are really asking, "How can I find guidance from the Lord for my daily choices and decisions?" Philip shows us how. It requires receptivity to the Spirit and obedience. Often the guidance we get does not fit with our practicality or prejudices. The key to understanding this passage is that the Greek words for *"south along the road which goes down from Jerusalem to Gaza"* also can mean "at high noon along the road." The Greek word *mesēmbría* can mean middle-day or south. Now Philip already knew that Gaza was south. He did not need that for guidance. And the instruction to go on the sun-baked Gaza road in the desert must have seemed strange.

The issue is obedience. We don't know what the Lord has planned in the circumstances into which he leads us. In this case with Philip, He had a meeting with an Ethiopian eunuch planned. The Lord knew that the officer was on his way home from Jerusalem to Ethiopia on that very road. Traveling at high noon on a desert road was no problem for the African. And the Lord wanted Philip at the right place and at the right time to meet him. The eternal life of a crucial person in the worldwide expansion of the movement was at stake.

The Lord often guides us to people and situations we wonder about at the time. Looking back, we can see that he used what was at the time a difficult order to follow but that blessings flowed from it. The Lord will use everything available to convince us of a direction—His indwelling Spirit, Scripture, consecrated thinking, our emotions when they are put at His disposal, the insights of people, and signs in the world around us. When we are willing, He will help us to want what He wants for us. He can steer us when we are on the move for Him. Guidance is difficult when we are stopped on dead center with our volitional gearshift set in reverse.

Philip *"arose and went"* (v. 27). There were no arguments or discussion of the hour of the day. Guidance comes from habitual prayer, Bible study, surrender to be used, and openness. Out of the flow, the next move in an ongoing obedience is baptized with a feeling of "rightness," not because it is logical but because closeness with the Lord has made it the thing we want to do. When an opportunity comes, we are ready. What happened to Philip because he obeyed has given us a rich treasure of how we can share our faith under the guidance of the Holy Spirit.

HOW TO SHARE OUR FAITH

[27]And behold, a man of Ethiopia, a eunuch of great authority under Candace the queen of the Ethiopians, who had charge of all her treasury, and had come to Jerusalem to worship, [28] was returning. And sitting in his chariot, he was reading Isaiah the prophet. [29] Then the Spirit said to Philip, "Go near and overtake this chariot."

[30] So Philip ran to him, and heard him reading the prophet Isaiah, and said, "Do you understand what you are reading?"

[31] And he said, "How can I, unless someone guides me?" And he asked Philip to come up and sit with him. [32] The place in the Scripture which he read was this:
"He was led as a sheep to the slaughter;
And as a lamb before its shearer is silent,
So He opened not His mouth.
[33] *In His humiliation His justice was taken away,*
And who will declare His generation?
For His life is taken from the earth."
[34] So the eunuch answered Philip and said, "I ask you, of whom does the prophet say this, of himself or of some other man?" [35] Then Philip opened his mouth, and beginning at this Scripture, preached Jesus to him. [36] Now as they went down the road, they came to some water. And the eunuch said, "See, here is water. What hinders me from being baptized?"

[37] Then Philip said, "If you believe with all your heart, you may."

And he answered and said, "I believe that Jesus Christ is the Son of God."

^{38} So he commanded the chariot to stand still. And both Philip and the eunuch went down into the water, and he baptized him. ^{39} Now when they came up out of the water, the Spirit of the Lord caught Philip away, so that the eunuch saw him no more; and he went on his way rejoicing. ^{40} But Philip was found at Azotus. And passing through, he preached in all the cities till he came to Caesarea.

—Acts 8:27b–40

The first discovery we make in the passage is that the Holy Spirit tailors the communicator's message to the particular needs of each person. The way Philip had preached to the Samaritans would not have worked with the Ethiopian. Luke tells us a great deal about this man's position, preparation, problems, and potential. We need to consider all these when we follow guidance to share our faith with a person. This man on the Gaza road was the secretary of the treasury of the Candace dynasty of Ethiopia. He was a eunuch who apparently had risen to great power as a leader in the queen's court. So much for his position.

The eunuch's preparation was that he obviously had come under the influence of monotheistic Judaism. Perhaps some of the Jews of the Dispersion had introduced him to the historic faith of the Hebrews. It would appear that he had become a proselyte because of his long journey from Ethiopia to Palestine to attend the services in the temple in Jerusalem and receive further instruction in the law. Luke tells us he had come to worship. The Greek word implies a pilgrimage. His problem was that all the services at the temple had not met his need. And the eunuch's potential was indicated by the fact that he kept reading Isaiah as he rode along. The Lord could use a man like that.

The second thing we learn about sharing our faith is the way the Holy Spirit guides us through ordinary warmth and concern for people. Philip's natural inclination was to care about the man. Think of all the "chance" encounters we have in which people will respond to genuine friendship. When Philip saw the eunuch's chariot, he was told to run alongside and engage the man in conversation. We can be sure that authentic interest in people is surely the Spirit's guidance. People don't need to hang an "I need Jesus!" sign around their necks; we can assume that.

What Philip said was an expression of interest in the man. People usually respond to the compliment of someone's wanting to know them and what they are doing. Find out what a person's interests are and you have hold of the protruding thread with which to unravel him or her and to know how to share Christ. Philip could see that what the Ethiopian was reading was a scroll of sacred Scripture. *"Do you understand what you are reading?"* (v. 30) was the sensitive question to ask. It implies, "Is that meaningful to you?" The response was immediate and filled with restlessness, discouragement, and frustration. *"How can I, unless someone guides me?"* The Greek word for "guide" is a technical word for authoritative teaching and interpretation. Apparently none of the scribes or Pharisees had taken time with the eunuch while he was in Jerusalem! The warm concern Philip had shown rewarded the deacon with an invitation to join the man in his chariot.

The third thing we discover about authentic evangelism is to start where people are in relationship to Christ and not where they should be. Philip takes the Ethiopian's lead. He didn't insist on first telling the man about what had just happened to him in Samaria or even about the Pentecost effluence, but met him at his level.

The eunuch was reading Isaiah 53:7–8—a great place to start to know about whom Isaiah was speaking. Who was this lamb led to the slaughter in the Isaiah passage?

The fourth key to communication is to allow the Holy Spirit to guide us in what to say and how to say it. When a person is open and ready, He will select from all we've learned in Scripture, verses memorized, and our personal experiences that which will aid the basic truth. Luke tells us that Philip opened his mouth. Why does he tell us that? The phrase implies that the Spirit guided his capacity of thought and articulation to help the Ethiopian. When we breathe the silent prayer, "Oh, Lord, use me; help me to say just the right thing at the right time and in the right way," He will.

We are confident that Philip had learned from the Samaritan experience and that he included the indwelling power of the Lord in his explanation of the steps of salvation. When they "happened" by some water, the eunuch asked to be baptized. We learn a most crucial key to sharing our faith from that. In the last stages of presenting Christ to an individual, it is absolutely essential to wait for the signs of the person's response and readiness. The most we should do is ask the gentle question, "How do you respond to what I've been saying?" A precipitous demand for a response in one-to-one evangelism can either turn a person off or result in his responding to our pressure and not to Christ. Often I'm led to say, "How would you like to have this love, joy, forgiveness, peace, and power we've been talking about?"

Philip never got to a question like that with the eunuch. He didn't have to. The eunuch asked. Philip now makes the crucial statement that brings forth the man's statement of faith which reflects so much about what Philip had been saying to him. As Luke tells us the man was baptized, suddenly we are struck with a question inside ourselves. "What if Philip had thought it foolish to go on the Gaza road at high noon? What about the people with whom we come in contact in less extraordinary circumstances?"

Philip is whisked off by the Spirit to the next assignment. The Lord had other work for him to do. And Ethiopia now had a Christian secretary of the treasury.

We'll meet Philip again. He continued his ministry as an evangelist, and Paul stopped at his home on his final trip to Jerusalem. But what turned Paul from being a persecutor of the church to becoming its most famous promoter is the exciting theme of the next phase of Luke's unfolding drama.

CHAPTER TEN—THE PERSECUTOR BECOMES A PROPAGATOR

ACTS 9:1–30

Scripture Outline

The Heavenly Vision (9:1–19)

Confirmation and Confrontation of the Vision (9:10–19)

News Too Good to Keep (9:20–25)

When We Need a Barnabas (9:26–30)

Paul is the most important human being who ever lived. He led the church into a worldwide movement, formulated its theology, and shaped its destiny. Without Paul, or someone like him, the infant church would not have grown into the spiritual and intellectual maturity which changed the course of history. And the only explanation of the dynamic of his leadership and the immensity of his gifts was that he was a man in Christ.

The first half of the Acts of the Holy Spirit is focused on the birth of the church. The second half is occupied by its expansion to the reaches of the then known world. The most crucial event of history, for which Jesus Christ lived, died, was resurrected, and glorified, was His infilling of a new humanity, the body of Christ. The second most strategic event was the conversion of Saul of Tarsus. And the profound secret of his watershed life was that Christ lived in him.

Life in Christ, Christ in Paul—that's the simple secret to climbing the heights of this Matterhorn of a man. His daring led the church to new frontiers, and his theology became the headwaters from which clear thinking has flowed. But to know Paul and not Paulism is to read carefully the account of his beloved friend to

161

whom he entrusted his biographical portrait. And Luke shows us the man—his hopes and visions, his victories and triumphs, his frustrations and failures. For Luke, Paul was an act of the Holy Spirit, the living, indwelling Christ. The Pharisee's conversion, character transformation, and intellectual remolding were distinctly the miracle of Spirit. Paul claimed nothing less or more. His life purpose and passion was, "For me to live is Christ" (Phil. 1:21).

THE HEAVENLY VISION

9:1 Then Saul, still breathing threats and murder against the disciples of the Lord, went to the high priest **2** and asked letters from him to the synagogues of Damascus, so that if he found any who were of the Way, whether men or women, he might bring them bound to Jerusalem.

3 As he journeyed he came near Damascus, and suddenly a light shone around him from heaven. **4** Then he fell to the ground, and heard a voice saying to him, "Saul, Saul, why are you persecuting Me?"

5 And he said, "Who are You, Lord?"

Then the Lord said, "I am Jesus, whom you are persecuting. It is hard for you to kick against the goads."

6 So he, trembling and astonished, said, "Lord, what do You want me to do?"

Then the Lord said to him, "Arise and go into the city, and you will be told what you must do."

7 And the men who journeyed with him stood speechless, hearing a voice but seeing no one. **8** Then Saul arose from the ground, and when his eyes were opened he saw no one. But they led him by the hand and brought him into Damascus. **9** And he was three days without sight, and neither ate nor drank.

—Acts 9:1–9

The mind of Saul of Tarsus was in turmoil as he traveled the six long days and nights from Jerusalem to Damascus. There was a growing uneasiness. Some of the exclamation points of his passionate determination to purge Israel of the followers of Jesus had turned into question marks. He had been shaken when his beloved and revered teacher Gamaliel was conciliatory to the disciples, warning the Sanhedrin not to be precipitous in their actions. Then he could not help admiring the resoluteness of these people. What was it about them? As a man of iron will, he had met his match in these seemingly undauntable people. How could belief in a dead Galilean carpenter produce that?

The Pharisee had known of Jesus during His ministry and knew well the circumstances surrounding His Crucifixion. As far as Saul was concerned, Jesus had been a political anarchist and a religious blasphemer. When he was appointed to head the effort to rid Jerusalem of His followers, he had taken the assignment with impassioned delight. The purpose matched his prejudices. But why had he gone overboard? Why was he so fanatical about this? Everything else in his life had been set aside for this one blinding rage he felt. His immense intellect ruminated over the strange mixture of thoughts and emotions that tumbled about inside of him. And then he remembered Stephen's face. That face! Why could he not get that face and his vision and prayer to Jesus off his mind?

Saul was both a Hebrew Pharisee and a man of the world. Born and raised by Hebrew parents in Hellenistic Tarsus, he had both Hebrew tradition and Greek culture flowing in his nature. At an early age, his parents' stature and resources, plus his own brilliance, had won him the sought-after privilege of studying under Gamaliel, the greatest Hebrew intellectual of the time. Saul had distinguished himself as a resourceful scholar and natural leader. He became a member of the strict sect of the Jewish religion called the Pharisees. They were committed to return the nation to impeccable obedience to the Law and the traditions. And yet, Saul had not lost his knowledge of and conditioning by the highly intellectual atmosphere of the Hellenistic world. Tarsus had one of the three greatest universities of the time, behind only Athens and Alexandria. Saul spoke fluent Greek, Hebrew, and Aramaic. He was exactly the kind of man Jesus needed to lead His movement. While Saul was tracking down His followers, the Lord was tracking him, waiting for the right moment. The Lord was setting the stage. The very one whose persecution had caused some of the Lord's people to flee to Damascus and start strong churches there would be central in the Lord's strategy for the future.

It was high noon when Saul and his men reached the outskirts of the city. The Pharisee was in deep thought when it happened. All of his persistent questions soon would be congealed into one great question that he would ask the rest of his life. Suddenly when Saul was nearing the edge of not being able to contain the turmoil inside him, a bolt of lightning flashed. He and the soldiers in his task force were thrown to the ground. Shaken and quivering with awe and wonder, Saul crouched, waiting for the thunder. It came not in a rumble in the sky, but in a powerful voice from heaven. Saul shuddered with the majesty and magnitude of the sound. *"Saul, Saul, why are you persecuting Me?"* (9:4). There was authority, judgment, grace, and urgency in that voice. *"Who are You, Lord?"* Saul replied with trembling voice. And then the answer came which the Pharisee would never forget. *"I am Jesus, whom you are persecuting. It is hard for you to kick against the goads."*

Goads? What were goads? The Greek word is *kéntron*, from the verb *kentéō*, which means to prick, to sting. What did the Lord mean? What was pricking and stinging Saul of Tarsus? Was it not the very misgivings and questions which had grown in his mind. This is the basis of the word picture I tried to paint about what was going on in Saul's mind. He was kicking against the promptings of the Spirit that were invading the thoughts of his mind. Preparation for any conversion begins with the Lord. But never more so than with this one perfectly suited to bridge the movement of His grace into both the Hebrew and Greek worlds.

The Lord was right—Saul had had unsettling thoughts, questions and misgivings which he had kicked against. All these coalesced into the one question he asked—a question indicating that it now had hit him with hurricane force that this was indeed none other than Jesus whom he had been persecuting. The followers of the Way were right after all. Jesus was alive! Only that would have caused the reaction in Saul. He was not easily intimidated. But *"trembling and astonished,"* he said, *"Lord, what do You want me to do?"* He would never stop asking that question all of his life. It became the secret of his guided life later on. It is our ultimate and obedient question in every situation.

The Lord could have effected Saul's complete conversion at that moment. But He had that planned in a way that would release Saul from an old life and the church from its fear of him.

When Saul arose from the ground, he was blind. He staggered about helplessly. What a pitiful picture—the arrogant, resolute, vigorous Saul of Tarsus being led into the city which he had planned to purge of the followers of the very One who had appeared and spoken to him. Near the end of his life he spoke of that encounter as a heavenly vision, so the blindness must have followed the hearing of the voice and seeing of the vision. The Lord had a plan. The scales over Saul's eyes would permit him to focus on nothing or no one for three days except the Lord who had appeared to him. Verse 9 reveals the dramatic scene of a capturer captured for a great purpose which he would soon discover: *"And he was three days without sight, and neither ate nor drank."*

We pause for a moment to reflect on what that dramatic encounter really means to us and the people to whom we communicate.

1. Life really begins with a divine encounter with Jesus Christ. We are either being prepared for that or we are living in the assurance of it.

2. The Lord prepares us for that encounter with the "goads" of questions which won't go away and a deep dis-ease which only He can resolve.

3. He is gracious to love us to the end of our own resources so that we can listen to what He has to say to us.

4. He has a plan for every life which we discover only after we have met Him. A guided life is a life in fellowship with Him.

5. He will use another person to confirm our encounter so that we can know both the joy of fellowship with Him and other believers. Conversion never happens in a vacuum of independence. It leads to a declaration of interdependence.

CONFIRMATION AND CONFORMATION OF THE VISION

[10] Now there was a certain disciple at Damascus named Ananias; and to him the Lord said in a vision, "Ananias."

And he said, "Here I am, Lord."

[11] So the Lord said to him, "Arise and go to the street called Straight, and inquire at the house of Judas for one called Saul of Tarsus, for behold, he is praying. [12] And in a vision he has seen a man named Ananias coming in and putting his hand on him, so that he might receive his sight."

[13] Then Ananias answered, "Lord, I have heard from many about this man, how much harm he has done to Your saints in Jerusalem. [14] And here he has authority from the chief priests to bind all who call on Your name."

[15] But the Lord said to him, "Go, for he is a chosen vessel of Mine to bear My name before Gentiles, kings, and the children of Israel. [16] For I will show him how many things he must suffer for My name's sake."

[17] And Ananias went his way and entered the house; and laying his hands on him he said, "Brother Saul, the Lord Jesus,

who appeared to you on the road as you came, has sent me that you may receive your sight and be filled with the Holy Spirit." [18] Immediately there fell from his eyes something like scales, and he received his sight at once; and he arose and was baptized.

[19] So when he had received food, he was strengthened. Then Saul spent some days with the disciples at Damascus.

—*Acts 9:10–19*

The only thing that came near matching the panic Saul felt on the road was the fear Ananias felt when the Lord appeared to the leader of the Damascus church and told him to go to the persecutor of the followers of the Way. Saul of Tarsus? Ananias probably knew that he was top on Saul's list for arrest and perhaps worse. He not only knew Saul, but knew the reason he had been on his way to Damascus. News like that travels ahead of a gestapo officer. Saul had had to get an order to purge the followers of Jesus at Damascus. According to Lake and Cadbury, the right of extradition of Jewish criminals had been given to the High Priest by Rome.[1] The historian Josephus makes reference to that kind of authority being given to Hyrcanus years before by Julius Caesar.[2] This means that Paul had to get permission for extradition of the Christians who had escaped his grasp in Jerusalem. The terrible news had leaked to the Christians and had preceded Saul's arrival. Ananias reminds the Lord about this and wonders about the safety of going to the feared persecutor. Putting ourselves inside his skin, we can imagine the fear which surged in him. Surely he feared a trick with a plot in it by clever Saul.

But the Lord had plans for Ananias and Saul. Ananias was to be a reconciler and bring an awesome message to his feared enemy. *"Go"* the Lord told Ananias, *"for he is a chosen vessel of Mine to bear My name before Gentiles, kings, and the children of Israel. For I will show him how many things he must suffer for My name's sake"* (v. 15).

How very gracious of the Lord to share His strategy for Saul in order to allay the fears in Ananias. Note that He did not tell Ananias to tell Saul all that He had planned. That would have been too much too soon for blinded Saul. The Lord seldom gives us our life plan all at once. He gives us just enough to help us set our long-range goals in Him and then walk in obedience each day.

One of the most moving scenes in all of Scripture is what happened when Ananias went to Saul. He found the feared persecutor alone, blind, and helpless. All the hurt and fright Ananias had felt for what this man had done to his brothers and sisters in Christ drained away. The same Lord who told him to go to Saul lived in him and had given him His own character traits of love and forgiveness. It was with the Lord's deep compassion and acceptance that Ananias could say, *"Brother Saul."* Brother? Yes, Ananias had taken the Lord's command seriously. How we need people to enact His love in a daring way by calling us by a name we have not yet earned or accepted for ourselves! Who needs that from you and me? From whom do we most need to receive that kind of reconciling assurance?

But Ananias's words were coupled with physical warmth. Imagine laying your hands on someone who you know had been on his way to arrest you! The Lord's messenger was faithful first to his reconciling assignment and then told Saul that he had been sent to him so that he might receive his sight and be filled with the Holy Spirit. As the Spirit of the Lord filled Saul with Himself, the scales fell off his eyes.

It was after the infilling that Saul was baptized. This indicates that baptism was an outer sign of the infilling, not the time of the infilling. That is in keeping with the early church's practice of baptism being a witness to the community of believers of the deep and inner bond of the Spirit's infilling.

Luke is the master of stating momentous truths as an aside. I keep wanting to insert exclamation points. Who can read this statement in verse 19 without a surge of amazement? *"Then Saul spent some days with the disciples who were at Damascus"(!).* The Lord was doing as much in the Damascus disciples as in Saul. Here is the church alive, indeed—a liberated Pharisee freed from hatred and disciples liberated from prejudice and fear.

NEWS TOO GOOD TO KEEP

[20] Immediately he preached the Christ in the synagogues, that He is the Son of God.

[21] Then all who heard were amazed, and said, "Is this not he who destroyed those who called on this name in Jerusalem, and has come here for that purpose, so that he might bring them bound to the chief priests?"

[22] But Saul increased all the more in strength, and confounded the Jews who dwelt in Damascus, proving that this Jesus is the Christ.

23 Now after many days were past, the Jews plotted to kill him. 24 But their plot became known to Saul. And they watched the gates day and night, to kill him. 25 Then the disciples took him by night and let him down through the wall in a large basket.

—Acts 9:20–25

Catch the intensity of the word *immediately*. Saul could not wait to go to the synagogues in Damascus to share the good news he had just received. It was too good to keep to himself. He came right to the point. Jesus is the Son of God. The King James has it "he preached the Christ . . . that He is the Son of God." The Greek text is that "he preached Jesus . . . that He is the Son of God." The New King James Version acknowledges that with the footnote. Actually it is stronger wording to say that Saul preached Jesus and identified Him as the one who is the Son of God. It is significant to note that this was the only time Saul/Paul used this particular messianic designation for Jesus Christ. This makes it all the more powerful here when spoken by a converted Pharisee known both for his brilliance and for his previous opposition to Jesus and His followers. The term "Son of God" was used for the Messiah as the true representative of God's people and as the anointed king of the kingdom of God. Saul could not have been more accurate, or bold. All his training in the sacred Scriptures leapt into use. "Listen! You've heard of Jesus. I know with assurance He is the Son of God."

The Jews in the synagogues were dumbfounded. *"Is this not he who destroyed those who called on this name in Jerusalem, and has come here for that purpose, so he might bring them bound to the chief priests?"* (v. 21). None other than Saul of Tarsus was saying Jesus was the Son of God. The persecutor was now a proponent!

Saul's immediate witness solidified his vision and strengthened his conviction. There could be no more effective place for him to establish his newfound faith than in the synagogues. He took his stand among his people. There was no turning back now.

When people receive Christ as Lord and Savior and are filled with His Spirit, it is crucial for them to tell the significant others in their lives. A public declaration accomplishes something for the one who shares his or her experience and those who hear. There is nothing so exciting and winsome as the witness of a new person in Christ. Some of the most exciting times for our church elders in Hollywood are when we meet each month with those who have been given the gift of faith to believe in Christ and have been filled with His Spirit. As one officer says often, "It's like starting all over for me each month when I hear these new Christians witness. That's what we're here for as a church!"

A great gift to the church is the excitement and enthusiasm of the newly born and filled. It is witnessing that quickens faith in others and often leads to their conversion when it is done in public worship. "Let the redeemed of the Lord say so" (Ps. 107:2)! Verse 22 focuses the Lord's power alive in Saul. Don't miss the fact that Saul's one message was "Jesus is the Christ." He never veered from that all through the rest of his ministry. Even when he dealt with profound theological issues in his epistles, he always came back to basics. And right from the beginning Saul used all of the brilliance of his intellect, all the training of his background, and all the determination of his will to serve the One who, out of limitless love, called him and filled him with His Spirit.

But Saul knew something else right from the beginning—the hostility of his own people. Eventually that would send him on his appointed task of reaching out to the Gentiles. The angry resistance he felt from the Jews right from the beginning was a foretaste of what he would know all his life. The escape in a basket over the wall in Damascus was only the first of many close scrapes with death. The Lord's prophetic statement to Ananias about the suffering Saul would endure had begun.

That too will happen to people whom we help become Christians. For some the joy of commitment to live for Christ is immediately mingled with the pain of rejection from family or friends. The impact of Acts 9:23–25 is in seeing how the followers of the Way endangered their lives to protect "Brother Saul." A part of our evangelism must be to follow through and stand with people as they take those first steps of growth and, often, encounter opposition. In our church we have a "Guardian Angel" program. Each new Christian is assigned a more mature member to see that he or she "makes it" through this crucial time. These Guardian Angels are what Barnabas was to Paul in the next section of this passage. The Son of Encouragement was back at work doing what awarded him the name.

WHEN WE NEED A BARNABAS

26 And when Saul had come to Jerusalem, he tried to join the disciples; but they were all afraid of him, and did not believe that he was a disciple. 27 But Barnabas took him and brought him to the apostles. And he declared to them how he

169

had seen the Lord on the road, and that He had spoken to him, and how he had preached boldly at Damascus in the name of Jesus. 28 So he was with them at Jerusalem, coming in and going out. 29 And he spoke boldly in the name of the Lord Jesus and disputed against the Hellenists, but they attempted to kill him. 30 When the brethren found out, they brought him down to Caesarea and sent him out to Tarsus.

—Acts 9:26–30

We need to check our chronology for the full impact of this portion of Chapter 9 of Acts. In checking Paul's personal account of what happened to him after his conversion, the meaning is enriched. Note Galatians 1:15–17: "But when it pleased God, who separated me from my mother's womb and called me through His grace, to reveal His Son in me that I might preach Him among the Gentiles, I did not immediately confer with flesh and blood, nor did I go up to Jerusalem to those who were apostles before me; but I went to Arabia, and returned again to Damascus." That means that after Saul left Damascus he went to the desert near the foot of Mount Sinai. We can identify with what happened there at that metaphor mountain of Israel's history. A new man in Christ meditated on the Law of Moses and reflected on what had happened to him on the Damascus Road. He was there for a long time before he made his first attempt to meet the apostles in Jerusalem.

The church in Jerusalem was not as flexible as the one in Damascus. The disciples there found it difficult to believe that Saul was one of them. We can empathize only if we try to recapture the feeling of fear the man Saul had generated in Jerusalem. It was there that he imprisoned followers of the Way and engineered Stephen's death. No wonder they were cautious!

But not Barnabas. His Holy Spirit gift was encouragement, as we have seen, and he put his own relationship with the apostles on the line. The Greek words translated *"but Barnabas took him and brought him to the apostles"* actually imply that he took Saul by the hand and led him in before the apostles to affirm his belief in his conversion and new life in Christ. How did Barnabas know that? Why was he so sure? I think it is because he sought Saul out when he heard that he was in Jerusalem. He had to know firsthand. And when he did, he had to be the reconciler—interceding, enabling, understanding. He was a peacemaker in the most creative way.

The few words, "but Barnabas took him by the hand," would make a great text for a separate sermon or class on this portion of

Acts. It focuses the calling we all have to be reconcilers. Where do we need to be a Barnabas? Where is there hostility and misunderstanding where we need to step in as an enabler of peace? It may mean going with a listening ear to both parties or to the group to allow them to talk out the difficulty. Going on from there, it means getting the people together for forgiveness and healing. It is the ministry of every Christian to be a Barnabas. Growing in Christ and being a peacemaker are inseparable. It means giving up the questionable luxuries of gossip and taking sides. But who needs these luxuries anyhow?

In the closing of this section we see Paul affirmed by the apostles and actively preaching in the city he knew so well. And the Hellenists were his main target. He was one of them. But the conflict became too great for Saul to remain in Jerusalem. He was sent off to his home city of Tarsus, where, if my calculation of the Galatian chronology is correct, he remained for ten years.

We are startled by that. Why so long? The Lord had work to do in the Pharisee. Saul needed to hammer out the implications of his experience for all of life. His theology needed to be refined and spelled out for all dimensions of thought. When he reappeared on the scene, he was ready. And out of the resources of those years, later he preached, wrote epistles, founded churches, trained leaders, and assured the future development of Christianity.

There are times in our lives when we are impatient to get on with what we believe God has called us to do. It is painful to wait. But the Lord knows what He is doing. Saul would have been less the man in Christ if he had not had that time of profound depth with the Lord. That's the salient point. Christ was life for Saul—in Tarsus, Philippi, Jerusalem, or Rome!

NOTES

1. Lake, Kirsopp, and Cadbury, Henry J., eds., *The Beginnings of Christianity,* vol. 4 (London: Macmillan and Company, 1933), p. 99.

2. Josephus, *Antiquities* XIV, 10, 2.

CHAPTER ELEVEN—THE EPICENTER IN THE ROCK

ACTS 9:31—11:30

Scripture Outline

Conditioned with Effectiveness (9:31–43)

An Uncommon Vision (10:1–16)

Beyond Wonder and Thought (10:17–23)

Pentecost in Caesarea (10:24–43)

The Gift of Tongues (10:44–48)

The Effects from the Epicenter (11:1–18)

They Were Called Christians (11:19–30)

While the Lord had Saul of Tarsus on the potter's wheel remolding his nature into a new man in Him, He was also at work in the other towering figure of the early church, Simon Bar-Jonah. What He did in Simon was to prepare the way for Saul's world-wide ministry.

The Lord had given Simon a new name years before. He was called *Kēphā* in Aramaic and *Pétros* in Greek. The name means rock. Jesus had said, "On this rock I will build My church" (Matt. 16:18). He did not mean just Simon the man alone, but his faith. That faith would be an example of the foundation of the church. Acts 9:32—11:30 records an earthquake whose force cut through both Peter the Rock and his faith from the epicenter. It split him open and moved the earth of his presuppositions. Consequently, it shifted the emphasis of the future of the church's mission. The church's seismographic calculations of the quake in Peter led to a new inclusiveness that moved Christianity beyond the confines of Judaism.

This passage introduces us to a distinctly different quality of guidance initiated by the acts of the Holy Spirit in the young church. I like to call it retrospective renaissance. The church determined what the Spirit wanted in renewal and reformation of old practices and customs in the future on the basis of what they observed Him doing in the present. The Lord was way out in front of His people, beckoning them on in the movement of His Spirit. They constantly were trying to catch up to know what He wanted in the light of careful observation of what He did. Old molds were shattered, walls of separation between people were razed, and the church was led beyond the exclusivity of its religion to an inclusive exclusivity—an inclusion of all races and national backgrounds and an exclusion of prejudice and judgmentalism. It didn't happen all at once, or without resistance and division, as we shall see. But the Lord had not come in the incarnation nor returned in the power of the Spirit to establish a new religion, or even just to renew Israel, but to save the world. The fear of breaking with the past was equaled only by the danger of starting a new religion. Christianity was and is a movement made up of Christ-centered, filled, transformed, and transforming people.

And to show the way, the Lord had to begin with Peter the Rock. The spiritual earthquake happened in him and then through him. He was at the epicenter of the force that created the chasm dividing the past from the future. While Saul prayed, Peter was used to open the way for a ministry to the world.

CONDITIONED WITH EFFECTIVENESS

31 Then the churches throughout all Judea, Galilee, and Samaria had peace and were edified. And walking in the fear of the Lord and in the comfort of the Holy Spirit, they were multiplied.

32 Now it came to pass, as Peter went through all parts of the country, that he also came down to the saints who dwelt in Lydda. 33 There he found a certain man named Aeneas, who had been bedridden eight years and was paralyzed. 34 And Peter said to him, "Aeneas, Jesus the Christ heals you. Arise and make your bed." Then he arose immediately. 35 So all who dwelt at Lydda and Sharon saw him and turned to the Lord.

36 At Joppa there was a certain disciple named Tabitha, which is translated Dorcas. This woman was full of good works and charitable deeds which she did. 37 But it happened in those days that she became sick and died. When they had

washed her, they laid her in an upper room. [38] And since Lydda was near Joppa, and the disciples had heard that Peter was there, they sent two men to him, imploring him not to delay in coming to them. [39] Then Peter arose and went with them. When he had come, they brought him to the upper room. And all the widows stood by him weeping, showing the tunics and garments which Dorcas had made while she was with them. [40] But Peter put them all out, and knelt down and prayed. And turning to the body he said, "Tabitha, arise." And she opened her eyes, and when she saw Peter she sat up. [41] Then he gave her his hand and lifted her up; and when he had called the saints and widows, he presented her alive. [42] And it became known throughout all Joppa, and many believed on the Lord. [43] So it was that he stayed many days in Joppa with Simon, a tanner.

—Acts 9:31–43

In this passage, I think that Luke was doing more than shifting his story line from Saul to Peter for a time. He was certainly doing that, but in addition he was showing us a principle about how the Holy Spirit works. The church was being conditioned by immense success in preparation for a new direction. The Spirit does that. There are times when failure is followed by new effectiveness for the Lord, but also He opens us to a new step of guidance through an authentic self-esteem that comes from knowing we are being used by Him in His kingdom purposes with people. This effectiveness then opens us up to new possibilities. There are times when, out of ineffectiveness, we cry out, "Lord, nothing is working; what do You want me to do?" And there are also times when we exclaim, "The Lord is on the move in our midst! What's next on His agenda?" The latter was true of the church in this brief passage. It led to the next step in the Lord's strategy.

In verse 31, we are told the ingredients of that blessed period. The church had followed the Lord's pre-Pentecost prophetic promise. They were His witnesses in Judea, Galilee, and Samaria. That faithfulness was rewarded with peace and with their continued growth as new creatures in Christ. The word used here for "edify" is from *oikodoméō,* meaning, literally, to build a house. The followers of Christ were being built into His likeness as people in whom He could dwell. The word implies teaching and instruction as the crucial elements of this building process. They were also being built together into a temple not built with hands.

The Lord was about to add some construction materials they would not have included in the building. The time of peace was preparation for that.

Note that their relationship with the Lord was marked by two things—fear and comfort. The words seem antithetical. But the meaning of fear here is awe and humble receptivity. And comfort, as we have seen, was rooted in the *parákletos,* the Spirit who stood by their side. The *paráklesis,* comfort, which the church was enjoying was because of the Lord's presence with them, in them, and between them. The verse is an excellent description of what the church is meant to be. The words "peace," "edification," "fear," and "comfort" would make a powerful flow of thought for a message on an effective church in preparation for a new level of adventure for, and with, the Lord.

The two accounts of Peter's gift of healing emphasize this special period of preparation. His gift of healing with individuals would soon be turned also to a sickness in the church's thinking and perception of its membership and future expansion. That would put him to the test. The Lord affirmed the gift he had in preparation for an even greater healing in which he would be pivotal. For that Peter would need a vision that would change his thinking about what he and the other Hebrew followers of Christ would have called "common."

AN UNCOMMON VISION

10:1 There was a certain man in Caesarea called Cornelius, a centurion of what was called the Italian Regiment, **2** a devout man and one who feared God with all his household, who gave alms generously to the people, and prayed to God always.
3 About the ninth hour of the day he saw clearly in a vision an angel of God coming in and saying to him, "Cornelius!"
4 And when he observed him, he was afraid, and said, "What is it, lord?"
So he said to him, "Your prayers and your alms have come up for a memorial before God. **5** Now send men to Joppa, and send for Simon whose surname is Peter. **6** He is lodging with Simon, a tanner, whose house is by the sea. He will tell you what you must do." **7** And when the angel who spoke to him had departed, Cornelius called two of his household servants and a devout soldier from among those who waited on him continually. **8** So when he had explained all these things to them, he sent them to Joppa.

⁹ The next day, as they went on their journey and drew near the city, Peter went up on the housetop to pray, about the sixth hour. ¹⁰ Then he became very hungry and wanted to eat; but while they made ready, he fell into a trance ¹¹ and saw heaven opened and an object like a great sheet bound at the four corners, descending to him and let down to the earth. ¹² In it were all kinds of four-footed animals of the earth, wild beasts, creeping things, and birds of the air. ¹³ And a voice came to him, "Rise, Peter; kill and eat."

¹⁴ But Peter said, "Not so, Lord! For I have never eaten anything common or unclean."

¹⁵ And a voice spoke to him again the second time, "What God has cleansed you must not call common." ¹⁶ This was done three times. And the object was taken up into heaven again.

—Acts 10:1–16

There are few passages that reveal the surprises of the Lord's guidance more than the two visions, one given to Cornelius and the other to Peter. They were part of one central vision the Lord had for His church. For us today the passage shows us that the Lord has a next step for each of us. He wants to give us more than we can imagine. He created a willingness in both Cornelius and Peter to want something more than they had experienced previously. I know that hunger. Don't you? The Lord defines the next step and then uses His sovereign power to arrange for the fulfillment of what He has prompted us to desire.

Cornelius is a classic example of this. As a whole, the tenth chapter tells us a great deal about this man. If all we had were verses 1 and 2, we would have enough to admire. Cornelius was a centurion, a Roman soldier in charge of one hundred men. He was a part of what was called the Italian cohort, a regiment of soldiers made up only of those who had distinguished themselves for gallantry and valor. The fact that he and his family were together in Caesarea means that he was either highly respected or was being rewarded for a special service to Caesar, or that he was retired. That he still had men at his command indicates the former. He was deeply respected by the Jews and had become a "God-fearer," a proselyte to Hebrew monotheism. His spiritual hunger was expressed by the regular disciplines of prayer and alms-giving. A remarkable man, he was one singled out by the Lord to be a personification of a truth He was going to teach Peter, and subsequently, the church. It was so crucial that He left nothing undone in His preparations.

There are times the Lord allows us to stumble onto what He's prepared. Other times He details His guidance in undeniably clear ways. In this case, He gave Cornelius a longing for Him and instructions to call for Peter; and to Peter gave a vision which became clear to the apostle through Cornelius's call. The Lord knew how to deal with a soldier who would respond to orders and a spiritually sensitive saint for whom a vision would delicately birth an idea in the tissues of his creative Hebrew brain.

Peter was a strong-willed man. The Lord had told him that He would build His church on the rock of the apostle's faith in Him. Now that faith had to be expanded to new vistas. That would not happen easily. Peter had to be made willing with a sure knowledge of what the Lord was doing as an undeniable sign of what He wanted His church to be and do. As Saint Bernard prayed years later, "Draw me, however unwilling, to make me willing; draw me, slow-footed, to make me run."

Simon had been drawn by the Spirit's guidance from one human need to another until he ended up in a village on the Mediterranean Coast called Joppa. There is evidence of the softening of his exclusive Hebraism in that he stayed at the home of Simon, a new believer who was a tanner. An orthodox Jew was not permitted to have any dealings with anyone who worked with dead animals. That's the reason that tanners had to live fifty cubits outside a village. This ritual uncleanness is clearly delineated in Numbers. But this tanner outside Joppa was different for Peter. The man was a believer in Christ, and Peter found in him a friend, in spite of the regulations. Peter was in process—on the way to freedom.

One day while he was at the tanner's house, Peter went up on the rooftop to pray. The question of the Gentiles was on his mind, sharpened by the obviously genuine faith of his host. Was the gospel exclusively for the Jews? Did a Gentile convert have to become a proselyte of Judaism prior to becoming a follower of the Lord?

While Peter prayed, he also waited for the noon meal to be prepared. Why else does Luke tell us the time of day? The vision the Lord gave him matched both the need of his mind and of his stomach. A vivid picture of a giant sheet with four corners was being let down on the earth. It was a mysterious vision indeed. The sheet contained all kinds of animals, reptiles, and birds, some of which Peter, as a strict and orthodox Hebrew, was not permitted to consume based on the food regulations of Leviticus 11 and Deuteronomy 14.

The sight of those forbidden foods was not nearly as startling as the Lord's command: *"Rise, Peter; kill and* eat" (Acts 10:13). Peter's strong will implemented his strong revulsion to things that years of conditioning had taught him were unclean. *"Not so, Lord! For I have never eaten anything common or unclean."* Quite a corrective to level on the Lord of creation! But it was a reaction of the moment, not a settled willfulness. The Lord spoke again; "What God has cleansed you must not call common." And to be sure he heard, the message was repeated two more times. The Lord wanted no confusion about that message. It was to be the basis of a renaissance that would shape the future of His movement.

The Lord was not contradicting Leviticus and Deuteronomy, or giving Peter a new diet, but getting through to him about the people he should love and reach with the gospel. The vision was parabolic, and like the Lord's parables during the incarnation, it had a simple and salient point. The church was not to call non-Hebrews common and make the body of Christ exclusively Hebrew. That took more than a parabolic vision to register on Peter's thinking. The Lord usually follows a concept with an experience in which our thinking and behavior can be altered by enacting the truth. And while Peter was having the vision, the Lord was also arranging for the situation in which the apostle would see more than a vision. He would see a Gentile centurion and his family uncommonly blessed.

A personal recapitulation of the meaning of this portion of the story is helpful. The Lord usually works in three ways in expanding our understanding of His will for us: first He creates a willingness; next He gives us a thought-reorienting truth out of the Scripture; and this is followed by a sign in our relationships or daily responsibilities. Something happens that gives us a confirmation of the truth. When all these line up, we can be sure we are on the way to a new discovery. Peter had had a growing uneasiness with exclusivism. The vision deepened that. The clinching confirmation was about to occur. This account thus far tells us four magnificent things about the Lord as the Holy Spirit: He is omnipresent, omnipotent, and omniscient. But He is also something else, which is the theme of this whole chapter. He is all-loving with a love that includes all people. It is His delight to surprise us with whom He chooses to love, call, and fill with His Spirit. Even a non-Hebrew centurion!

BEYOND WONDER AND THOUGHT

¹⁷ Now while Peter wondered within himself what this vision which he had seen meant, behold, the men who had been sent from Cornelius had made inquiry for Simon's house, and stood before the gate. ¹⁸ And they called and asked whether Simon, whose surname was Peter, was lodging there.

¹⁹ While Peter thought about the vision, the Spirit said to him, "Behold, three men are seeking you. ²⁰ Arise therefore, go down and go with them, doubting nothing; for I have sent them."

²¹ Then Peter went down to the men who had been sent to him from Cornelius, and said, "Yes, I am he whom you seek. For what reason have you come?"

²² And they said, "Cornelius the centurion, a just man, one who fears God and has a good reputation among all the nation of the Jews, was divinely instructed by a holy angel to summon you to his house, and to hear words from you."
²³ Then he invited them in and lodged them.

On the next day Peter went away with them, and some brethren from Joppa accompanied him.

—Acts 10:17–23

Peter *"wondered"* about the vision. The Greek word is *diēpórei,* the imperfect of *diaporéō,* meaning "perplexed." He was completely at a loss to know what he should do about the astounding truth the vision had revealed. Then we are told that he *"thought"* about the vision. Here the Greek word, *dienthu-mouménou,* is a double compound, meaning that he revolved the truths in his mind, over and over again, through and through, in and out, in an effort to understand the meaning of the strange revelation. As he wondered and thought, his main concern was what he should do about what he had experienced.

The Lord was taking no chances. He did not want a long reflective period with no action. He wanted Peter to get moving on the revelation of His inclusive love. While Peter wondered and thought, the Lord already had arranged the action step to be taken. The Lord's prevenience had precipitated the need for obedience. At the very time Peter was receiving the vision, emissaries from Cornelius were on the way. And while he was contemplating what the vision meant, the men were at the gate. And so that Peter would waste no time ruminating over who they were, the Spirit told him that he should get off the rooftop of contemplation and go with them, *"doubting nothing."* The apostle had all he needed: the inspiration of the vision, the interpretation of the vision, and an opportunity for the implementation of the vision.

This passage gives us a splendid vehicle to communicate the strategy of revelation. The Lord couples insight and instigation. He shows us truth and gives us an opportunity to act on what we've learned. We need to share with people the implication of this for daily living. Following personal Bible study, a class, or sermon, the Lord usually provides the situation or circumstances of living the discovery the exposition has made clear. Action is an essential stage of learning. We know what we've acted. The times between study periods in the Word will be filled with the Lord's perfectly timed, prearranged opportunities to act on what we've learned.

When this alternating balance between hearing and doing becomes real to us as communicators, we will be able to share it with our listeners. In my own life, the Lord usually gives me a chance to experience the truth I want to present prior to the teaching or preaching of it. That allows me to do so much more than tell people what the Scripture says. It provides the personal illustrations which make the exposition live with intensity. We only know what we've lived. And people can appropriate only so much truth as they are shown how to implement.

When I finish the outline of my sermons for a year ahead, I know what will be my autobiography for that year. The Lord will put me through the experiences which will incarnate the basic themes in real living. That gives me the authority to teach and preach authentically. It also provides me with an action-step challenge for my message. The task is not to ask people what they are going to do about what has been taught, but to help them await expectantly the opportunities the Lord will arrange. The Lord seldom gives vision without the challenge to live that vision. And because He knows our temptation to ponder and think too long, He presses us with an undeniable opportunity. It may come in a person who needs what we've learned, a problem that can be solved with the insight we've discovered, or with a next step in His strategy for us that must be taken because of the liberating truth that has dawned upon us.

This gives us an awesome sense of how the Lord continues His creative, redemptive work. Because He knows the future, He is arranging the timing of both our insight and the circumstances in which we will grow by acting on it.

The conclusion of a message should be to heighten for our listeners an anticipation and awareness of the Lord's "coincidences." Often, I end a time of teaching or preaching with something like this: "We've been given a momentous, mind-reorienting truth in the passage we have considered today. That truth will become part of the fiber of our character as we live it. The Lord who made it real to us will provide perfectly timed opportunities. Expect them. Welcome them as gifts. Look for them with expectancy. When they happen, know that the Lord has prepared you for what He has prepared for your ministry."

In smaller, more informal groups where we are teaching or leading discussion of the Bible, it is helpful to enable people to share what has happened to them between sessions. Most of us need time to process truth. Often, a question like this helps: "During the past week, what opportunities has the Lord provided to live what we talked about in our exposition last week?" The sharing of the responses with the group will encourage others, and often, it will alert them to opportunities they may have missed.

In the context of worship, witnessing can help bring reality to the truth that has been preached. When a member shares the implementation of some inspiration from the pulpit, it challenges others to think about how they are living what they are receiving week after week. A few months ago, a member of my church gave a brief witness about what had happened to him in response to a message I had preached on "The Five Steps to Financial Freedom." The witness had greater impact than the sermon! The proclamation of the Word is not limited to the pulpit.

This passage from Acts prompts us to wonder who, or what, is waiting at the gate while we wonder and think, putting off doing something about the truth the Lord has given us.

Peter responded with action. He received the Gentile visitors and invited them to stay overnight in Simon's home. The earthquake had begun. The Rock was splitting wide open at the epicenter! We are told that he *"lodged"* with Cornelius's men. The Greek active voice is used rather than the passive voice of Acts 10:6. Peter was performing the action rather than being the recipient of it. He was the initiator, instigator, of the invitation and hospitality.

This helps us to understand that in response to a vision of truth there are little acts of obedience which open the way to more crucial opportunities. The Lord gave Peter a chance to try on his newfound wisdom in his attitude to the Gentile messengers. If Peter had resorted to attitudes of Hebrew exclusivism toward the messengers, he might not have had the opportunity to meet the centurion who had sent them, or to cooperate with the Lord who was staging the whole breakthrough of Christianity to the Gentile world!

PENTECOST IN CAESAREA

[24] And the following day they entered Caesarea. Now Cornelius was waiting for them, and had called together his relatives and close friends. [25] As Peter was coming in, Cornelius met him and fell down at his feet and worshiped him. [26] But Peter lifted him up, saying, "Stand up; I myself am also a man." [27] And as he talked with him, he went in and found many who had come together.

[28] Then he said to them, "You know how unlawful it is for a Jewish man to keep company with or go to one of another nation. But God has shown me that I should not call any man common or unclean. [29] Therefore I came without objection as soon as I was sent for. I ask, then, for what reason have you sent for me?"

[30] So Cornelius said, "Four days ago I was fasting until this hour; and at the ninth hour I prayed in my house, and behold, a man stood before me in bright clothing, [31] and said, 'Cornelius, your prayer has been heard, and your alms are remembered in the sight of God. [32] Send therefore to Joppa and call Simon here, whose surname is Peter. He is lodging in the house of Simon, a tanner, by the sea. When he comes, he will speak to you.' [33] So I sent to you immediately, and you have done well to come. Now therefore, we are all present before God, to hear all the things commanded you by God."

[34] Then Peter opened his mouth and said: "In truth I perceive that God shows no partiality. [35] But in every nation whoever fears Him and works righteousness is accepted by Him. [36] The word which God sent to the children of Israel, preaching peace through Jesus Christ—He is Lord of all— [37] that word you know, which was proclaimed throughout all Judea, and began from Galilee after the baptism which John preached: [38] how God anointed Jesus of Nazareth with the Holy Spirit and with power, who went about doing good and healing all who were oppressed by the devil, for God was with Him. [39] And we are witnesses of all things which He did both in the land of the Jews and in Jerusalem, whom they killed by hanging on a tree. [40] Him God raised up on the third day, and

showed Him openly, [41] not to all the people, but to witnesses chosen before by God, even to us who ate and drank with Him after He arose from the dead. [42] And He commanded us to preach to the people, and to testify that it is He who was ordained by God to be Judge of the living and the dead. [43] To Him all the prophets witness that, through His name, whoever believes in Him will receive remission of sins."

—*Acts 10:24–43*

The travel along the road between Joppa and Caesarea gave Peter time to collect himself. Was the vision of the sheet let down from heaven a sign of Cornelius? Was the centurion like the previously forbidden food? Peter wondered. A sense of excited expectation possessed him as he neared the revered Roman's home.

If ever there was a group ready for whatever the Lord has made ready, it was Cornelius and his family. The whole family not only shared the centurion's belief, but also his longing for something more.

When Peter entered the house, Cornelius made obeisance. The centurion's pent-up anticipation and all he had heard about Peter's spiritual power made him more than a gracious host. He revered the apostle. That gave Peter an opening he needed. Both he and Cornelius were on level ground in the presence of the only One worthy of worship.

That led naturally for Peter to begin to explain his presence. Why did he do that? It sounded like a putdown of his gracious host. Note verse 45: *"And those of the circumcision who believed"* indicates that Peter had with him some of the conservative group of Hebrews who believed that the only way to Christ was through the full participation *first* in Hebraism, including all the rites and rituals of Israel, particularly circumcision. Under pressure from that group, Peter gave in to the need for a declaratory, but defensive statement. After he got past that deferential nod to the circumcision party, he pressed on to the real reason he was there. What he preached was a part of his own growing realization that the Lord shows no partiality.

"In truth, I perceive that God shows no partiality" (v. 34). The word "perceive" translates the verb *katalambánō,* meaning "to take hold of," "to grasp with the mind." Combined with the verb form and tense, it means that the truth had been dawning on him. Indeed it had! There before his receptive audience, Peter was sure of what he had suspected the vision had meant. That's quite

a shift: along with the church as a whole he had believed that one must become a full-fledged Hebrew before being permitted to receive the power of Christ.

It is exciting to see how Peter packed so much into a short message. We sometimes confuse length with effectiveness. Not so for the apostle, who was filled with the incisiveness and guidance of the Holy Spirit. He covers the ground: who Christ is, what He did, the power of the Resurrection, divine election of those set free to believe, and the offer of forgiveness of sin. I will resist the urge to "exposit his exposition" but will underscore it as a propitious passage for preparing people to experience the full power of the "matchless" gospel.

Before Peter got to the Pentecost effluence as part of his message, it happened. We feel the impinging Spirit waiting for Peter to explain that. The climactic statement that whoever believes in Christ will receive remission of sins brought a deep desire in the hearts and minds of Cornelius and his household. And the Holy Spirit fell upon them. the way that happened is a good lesson that we cannot administrate Pentecost; "the wind blows where it wills." At the same time, we should not be surprised when it happens. When we communicate the gospel, the gift of faith to respond is given, and the infilling of the Spirit follows. We should expect it; thank the Lord in advance for it. This would be a good passage for required reading or prayer in every robing room for clergy before they enter the sanctuary!

THE GIFT OF TONGUES

[44] While Peter was still speaking these words, the Holy Spirit fell upon all those who heard the word. [45] And those of the circumcision who believed were astonished, as many as came with Peter, because the gift of the Holy Spirit had been poured out on the Gentiles also. [46] For they heard them speak with tongues and magnify God.

Then Peter answered, [47] "Can anyone forbid water, that these should not be baptized who have received the Holy Spirit just as we have?" [48] And he commanded them to be baptized in the name of the Lord. Then they asked him to stay a few days.

—*Acts 10:44–48*

One of the outward signs of Christ's indwelling power in the Holy Spirit was that Cornelius and his household spoke in tongues. Peter's response is that they have received the Holy Spirit as had he and the other believers who were present. Note that Luke does not use his carefully selected word for the Pentecost speaking in "other" tongues. Here they spoke with tongues and magnified God. That's what the gift of tongues was given for—to magnify God. Neither Peter not the others tried to induce the gift, nor did they make it a requirement. The Spirit did it. He gave them an assurance of His presence in them, an undeniable gift of faith to receive the gospel, *and then,* he gave them the freedom, the release to make words of praise in an ecstatic language. They were caught up in uncontainable joy and adoration.

Looking back on what we said earlier about the control of the will over the signals of the cerebral cortex of the brain, we read with awe the account of these yielded and exuberant Romans. The Lord left nothing out of what He gave them. He wanted both Peter and the circumcision party that was present to know that these Gentiles had been given the full blessing they also had experienced. The Lord did not want the legalists in attendance to return to Jerusalem saying, "They were blessed, but they didn't speak in tongues!"

The important thing for us is not to make a rule out of this passage any more than we did the two-part blessing of the Samaritans in Acts 8. What is crucial is the praise that was expressed. It is not for us to legislate that it must be done with or without tongues. The evidence of salvation is praise and subsequent discipleship.

The gift of tongues is a gift offered to all Christians; it is required of none. I am thankful for the gift. I did not seek it or try to produce it. Some months after the infilling of Christ's Spirit I described earlier, the gift was given. It came at a time of yieldedness and a longing for all the Lord wanted to give. One day twenty-eight years ago in a special service for the healing of the needs of people, I was praying quietly and individually for a woman who had great physical and emotional needs. As I was praying, I felt a surge within me of power, praise, and joy. The words of a language I could not identify, or even want to try, came flowing forth quietly. The woman does not remember hearing them. What she remembers to this day is that a warmth pervaded her body and she was healed.

After the service, I went back to my study and sat quietly praying, thanking the Lord for the power to praise Him. And again the flow of joyous sounds came from my released tongue. Now these many years later, the gift is stronger than ever and is frequently the special gift of release in my prayers. Often when faced with a complex problem, the prayers about it are interrupted by the gift accompanied by the gift of interpretation. The answer I had not been able to reason out is given.

The same thing happens in study for the exposition of Scripture. When I feel that there is a deeper truth eluding my intellect, training, and experience, I lean back, pray quietly, and allow my will to yield to the implanting of the gift of wisdom. This is often followed by praise in tongues. And the insight given in those times is often the portion of the preaching or teaching that brings the comment, "How did you know what I was feeling and going through? You spoke to my need as if I had been the only person here." Or, "Where did you find that insight into that passage? I've never thought of that before." I am quick to respond, "Neither had I. It was a gift!"

The water baptism of Cornelius and his household must have been one of the most joyous and moving in history. It was the outward sign of the inner Spirit baptism which had taken place. In it, history was being made and, as a result of it, the Christian church took a whole new direction.

The fact that the church in Jerusalem knew about what had happened to Cornelius and his household before the time Peter arrived to tell the good news, indicates that some of the circumcision party skipped out the side door to get to Jerusalem to tell the apostles and leaders of the church what had happened. But, as is often the case, they were critical and told only that Peter had been with uncircumcised Gentiles and had eaten with them. The empowered preaching of the gospel, the outpouring of the Holy Spirit, and the evidence of praise were forgotten. Why? Jealousy or legalism? Perhaps both, and that is a nasty brew when ladled with pride.

THE EFFECTS FROM THE EPICENTER

11:1 Now the apostles and brethren who were in Judea heard that the Gentiles had also received the word of God.
2 And when Peter came up to Jerusalem, those of the circumcision contended with him, 3 saying, "You went in to uncircumcised men and ate with them!"
4 But Peter explained it to them in order from the beginning, saying: 5 "I was in the city of Joppa praying; and in a trance I saw a vision, an object descending like a great sheet, let down from heaven by four corners; and it came to me.
6 When I observed it intently and considered, I saw four-footed animals of the earth, wild beasts, creeping things, and birds of

the air. [7] And I heard a voice saying to me, 'Rise, Peter; kill and eat.' [8] But I said, 'Not so, Lord! For nothing common or unclean has at any time entered my mouth.' [9] But the voice answered me again from heaven, 'What God has cleansed you must not call common.'[10] Now this was done three times, and all were drawn up again into heaven. [11] At that very moment, three men stood before the house where I was, having been sent to me from Caesarea. [12] Then the Spirit told me to go with them, doubting nothing. Moreover these six brethren accompanied me, and we entered the man's house. [13] And he told us how he had seen an angel standing in his house, who said to him, 'Send men to Joppa, and call for Simon whose surname is Peter, [14] who will tell you words by which you and all your household will be saved.' [15] And as I began to speak, the Holy Spirit fell upon them, as upon us at the beginning. [16] Then I remembered the word of the Lord, how He said, 'John indeed baptized with water, but you shall be baptized with the Holy Spirit.' [17] If therefore God gave them the same gift as He gave us when we believed on the Lord Jesus Christ, who was I that I could withstand God?"

[18] When they heard these things they became silent; and they glorified God, saying, "Then God has also granted to the Gentiles repentance to life."

—Acts 11:1–18

One day I stood with a friend looking into the trench which had resulted from an earthquake. My friend said, "Look at that! Something happened here." Indeed it had. A fault separated what had been solidly a part of a northern California field. It was too wide to leap across.

That same sort of separation happened to Peter and subsequently the church. It divided their history from the time of being a sect of Judaism to becoming an inclusive intersocial, interracial, and eventually, international movement.

The other apostles had been briefed, and they began their interrogation of Peter with an accusation, not an affirmation—in fact, not even a question. But something had happened to Peter, and he could not contain the blessing. In good Hebrew style, he began at the beginning and gave all the salient details. The same Holy Spirit who blessed at Caesarea was also at work in the minds of the other apostles. They loved Peter and believed in him. They gave him a good hearing. His question *'Who was I that I could withstand God?"* (v. 17) was the clincher. And who were the other apostles to withstand Him either? They glorified the Lord and with reflective analysis received the guidance that the Way was open for all people: *"Then God has also granted to the Gentiles repentance to life."*

The shock at the epicenter had spread through the leadership of the church. They had to admit in astonishment what my friend said about the fault: "Something happened in Caesarea!"

What are the implications of this for us and our communication? There's a great difference between having the Lord on our agenda and being on His. What would it take to shift the epicenter? Further, the Lord is preparing a next step for each of us. It may be the same one the church and Peter needed to take in order to become inclusive rather than remain exclusive of certain types or kinds of people or groups. And then this passage gives us the assurance that the Lord will move us on in our growth and that the one place He'll never allow us to stay is where we are. But be sure to catch the full impact of the way the Lord works. He puts the "pricks" in our consciousness and unsettles us with the desire of something more of what He wants to give. Most of all, whatever He calls us to do as our next step in growth will further involve us with people who need Him more than they need their next breath. And Cornelius's messengers are waiting, knocking at our door!

THEY WERE CALLED CHRISTIANS

[19] Now those who were scattered after the persecution that arose over Stephen traveled as far as Phoenicia, Cyprus, and Antioch, preaching the word to no one but the Jews only. [20] But some of them were men from Cyprus and Cyrene, who, when they had come to Antioch, spoke to the Hellenists, preaching the Lord Jesus. [21] And the hand of the Lord was with them, and a great number believed and turned to the Lord.

[22] Then news of these things came to the ears of the church in Jerusalem, and they sent out Barnabas to go as far as Antioch. [23] When he came and had seen the grace of God, he was glad, and encouraged them all that with purpose of heart they should continue with the Lord. [24] For he was a good man, full of the Holy Spirit and of faith. And a great many people were added to the Lord.

[25] Then Barnabas departed for Tarsus to seek Saul. [26] And when he had found him, he brought him to Antioch. So it was

that for a whole year they assembled with the church and taught a great many people. And the disciples were first called Christians in Antioch.

27 And in these days prophets came from Jerusalem to Antioch. 28 Then one of them, named Agabus, stood up and showed by the Spirit that there was going to be a great famine throughout all the world, which also happened in the days of Claudius Caesar. 29 Then the disciples, each according to his ability, determined to send relief to the brethren dwelling in Judea. 30 This they also did, and sent it to the elders by the hands of Barnabas and Saul.

—Acts 11:19–30

The surprising twist of this passage provides a startling conclusion to this section of our survey of the Acts of the Holy Spirit. It points out that after the church made the first step of including the Gentiles as recipients of the grace of God, an effectiveness resulted with one of the most hostile groups in Israel. Remember the Hellenists? Remember what happened to Stephen and then to Saul when he returned to Jerusalem as a converted follower of the Way? The Hellenists were the ones with whom Saul disputed even though he was one of them as a Greek-speaking Jew. They sought to kill him and were the reason he had to escape the Holy City.

A mysterious twist of early church history occurred when some of the believers who had scattered because of Saul's preconversion purge of Jerusalem went as far as the eastern tip of the Mediterranean to a city called Antioch. At the same time that the apostles at Jerusalem were guided in their decision about the Gentiles, these displaced believers in Antioch began preaching Christ to the Hellenist Jews there. The Lord blessed their efforts. Was there a correlation between that blessing and the one that happened in the guided conclusion reached by the church in Jerusalem? I think so. The Lord pours out His blessing on the church wherever it responds to His guidance and moves on in faithful obedience.

Interesting. The apostles sent Barnabas, the encourager, to check on the power of evangelism that had been released in Antioch. In his customary Spirit-inspired affirmation, he rejoiced at what the followers of the Way were doing there. But he also discerned that they needed help in that secular city where political intrigue, cults, and sensuality abounded. Who could do that? Who had the intellectual training, Roman citizenship, and spiritual power, to establish a beachhead there? Who but Saul of Tarsus?

Barnabas went to Tarsus to call the meditating Saul into active ministry. And the years of preparation had made him ready. His mind was alert with Christ; his thinking was fashioned around the mind of Christ; and his will was under the control of his new and indwelling Lord. Saul responded with vigor and enthusiasm, and the missionary team of Saul and Barnabas was formed.

They preached for a full year in the city of Antioch. It was a good place to begin. If they could win converts and establish a church there, anything was possible. The city was ranked third in prominence to Rome and Alexandria. It was called one of the "eyes" of Asia in the far-flung Roman Empire, and a Roman prefect was stationed there to assure the power of Rome in the area. The culture of the city was Greek. Cosmopolitan and metropolitan in spirit and size, it was also one of the most corrupt cities of the then-known world. Ritual prostitution in the temple of Daphne characterized the sensual orientation of the morals of the city. And it was in that atmosphere that Paul began his ministry of preaching Christ!

It is significant that the Lord chose this time and place to begin the penetration of the Gentile world. The church in Jerusalem had said "Yes!" to His inclusive guidance. The next step was on the way! And it was at Antioch that the followers of Christ were first called Christians. It was not the church's idea. The people in Antioch coined the name. The suffix "ian" meant "belonging to" or "of the part of" or "a partisan of." Indeed they were all these, and more. The coined name was really a great compliment. Paul's vital preaching of Christ, the new life "in Christ," and the power of His indwelling as the secret of lasting joy and peace, had led non-Jews, Greeks, Romans, rich and poor, prominent citizens and converted prostitutes, into a strong and inclusive church.

It was so strong, in fact, that when a famine hit Jerusalem, and the church there was in desperate straits, it was the church at Antioch that sent an offering. The first missionary offering was sent to the believers in Jerusalem by a church made up of the inclusive fellowship that the Lord had given them the vision to see as His will. What an exciting confluence of circumstances.

The new age of the church had begun. No wonder they were called Christians. Perhaps for the first time their inclusive faith deserved the title!

CHAPTER TWELVE—UNRECOGNIZED ANSWERS TO PRAYER

ACTS 12:1–24

Scripture Outline

Diminished Expectation (12:1–5)

A Prayer Answer on Two Feet (12:6–12)

The Answer Kept Knocking (12:13–24)

Mark Twain once said, "The secret of humor itself is not joy but sorrow. There is no humor in heaven." I don't agree. The Lord shares our sorrows and never laughs at us. But surely He laughs with us when we discover that our sense of unanswered prayer in a situation was only that we had not recognized the answer He'd given already. When we realize that the answer was there all along, we laugh at our anxious lack of expectation.

I think the Lord enjoys the laugh with us. He delights to surprise us with answers that are beyond our level of expectation. Then when we finally realize what He did, we are amazed. As a friend of mine said, "While I was praying expecting very little, God already had done something great—so great that I had a hard time accepting the answer. God does have a sense of humor, doesn't He?" He joined God in the laughter of heaven.

Luke interrupts his intense account of the birth and expansion of the church to give us some comic relief. He enjoys telling these accounts of the interventions of the Lord which are answers to the very prayers His people are still praying. The account of Peter's release from prison while the Christians prayed, and their inability to recognize the answer when it came, is told very humorously. We laugh through it with Luke and then suddenly realize he's helped us laugh at ourselves.

A vital dynamic in great communication is the creative use of humor. It frees us to laugh at ourselves and with people. It's best not to introduce it by the aside, "Now I'm going to tell you a very funny story." That puts our hearers on the defensive to decide just how funny it was! The comic who was introduced as the funniest man in the world couldn't get a laugh out of the crowd that was determined not to respond because of the exaggerated introduction.

Luke does not tell us he is going to be humorous. He just does it. Remember that this was written to a man he was trying to introduce to the deeper dimension of the indwelling Lord. Why a story on the church's ineptness at recognizing an answer? Often the best way to communicate the power of Christ's life in us is to share our own humanness in growth. When this is done with humor, our own humanity is established and we can move on with our listeners to discover what the Lord is saying to both communicator and listener.

DIMINISHED EXPECTATION

12:1 Now about that time Herod the king stretched out his hand to harass some from the church. ² Then he killed James the brother of John with the sword. ³ And because he saw that it pleased the Jews, he proceeded further to seize Peter also. Now it was during the Days of Unleavened Bread. ⁴ So when he had arrested him, he put him in prison, and delivered him to four squads of soldiers to keep him, intending to bring him before the people after Passover.

⁵ Peter was therefore kept in prison, but constant prayer was offered to God for him by the church.

—*Acts 12:1–5*

It was a discouraging time for the church in Jerusalem. King Herod had discovered how to gain popularity and support from the Jews by persecuting the Christians. For a man as dissolute as he, that's heady wine. Herod Agrippa I was a nephew of Herod Antipas who had murdered John the Baptist, and grandson of Herod the Great. His opportunistic approach to leadership began during his training at Rome with the influence of Caligula, the selfish and egotistic son of the emperor. Later, this Herod was appointed to rule in Palestine and was given power in stages, until he ruled over the largest realm of any man since his grandfather.

The secret of his success was that he learned how to cultivate the favor of the Jews. They had consistently persecuted the church, and the loss of Saul of Tarsus as chief gestapo officer must have enraged them. Herod arrested James and had him beheaded. That brought him such acclaim from the leaders of Israel that he went after another principal leader of the Christians. Simon Peter was arrested and put in prison. And Herod, knowing of his escape once before, took no chances. Luke prepares us for the wonder, and the humor, of what happened later, by telling us the extent of the king's precaution to keep Peter in prison before he followed through on his obvious intention to behead him. It was Passover, and the time was not most propitious for his purposes. He appointed four squads to guard one man! A squad had four soldiers in it, so there were sixteen guards for one spiritual leader who had broken no law. A bit of background study heightens how these guards would have functioned. They probably served on three-hour watches, with two guards chained to the prisoner and two at the door. If the four squads meant a rotation of four men every three hours, that was precaution enough, but it may have meant that there were sixteen at a time!

All this is to point up the human impossibility of escape. There was nothing the church could do except pray. Except pray? Many previously answered prayers should have told the Christians that there is no more powerful weapon! The Christians knew what Herod intended to do. How could they face the future without their beloved Peter? But note that they did not pray for a miraculous release. Luke tells us that *"constant prayer was offered to God for him by the church"* (v. 5).

That shows us the diminished expectation the church was experiencing. There were no bold prayers in the name of Jesus for Peter's release. They asked that he be sustained and strengthened, but in the light of Luke's careful accounts of specific prayers and astounding answers all through Acts, we are fairly confident that he would have used this as a further evidence of how intercessory prayer was answered.

But as the story is related by Luke, it not only sets up the subsequent humor, but it involves us in empathy for the church. One of the great problems we all face is not how to pray, but what to pray. When a person we love is troubled, we wonder what is best. We are reluctant to be specific in our intercession because we fear telling God what we think best. We get into the muddle of what's our will versus what is God's will, as if the two could not be the same.

Years of trying to learn how and what to pray for others have taught me to spend more time listening to what the Lord wants me to ask than in asking. Then the asking can be what He is more ready to give than I may have had the courage to ask.

Discouragement over what we perceive as unanswered prayer in the past wilts our willingness to pray boldly. We assume that there was no answer because what happened was not what we wanted. Our limited view of time and eternity narrows our own perception of what an answer should be. Even after years of seeing God use what we thought were problems for a greater potential, we forget that experience and get caught in judging what God will do in a present situation on the basis of what we thought He should have done previously, but didn't. This, perhaps, was what the church in Jerusalem was facing. "We prayed for James and he was beheaded; what else can we expect for Peter?"

A woman came to see me about her inability to pray for her sick husband. They had been married for a few brief years. She had lost a previous husband through cancer. She prayed for him and he died. She felt panicked not only by the danger of further loss, but by "failure" of her prayers for her first husband. What she could not trust was God's sovereignty—that He is all-powerful to deal with each situation according to a greater plan than we can fathom. The significant difference between the two men was that her first husband was a Christian; her ailing second was not. Then I asked her what she would pray if she did not limit God by what she accused Him of not doing when she asked before. Her reply was very revealing. "I've thought a lot about that," she said. "I'd ask that the Lord bring him to a relationship with Him, and I'd ask that nothing happen to him until he was sure of that."

I told her that all that thinking about what to pray had been prayer in itself. The Lord was getting her ready to ask. Her prayer was answered. He became a Christian and is alive today.

Expectation is a crucial part of dynamic prayer. But it must be built on the insight and guidance of prolonged prayer to know how to pray. Building our prayers on unguided, negative expectations is disastrous. We expect far too little, we ask for it, and then are disappointed that the Lord didn't do better for us.

The formula for creative intercessory prayer is: listen carefully, ask boldly, trust completely, and know that the answer is part of the tapestry of God's greater plan. He uses everything for His glory and our growth, if we allow Him.

A PRAYER ANSWER ON TWO FEET

6 And when Herod was about to bring him out, that night Peter was sleeping, bound with two chains between two soldiers; and the guards before the door were keeping the prison.

[7] Now behold, an angel of the Lord stood by him, and a light shone in the prison; and he struck Peter on the side and raised him up, saying, "Arise quickly!" And his chains fell off his hands. [8] Then the angel said to him, "Gird yourself and tie on your sandals"; and so he did. And he said to him, "Put on your garment and follow me." [9] So he went out and followed him, and did not know that what was done by the angel was real, but thought he was seeing a vision. [10] When they were past the first and the second guard posts, they came to the iron gate that leads to the city, which opened to them of its own accord; and they went out and went down one street, and immediately the angel departed from him.

[11] And when Peter had come to himself, he said, "Now I know for certain that the Lord has sent His angel, and has delivered me from the hand of Herod and from all the expectation of the Jewish people."

[12] So, when he had considered this, he came to the house of Mary, the mother of John whose surname was Mark, where many were gathered together praying.

—Acts 12:6–12

The Lord's timing was right on schedule. On the night before *"Herod was about to bring [Peter] out,"* the angel of the Lord appeared in the prison to set him free. The Greek implies that it was the night before his execution was planned. The sleeping apostle did not wake easily. What a splendid picture of trust and serenity! He was not anxious about the next day. Death held no power for this Christ-filled man, except a deeper union with Him. He was fast asleep in the relationship which had begun when he heard the Lord's commanding words, "Come follow Me!" and since Pentecost, he had lived in the inner resources of the flow of His Spirit. Peter was sleeping in the same mysterious confidence in which he had lived since the infilling of Christ's Spirit. If it was his time to die, so be it. If not, the Lord would intervene.

The description of that intervention is humorous. Apparently Peter did not respond to the call of his name. The angel struck the apostle a smart blow on the side to move him from his confident sleep. And then he had to lead the sleeping saint each step of the way, giving instructions to him for putting on his sandals and robe. What is implied was that he was in a half-awake trance. The tall, robust fisherman was cared for like a little child. We laugh as we read the humorous account.

What happened was a three-part miracle. The first part was to get Peter out of the chains fettered to the arms of the two guards; the second was to get him past the guard posts; and the third was to get him through the iron gate of the wall surrounding the whole prison. The angel accomplished all three without the guards being roused. It wasn't until Peter and the angel were out of the prison and down the street that he fully woke up! His waking thought was one of praise for the miracle. "Only the Lord could do this! He must have sent His angel."

Indeed He had. And I think the whole company of heaven was watching that night. "The great cloud of witnesses," the heavenly cheering section, was pulling for the success of the event. And I think they laughed as the leaders of Israel were outsmarted one more time, and Herod was denied one more manipulative deed to keep his power. Also, it must have been a very humorous thing to see the church continuing to pray with little expectation while Peter was already out of the prison!

Peter's second thought after praise to the Lord was as customary as the first. He wanted to share the joy with his sisters and brothers in Christ. Since Pentecost, he had kept neither his joys nor his failures to himself. That was one of the remarkable manifestations of the Spirit in Peter. Christ in him and Christ in the fellowship were the two great realities for his life. And so, he made his way to the home of Barnabas's aunt, the mother of John Mark, the site of the Upper Room. Peter was the answer to prayer on two feet walking. Or did he run, full of excitement and the sheer delight of being the Lord's surprise in answer to the prayers still being prayed?

THE ANSWER KEPT KNOCKING

13 And as Peter knocked at the door of the gate, a girl named Rhoda came to answer. 14 When she recognized Peter's voice, because of her gladness she did not open the gate, but ran in and announced that Peter stood before the gate. 15 But they said to her, "You are beside yourself!" Yet she kept insisting that it was so. So they said, "It is his angel."

16 Now Peter continued knocking; and when they opened the door and saw him, they were astonished. 17 But motioning to them with his hand to keep silent, he declared to them how the Lord had brought him out of the prison. And he said, "Go, tell these things to James and to the brethren." And he departed and went to another place.

¹⁸ Then, as soon as it was day, there was no small stir among the soldiers about what had become of Peter. ¹⁹ But when Herod had searched for him and not found him, he examined the guards and commanded that they should be put to death.

And he went down from Judea to Caesarea, and stayed there.

²⁰ Now Herod had been very angry with the people of Tyre and Sidon; but they came to him with one accord, and having made Blastus the king's personal aide their friend, they asked for peace, because their country was supplied with food by the king's country.

²¹ So on a set day Herod, arrayed in royal apparel, sat on his throne and gave an oration to them. ²² And the people kept shouting, "The voice of a god and not of a man!" ²³ Then immediately an angel of the Lord struck him, because he did not give glory to God. And he was eaten by worms and died.

²⁴ But the word of God grew and multiplied.

—Acts 12:13–24

An outer court probably separated Mark's home from the street. The heavy wooden gate was the only way inside, and it was tightly locked. These were dangerous days for those early Christians. Every precaution for safety was taken; at least there would be an early warning of the intrusion of Herod's soldiers or the temple guard. Peter knocked, and waited. A young woman by the name of Rhoda was sent by the praying fellowship to see who was interrupting their prayers for Peter. He urged her to open the gate. Strange twist. She was so amazed at recognizing Peter's voice on the other side of the gate, she could not open the lock!

What follows is a comic scene of Rhoda running back and forth trying to communicate her excitement. She was awestruck! The very person for whom she had been praying on that night before his sure execution was standing outside the gate. When she finally was able to pull herself together long enough to put into words the unbelievable fact of Peter at the gate, she blurted out the news.

The response of the fellowship is equally humorous. They simply did not believe Rhoda. *"You are beside yourself!"* (v. 15). The use of the word *chōrís,* which means to have lost touch with reality, or to be apart from what was realistically possible, shows how resigned they were to Peter's death. When she persisted, interrupting their prayers for the one she knew was below at the gate, they exasperatedly said, "Oh, you must have seen his angel." They expected the worst and found it impossible to accept God's best. The discussion of Rhoda's insistence was probably based on one or two of the following possibilities. There was an idea commonly held at that time in Israel's religion that each person had a guardian angel. If it was Peter's angel at the gate, they were probably disturbed that he was not busy doing what they had been praying so arduously for in the strengthening and protection of the apostle. The other possibility is worse. Perhaps they assumed that Peter already had been beheaded and that it was his spirit manifestation coming to comfort them. If neither of these expositional suppositions is correct, what is sure is that they did not believe it was Peter.

The key phrase of the whole passage, found in verse 16, provides an exciting text for teaching or preaching: *"Now Peter continued knocking."* The tense in the Greek tells us that he persisted continuously. The praise with which he was filled and which he wanted to share was about to be turned into impatience with the long wait while the fellowship tried to calm down Rhoda. Remember, he was an escaped prisoner. How long would it be before the search party was sent out? The church was so occupied with prayer for Peter that he was kept out on the street where the sound of soldiers' feet and rattling of armor could mean a miracle denied and negated. I think Peter's persistent knocking thundered to pounding that reached the ears, and finally the conscious thinking, of the Christians at prayer.

When finally they opened the gate, the praying fellowship saw Peter and was astonished. I am pleased that Luke tells us that Peter had to motion them to be silent. I hope it was praise he silenced and not further need for assurance that it was really he. He told them the wondrous story and then left to find a place of hiding.

Herod's reaction to Peter's escape was so violent that he killed the guards who had been stationed to assure that he did not get out of the evil king's grasp. He had lost a chance to placate the Jews and divert their attention from the famine. His frustration was sublimated by a trip to Caesarea. There his arrogance was displayed again. The people of Tyre and Sidon needed his favor, and his pretentious oration to them brought further solicitous shouts, *"The voice of a god and not of a man!"* (v. 22). That says more about Herod than about the people who needed his favor. This was what the king wanted to hear. Since his boyhood days with his friend Caligula in Rome, he wanted the god-like power of the Caesars. Caligula went mad and Herod was eaten by worms. A fitting kind of death for a man who had eaten on his own soul all of his life!

I don't know about you, but I'm still chuckling about what happened at the gate of John Mark's house. After enjoying the laughter's full relaxing effect, we are able to appropriate what the story has said to us.

1. Expectation is the gift we offer the Lord in response to His gift of prayer. It is what we bring as an offering for our communication with Him. Expectation is a blend of confident trust and sanctified imagination. It gives us the capacity to ask the Lord for what He wants to give.

2. The Lord answers all prayer. Knowing so much more than we do, He grants some, refuses others, and delays still others. A delay is an answer! To have what He wants for us without His timing would be disastrous.

3. Often the answer we've been praying for is staring us in the face. Sometimes the Lord responds with a portion of the answer which requires joyous acceptance and implementation before we can appropriate the whole. We cannot receive the rest until we act on the first step.

4. There are times when we are so intent on praying that the prayer is all talking and no listening. The answer is knocking!

Chapter Thirteen—The First Missionary Journey

Acts 12:25—14:28

Scripture Outline

An Inner Call and an Outer Confirmation (12:25—13:3)

A Double Name for a Two-Pronged Thrust (13:4–12)

What It Means to Be Truly Free (13:13–52)

How to Handle Rejection (14:1–28)

James S. Stewart ended the introduction to his Cunningham Lectures on Paul, which later became his vital book *A Man in Christ,* with an insightful statement that helps us appreciate what we are about to discover in our survey of the first missionary journey. Dr. Stewart was a busy and involved local church pastor at the time he delivered the lectures. His comment focuses our need to keep that rare blend of in-depth preparation plus involvement with people.

"The preparation of the lectures and the actual writing of the book," Stewart said, "have gone on amid the absorbing and incessant claims of congregational work in a busy parish. But I would believe that, for one who seeks to interpret the vital religion of Paul (a religion, it should never be forgotten, hammered out in the turmoil of the mission field), the daily pressure of the demands of the active ministry may not be altogether a disadvantage."[1]

That insight prepares us for the discovery of the most effective way to appreciate the deeper meaning of each section of the rest of Acts, and particularly the impact of the missionary journeys. What Paul preached along the way gives us an example of how the long time of preparation in Tarsus provided the raw material for dynamic communication with real people. Luke gives us the advantage of being able to capture the human situation in each city or village and see how the Holy Spirit guided Paul to exactly what was needed. Once we do that, we will be able to communicate to others the answers to these key questions for the exposition of the remainder of Acts:

1. What did Paul find in each city?

2. What did he preach in response?

3. What happened?

4. What does it mean to us today?

AN INNER CALL AND AN OUTER CONFIRMATION

25 And Barnabas and Saul returned from Jerusalem when they had fulfilled their ministry, and they also took with them John whose surname was Mark.
13:1 Now in the church that was at Antioch there were certain prophets and teachers: Barnabas, Simeon who was called Niger, Lucius of Cyrene, Manaen who had been brought up with Herod the tetrarch, and Saul. 2 As they ministered to the Lord and fasted, the Holy Spirit said, "Now separate to Me Barnabas and Saul for the work to which I have called them." 3 Then, having fasted and prayed, and laid hands on them, they sent them away.

—Acts 12:25—13:3

The crucial aspect of this passage for us is that the prophets and teachers of the Antioch church were led by the Spirit to separate Paul and Barnabas for a work to which they already had been called by the same Spirit. The word for "called" in *"Now separate to Me Barnabas and Saul for the work to which I have called them"* (13:2) is *proskéklēmai,* in the perfect tense, meaning that the two had an inner call which the church recognized by releasing them to the task. It was not first the idea of the church. The responsibility of the church was to recognize what the Spirit had accomplished in creating the desire and clarifying the direction.

Both are part of discovering the will of the Lord in our own lives. We all need trusted friends whose authentic relationship with the Lord prepares them to be channels of the Spirit to confirm in us what we are to do. Over the years I have found that my best decisions have been made when I thought and felt a direction through prolonged prayer and consecrated thinking, and then waited for a spontaneous, unsolicited affirmation of that through some person who I know prays for me consistently. The combination seldom fails to be right.

The teachers and prophets of Antioch are an interesting mixture. They show what an interracial, crosscultural church had grown up in that metropolitan city which from this point on became the headquarters of missionary Christianity. The Lord had called into the fellowship and into leadership positions people from several nations. A fellowship from the then-known world could be led to the decision of wanting to reach the world. This could never have happened in the Jerusalem church.

The Lord knew what He was doing! Note the magnificent mixture:

Barnabas, who had the rich background of the infant church in Jerusalem from Pentecost or shortly thereafter; Simeon, also called Niger, a Latin name showing two strong cultures in one person; Lucius of Cyrene, also a Latin name, clearly identified as coming from North Africa; Manaen, who had been raised *(súntrophos)* in the court of Herod the tetrarch (that is, the court of Herod Antipas, father of Agrippa); and Saul, the converted Pharisee. It was a world fellowship to start a world movement. Even Mark, brought from Jerusalem, would add his own contribution later. As the Lord had gotten those men ready for world mission, so too, He would use the failures and difficulties such as Mark would face to get him ready to write the first Gospel.

The Lord prepares us for the strategic opportunities each of us has. This analysis of the leadership of Antioch in Syria leads us to pray, "Lord, thank You for calling us to be Your people, indwelt by Your Spirit, and prepared for our mission by everything we have been through. Use what we are now discovering and going through for the next step of Your strategy for us!"

To be in Christ is to be in mission. The ministry is for all the people of God—whether we are called to stay in Antioch, or move out in a special missionary journey in response to a call. The adventure is Christ, in Antioch or on to Cyprus!

A DOUBLE NAME FOR A TWO-PRONGED THRUST

[4] So, being sent out by the Holy Spirit, they went down to Seleucia, and from there they sailed to Cyprus. [5] And when they arrived in Salamis, they preached the word of God in the synagogues of the Jews. They also had John as their assistant.

⁶ Now when they had gone through the island to Paphos, they found a certain sorcerer, a false prophet, a Jew whose name was Bar-Jesus, ⁷ who was with the proconsul, Sergius Paulus, an intelligent man. This man called for Barnabas and Saul and sought to hear the word of God. ⁸ But Elymas the sorcerer (for so his name is translated) withstood them, seeking to turn the proconsul away from the faith. ⁹ Then Saul, who also is called Paul, filled with the Holy Spirit, looked intently at him ¹⁰ and said, "O full of all deceit and all fraud, you son of the devil, you enemy of all righteousness, will you not cease perverting the straight ways of the Lord? ¹¹ And now, indeed, the hand of the Lord is upon you, and you shall be blind, not seeing the sun for a time."

And immediately a dark mist fell on him, and he went around seeking someone to lead him by the hand. ¹² Then the proconsul believed, when he saw what had been done, being astonished at the teaching of the Lord.

—*Acts 13:4–12*

Luke uses the occasion of describing the ministry in Paphos, a port on the island of Cyprus, to introduce Saul's name as a Roman citizen. Being born and raised in Tarsus during the Roman occupation there gave him that crucial credential. Paul was his Latin or Roman name, Saul his Jewish name; Greek culture was his conditioning, Hebraism his training, and life in Christ his purpose and passion. A man for all nations and all seasons.

In this passage we see a "Saul-Paul," two-pronged thrust for two very different people. As a Jew he confronted the troubled Jewish man by the name of Bar-Jesus who was a false prophet and a sorcerer; and as a Roman he influenced the life of a Roman proconsul named Sergius Paulus. We can understand why Paul used his Roman name and background to establish a relationship with the intellectual proconsul. He told him about Jesus Christ and the man showed signs of becoming a believer. Then Bar-Jesus, who had apparently been the proconsul's mentor up to that time, jealously stepped in to prevent Paul from converting him. Paul's background in the Hebrew faith enabled him to see the exact nature of the false prophet's distortion. He was obviously demon-possessed. Paul took the radical action of asking the Holy Spirit temporarily to blind him. He confronted Bar-Jesus with his spiritual blindness by imposing upon him a short-term physical blindness. Paul remembered the life-changing impact of his own blinding after the Damascus Road experience. The false prophet lost his influence on the city and over the proconsul. As a result Paul led Paulus to Christ. The mission had begun!

Just as Paul's many-faceted background contributed to his call, so too every phase of his preparation in Tarsus, and his familiarity with Greek culture and the Roman world, prepared him to speak to different people at many different levels.

The more varied our background as communicators today, the better. And the more diversified our interests, the more people we can touch. Our training, cultural background, national heritage, hobbies, and sports activities put us in touch with a wide variety of people. Also, our illustrative material can be drawn from these many worlds. People are like islands: you have to row around them before you know where to land. But once the point of contact is established, communication between persons can begin and soon the opportunity to share "the reason for the hope that is within you" will be provided.

Paul must have been gratified that his first prolonged stop on the journey resulted in a brilliant intellectual's coming to Christ (v. 7), and to both abundant and eternal life. Luke does not tell us what happened to Bar-Jesus. Perhaps he was helped by the new man inside the proconsul. We do not know. But it is moving today to see a chapel on the coast where ancient Paphos stood. When I visited the chapel recently, I sat for a long time and thought about what happened there so many years ago. Then I thought about both Paul and Paulus as a part of the company of heaven with whom I was honored to praise the reigning Christ!

WHAT IT MEANS TO BE TRULY FREE

13 Now when Paul and his party set sail from Paphos, they came to Perga in Pamphylia; and John, departing from them, returned to Jerusalem. 14 But when they departed from Perga, they came to Antioch in Pisidia, and went into the synagogue on the Sabbath day and sat down. 15 And after the reading of the Law and the Prophets, the rulers of the synagogue sent to them, saying, "Men and brethren, if you have any word of exhortation for the people, say on."

16 Then Paul stood up, and motioning with his hand said, "Men of Israel, and you who fear God, listen: 17 The God of this people Israel chose our fathers, and exalted the people

when they dwelt as strangers in the land of Egypt, and with an uplifted arm He brought them out of it. [18] Now for a time of about forty years He put up with their ways in the wilderness. [19] And when He had destroyed seven nations in the land of Canaan, He distributed their land to them by allotment.

[20] "After that He gave them judges for about four hundred and fifty years, until Samuel the prophet. [21] And afterward they asked for a king; so God gave them Saul the son of Kish, a man of the tribe of Benjamin, for forty years. [22] And when He had removed him, He raised up for them David as king, to whom also He gave testimony and said, 'I have found David the son of Jesse, a man after My own heart, who will do all My will.' [23] From this man's seed, according to the promise, God raised up for Israel a Savior—Jesus— [24] after John had first preached, before His coming, the baptism of repentance to all the people of Israel. [25] And as John was finishing his course, he said, 'Who do you think I am? I am not He. But behold, there comes One after me, the sandals of whose feet I am not worthy to loose.'

[26] "Men and brethren, sons of the family of Abraham, and those among you who fear God, to you the word of this salvation has been sent. [27] For those who dwell in Jerusalem, and their rulers, because they did not know Him, nor even the voices of the Prophets which are read every Sabbath, have fulfilled them in condemning Him. [28] And though they found no cause for death in Him, they asked Pilate that He should be put to death. [29] Now when they had fulfilled all that was written concerning Him, they took Him down from the tree and laid Him in a tomb. [30] But God raised Him from the dead. [31] He was seen for many days by those who came up with Him from Galilee to Jerusalem, who are His witnesses to the people. [32] And we declare to you glad tidings— that promise which was made to the fathers. [33] God has fulfilled this for us their children, in that He has raised up Jesus. As it is also written in the second Psalm:

'You are My Son,
Today I have begotten You.'

[34] And that He raised Him from the dead, no more to return to corruption, He has spoken thus:

'I will give you the sure mercies of David.'

[35] Therefore He also says in another Psalm:

'You will not allow Your Holy One to see corruption.'

[36] "For David, after he had served his own generation by the will of God, fell asleep, was buried with his fathers, and saw corruption; [37] but He whom God raised up saw no corruption. [38] Therefore let it be known to you, brethren, that through this Man is preached to you the forgiveness of sins; [39] and by Him everyone who believes is justified from all things from which you could not be justified by the law of Moses. [40] Beware therefore, lest what has been spoken in the prophets come upon you:

[41] *'Behold, you despisers,*
Marvel and perish!
For I work a work in your days,
A work which you will by no means believe,
Though one were to declare it to you.'"

[42] So when the Jews went out of the synagogue, the Gentiles begged that these words might be preached to them the next Sabbath. [43] Now when the congregation had broken up, many of the Jews and devout proselytes followed Paul and Barnabas, who, speaking to them, persuaded them to continue in the grace of God.

[44] On the next Sabbath almost the whole city came together to hear the word of God. [45] But when the Jews saw the multitudes, they were filled with envy; and contradicting and blaspheming, they opposed the things spoken by Paul. [46] Then Paul and Barnabas grew bold and said, "It was necessary that the word of God should be spoken to you first; but since you reject it, and judge yourselves unworthy of everlasting life, behold, we turn to the Gentiles. [47] For so the Lord has commanded us:

'I have set you as a light to the Gentiles,
That you should be for salvation to the ends of the earth.'"

[48] Now when the Gentiles heard this, they were glad and glorified the word of the Lord. And as many as had been appointed to eternal life believed.

[49] And the word of the Lord was being spread throughout all the region. [50] But the Jews stirred up the devout and prominent women and the chief men of the city, raised up persecution against Paul and Barnabas, and expelled them from their region. [51] But they shook off the dust from their feet against them, and came to Iconium. [52] And the disciples were filled with joy and with the Holy Spirit.

—Acts 13:13–52

William Ramsay, in *St. Paul the Traveler and Roman Citizen*, gives some very useful information about the location of this Antioch. The province of Pisidia was not formed until A.D. 295. Antioch was in Phrygia. Pisidia at Paul's time was a city in the geographical area of the Roman Empire called Phrygia. What is meant here in the Acts reference is Antioch near Pisidia the city. "Pisidian Antioch" was Luke's way of distinguishing it from several other Antiochs of the time.

What happened to Paul and his companions on the way to Antioch had a profound effect, I believe, on what he said and did there. It had been a long, tiring sea voyage from Cyprus to Attalia, a seaport in the district of Pamphylia, on the southern coast of what is Turkey today. After landing there, Paul, Barnabas, and John Mark made their way a few miles north to Perga. Two disturbing things happened to Paul there. He contracted a physical disease, and Mark left him and Barnabas to return to Jerusalem. The disease is not identified, but it was extremely painful. Most biblical authorities identify it with a form of malaria, which was prevalent at the time around the lowlands of Perga. Others have suggested he had painful eye trouble because of the reference in the Galatian letter, written to the cities he visited in that area after his sickness. "And my trial which was in my flesh you did not despise or reject, but you received me as an angel of God, even as Christ Jesus. What then was the blessing you enjoyed? For I bear you witness that, if possible, you would have plucked out your own eyes and given them to me" (Gal. 4:14–15). This may be Pauline hyperbole or a statement of his condition. Perhaps we do not need to decide. The virulent form of malaria he would have contracted in that area of Perga caused severe headaches which were like a white-hot poker driven through the cranium. Paul was a sick man, whatever the disease was called. He called it a "thorn in his flesh" (2 Cor. 12:7) and struggled with the Lord to have it removed. It was then that he learned that Jesus Christ alone was sufficient for him. We believe that Paul's decision to go to Antioch, 3,600 feet high in the mountains, was to recover.

Added to this, Paul went through the difficult relational problems with Mark. The young man defected the missionary team and went back home. The break also must have caused tensions with Barnabas and Paul which later, at the beginning of another journey, caused a split between them. Barnabas was a relative of Mark and his gracious nature would have caused deep grief over the departure of his young cousin. We do not know what caused the breakup. Mark's immaturity in Christ, the strangeness of the foreign territory, the demands of travel? Or was it Paul's rigorous and vigilant commitment to the mission? Then too, Paul was facing physical difficulties which may have made him less than patient. Whatever the cause, the breakup was painful for all three, and it had repercussions for years to come until they were reconciled late in Paul's life. Both Mark and Paul had failed with each other, and yet I believe the failure led to a much more powerful preaching of the gospel when Paul and Barnabas arrived at Antioch.

All this is what Paul brought to Antioch. It shaped both his message and his attitude. Vulnerability deepened his forceful style, and Christ's suffering was a fresh, personal experience. He found a ready audience of Jews and "God-fearing" proselytes. The city heard him gladly when he preached in the synagogue. It was here in an initially receptive atmosphere that Paul preached the first full sermon that has been recorded for us.

Up to this point, we have had one-line synopses of what Paul said in the synagogues of Damascus and Jerusalem, or to the people in Syrian Antioch. Now, as a part of this first missionary journey, we have a chance to be part of the synagogue in Antioch in Phrygia to listen to a comprehensive, theologically developed communication of what Jesus Christ has done to set us free.

The key verses for exposition of this portion of Acts 13 are 38 and 39. Everything Paul had said up to that point led to the thrust of the verses, and everything that happened in Antioch was because of it. In preparation, he showed how Jesus was the Messiah promised by David, predicted by the prophets, and foretold by John the Baptist. Then he showed what must have been the result of his thought and prayer in those years of waiting in Tarsus. He combined the essence of Jesus' teaching on faith and the Old Testament concept of justification, presenting them together under the offer of forgiveness of sin and true freedom. In Christ's death and Resurrection God has established our acceptance by Him, something that the Law and the sacrificial system of Israel could not do. Here is the powerful concept of justification by faith alone which becomes Paul's central theme and later is refined in Romans, Galatians, and Colossians. *"Therefore let it be known to you, brethren, that through this Man is preached to you the forgiveness of sins; and by Him everyone who believes is justified from all things from which you could not be justified by the law of Moses"* (13:38–39).

The basic meaning is that it is by faith, and not the works of the Law of Moses, that a person is justified, acquitted, forgiven, and set free. The Law could not justify anyone, for all have broken it, but forgiveness is offered through the death and Resurrection of Jesus. Paul's statement does not mean that the Law justified in some things and Jesus took care of the rest. *"All things"* is inclusive grace. The Law was not offered to be our justification. By its very nature law cannot be acquittal, for the Law establishes the way a righteous God wants His people to live with Him and each other.

Ideally, living the Law to perfection, a person would not need justification, but no one had ever lived it to perfection. The sacrifices were an incomplete source of justification and thus led to the prediction of the prophets that God Himself would provide the way of a complete acquittal for sins. This, says Paul, has been done in Jesus Christ, God's Messiah, the ultimate sacrifice for sins and the freedom from the failure all have incurred in trying to live the absolute demands of the Law. The ASV thus translates the word "justify" as freedom, "That everyone who believes is freed from all things, from which you could not be freed through the Law of Moses." This freedom is the result of faith and not the works detailed in the Law. The Greek used here for "justify" is *dikaiōthenai,* from *dikaióō,* to deem right, accept, acquit.

Paul has revealed to the Antioch synagogue the revolutionary truth the Lord made clear to him. The more clearly developed form of this came later, as we see in Romans 3 and Galatians 2:16; 3:10–11; 5:4. But here, in its unpolished form, it is the cause of a tremendous response in the city. The people in the synagogue, Jews and Gentile proselytes, hear him gladly and ask for him to speak in the next synagogue service the following week. The news of his exciting preaching, and this liberating gospel of justification, spreads throughout the city. When the synagogue meets again, almost the whole city turns out to hear more of this liberating news. The difference is that the crowd which was attracted included Gentiles in addition to the proselytes to the Jewish religion. That was more than the Jews could take. Out of envy, not just the purity of the synagogue and their religion, they opposed Paul and Barnabas bitterly.

The violent reaction led Paul to a watershed which we are sure he had been approaching in his mind. It would be reiterated often in the future: because of the resistance of the Jews he would turn to the Gentiles. His historic statement was a further widening of the shock from the epicenter that began in Peter. But note that Paul says that it was necessary that the Word of God should first be spoken to the Jews. If he had begun with the Gentiles, he would never have had any hearing from the synagogue. The leaders of the Jews in Antioch had had enough: they raised up a persecution movement. Paul and Barnabas enacted Jesus' recommendation that when an authentic effort is made and hostile rejection occurs, one should shake the dust off his feet and get on to the people waiting to hear elsewhere.

But there's no need for Paul to shake the dust off his feet in response to our reaction to what he has said. We hear him not just gladly, but with rapt attention. His is liberating news we need to hear again every day, and recover as the basis of our freedom as persons almost every hour.

Luke reminds us that the ability to hear and appreciate our freedom through faith in the justification of the cross is by the Lord's election. Verse 48 tells us that those who *"had been appointed to eternal life believed."* That too is a part of the work of His Spirit. It is not a source of arrogance but profound humility. We choose because we were chosen and given the gift of faith to accept the grace offered because we were declared accepted on Calvary. We reach out to grasp the gift because the Lord already had a firm grasp on us and are filled with His Spirit because it was His good pleasure to give Himself to us. It is all His doing from beginning to end. And the same Spirit at work in Antioch then will be at work when we communicate, *if* we offer the same basic message of justification by faith alone and the freedom which is available as a gift of the Lord. But even the desire to offer people nothing less than what will satisfy their aching hunger is the result of His Spirit at work in us as communicators.

Paul has given us a basis of asking ourselves: to what extent has the assurance of justification by faith alone become the basis of our inner security with the Lord? Do we live as people who know that we've been acquitted, forgiven, reconciled once and for all by Christ's death and Resurrection? Has this resulted in freedom from guilt and compulsive ways of trying to make ourselves right with the Lord by our own efforts? Are we liberated from having to win His approval and the acceptance of others?

The message at Antioch brings us back to the core of our spiritual, psychological, and interpersonal liberation. We are loved and forgiven just as we are, not for what we have been or will do. God is for us, not against us. His grace is not conditioned by our performance. But is that our working, daily, moment-by-moment security?

When Rembrandt painted his famous portrayal of the Crucifixion, he painted his own face into one of the crowd at the foot of the Cross. He expressed the longing we all feel to be there hourly to recover the amazing gift of unconditional love through the Savior's death on the Cross.

We are like the man overheard by H. Wheeler Robinson in a Paris cathedral as the words "Christ have mercy, God have mercy, upon us," were sung. The man was wringing his hat in his hand, saying, "If only He could, if only He could." But He can, and will—not only in each new failure or sin, but as the bedrock of a new liberation to live as free, forgiven people. As Paul wrote to the people in this area long after his visit, "For freedom Christ has set us free" (Gal. 5:1, RSV).

Paul was the most free human being who ever lived. And it is a significant thing to us as communicators that his first recorded public declaration of the source of that freedom came after a sickness which thundered loudly the meaning of Christ's total suffering, and a broken relationship with a frightened young man, which reaffirmed his own humanity and inadequacy apart from Christ.

A communicator has no greater need than to discover repeatedly this healing assurance in his or her own life. It results in a freedom from defensiveness, a winsome joy that is contagious, and a message that matches the deepest need in the minds and hearts of our listeners, as well as those with whom we have one-to-one conversations about Christ's emancipation from guilt and self-justification.

Writing this in the early morning hours as the sun is rising, I have come to an important realization. Even after thirty years of study, teaching, and preaching, feeling myself a part of that Antioch synagogue listening to Paul has set me free again—this time from the residue of yesterday's efforts to justify myself in so many little ways that had resulted in less than vibrant joy as I began to work today. Then, as I listened and tried to imagine how those people felt when they heard this good news for the first time, I too was in Rembrandt's painting. It's been thirty-three years since I first heard that liberating truth as a young, insecure college student. And yet it was all fresh and new this morning. A new day, a new beginning. And the rest of life? Thousands more sunrises and opportunities to know I am loved as I am and therefore don't have to remain as I was!

A member of my congregation ran up to me recently with the exciting news, "We've got a new teacher in our church school class!" I tried to collect my thoughts about any change in the teaching staff of that class. When she went on, I knew what she meant. The teacher who taught that class was a member of the laity from the television world. His first experience of Christ, years before, had been renewed in a fresh rediscovery of freedom through justification by faith alone. This had made him a more impelling teacher than ever. Indeed, there was a new teacher in that class!

The startling truth is that the hunger of Christians and non-Christians alike is for this essential of our faith. Just as breakfast cannot suffice for the hunger of noontime or our present breath for the next, our continuing freedom is dependent on a consistent rediscovery of our forgiveness, that we are loved unconditionally, and that there is no need to justify ourselves. That alone is the source of an artesian joy which flows from the limitless grace of our Lord.

The Antioch ministry, which ended in conflict and persecution, sounds that note of joy. The disciples shook the dust off their feet and went on their way *"filled with joy and with the Holy Spirit"* (13:52). The rejection denied Paul and Barnabas the lesser emotion of happiness and in its place they knew joy, the outward manifestation of the inner experience of grace. The joy they knew and felt was not just *given* by the Lord's Spirit. It *was* the Lord's Spirit welling up within them. And Paul and Barnabas would need that for the challenge and difficulties that lay ahead of them. The reactions of people—acceptance or rejection—could never be the basis of their joy.

HOW TO HANDLE REJECTION

14:1 Now it happened in Iconium that they went together to the synagogue of the Jews, and so spoke that a great multitude both of the Jews and of the Greeks believed. 2 But the unbelieving Jews stirred up the Gentiles and poisoned their minds against the brethren. 3 Therefore they stayed there a long time, speaking boldly in the Lord, who was bearing witness to the word of His grace, granting signs and wonders to be done by their hands.

4 But the multitude of the city was divided: part sided with the Jews, and part with the apostles. 5 And when a violent attempt was made by both the Gentiles and Jews, with their rulers, to abuse and stone them, 6 they became aware of it and fled to Lystra and Derbe, cities of Lycaonia, and to the

surrounding region. ⁷ And they were preaching the gospel there.

⁸ And in Lystra a certain man without strength in his feet was sitting, a cripple from his mother's womb, who had never walked. ⁹ This man heard Paul speaking. Paul, observing him intently and seeing that he had faith to be healed, ¹⁰ said with a loud voice, "Stand up straight on your feet!" And he leaped and walked. ¹¹ Now when the people saw what Paul had done, they raised their voices, saying in the Lycaonian language, "The gods have come down to us in the likeness of men!" ¹² And Barnabas they called Zeus, and Paul, Hermes, because he was the chief speaker. ¹³ Then the priest of Zeus, whose temple was in front of their city, brought oxen and garlands to the gates, intending to sacrifice with the multitudes.

¹⁴ But when the apostles Barnabas and Paul heard this, they tore their clothes and ran in among the multitude, crying out ¹⁵ and saying, "Men, why are you doing these things? We also are men with the same nature as you, and preach to you that you should turn from these useless things to the living God, who made the heaven, the earth, the sea, and all things that are in them, ¹⁶ who in bygone generations allowed all nations to walk in their own ways. ¹⁷ Nevertheless He did not leave Himself without witness, in that He did good, gave us rain from heaven and fruitful seasons, filling our hearts with food and gladness." ¹⁸ And with these sayings they could scarcely restrain the multitudes from sacrificing to them.

¹⁹ Then Jews from Antioch and Iconium came there; and having persuaded the multitudes, they stoned Paul and dragged him out of the city, supposing him to be dead. ²⁰ However, when the disciples gathered around him, he rose up and went into the city. And the next day he departed with Barnabas to Derbe.

²¹ And when they had preached the gospel to that city and made many disciples, they returned to Lystra, Iconium, and Antioch, ²² strengthening the souls of the disciples, exhorting them to continue in the faith, and saying, "We must through many tribulations enter the kingdom of God." ²³ So when they had appointed elders in every church, and prayed with fasting, they commended them to the Lord in whom they had believed. ²⁴ And after they had passed through Pisidia, they came to Pamphylia. ²⁵ Now when they had preached the word in Perga, they went down to Attalia. ²⁶ From there they

sailed to Antioch, where they had been commended to the grace of God for the work which they had completed.

[27] Now when they had come and gathered the church together, they reported all that God had done with them, and that He had opened the door of faith to the Gentiles. [28] So they stayed there a long time with the disciples.

—Acts 14:1–28

Christians, and especially Christian communicators, must eventually discover how to deal with the many kinds of rejection. Acts 14 provides a basis of looking into the different expressions on the face of the old enemy—discouragement, caused by people's rejection. None of us escapes. People are complicated and their reactions are fickle. We should know—each of us is one of them! Freedom from people and their responses is essential to our effectiveness with them. In the three cities visited in Acts 14, we observe the missionaries' response to rejection in various forms and see how they had a long memory when it came to the gospel and a short memory about people's reactions.

Pressing on into the district of Lycaonia, Paul and Barnabas came to the city of Iconium. Filled with the joy of the Holy Spirit, they repeated the pattern of Antioch, going first to the synagogue and making a forceful presentation of the gospel, and then dealing with the strange mixture of tremendous acceptance and terrible rejection. They did not allow the latter to diminish their efforts to work tirelessly with the first.

That points up a problem with which we all wrestle. One rejection can tip the scales weighted with hundreds of affirmations. Satan's trick is to preoccupy us with a rejection so that we forget the positive responses. As a young pastor, before I discovered the security of Christ's indwelling Spirit, one cranky comment from a church member after the Sunday morning worship would obsess my mind to the exclusion of dozens of people who told me that the sermon had introduced them to Christ or helped them in their living of the adventure in Him. I would brood for hours on Sunday afternoon. My wife, Mary Jane, would ask, "Didn't anyone express affirmation?" My response would be to briefly acknowledge that and then to go back to picking away at what my friend Marilee Zdenek calls "splinters in our pride."[2] One day a physician friend of mine said bluntly, "Lloyd, you're going to have to learn how to deal with rejection if you want to work with people." Another splinter! But when those splinters collected and festered, they were the cause of an overall low-grade spiritual fever that was doing what a slight physical fever does—I was not sick enough to go to bed, nor well enough to be effective.

This was part of what led me to my search for the power of the Holy Spirit. The strange thing was that after an infilling of the Lord's Spirit, I was more sensitive, and less sensitive, all at the same time. Christ's Spirit broke me open to people and their needs. I became aware that often rejection was a plea for help from people. In other cases, it was legitimate objection to areas where I needed to grow. In the very least, it was an invitation to be taken seriously.

As I grew in dependence on Christ's inner Spirit, I became less sensitive. I was the most surprised of all. The secret was in discovering the causes of rejection. In most cases the Lord had put a solid hook into people's souls, and, if my calling was to fish for people, a tug on the line was a sign that the fun of landing the person had begun. As an enthusiastic fresh and salt water fisherman, I'm always delighted when a fish really takes the bait. These kinds never leap into the boat! They have to be worked with for a long time before they can be brought alongside and netted.

Iconium displays the freedom Paul and Barnabas had from negating the work they were called to with those who responded, as they avoided becoming overly obsessed with those who didn't. In fact, they came to realize that a sign of the Spirit's blessing was opposition. When the situation became dangerous, as it did in Iconium, the two conditioned athletes in the Spirit received a "second breath" and ran on with the Master to the next city.

In Iconium the Gentiles heard Paul and Barnabas readily. In Lystra, they heard them too readily. This too was a subtle form of rejection. Some people try to divide and conquer; others simply include and conquer. That was the manipulative form of passive resistance to the gospel in Lystra. Look carefully at how it happened, for that clever tactic is still in vogue today!

A lame man who had the same physical prognosis as the lame man we met earlier who was healed by Peter and John at the gate in the temple caught the attention of Paul as he preached. He didn't cry out like the beggar. Instead, his face radiated the obvious sign of the gift of faith being planted in his mind as he heard the gospel. Paul stopped speaking and commanded the man to stand up and walk. The gift of faith in Christ was coupled with the gift of healing, and the man stood up and walked.

This brought a tremendous response from the people of Lystra—the wrong kind. In their native Lycaonian language they burst out what they felt was the finest accolade they could give, *"The gods have come down to us in the likeness of men!"* (14:11).

A careful study of the Roman literature of the time helps us identify what was happening. There was an ancient myth[3] that Zeus and Hermes had come to that region disguised as mortals. The community—except for one couple, Philemon and Baucis—rejected them. The two gods sent judgment on the area except for the old couple, who were rewarded for their receptive welcome by being made guardians of a magnificent temple on the outskirts of Lystra. Later, when the couple died, they were turned into two giant trees as memorials of their kind deeds. The legend had become part of the folklore of Lystra, and the people identified Zeus and Hermes with Paul and Barnabas! When they saw the healing of the lame man, they exclaimed that the two gods had returned. They were going to take no chances this time. They gave Paul and Barnabas the key to the city and a welcome befitting the gods they supposed them to be. Tall and robust Barnabas was deified as Zeus, the head of the pantheon, because of his physical stature; and Paul, because of his ability to speak, they called Hermes, the god of eloquence and rhetoric.

When it dawned on Paul and Barnabas what was happening, they were horrified. They had been syncretized into the Greek pantheon! The people had not heard the gospel; they had made gods out of them. Paul used the challenge. Beginning with the false assumption, he told them that they too were human beings like the people of Lystra and had come not to be gods but to lead them to the living God.

Paul never finished his sermon. He didn't even get past the introduction! When he talked about God's goodness as the Creator and Sustainer of all and the Giver of rain and fruitful seasons, filling hearts with good and gladness, that's all the Lycaonians needed to hear. Really, that's all they wanted to hear. Anything more might change the illusion they had created. The multitudes wanted to offer sacrifices to them. Paul was never given a chance to tell them about his Lord, the living sacrifice for their sins.

Meanwhile, back to you and me—what does this form of rejection mean to us? It alarms us with the danger of people fitting the Christ and gospel we preach and teach into their own religious and cultural presuppositions, and never hearing us. It also rattles our teeth with the way people make heroes of the communicators as the best defense against hearing what they are really saying. We've all had it happen.

This is one of the most enticing temptations for us. Leaders can become diminutive gods for people. We are in danger only when we do not recognize what's happening and feed on the accolades instead of Christ. The only cure is pressing on to challenges He has for us that are greater than the talents people tell us we have. That throws us back on His everlasting arms instead of the possessive grasp of people. Don't pray for humility; that's the worst kind of pride. The sure cure is to ask the Lord, not for tasks equal to our abilities, but for power to meet the impossibilities He gives. Calling our hero worshipers into the challenge with us will not diminish our leadership, but will show them the secret of our power that can be theirs also—the indwelling Christ!

The Lystrians' desire to sacrifice to Paul and Barnabas was short-lived. Hostile Jews from Antioch and Iconium turned an adoring city of potential sacrificers to the missionaries into a lynch mob. It was a good thing Paul and Barnabas had not been beguiled by the misdirected adulation for them. People who deify human leaders also turn on them when those leaders don't submit to fitting into molds the manipulative deifiers have in mind.

The sin of our human nature lies in the struggle for power. Without a profound inner transformation, we all want control. When people feel the impotence of their own ability to control, they will try to do it through their leaders. This is what causes factions in churches. The old game of "capture the leader" is boiling when the attention is off Christ, and human ability rather than His Spirit is the focus. Leaders are pitted against each other whenever the lust for control has not been healed by making Christ the leader!

Paul was dragged out of the city, stoned, and left for dead. We wonder if he thought about Stephen and that face he'd never forgotten. But Paul was not alone as Stephen had been. Another group, not yet courageous enough to intervene, stood at a distance. When the lynch mob left, thinking they had gotten rid of Paul forever, a band of disciples came and gathered around him. Luke leaves it to our creative reflection to decide where they came from. Lystra? Were there others along with the lame man who heard the gospel and became disciples? Iconium and Antioch? A better choice. Paul and Barnabas had stayed in two cities long enough for new converts to be matured into the quality of believers Luke would call disciples. Probably what happened was that when the force of hostile people was mounted in Antioch and then Iconium, picking up the stream of anger as they made their way to Lystra, the disciples also gathered a group to follow closely behind to see what they could do to help their beloved (but not deified!) mentors in the faith.

What did they do when they were gathered around the bruised and battered Paul who had been left for dead? They prayed! Obviously they prayed for the apostle and he rose up. What a blessing for those young Christians! They had been given the Holy Spirit's gift of faith and healing.

Raised up by their prayers, Paul strode back into the city and got Barnabas, and with the joy of the Spirit's intervening power sounding in their hearts, they exhibited the raw courage to go right back into the jaws of the enemy in the cities of Antioch and Iconium. The miracle of Paul's resuscitation after the stoning gave him a credential no one dared question. He and Barnabas were free to solidify their evangelism, train new believers, and organize strong churches.

The organization of the churches is shown us by Luke. In each of the churches elders were trained and appointed. The Greek word in verse 23 for elders is *presbutérous,* which was originally used for older persons. The term was also used for the leaders of Israel. In the case of the elders appointed for these churches, they were mature believers who were put in charge of the spiritual life of the congregation. The form of church government in many churches today is based on this practice which was further developed in subsequent years of the first century.

In the New Testament church, various names are used for those elected to leadership. Building on the Hebrew tradition, there were *presbúteroi,* after the model in Jerusalem. At Ephesus and Philippi they were called *epískopoi,* bishops or overseers, and at Rome and Thessalonica they were called *proístamenoi,* leaders. Generally the Jewish communities used the term elders and the Greek communities, bishops.

After Paul and Barnabas were sure that the work they had begun was fully established, they made the long journey back to Syrian Antioch. The beachhead in the Gentile world was established. It had been a long and fruitful adventure, marked by the wondrous blend of physical sickness, pain, rejection, along with the converts who would live forever, the strong churches which would grow, and the greatest satisfaction any Christian in any age can know—that he or she communicated the gospel!

NOTES

1. James S. Stewart, *A Man in Christ: The Vital Elements of St. Paul's Religion* (Grand Rapids: Baker Book House, reprint 1975), p. 8.

2. Marilee Zdenek, *Splinters in My Pride* (Waco, Tex.: Word Books, 1979).

3. The reference is to a passage in Ovid *Metamorphosis* VIII.

CHAPTER FOURTEEN—THE STRUGGLE FOR FAITH

ACTS 15:1–41

Scripture Outline
A Ladder or a Leap (15:1–5)
When Good People Disagree (15:6–29)
Harder to Live Than Decide (15:30–41)

The title of this chapter is a contradiction of terms—purposely. Faith itself is not the struggle; it is a gift of the Lord to enable us to respond to His love. The struggle is to live by faith alone as the basis of our righteousness with Him. It is difficult for us to be convinced that something more is not also necessary for our justification, and not only for our own but for others. Our temptation is to establish standards, practices, and regulations in addition to faith. Self-justification and judgmentalism result.

We are not alone. The early church struggled for faith. That's the central issue of Acts 15. The epicenter we talked about earlier was still being straddled by many in the church with one foot in Judaism and the other at the foot of the cross. The gap was widening. Peter's experience with Cornelius and the Jerusalem church's final affirmation of the fact that the Holy Spirit had blessed the Gentile were only a beginning. It was one thing to confirm offering the gospel to one who was a "God-fearer," but quite another to offer Christ to Gentiles who were not first initiated into the Law of Moses.

If Peter's experience was the beginning of the epicenter, Paul's preaching to the Gentiles and disregard for insisting that they become obedient to all the requirements of the Mosaic Law widened the cleavage between two distinct groups within the church. There were Paul and his followers who believed that it was by faith alone that a person was justified; and the Pharisee party made up of converted Pharisees who asserted that Gentiles must become full participants in Hebraic legalism and customs in addition to faith in Christ as the fulfillment of the promise for *Israel's* Messiah. Their disciples, even more intractable, were the Judaizers.

Now you can see why I have used the words "the struggle for faith." The great challenge of Paul's life was the struggle to keep faith in Christ, and not fulfilling the Mosaic Law, as the only basis of salvation.

Many preachers and teachers who exposit Acts either skip the fifteenth chapter or pass over it lightly. They find it difficult to look at the wrangles of the early church and a meeting of church leaders in Jerusalem and find the lessons there that apply to contemporary life in the cybernetic, computerized world of the concrete jungle. And yet, every generation has to go back and remake for itself the decision arrived at in Jerusalem at that summit meeting we are about to consider. The struggle for faith alone for justification is as real today as it was for Luther and Calvin during the watershed days of the Reformation. It is a struggle in our time, not only for the organized church, but for each of us, every day, and in most hours of every day. We ask, Isn't there something else I can do or be to be sure of God's approval? The struggle for faith alone never ends. It's a part of our own inability to accept a gift. And deeper than that: we want to be loved because of what we do for God. Unconditional love is both difficult to receive, and at times, almost impossible for us to extend to others. Acts 15 is as real as this morning's headlines.

Background is necessary to understand the issues that led up to the historic decision of the Jerusalem Council. Our tendency is to join Paul's team before we understand the opposition. In daily living we may find ourselves much more comfortable with the Pharisee's party or even with their vigilantes, the Judaizers. Let's think for a moment from inside their minds. Empathetical identification will not only give us perspective of their point of view; it may help us to join Paul in his struggle for faith as much more committed teammates.

A LADDER OR A LEAP

15:1 And certain men came down from Judea and taught the brethren, "Unless you are circumcised according to the custom of Moses, you cannot be saved." [2] Therefore, when Paul and Barnabas had no small dissension and dispute with them, they determined that Paul and Barnabas and certain others of them should go up to Jerusalem, to the apostles and elders, about this question.

³ So, being sent on their way by the church, they passed through Phoenicia and Samaria, describing the conversion of the Gentiles; and they caused great joy to all the brethren. ⁴ And when they had come to Jerusalem, they were received by the church and the apostles and the elders; and they reported all things that God had done with them. ⁵ But some of the sect of the Pharisees who believed rose up, saying, "It is necessary to circumcise them, and to command them to keep the law of Moses."

—*Acts 15:1–5*

The Christian Pharisees and the circumcision party from Judea were not all bad. They believed that God's strategy for history had been in and through His chosen people, the Jews. He had given them the Ten Commandments and the basics of how to live as His people in the regulations given through Moses. Circumcision became the catchall word for obedience to the Law. And Law meant everything from taking no other god before the Lord to the most minute details for cleanliness. The people of Israel would not have survived as a distinct people without the Decalogue, and also the laws were very practical regulations for health and survival. The difficulty occurred when the Law became a ladder to be climbed to salvation. Rather than seeing the Law as an expression of God's love for His people, it became something they must do in order to be loved. It offered the security and assurance that if the Law was fulfilled impeccably then they could be sure that they were right with God. But He never intended that the keeping of the Law should be a substitute for Him.

Let me illustrate it in human terms of the relationship of a parent and a child. The parent knows from experience that there are basics of living which work for welfare and happiness. Learning obedience to the parent is necessary preparation for self-discipline. Then out of love the parent lays down certain regulations for the child's welfare. They are not to be a burden but a guide to a responsible and rewarding life. To stress the importance, they are enforced so that they become part of the character of the child, for the child's welfare. For the child they become "oughts" which, when done, bring approval from the parent. The idea is developed early that earning that approval brings a feeling of pleasure from the parent and in the child.

Now, the parent never intended that the basis for living become a substitution for a loving, affectionate relationship between him or her and the child. But even when the parent has not said it or even implied it, the "Daddy-won't-love-me-unless-I-do-what-he's-said" syndrome sets in. That causes two reactions. Some children desire to please so much that they make every effort to do what's been established as the "you-oughts" of life. Others must test every regulation and break most of them to assert independence and, really, to test the extent of the parent's love.

Now press the analogy one step further. What if the child who has kept the rules sees the other child break them or bypass them? And then what happens if the obedient child is told that the parent accepted and loved the disobedient child? "This cannot be! Everything I've done has been right. My father would not allow that! Everything that's important has been bypassed. All that I've done to please my father has been neglected. My brother must do what's required before he can expect to be loved."

I've purposely oversimplified in that analogy. The reason is that I believe there is a child inside the most sophisticated of us adults. Our sense of justice rooted in the "obey-to-please" principle, becomes our security. And it's projected onto God as a cosmic parent figure. How could God offer a relationship of love to anyone who doesn't meet the requirements I have tried to live up to all through the years?

The controversy between Paul's insistence that faith alone justifies and the Christian Pharisees' idea that God would not set aside the Law in receiving a Gentile believer, is really the parable of the prodigal son written large in a gigantic social issue. Most of the converted Pharisees did not want to exclude the Gentiles; they simply wanted them to play by the rules and keep the Law God had given them through Moses. Some of them didn't even want to require full initiation into Hebraic disciplines before a Gentile could become a Christian. But inclusion in the church was something different. The Christian Pharisees were all agreed that becoming a Jew in every sense was required for membership in the church. The requirements for a Gentile to become a proselyte to Hebraism were transferred as the absolute minimum for becoming a fellow participant in the body. The Christian Pharisees were elder brothers who not only had kept the rules, but insisted that they knew what was required by the Father to please Him.

We are getting closer to the core of the issue that gripped the church in a hammerlock of inability to reach the Gentile world. Christ was the Jewish Messiah for the Hebrew Christians. He was the assurance that God was faithful to His promises. Their basic conviction was not the idea of God's unconditional love but His faithfulness in coming in the Messiah as He said He would. And the Messiah Himself had clearly said that He came not to destroy the Law but to fulfill it. That meant the Law plus Christ as a basis of salvation.

Now we can see why Paul's preaching to the Gentiles and receiving them into full membership in the church was so shocking and abhorrent to the Pharisees' party and the Judaizers. He had to be stopped! They organized their forces for a once-and-for-all confrontation. They came from Judea with a flat and immutable contradiction to Paul's ministry: *"Unless you are circumcised according to the custom of Moses you cannot be saved"* (v. 1). It was not the physical act of circumcision alone, but the instruction in the Law and the pledge to keep it, which preceded the ritual that they had in mind. They were saying something very different about God from what Paul was saying. God's love was not unconditional. Jesus Christ was *part* of the ladder to salvation, not the *only* way!

That kind of thinking is not limited to first-century Christianity. It is around in subtle, and some blatant, forms today. We have our standards and values which others must meet in order to be accepted. And most of those standards are excellent and probably are rooted in parental and cultural conditioning. But are they conditions to our acceptance of others? When people fail to keep our rules, it's difficult for us to believe they also know *our* Christ!

As a solid, responsible Presbyterian said after hearing a witness of a new Christian whose lifestyle did not measure up to what was important in the man's code of impeccable performance, "How can that guy stand up there and say he's a Christian? He's bypassed everything I've believed important to get to his 'experience' of Christ!"

Paul knew that the harassment of the Judaizers had to be dealt with for the future of the expansion of Christianity into the Gentile world. He did not negate the Law. What he did negate was the idea that it was the basis of salvation and a requirement of the Gentile converts for being made full members in the body of Christ. Paul and Barnabas decided to go to Jerusalem to get a further decision to augment the one made in affirmation of Cornelius's conversion, filling by the Spirit, and baptism by Peter.

WHEN GOOD PEOPLE DISAGREE

[6] Now the apostles and elders came together to consider this matter. [7] And when there had been much dispute, Peter rose up

and said to them: "Men and brethren, you know that a good while ago God chose among us, that by my mouth the Gentiles should hear the word of the gospel and believe. [8] So God, who knows the heart, acknowledged them by giving them the Holy Spirit, just as He did to us, [9] and made no distinction between us and them, purifying their hearts by faith. [10] Now therefore, why do you test God by putting a yoke on the neck of the disciples which neither our fathers nor we were able to bear? [11] But we believe that through the grace of the Lord Jesus Christ we shall be saved in the same manner as they."

[12] Then all the multitude kept silent and listened to Barnabas and Paul declaring how many miracles and wonders God had worked through them among the Gentiles. [13] And after they had become silent, James answered, saying, "Men and brethren, listen to me: [14] Simon has declared how God at the first visited the Gentiles to take out of them a people for His name. [15] And with this the words of the prophets agree, just as it is written:

[16] *'After this I will return*
And will rebuild the tabernacle of David, which has fallen
down;
I will rebuild its ruins,
And I will set it up;
[17] *So that the rest of mankind may seek the* LORD,
Even all the Gentiles who are called by My name,
Says the LORD *WHO DOES ALL THESE THINGS.'*
[18] "Known to God from eternity are all His works.

[19] Therefore I judge that we should not trouble those from among the Gentiles who are turning to God, [20] but that we write to them to abstain from things polluted by idols, from sexual immorality, from things strangled, and from blood. [21] For Moses has had throughout many generations those who preach him in every city, being read in the synagogues every Sabbath."

[22] Then it pleased the apostles and elders, with the whole church, to send chosen men of their own company to Antioch with Paul and Barnabas, namely, Judas who was also named Barsabas, and Silas, leading men among the brethren.

[23] They wrote this letter by them:

The apostles, the elders, and the brethren,

To the brethren who are of the Gentiles in Antioch, Syria, and Cilicia:

Greetings.

24 Since we have heard that some who went out from us have troubled you with words, unsettling your souls, saying, "You must be circumcised and keep the law"—to whom we gave no such commandment— 25 it seemed good to us, being assembled with one accord, to send chosen men to you with our beloved Barnabas and Paul, 26 men who have risked their lives for the name of our Lord Jesus Christ. 27 We have therefore sent Judas and Silas, who will also report the same things by word of mouth. 28 For it seemed good to the Holy Spirit, and to us, to lay upon you no greater burden than these necessary things: 29 that you abstain from things offered to idols, from blood, from things strangled, and from sexual immorality. If you keep yourselves from these, you will do well.

Farewell.

—Acts 15:6–29

The Jerusalem Council was not made up of the "good guys" and the "bad guys." They were all good people, all converted to Christ, *and* all sure they were right. Have you ever been in a situation like that? The Scripture we have just read shows us that conflict between believers is not the exclusive problem of your church board . . . or of your church members . . . or of your family and friends. That kind of honesty helps us to learn from how the early church leaders worked through to the most important decision ever made for the future of the Christian movement. Here's how they did it.

1. They did not deny differences. So often we think that a sign of fellowship is that everyone agrees on everything. True fellowship is working through differences to the mind of Christ.

2. They boldly and strongly stated their differing ideas. Luke tells us in verse 7 that there was *"much dispute."* The Greek word used here, *zētéseōs,* denotes a heated debate, not just an exchange of opinions. Sometimes it is absolutely crucial to allow differences to surface before people are free to seek the Lord's will together. As one woman said in a meeting I attended, "Don't interrupt me. Let me have my say and then I'll feel better and hope we can find a solution together."

3. The people aired their feelings before the leaders spoke. Peter, Barnabas, Paul, and James spoke *after* listening to the opposition

report. They did not limit expression by a foregone conclusion established in introductory remarks. Nothing causes angry feelings and inconclusive decisions more than a leader who sand-bags the meeting with what he or she expects as the result of the discussion or debate.

4. What seemed good to the Holy Spirit and to the group at the conclusion was the basis of the decision. The Holy Spirit can use all present to communicate a better strategy than any one person can discover alone. Church government is not representative administration in the sense that officers are elected to represent the point of a faction or group within the church. They should be elected because they are the quality of people who will, with open minds, seek the mind of the Holy Spirit, and not the prescribed views of a segment of the church.

After the issue had been aired about the Gentile conversion *and* inclusion in the church by Paul and Barnabas, Peter rose and spoke. He reviewed what had happened when the Holy Spirit opened the door to the Gentiles by the blessing poured out on Cornelius and his household. It is interesting to note that the reference to a *"good while ago"* (v. 7) in the dating of the event, in the Greek indicates a significant lapse of time, as in our idiom, "in the early days."[1] This implies a lapse of as much as ten years. The previous decision of the leaders of the church had a long time to simmer. Inside the protagonists it had come to a boiling point. This helps us to understand that legislation does not always mean implementation.

The significant contribution of Peter was to call the assembly back to what the Lord did through the Holy Spirit. He gave Cornelius the gift of faith and the infilling. Then the key thrust: *"and made no distinction between us and them, purifying their hearts by faith"* (v. 8). The struggle for faith as the issue was formed. To purify by faith was the same as to purify by sacrifice. What the Gentiles were given was the gift of righteousness with God, previously understood to come only with circumcision and sacrificial oblation. Why then put a human yoke on those new Gentile Christians which not even the Hebrews had been able to live faithfully? Grace had broken into the meeting through a man who knew human frailty. In substance Peter is saying, "We Hebrews have not kept the Law ourselves; why now put it on the necks of new converts?"

The idea of the yoke in that time refers to a learning experience. Jesus had said, "Take my yoke upon you and learn of Me."

The reference is to the training yoke of oxen. One side had a smaller yoke for the young ox being trained and a larger one for the older, stronger ox. The trainee learned by keeping pace with the training ox. Perhaps Peter is saying, "Why require training in the Law when that brought us neither the peace nor power of God?" The salient concern was salvation, and the Hebrews had come no closer to that because of the Law. The grace of the Lord Jesus had saved them—not their own effort to keep the Law. Not the Law and Christ, but Christ only!

That argument brought silence and a receptive hearing of Paul and Barnabas. Once again they reasoned for the guidance of the Holy Spirit with what we called earlier, retrospective analysis. What the Spirit had done and was doing was the only way to know what He wanted to do. It was obvious that He was giving the gift of faith to Gentiles.

James, the brother of the Lord, who had risen to power in the Jerusalem church was obviously the person in charge of the meeting, for he spoke last and crystallized what he had heard the Holy Spirit saying to the group. He followed his Brother's custom of rooting what he said in the Scripture. His authority was Amos 9:11–12, the clear prediction of God's intention to call the rest of mankind to Himself: *"'Even all the Gentiles who are called by My name, says the LORD who does all these things'"* (v. 17). On the basis of that James offered a recommendation. The verb used, *kríno*, would suggest his guided, personal opinion—*èg ôkríno* "I judge" (v. 19). The spirit of his comments was then expressed in the letter that was sent out, *"It seemed good to the Holy Spirit, and to us"* (v. 28). Circumcision and the ritual requirements of the Hebrew religion should not be imposed on the Gentiles. Only an appropriate conduct after conversion should be expected. The Gentile converts should abstain from foods previously sacrificed to idols, from strangled animals which still contained blood, and from fornication. We can imagine, from our experience in group decisions, they probably started with the whole list of hundreds of the Leviticus regulations, and ended up with those they felt were absolutely required for purity of life. They also were concerned about unnecessarily offending Jews scattered in the Gentile world by a flagrant disregard for those rules which were so sacred to them. This is an excellent display of the Holy Spirit's gift of wisdom through human channels. A letter was drafted explaining this action, and a group including Paul and Barnabas was elected to distribute it to the church.

The Holy Spirit had won the struggle for faith as the only basis of salvation. Paul could hardly wait to get back to the churches in Galatia to tell the Gentiles of the victory that had been won. Later, when he learned that the Judaizers were still hassling his beloved friends, he wrote the Epistle to the Galatians. The whole epistle should be read as a part of our understanding of the momentous decision that had been made in Jerusalem.

The impact of this for our lives is undeniable. Our righteousness with God is through faith and not the compulsive fulfillment of our own idea of what He requires. This does not mean that there are no disciplines for our living of our faith. What it does mean is that faith brings us into fellowship with God, who through His indwelling Spirit then gives us the power to do what He has lovingly provided us in the Ten Commandments and in Christ's message as a chart for living. But now we live the Commandments, the great commandment to love God, ourselves, and others, and the Sermon on the Mount, not to be approved but because we already are approved. On the basis of that approval we can evaluate what behavior is best for the Lord's glory and our growth. And we do it all in the amazed awareness that He loves us right now as much as He ever will! That will take a whole life-time and all of eternity to fathom.

Thus armed, we can confront the Judaizing tendencies in our attitudes to other people. Whom have we held off from Christ or from fellowship with us because they don't measure up? What cultural or religious customs have we added to the gospel as requirements before we give people our approval? What nonbiblical standard of conduct have we blended with our own authority and used to determine whether a person is, or is not, an acceptable Christian? And what tenet of theology or precious aspect of our own experience have we used to lever people? These questions help me, and I hope you, to admit the struggle we all go through to live by faith alone as our justification with God and our evaluation of the spirituality of others. Our hope is that the Lord's unmerited grace will make us resign from the Judaizers and join Paul in reaching others with unqualified, non-judgmental love.

HARDER TO LIVE THAN DECIDE

30 So when they were sent off, they came to Antioch; and when they had gathered the multitude together, they delivered the letter. 31 When they had read it, they rejoiced over its encouragement. 32 Now Judas and Silas, themselves being

232

prophets also, exhorted and strengthened the brethren with many words. ³³ And after they had stayed there for a time, they were sent back with greetings from the brethren to the apostles.

³⁴ However, it seemed good to Silas to remain there. ³⁵ Paul and Barnabas also remained in Antioch, teaching and preaching the word of the Lord, with many others also.

³⁶ Then after some days Paul said to Barnabas, "Let us now go back and visit our brethren in every city where we have preached the word of the Lord, and see how they are doing." ³⁷ Now Barnabas was determined to take with them John called Mark. ³⁸ But Paul insisted that they should not take with them the one who had departed from them in Pamphylia, and had not gone with them to the work. ³⁹ Then the contention became so sharp that they parted from one another. And so Barnabas took Mark and sailed to Cyprus; ⁴⁰ but Paul chose Silas and departed, being commended by the brethren to the grace of God. ⁴¹ And he went through Syria and Cilicia, strengthening the churches.

—*Acts 15:30–41*

The questions we asked in the previous section, focused on the Jerusalem conference, are an accountability test. Belief and action are hard to keep together. They were for Paul, too. I have included the preparations for the second missionary journey in this chapter because they help us to see that the challenge of unconditional love is easier to meet in deciding legislation for a group than it is in our relationships with individuals.

For Paul, the triumph of Jerusalem was followed by the tragedy of his own attitudes toward Mark. The rift between him and Barnabas over Mark caused that dynamic team to split up. They were so perfectly matched by talents, temperament, and Holy Spirit gifts; each needed the other. Yet when Barnabas, in his customary forgiving, accepting, affirming nature, wanted to take Mark along on the second journey, Paul balked. The young man had not measured up before, and he probably would do no better a second time—qualified love. The Scripture is very pointed in the Greek and our English translation, telling us *"Barnabas was determined to take with them John called Mark"* (v. 37). The Greek word for "determined" is from *boúlomai,* meaning to be minded with strong purpose. This is the same root we noted in chapter 2 of Acts for the immutable, irrevocable purpose of God. Barnabas was intractable in his position. Paul was equally strong-minded. He did not want a missionary dropout along again!

The two strong wills clashed sharply, and Luke is very honest in allowing us to see the humanity of two men he admired so much. The contention over Mark became *"so sharp that they parted from one another"* (v. 39). The word translated "sharp" has the root meaning of cutting, "as with a sword or a sickle." The two missionaries who had just won a battle for faith and unqualified love for the Gentiles cut one another off and saw no recourse but to part company and go off in two directions. We wonder if Mark overheard the two great men wrangle.

We are left to think about the Lord's will in all of this matter. Did He intend for Paul and Barnabas to split up? I hardly think so. His intentional will was that they should remain together. His circumstantial will brought good out of the incident in spite of the failure of both men to agree on what to do with someone who had failed. Amazing! And yet, the Lord used the shattered pieces and used the time Mark had alone with Barnabas and then with Peter to help him grow into the mature man who wrote the first Gospel. The Lord could have accomplished that without the tragic break-up of the Paul-Barnabas team. He could have gotten Mark and Peter together for the apostle to give the young man the first-hand account of Jesus' life and message. But our Lord can use our own mistakes to weave the dark threads of failure into the tapestry to highlight by contrast the bright strands of victory.

Note in verse 34 how the Holy Spirit planned ahead: *"However, it seemed good to Silas to remain there."* Silas had come to Antioch as part of the group appointed by the Jerusalem Council to help interpret the action of the Council to the churches. We are told that he joined a man by the name of Judas and preached and built up the fellowship in the context of the new freedom afforded by the Jerusalem decision for the evangelization of the Gentiles. Then the rest of the group from Jerusalem were sent back. It did not seem right in Silas's mind to go with them. Why? Luke does not explain Silas's reasoning. What we do know is that the inner urge to stay made him available to step in and take Barnabas's place. Paul selected him and he was in the right place at the right time.

We press on now with a squint at our own feet of clay, feeling a measure of relief that two of the greatest men of history were not totally unlike ourselves. But before that gives us an excuse, we are challenged by the fact that both Paul and Barnabas moved on to their new, but separate callings. The reconciliation of the two of them, and of Paul with Mark, would come later. Unconditional love won in the end; Colossians 4:15 is evidence of that. When Paul was in prison in Rome, Mark was with him, and the great apostle commended him to the church in Colossae.

It is a challenge to realize that we don't have to wait until the end of our lives to experience reconciliations. As I've moved through this chapter of Acts, I've realized areas where I'm struggling to keep faith as my only confidence with God, and relationships where my standards for people have blocked unconditional love. What about you? The Council of Jerusalem not only changed the future of the expansion of the church. If we deal with the same issue, it will change us and our churches. And if we fail again? The Lord will use even that if we surrender it to Him with faith in His mercy!

NOTE

1. F. F. Bruce, *The Acts of the Apostles,* p. 292.

CHAPTER FIFTEEN—FREEDOM AND FLEXIBILITY IN THE SPIRIT
ACTS 16:1—18:23

Scripture Outline

Freedom and Flexibility (16:1–5)

When No Is Part of a Yes (16:6–10)

The European Beachhead in a Little Rome (16:11–40)

Turning the World Upside Down (17:1–9)

Fair-Minded Bereans (17:10–15)

To the Unknown God (17:16–34)

How the Lord Helps When We Are Discouraged (18:1–23)

In the second missionary journey we are given an excellent opportunity to observe how the Holy Spirit guides. A different Paul emerges from the victory of the Jerusalem conference and the sobering loss of Barnabas. He is both more determined than ever in his purpose, and more dependent on the Spirit's power. Therefore we can see what the Spirit can do with a humble, receptive, and ready mind. The Spirit opens and closes doors, says no to some possibilities and makes that a part of an ultimate yes. Because Paul has his purpose to communicate Christ resolutely clear and his plan to reach the Gentiles as the pivot of his surrendered will, he is open to receive the power of daily, moment-by-moment guidance.

In this chapter we will consider all of the second missionary journey. Each section of our exposition is worthy of a separate chapter. For the communicator preaching or teaching Acts, the journey may be considered as a whole or as part of a shorter survey course or series of messages, or each section of our division of the material may be used as a separate presentation. I believe the latter is preferable because of the rich resources available for exposition. The urgent question among Christians today is to discover the Spirit's guidance in their lives.

FREEDOM AND FLEXIBILITY

16:1 Then he came to Derbe and Lystra. And behold, a certain disciple was there, named Timothy, the son of a certain Jewish woman who believed, but his father was Greek. ² He was well spoken of by the brethren who were at Lystra and Iconium. ³ Paul wanted to have him go on with him. And he took him and circumcised him because of the Jews who were in that region, for they all knew that his father was Greek. ⁴ And as they went through the cities, they delivered to them the decrees to keep, which were determined by the apostles and elders at Jerusalem. ⁵ So the churches were strengthened in the faith, and increased in number daily.

—Acts 16:1-5

We have seen how the Spirit had Silas in the wings. He was able to drop everything and respond to the call to go with Paul. Note how free these early Christians were. They could be open to changes of plans because their purpose was clear. Daily guidance is given to those who are set in the ultimate will of God. Silas was ready to start off on foot with Paul to visit the Galatian churches. But the Spirit had so much more in mind than that! How He accomplished it has great impact on how He guides us today.

Paul and Silas moved north around the tip of the Mediterranean and then westward to the cities of Derbe and Lystra. You will note that the order of the cities listed in the Galatian district is reversed in the second journey. In the first they had been approached from the west instead of the east.

We can imagine the mixture of feelings in Paul when he returned to Lystra. Here he and Barnabas had just barely escaped coronation as Hermes and Zeus. There had seemed to be so little response there and the ministry ended with Paul's being stoned. But one young man and his mother were the fruit of that turbulent time of ministry. The young man's name was Timothy. His mother, Eunice (2 Tim. 1:5), was a Jew and his father was Greek. Under Paul's preaching, Timothy and his mother had received the gift of faith and had become committed disciples. We wonder if the young man was a part of that circle of disciples who stood around the bloody and beaten Paul after the stoning and prayed for him. He certainly had felt the impact of Paul's life afterward and became part of the strong church left in Lystra after the missionaries had returned to Syrian Antioch. In the interval, he had continued to grow in Christ and was ready to respond when Paul called him to join him and Silas as they pressed on to other cities. Silas had taken Barnabas's place; now here was a young man to step in and assume the role Mark had not played in Paul's life.

We feel Paul's determination to amend for his failure with Mark in his training of young Timothy. The Holy Spirit always gives us another chance!

Paul's freedom and flexibility under the guidance of the Spirit were shown by his circumcision of Timothy. Because Timothy's father was Greek, he had not been circumcised. But Paul had no need to flaunt his victory in Jerusalem by having an uncircumcised half-Jew as his traveling companion. He wanted no impediment in his ministry with the Jews whom he would meet along the way in his campaign to reach the Gentile world. Note that Paul's greatness in the Spirit was that He could fulfill regulations he no longer felt were necessary to him in order to win people for whom they were still the crucial issue. When we win a strategic battle, we are liberated from the necessity of parading that victory before those who lost. As a great communicator, Paul knew that he had to build bridges and identify with the feelings of those who were smarting under the defeat.

The circumcision of Timothy shows us something else. Paul did not disregard the Law of Moses and repeatedly in his ministry in succeeding years showed his faithfulness to customs and traditions. Though they were not required before faith or justification, they could be helpful expressions of that faith. Paul was free to be "all things to all men, that I might by all means save some" (1 Cor. 9:22). That's freedom and flexibility.

WHEN NO IS PART OF A YES

⁶ Now when they had gone through Phrygia and the region of Galatia, they were forbidden by the Holy Spirit to preach the word in Asia. ⁷ After they had come to Mysia, they tried to go into Bithynia, but the Spirit did not permit them. ⁸ So passing by Mysia, they came down to Troas. ⁹ And a vision appeared to Paul in the night. A man of Macedonia stood and pleaded with him, saying, "Come over to Macedonia

and help us." [10] Now after he had seen the vision, immediately we sought to go to Macedonia, concluding that the Lord had called us to preach the gospel to them.

—*Acts 16:6–10*

Paul's idea was to go to the Roman province of Asia, not to be confused with what we think of today as Asia. Roman Asia was the province west of Pamphylia extending over to the eastern coast of the Aegean Sea. The apostle was convinced that was the next step of strategy for reaching the Gentile world. Luke tells us that Paul and his companions were forbidden to go there. The Greek word translated "forbidden" is *kōluthéntes,* the aorist past participle of *kōlúō,* "to hinder," expressing antecedent action. It was prior to entering Asia that the Spirit guided Paul's mind, feelings, and reactions to coalesce in a decision that it was not His will and guidance to enter Asia. A door was closed.

When we are in the flow of the Spirit, He will use all our intellectual and emotional capacities to communicate the rightness or wrongness of a direction. When our purpose and long-range goals are clear, we can dare to trust our consecrated thinking and responses of our emotions. The Spirit trusts us more than we trust Him at times. Elaborate theories have been developed as to why Paul didn't go into Asia: Some say he became ill again and thought it best not to go. Others have suggested it was because he learned that the Judaizers were waiting to disturb his preaching there. Still others have conjectured an experience matching that of the Damascus Road. These theories all deny what I think Luke is trying to communicate about guidance. Paul was a Spirit-sensitized man who had no need to wring his hands and say, "Oh, I wish I knew what the Spirit is telling me to do." There was not in him any of that self-will seeking to conscript the Spirit. Paul was prayer-saturated; all of life was communication with the Spirit. He took it as a part of the Spirit-filled life that his thoughts and feelings were marshaled in service to his Lord. The problems he had had back in Antioch of Syria with Barnabas had made him all the more determined to be a man in Christ in whom His Spirit could live. For Paul, a "no" from the Lord about Asia meant it was part of a greater "yes" that was soon to be revealed. Freedom and flexibility.

When the door to Asia was shut, Paul simply continued moving on to new cities in Galatia following the mandate of his essential purpose of preaching Christ and his basic plan of reaching the Gentiles. He knew the power of guidance would be given. He did not sit on the Asian border contemplating the will of God but took the opportunity to reach the many people in the other cities of Galatia. When he and his friends approached the border of Mysia, they wanted to go northeast into the wilderness area of Bithynia. The Spirit of Jesus did not allow them. In this case the Greek verb is in the present active form. The former prohibition was given prior to their getting to Asia, whereas this guidance was given as they were at the very point of entering Bithynia. Another door was closed. From that geographical point, there was one alternative which seemed best. Surely they were not to turn back. Surely the Spirit had not brought them that far without something planned for them. They did what clear thinking suggested was best: they headed east to Troas on the Aegean coast. That thinking too is a part of guidance for a person who has surrendered his or her mind to the Lord's use.

In Troas the Lord used still another method of communicating His guidance to the apostle. A Macedonian man appeared in a dream with an urgent plea, *"Come over to Macedonia and help us"* (v. 9). When Paul awoke, he knew the last months had been for a purpose. The "no" of the Spirit did lead to a "yes" of clear direction. The Greek word used to describe the congealing of this realization is "concluding," *sumbibázontes.* The present active participle of *sumbibazō,* it means to come together, to coalesce, bind or knit together, to see the way things agree, pointing a direction. The use of the word suggests that the dream was a confirmation of a growing conviction.

The time in Troas had been an opportunity to meet a Greek who joined the three missionaries. He was undoubtedly a disciple of Christ prior to the meeting or Acts would not have missed the chance to tell us about that. What Paul brought together, I think, was the need in Macedonia that this man explained. "Is that what the Lord has been trying to say to us?" they may have wondered. The dream made that possibility a conclusion. The Greek was a physician by the name of Luke! It is at this point in Acts that the pronouns change from third person "they" to first person plural "we." Secondhand reports become eyewitness accounts. Luke became a close, trusted friend of the apostle and continued with him to the end of his life.

Reflect for a moment on the different terms used to describe the presence of the living Christ. The Holy Spirit forbade Paul and his companions to go into Asia; the Spirit didn't permit them to go into Bithynia; and the Lord was the source of the conclusion to go to Macedonia. This is not a careless interchange of designations of the deity, but an affirmation of the oneness of the Spirit, Holy Spirit, and the Lord—Immanuel continuing His ministry!

Let's recapitulate briefly what this section tells us about guidance:

1. It is discovered in the flow of the Spirit while we are being carried along in His fast-moving currents.

2. In the flow, through consistent prayer and openness expressed in complete willingness the Spirit will use our thinking, feelings, and the confluence of circumstances to make His guidance clear.

3. The Spirit has assumed the responsibility to guide us. Therefore we can accustom ourselves to recognize the hand of the Lord in everything that happens.

4. This leads to humble praise that we have been created capable of being guided rather than the arrogance to think that we have been given clairvoyance or fortune-telling abilities.

The point is that the powerful, infilling Lord is able—able to get you and me to our Troas by whatever means He decides to use. And to be in Troas with the Lord is sublimely better than to be anyplace else without Him!

Verse 11 is a bridge between the Macedonian call and the sail across the northeastern portion of the Aegean to Samothrace and Neapolis. It will be included in our next section of the sixteenth chapter, but it provides a fitting conclusion on this portion of our study of guidance. There had been times when the wind of the Spirit had seemed against Paul and his friends. He caused them to alter course as He became a headwind against the bow of their strong ideas of direction. However, when the guidance became clear to head for Europe, the wind was at their backs. The clear and decisive direction had been given. Now the wind carried them rather than resisting their wrong direction. Luke uses a Greek nautical phrase to describe the difference: *"we ran a straight course"* (v. 11), meaning that they were out ahead of the wind, with a following sea pressing their ship rapidly through the sea. Any sailor knows what a difference it makes to be carried by the wind and waves rather than going against them.

Recently, I shared in leading the worship in which my son, Scott, was married to a young woman of Irish descent. It seemed appropriate to end the service with the blessing that affirmed their Celtic heritages. The closing line expressed my deep prayer benediction for them from Saint Patrick: "And may the wind always be at your back." And that's my hope for my own life and for every person who seeks guidance from the *ruach* of the Lord. But even when He's against our bow, we know it's only so we can shift course a bit, and then we also appreciate the times when He is at our backs!

THE EUROPEAN BEACHHEAD IN A LITTLE ROME

[11] Therefore, sailing from Troas, we ran a straight course to Samothrace, and the next day came to Neapolis, [12] and from there to Philippi, which is the foremost city of that part of Macedonia, a colony. And we were staying in that city for some days. [13] And on the Sabbath day we went out of the city to the riverside, where prayer was customarily made; and we sat down and spoke to the women who met there. [14] Now a certain woman named Lydia heard us. She was a seller of purple from the city of Thyatira, who worshiped God. The Lord opened her heart to heed the things spoken by Paul. [15] And when she and her household were baptized, she begged us, saying, "If you have judged me to be faithful to the Lord, come to my house and stay." So she persuaded us.

[16] Now it happened, as we went to prayer, that a certain slave girl possessed with a spirit of divination met us, who brought her masters much profit by fortune-telling. [17] This girl followed Paul and us, and cried out, saying, "These men are the servants of the Most High God, who proclaim to us the way of salvation." [18] And this she did for many days.

But Paul, greatly annoyed, turned and said to the spirit, "I command you in the name of Jesus Christ to come out of her." And he came out that very hour. [19] But when her masters saw that their hope of profit was gone, they seized Paul and Silas and dragged them into the marketplace to the authorities.

[20] And they brought them to the magistrates, and said, "These men, being Jews, exceedingly trouble our city; [21] and they teach customs which are not lawful for us, being Romans, to receive or observe." [22] Then the multitude rose up together against them; and the magistrates tore off their clothes and commanded them to be beaten with rods. [23] And when they had laid many stripes on them, they threw them into prison, commanding the jailer to keep them securely. [24] Having received such a charge, he put them into the inner prison and fastened their feet in the stocks.

²⁵ But at midnight Paul and Silas were praying and singing hymns to God, and the prisoners were listening to them. ²⁶ Suddenly there was a great earthquake, so that the foundations of the prison were shaken; and immediately all the doors were opened and everyone's chains were loosed. ²⁷ And the keeper of the prison, awaking from sleep and seeing the prison doors open, supposing the prisoners had fled, drew his sword and was about to kill himself. ²⁸ But Paul called with a loud voice, saying, "Do yourself no harm, for we are all here."

²⁹ Then he called for a light, ran in, and fell down trembling before Paul and Silas. ³⁰ And he brought them out and said, "Sirs, what must I do to be saved?"

³¹ So they said, "Believe on the Lord Jesus Christ, and you will be saved, you and your household." ³² Then they spoke the word of the Lord to him and to all who were in his house. ³³ And he took them the same hour of the night and washed their stripes. And immediately he and all his family were baptized. ³⁴ Now when he had brought them into his house, he set food before them; and he rejoiced, having believed in God with all his household.

³⁵ And when it was day, the magistrates sent the officers, saying, "Let those men go."

³⁶ So the keeper of the prison reported these words to Paul, saying, "The magistrates have sent to let you go. Now therefore depart, and go in peace."

³⁷ But Paul said to them, "They have beaten us openly, uncondemned Romans, and have thrown us into prison. And now do they put us out secretly? No indeed! Let them come themselves and get us out."

³⁸ And the officers told these words to the magistrates, and they were afraid when they heard that they were Romans. ³⁹ Then they came and pleaded with them and brought them out, and asked them to depart from the city. ⁴⁰ So they went out of the prison and entered the house of Lydia; and when they had seen the brethren, they encouraged them and departed.

—Acts 16:11-40

I will never forget the excitement I felt when I drove my little rented car into Neapolis on the Aegean coast of northern Greece. I had the whole day ahead for a prayerful reflection of Paul's ministry in Philippi. My desire was to take the same route through the cut in the mountains from the place where Paul and his three friends landed in Macedonia and walked on to Philippi. My consideration of the strategic ministry in Philippi began as the road through the seaside cut in the mountains merged with a modern road built over the ancient Egnatian Way, the Roman highway connecting the Aegean with the Adriatic Sea. I could picture Roman chariots and marching legions as I drove along and reached the ruins of the city of ancient Philippi. How strategically Philippi was located, with the Roman road running straight through the center. Anything that happened there would reach the world. As I climbed around the ruins, locating the parts of the ancient city, I gathered my thoughts concerning the background of what was known in Paul's day as a little Rome.

The Roman colony had been occupied by veteran Roman soldiers who were sent there as colonizers. This was considered a reward for faithful service to Caesar. These distinguished legionnaires brought with them the customs, language, and ambience of Rome. A magnificent city of Roman buildings, columns, and an amphitheatre was built. The city became an outpost of Rome in Macedonia, and the citizens were given the rights and privileges they would have had living in Rome itself.

A handful of Jews also lived there and worshiped at a place of prayer by the riverbank. There was no synagogue. Since it took ten Jewish men to organize a synagogue, the number of Jews there must have been very small. Apparently Jews were not welcome in Philippi, and this may give us an indication of the subsequent anti-Semitic charges brought against Paul.

The preaching of the gospel began with the little band of women at a riverbank prayer center used by the Jewish women. One woman, Lydia, was the first convert, and she was baptized, along with her family.

Paul and his fellow missionaries were plummeted into unsolicited prominence by a slave girl with the power of soothsaying. She followed them about, shouting, *"These men are the servants of the Most High God, who proclaim to us the way of salvation"* (v. 17). She was right, but a demon-possessed fortune-teller would not have been Paul's choice for the announcement to the city of why he had come. He could discern the difference between demonic possession and the authentic, Holy Spirit gift of prophecy. The Christian evangelists were not only hassled by the Judaizers throughout their ministry; they also became the target of Satan's harassment. It would have been tragic to have Satan announce his preaching of Christ in Philippi. The evil one was working at his old tricks in seeking to capture and control events. The channel of his influence was a deranged woman, but her soothsaying powers were given honor in those days. People believed that the loss of a person's wits often meant that the mind of the gods had been placed within them and what they said was a message about the future from the gods. Luke's Greek actually means that the woman had a spirit, a python: *ōchousan pneûma púthōna.* The idea came from the god Apollo who was supposedly embodied in a snake at Delphi, also called Pytho. From that, anyone with soothsaying or ventriloquist capacities was called a pytho.

The truth of the matter, however, was that the woman was possessed by Satanic power and Paul's ministry was being disturbed by an unwanted benediction of Satan on his communication of Christ. The apostle prayed a prayer of exorcism in the name of Jesus Christ. The woman was set free of her possession and healed by the power of the Lord. What Paul did not know before, he soon found out. The woman was owned by some men who made profit from her soothsaying. Having lost their source of revenue, they had Paul and Silas arrested and brought them before the authorities of the city. They were beaten and put into prison.

It was a good thing Paul and his friend Silas did not count on lack of adversity as a sign of the guidance of the Spirit. There was no "What did I do to deserve this?" or "The Holy Spirit must have departed or this wouldn't have happened!" Rather, they went into the prison anticipating what this set of circumstances would bring in the Holy Spirit's strategy. Praise was their response, and at midnight they were singing hymns. It is a special delight to read the Psalms as a part of our devotions and wonder which ones were sung that night. I sat in the excavation of that prison room. On the wall is a plaque with the inscription, "For me to live is Christ," from Paul's letter later written to the church at Philippi. That was the basis of their "songs in the night." The Lord would intervene . . . but if not . . . "to die is gain"—the other half of Philippians 1:21. But the Lord had so much more ahead than a stop in a Roman colony in Macedonia. While Paul and Silas were singing, an earthquake struck and broke open their stocks and set them free.

Paul and Silas were ready for the blessing that came out of the difficulty. The Philippian jailer was converted, and he and his family were baptized in Christ's name as an outward sign of His new indwelling in them. Along with Lydia and the others who were introduced to Christ during the brief time Paul was there, they formed a strong church which grew. It was to these beloved friends that Paul wrote the Philippian epistle which expressed so much tender love and encouragement. The Holy Spirit had guided with courage in adversity and then an earthquake intervention which released not only Paul and Silas from prison but also the jailer. He was set free to accept Christ and become a pillar of the new church. The Roman columns of Philippi are crumbling; this pillar lives in eternity because of Paul's witness to him.

Notice how Paul once again uses his Roman citizenship to the advantage of the ministry of Christ. He knew that the word would spread from Philippi to the Roman world. His creative self-esteem in Christ would not allow the magistrate to send him off as an itinerant Jew who had exorcised a slave girl. A Roman citizen had preached Christ in their city, and they could not dismiss him summarily. Under the guidance of the Holy Spirit we are liberated to use all things to His glory. Just as He utilizes every aspect of our background in the ministry, so too we can marshal all that we have to demand respect for our message. That too is part of freedom and flexibility.

TURNING THE WORLD UPSIDE DOWN

17:1 Now when they had passed through Amphipolis and Apollonia, they came to Thessalonica, where there was a synagogue of the Jews. ² Then Paul, as his custom was, went in to them, and for three Sabbaths reasoned with them from the Scriptures, ³ explaining and demonstrating that the Christ had to suffer and rise again from the dead, and saying, "This Jesus whom I preach to you is the Christ." ⁴ And some of them were persuaded; and a great multitude of the devout Greeks, and not a few of the leading women, joined Paul and Silas.

⁵ But the Jews who were not persuaded, becoming envious, took some of the evil men from the marketplace, and gathering a mob, set all the city in an uproar and attacked the house of Jason, and sought to bring them out to the people.
⁶ But when they did not find them, they dragged Jason and some brethren to the rulers of the city, crying out, "These who have turned the world upside down have come here too.
⁷ Jason has harbored them, and these are all acting contrary to the decrees of Caesar, saying there is another king—Jesus."
⁸ And they troubled the crowd and the rulers of the city when

they heard these things. [9] So when they had taken security from Jason and the rest, they let them go.

—Acts 17:1–9

Paul, Silas, Timothy, and Luke left Philippi more convinced than ever that Christ only was their essential message. They made their way through the mountains of Macedonia along the Egnatian Way, through the cities of Amphipolis and Apollonia to the capital city of Macedonia. That is an arduous winding road through rugged mountain passes. As I drove over it, I reflected on the anticipation the four missionaries must have felt as they considered the strategic city that lay ahead. I imagine that Paul and Luke pooled their information. Luke knew that the flourishing commercial seaport city was one of the major trading and shipping centers of the world. Among the population were tough-minded, rugged southern Europeans, seamen from all over the world, and merchants known for their sharp-dealing methods. Thessalonica was a "free city" with its own constitution and magistrates called politarchs. Paul was aware that Thessalonica had a thriving population of Jews and a strong synagogue. What the Holy Spirit knew was that He had a crucial ministry ahead for the four men that would focus a message of conversion and give birth to a strong church.

After the arduous journey through the mountains, Paul and his friends entered the city with confident anticipation and began ministry in the synagogue. (Reading 1 and 2 Thessalonians along with this portion of Acts heightens what Paul said and what happened there.)

This was the place where opponents of the itinerant evangelists gave them the accolade, *"These who have turned the world upside down have come here too "*(v. 6). The news had preceded the evangelists from Philippi, but also seamen had brought the word about the Christians from Palestine and Syria, as well as wherever the followers of Jesus Christ had made their impact on the then-known world. Paul could be called one who turned the world upside down because of what he preached and the results from Thessalonica alone. In his first epistle to the Thessalonians, he says, "For from you the word of the Lord has sounded forth, not only in Macedonia and Achaia, but also in every place. Your faith toward God has gone out, so that we do not need to say anything. For they themselves declare concerning us what manner of entry we had to you, and how you turned to God from idols to serve the living and true God" (1 Thess. 1:8–9).

Paul turned the world upside down because of the people who responded and *turned* to the Lord. There are two different words used in the Greek in the Acts and the Thessalonian passages. In Acts 17:6 the word for "turned" is *anastatōsantes*, from *anastatóō*, to stir up, unsettle, or excite. In 1 Thessalonians 1:9, however, the word for "turned" is *epestrépsate*, from *epistréphō*, to turn to, or turn again, and it is in the aorist tense, indicating an immediate and decisive turn as a part of a deliberate decision. The preaching of the gospel does stir up, excite, and unsettle old values and securities demanding a decision, a turn around.

This background helps us to appreciate the radical (to the roots) kind of message Paul was led to preach. He reached the deepest needs of people in Thessalonica with the preaching of Jesus Christ as the only basis of abundant life now and eternal life forever. Acts 17:4 indicates that some of the Jews were persuaded; but a great multitude of the devout Greeks, including some of the leading women, turned around through a liberating conversion experience. The pivot of life must be turned from self-control to Christ, or there is no real beginning. Nothing is more frustrating than trying to grow in a life one has not really begun.

All that we've said about the Spirit-filled life must begin with an incisive confrontation of the real self with the living Christ. We may ease into the preparation for that, which may take years, but there has to be that point when we give as much as we know of ourselves as we know at that time of Christ as Lord. Everyone who claims to be a Christian ought to be able to point to that time, or it is still ahead. I believe this accounts for the great numbers of church people today who are claiming to have been "born again" or to have had experiences of being "baptized by the Holy Spirit." Up to that point their faith was bland or dull. Often they find their new experience difficult to explain to fellow church members and friends. What happened is that for the first time they were turned by an upset of their settled security, and at the same time were turned around by Christ from a life in their own direction to a life under the direction of His Spirit. This passage in Acts, when considered along with the Thessalonian epistles, gives the expositor a powerful opportunity to graciously confront any of his or her listeners with the absolute necessity of a U-turn conversion. Also, a church that requires a period of instruction before people join the church, even for transfers of membership, can discover and help those people who need a decisive liberation of the will to turn around.

Paul's message not only brought conversion but hostility. Again, envy among the Jews in the synagogue was the cause. They gathered a mob from the marketplace next to the docks of the port. They were the *agoraíon* from the word *agorá,* meaning marketplace. These were bartering sailors and drifters. They set the city in an uproar.

Two summers ago, as a part of my preparation for writing this commentary, I spent a prolonged period of my study time in Thessalonike (modern Thessalonica) and observed the same type of men around the docks. It was difficult to win their trust or even a conversation. I would not have wanted to be the target of an organized effort of these men to put me out of the city. But that's exactly what the Jews had in mind when they gathered the mob to assault the apostle Paul.

One of the U-turn converts of the ministry was a man named Jason. Apparently his home had become a kind of base of operations for the newly formed church. When the mob could not find Paul and his fellow missionaries, they dragged Jason and some of the other converts to the magistrates. These *politarchos* were local magistrates dependent upon cooperation with the Romans in the management of the "free city." The charge brought against Paul and his fellow workers, and secondarily against Jason for harboring them, was not only that they were upsetters of the world, but that they claimed Jesus, and not Caesar, was king. The status of Thessalonica as a "free city" would be threatened if that went on. The mob had been carefully trained by the Jews about what to say. But since they had not been able to find Paul and the others, the magistrate could dp nothing but take a security bond from Jason, thus making him responsible for the missionaries' future actions.

With that Luke's account of the ministry in Thessalonica comes to an abrupt close. Paul and Silas were secretly sent on their way by a firmly established church. But these new and beloved converts were never off the apostle's mind. That's the reason he wrote what I believe to be the first of his epistles to the new church in Thessalonica from Corinth a brief time later. The letters review Paul's essential message: the Lordship of Christ, conversion, the blessing of His Spirit, how to pray, and how to live in the spontaneity of the Spirit without quenching His inner fire.

FAIR-MINDED BEREANS

[10] Then the brethren immediately sent Paul and Silas away by night to Berea. When they arrived, they went into the synagogue of the Jews. [11] These were more fair-minded than those in Thessalonica, in that they received the word with all readiness, and searched the Scriptures daily to find out whether these things were so. [12] Therefore many of them believed, and also not a few of the Greeks, prominent women as well as men. [13] But when the Jews from Thessalonica learned that the word of God was preached by Paul at Berea, they came there also and stirred up the crowds. [14] Then immediately the brethren sent Paul away, to go to the sea; but both Silas and Timothy remained there. [15] So those who conducted Paul brought him to Athens; and receiving a command for Silas and Timothy to come to him with all speed, they departed.

—Acts 17:10–15

Sixty miles away, the Holy Spirit had a receptive city waiting, to balance for a brief time the rejection of the Jews at Thessalonica. There Paul and Silas, along with Timothy and Luke, found fair-minded people with a readiness to receive the Good News of the gospel. Luke paid them quite a compliment by using a Greek word, *eugenésteroi,* from *eugenés,* meaning "noble," "generous," "free from prejudice," or, as in the case of the NKJV, *"fair-minded."* This was expressed in a readiness to listen and search the Scriptures to see if what Paul was saying was true. The name "Berean" has meant just that ever since. We have a class in our congregation called "The Bereans," made up of young adults who display these same qualities.

The apostle's pleasant experience with the Bereans was short-lived. The envious Jewish leaders from Thessalonica dogged his steps and disrupted the receptivity. The brief respite before they came gave Paul time to collect his strength and be ready for the vigorous demands of the challenge of Athens, then the intellectual capital of the world. He went on with Luke, for the account in Athens reads as if Luke had been an eye-witness, while Timothy and Silas remained in Berea for a time and then went back to Thessalonica to strengthen the church there. It is interesting that in the cities where there was the greatest resistance, some of the strongest churches were born, a fact that frees us of the misconception that a sign of the Holy Spirit's power is ease and lack of conflict. A strong church grew in Thessalonica in adversity, whereas none was born in Berea.

TO THE UNKNOWN GOD

16 Now while Paul waited for them at Athens, his spirit was provoked within him when he saw that the city was given over to idols. 17 Therefore he reasoned in the synagogue with the Jews and with the Gentile worshipers, and in the marketplace daily with those who happened to be there. 18 Then certain Epicurean and Stoic philosophers encountered him. And some said, "What does this babbler want to say?"

Others said, "He seems to be a proclaimer of foreign gods," because he preached to them Jesus and the resurrection.

19 And they took him and brought him to the Areopagus, saying, "May we know what this new doctrine is of which you speak? 20 For you are bringing some strange things to our ears. Therefore we want to know what these things mean." 21 For all the Athenians and the foreigners who were there spent their time in nothing else but either to tell or to hear some new thing.

22 Then Paul stood in the midst of the Areopagus and said, "Men of Athens, I perceive that in all things you are very religious; 23 for as I was passing through and considering the objects of your worship, I even found an altar with this inscription:

TO THE UNKNOWN GOD.

Therefore, the One whom you worship without knowing, Him I proclaim to you: 24 God, who made the world and everything in it, since He is Lord of heaven and earth, does not dwell in temples made with hands. 25 Nor is He worshiped with men's hands, as though He needed anything, since He gives to all life, breath, and all things. 26 And He has made from one blood every nation of men to dwell on all the face of the earth, and has determined their preappointed times and the boundaries of their dwellings, 27 so that they should seek the Lord, in the hope that they might grope for Him and find Him, though He is not far from each one of us; 28 for in Him we live and move and have our being, as also some of your own poets have said, 'For we are also His offspring.'

29 Therefore, since we are the offspring of God, we ought not to think that the Divine Nature is like gold or silver or stone, something shaped by art and man's devising. 30 Truly, these

times of ignorance God overlooked, but now commands all men everywhere to repent, [31] because He has appointed a day on which He will judge the world in righteousness by the Man whom He has ordained. He has given assurance of this to all by raising Him from the dead."

[32] And when they heard of the resurrection of the dead, some mocked, while others said, "We will hear you again on this matter." [33] So Paul departed from among them.

[34] However, some men joined him and believed, among them Dionysius the Areopagite, a woman named Damaris, and others with them.

—Acts 17:16–34

In Athens, the center of culture, religion, and philosophy, Paul was not troubled by the leaders of the Jews or by Judaizers. He did, however, discover the difficulties of confronting the intellectual community with the gospel, and in particular, the Resurrection. He resisted the temptation of diluting his message. He was disturbed by the idols of the city, particularly one called *"To the Unknown God."* Though he began his ministry with the Jews and Gentile proselytes, it wasn't long before Paul caught the attention of the philosophers. His preaching in the *agora,* the marketplace, soon had the intellectual community's interest and strong reaction.

Two philosophic schools dominated the city's thought. The Epicureans asserted that happiness and pleasure were the two principal aims of a tranquil life. They believed that everything happened by chance; the gods were remote and uninvolved, so there was no need for concern or anxiety. Life was to be lived free of passion, pain, and fear of any kind. Three cardinal words focus their lifestyle: eat, drink, and be merry. The Stoics, who took their name from the Stoa Poikile (the Painted Porch), where their founder Zeno taught, could not have been more opposite. For them, all of life was determined by the gods. It had to be lived according to the laws of nature completely free of emotional involvement. The Stoics' goal was to accept nature and live in it without intensity. They were pantheistic, seeing all as an expression of their gods.

Now we can see why Paul's preaching of Jesus and the Resurrection (v. 18) caused such a stir in Athens. Their charge against him must have troubled the highly intellectually trained Paul. They called him a *"babbler"* and a *"proclaimer of foreign gods."* The word "babbler," which translates *spermológos,* meaning "seed-picker," comes from Athenian slang referring to birds which flitted about picking up seeds. That idea was applied to people who hung around the marketplace picking up scraps of information. At this time, it meant one who picked up bits of knowledge from lectures, but had no clearly developed thought of his own. It was a synonym for an undisciplined plagiarist.[1]

No accusation could have been more demeaning to Paul's intellectual integrity—except to have said that he was a proclaimer of foreign gods. For him, Jesus Christ was the revelation of the only true God, the Lord of all creation and the author of all truth.

The accusations were wide of the truth on both accounts. Paul was not a gatherer of bits of thought, but a man with one central thought. We admire his openness to the Holy Spirit to stick to his message of Jesus and the Resurrection. So often Christian intellectuals make such an effort to establish their scholarly credentials that they try to out-intellectualize the intellectuals.

Paul was brought before the Areopagus, the same court that had tried and condemned Socrates to death centuries before. Now in democratic Athens, the power of the courts was limited to being a sort of philosophic review board for the intellectual and moral quality of the city. It had the authority to control who lectured in the city and to bring any lecturer before the philosophers to pass on his credentials and content. Before the court which met on Mars Hill, Paul used the opportunity to communicate in a very dynamic way.

He began where the philosophers were. Taking the altar of the Unknown God as his metaphor and his authority, he proceeded to tell the intellectuals who this God really is: He is the Creator and source of all life—the one who guides all history and on whom all life depends. By grace He is not the object of mankind's search but the One in search of His people. He is the one in whom *"we live and move and have our being"* (v. 28). Paul exposed the extent of his classical training by quoting from one of their own poets, as he used for his own purposes a phrase from Minos's address to his father Zeus, "Thou art risen and alive for ever, for in thee we live and move and have our being." And the *"and we are also His offspring"* comes from a work of Epimenides the Cretan. Paul knew his literature!

With these references he moved on to his target—Jesus Christ in whom the living God has been revealed. Through Him the world will be judged. His authority has been validated in having been raised from the dead. Paul got as far as the Resurrection, but that was more than his hearers were willing to consider. Luke tells us that *"all the Atheneans and the foreigners who were there spent their time in nothing else but either to tell or to hear some new thing"* (v. 21). This was too new, and too specific for either the Epicureans or the Stoics. Some mocked; others put him off, saying, *"We will hear you again on this matter"* (v. 32). The brilliant, converted, and Christ-filled Pharisee was too much for them when he talked of judgment and Resurrection.

Before Paul departed, the seemingly unproductive time with the philosophers had not been without some results. Dionysius, a member of the Areopagan court, became a believer. Given the erudite and intellectual haughtiness of the court, that's not a bad average. Luke tells us that a woman by the name of Damaris also became a believer along with others in the city. All was not lost. A church began to grow from that meager beginning. Paul had not compromised his message and had been guided by the Spirit's freedom and flexibility to communicate differently to people with very different grids of resistance over their minds.

HOW THE LORD HELPS WHEN WE ARE DISCOURAGED

18:1 After these things Paul departed from Athens and went to Corinth. **2** And he found a certain Jew named Aquila, born in Pontus, who had recently come from Italy with his wife Priscilla (because Claudius had commanded all the Jews to depart from Rome); and he came to them. **3** So, because he was of the same trade, he stayed with them and worked; for by occupation they were tentmakers. **4** And he reasoned in the synagogue every Sabbath, and persuaded both Jews and Greeks.

5 When Silas and Timothy had come from Macedonia, Paul was compelled by the Spirit, and testified to the Jews that Jesus is the Christ. **6** But when they opposed him and blasphemed, he shook his garments and said to them, "Your blood be upon your own heads; I am clean. From now on I will go to the Gentiles." **7** And he departed from there and entered the house of a certain man named Justus, one who worshiped God, whose house was next door to the synagogue. **8** Then Crispus, the ruler of the synagogue, believed on the Lord with all his household. And many of the Corinthians, hearing, believed and were baptized.

9 Now the Lord spoke to Paul in the night by a vision, "Do not be afraid, but speak, and do not keep silent; 10 for I am with you, and no one will attack you to hurt you; for I have many people in this city." 11 And he continued there a year and six months, teaching the word of God among them.

12 When Gallio was proconsul of Achaia, the Jews with one accord rose up against Paul and brought him to the judgment seat, 13 saying, "This fellow persuades men to worship God contrary to the law."

14 And when Paul was about to open his mouth, Gallio said to the Jews, "If it were a matter of wrongdoing or wicked crimes, O Jews, there would be reason why I should bear with you. 15 But if it is a question of words and names and your own law, look to it yourselves; for I do not want to be a judge of such matters." 16 And he drove them from the judgment seat. 17 Then all the Greeks took Sosthenes, the ruler of the synagogue, and beat him before the judgment seat. But Gallio took no notice of these things.

18 So Paul still remained a good while. Then he took leave of the brethren and sailed for Syria, and Priscilla and Aquila were with him. He had his hair cut off at Cenchrea, for he had taken a vow. 19 And he came to Ephesus, and left them there; but he himself entered the synagogue and reasoned with the Jews. 20 When they asked him to stay a longer time with them, he did not consent, 21 but took leave of them, saying, "I must by all means keep this coming feast in Jerusalem; but I will return again to you, God willing." And he sailed from Ephesus.

22 And when he had landed at Caesarea, and gone up and greeted the church, he went down to Antioch. 23 After he had spent some time there, he departed and went over the region of Galatia and Phrygia in order, strengthening all the disciples.

—Acts 18:1–23

The account of Paul's time in Corinth is not only a record of how the Spirit ministered *through* him, but also a stirring description of how He ministered *to* him. The passage is an excellent basis for an in-depth study of the causes and cures of discouragement.

1. *A candidate for discouragement.* Paul's fifty-mile walk from Athens to Corinth must have been filled with the discouragement of so little response in the intellectual capital of the world. We gain insight into

the apostle's inner feelings when he arrived at Corinth from the second chapter of his first letter later written to the church established while he was there.

> And I, brethren, when I came to you, did not come with excellence of speech or of wisdom declaring to you the testimony of God. For I determined not to know anything among you except Jesus Christ and Him crucified. I was with you in weakness, in fear, and in much trembling. And my speech and my preaching were not with persuasive words of human wisdom, but in demonstration of the Spirit and of power, that your faith should not be in the wisdom of men but in the power of God (1 Cor. 2:1–5).

Obviously, Paul's reaction to the philosophers in Athens led him to both discouragement and a new determination. The Spirit allowed the great apostle to get in touch with his feelings. In the future he would get to the Cross and the Resurrection more directly and quickly. He would not rely on lofty words of wisdom as he had in Athens. It is difficult to establish that we are clever and at the same time communicate the crucified and risen Savior.

There was further discouragement awaiting the travel-weary apostle when he arrived in Corinth. He had been driven out of Macedonia and barely tolerated in Athens. In Corinth, he met the same hostility he had experienced before from the Jews. We sense the fuse of his patience burning very short when he exclaims, *"Your blood be upon your own heads; I am clean. From now on I will go to the Gentiles"* (v. 6).

The ambience of Corinth itself didn't help. Materialism, vice, sensualism were present at every turn. The cosmopolitan city was dominated by the Temple of Aphrodite towering over the city on the Acrocorinthus. It had one thousand consecrated prostitutes. That developed the synonym, *corinthianize,* for fornication used in that time. This "vanity fair" of the Roman world was the capital of the province of Achaia and the leading commercial city of Greece. The marketplace was a center of trading for the world's merchants from everywhere—from Africa to Syria and from Europe to Egypt—selling everything from Arabian balsam, Phoenician dates, Babylonian ivory, Egyptian papyrus, Cilician goat's hair, Lycaonian wool, to Phrygian slaves. As Paul looked around at the sensuality and crass commercialism, we are sure he wondered about strategy again in this pagan city. Indeed, the bold apostle was a candidate for discouragement.

This review of what Paul found in Corinth and what he felt in himself is a helpful parallel to identify the things that make us discouraged today. The negative attitudes of people, the sin and suffering around us, and the sheer exhaustion of working hard for the Lord are elements of a kind of Elijah complex we all experience at times. It is the "I,-even-I-only,-am-left-among-the-faithful" kind of syndrome. But the same Lord who got Elijah back on his feet was also working in His diminished apostle.

2. *The Lord's cures for discouragement.* The Lord did three things to give new strength and courage to Paul while he was at Corinth. He gave him the gift of new friends, a vision to recall him to be a visionary, and a specific, perfectly timed intervention. He does no less for us today.

First, knowing what Paul was to face in Corinth, the Lord gave him new friends who shared Christ and his avocation of tent-making. Aquila and Priscilla were Hebrew Christians who, after having been driven out of Rome by Claudius, had fled as far as Corinth. They extended hospitality to Paul and an opportunity for the release of work with his hands. In the frustration of the persistently incomplete in ministry, the Lord often gives a spiritual leader the opportunity to relax and recuperate with something to do that can be finished. But it was working with understanding friends that gave Paul a chance to rebuild his energies.

When he began to preach again, Paul's ministry in Corinth brought both tremendous response and vitriolic rejection. Crispus, the ruler of the synagogue, was converted along with his household. That crystallized the issue with the Jews, and the attack was on again. But so was the Spirit power in Paul's preaching. A large number heard and believed the apostle's straightforward presentation of the gospel. When the conflict with the Jews reached a boiling point in Corinth, the Lord gave His second cure for discouragement.

The appearance of the Lord in a vision tells us further about the apostle's condition. What the Lord said indicates what the weary missionary was going through. He was afraid, tempted not to speak in the light of the conflict, in need of a fresh encounter with Christ, and he longed for the assurance that the church would survive in Corinth. The Lord put His tender touch on the raw nerve in the apostle. What He said to him, He says to us in those times of depletion and discouragement: *"Do not be afraid, but speak, and do not keep silent; for I am with you, and no one will attack you to hurt you; for I have many people in this city"* (vv. 9–10).

This is a five-part prescription for curing discouragement:

1. A deeper love to replace a greater fear.

2. A gift of courage to replace caution.

3. An abiding Presence in alarming perplexities.

4. An unlimited help against ultimate hurts.

5. A freedom from loneliness in fellowship with Christ's friends.

That put things back into perspective for Paul. He was far too well along in the Christian life to fear the temporary things that could panic most persons. His fear was that continued success in preaching the gospel would bring further hostility. He had been beaten, imprisoned, chased out of cities, and persistently pursued by the Judaizers.

There's only one cure for that kind of fear—love. Paul had a deep need for a revival of the love relationship of acceptance and assurance that the Lord had given him each step of the way. Only love can exorcise fear. Fear is always the absence of knowing we are loved. The apostle needed to know that he was loved for who he was and not for what he was doing.

A renewal of that basic grace would replace the caution with courage. Daring to preach regardless of the danger would open Paul again to the fresh flow of power. Silence would shut off the channel. Paul was blessed as he blessed others by boldly sharing the gospel.

But he could do that only as he kept his eyes riveted on Christ and not the perplexities. Analysis of problems is perilous without a sense of the Presence. Jesus' promise to the disciples (Matt. 28:20) is reaffirmed for Paul, "I am with you." The Lord of the Damascus Road, the Tarsus quiet, the Jerusalem Council, the earthquake at Philippi was also the source of strength for Corinth.

With that assurance, nothing ultimately could hurt Paul. Notice that the Lord didn't promise freedom from further attack. What He did promise was that no one could hurt him. What did the Lord mean? Paul had further physical harm done him throughout the rest of his ministry. But it could not *hurt* him. He was safe for eternity. The difficulties would not mar that inner security between Paul and his Lord. The point is that for a time the apostle had had enough, and the Lord stepped in to assure him that he would not have to face more than he could bear.

And further, Paul was not alone. The Lord had surrounded him with a strong force of faithful people. There were Silas, Timothy, and Luke. To meet the special time of need, these three were joined by Aquila and Priscilla. Then there was Justus, who had taken his stand for Christ at the cost of losing his position of prestige. And added to all these were the new converts to Christ who would not let Him down by forsaking His apostle. The Lord was gathering His people in support of His chosen and appointed vessel.

The Lord seldom solves the problem of discouragement without using His people to remind us that we are loved by Him through them. In fact, nothing deepens fellowship more than our honest confession of need and frustration. We can imagine that Paul fostered respect and admiration more than tender feelings of wanting to comfort him. His time of vulnerability reminded him that the qualification for ministry is the willingness to be ministered to in the fellowship.

But the Lord's reference to the *"many people"* (v. 10) that He had in the city also included a strategically placed proconsul whom He would use when the leaders of the Jews further precipitated their attack on Paul. Little did Gallio know that his appointment by Rome to serve in Corinth was to be used by the Lord to save His apostle. Gallio was proconsul of Achaia for about a year from A.D. 51–52 according to an inscription from Delphi. He was the brother of Seneca, the philosopher. Since Paul was in Corinth for eighteen months, Gallio must have arrived after the apostle. Apparently the proconsul had had his previous encounters with the synagogue leaders during his time in Corinth. When Paul was brought before him and the charge was made, Gallio didn't wait to hear the apostle's defense. In fact, Luke implies that the proconsul interrupted him just as he was about to speak. If the Jews had brought a real case of wrongdoing or wicked crime, that would have been fine; but one more dispute over words was more then Gallio wanted to hear. They should decide the matter for themselves. Here was the Lord's perfectly timed intervention through a hardened Roman officer who probably wished he was back at Rome rather than in tumultuous Corinth arguing with Jewish dissidents. He washed his hands of the case and dismissed the court.

His decision and attitude unleashed hostilities other than those felt by the Jewish leaders against Paul. The Greeks of Corinth took Gallio's lead as an excuse to beat Sosthenes, the ruler of the synagogue. The act of violence was overlooked by Gallio—an unexpected twist of events. Probably the Jews did not accept Gallio's decision and remained in the judgment seat area. When the Greeks tried to clear the area, violence broke out.

Indeed, the Lord did have many people in Corinth! Even a Roman official who didn't know that he was an instrument of intervention. But that's the serendipitous way the Lord works. The decision of Gallio made it possible for Paul to remain in Corinth a *"good while"* (v. 18) longer until his work was finished. This time was probably in addition to the eighteen months mentioned in verse 11. The time in Corinth was one of the most strategic in the apostle's ministry. He preached, taught, wrote the Thessalonian epistles, and was reconfirmed in his call and relationship with the Lord. The time of discouragement was over. The freedom and flexibility of the Spirit returned.

Luke's account of the conclusion of the second missionary journey carries an insight into Paul's mind and heart when he left Corinth. We are told that he took Priscilla and Aquila with him to the port of Cenchrea to get a ship to Caesarea to go on to Jerusalem for the feast. Now Luke tells us an interesting thing: Paul had his hair cut before boarding the ship. This would have been a part of the Nazarite vow in preparation for Jerusalem. The vow had originally been a lifetime of abstinence from wine and the shaving of the head. In Paul's day it was limited to thirty days. The hair was cut and offered as part of a sacrifice at Jerusalem. If a Jew began the thirty-day period away from Jerusalem, the hair was cut and saved until he reached Jerusalem, at which time his head would be shaved.

Paul had been through a difficult time and the Lord had helped him out of his valley. In performing this Nazarite vow, he expressed his gratitude and his recommitment to his central purpose and plan, and at the same time reaffirmed rather than negated his Hebrew heritage. If he had begun the vow in Corinth it would be all the more significant as a testimony to the Jews there. That would mean that the hair cutting at Cenchrea was the completion of the thirty days. The inner man in Paul longed to be back in Jerusalem. The hostility of his fellow Jews had made him feel like an expatriate in exile from his cherished heritage. Paul wanted to go home.

When the ship stopped at Ephesus, Paul, Priscilla, and Aquila got off briefly for a visit to the city. The apostle could not stay away from the synagogue and one further opportunity to communicate Christ. The response was positive and the people wanted him to stay, but his heart was in Jerusalem. He promised to return and sailed off for Caesarea. Acts 18:22 tells us that after he landed there he went *"up and greeted the church."* I believe this refers to the church at Jerusalem. After that he returned to Antioch of Syria. We are sure that the time in Jerusalem and among his beloved friends in Antioch was healing and renewing.

There is a sense of delay in the time at Antioch. Paul's plan to return immediately to Ephesus seems to have been interrupted by something demanding his attention. It is my supposition that Timothy had returned home to Lystra and learned of the upsetting tactics of the Judaizers among the Galatian churches. That suggests that perhaps the Galatian letter was written from Antioch as an antidote to the virulent poison the Judaizers were inflicting on the churches. After that Paul could not resist going to his friends personally to strengthen them in Christ. The route for the return to Ephesus was through Galatia and Phrygia.

We have lived in the apostle's skin through propitious and perilous days. We've been with him in success and failure, delight and discouragement. And through it all, we have discovered again for ourselves that the Lord is faithful. He will not leave or forsake us. As communicators, in our own set of mixed bane and blessing, we have been reminded not to be afraid, for the Lord is with us; to speak and not be silent, regardless of the difficulties; and to count on a life full of surprising interventions which the Lord will enable through people who are being prepared right now to help us. That is the true and lasting liberation from caution or reserve and the source of a constant flow of freedom and flexibility in our life and in His Spirit.

NOTE

1. W. M. Ramsay, *Saint Paul the Traveler and the Roman Citizen* (Grand Rapids: Baker Book House, reprint 1949), p. 246.

CHAPTER SIXTEEN—INTRODUCING RELIGIOUS PEOPLE TO THE LORD
ACTS 18:24—19:7

Scripture Outline
> What Apollos Had (18:24–26a)
> What Apollos Needed and Received (18:26b–28)
> What Did You Receive When You Believed? (19:1–7)

Perhaps the greatest challenge we all face as communicators is to introduce religious people to grace and the power of the indwelling Christ. Religion is man's effort to be righteous and adequate on the basis of self-effort and to live life dependent upon self-sufficiency. It is the strenuous desire to live for the Lord rather than by His power. Our churches are filled with good, moral, respectable people. They have domesticated the gospel into a set of rules and regulations, rites and rituals, which can be accomplished with little contact with, or need for, the Lord. The church for them has become a culturally conditioned institution of cherished programs, traditions, and procedures. The result is a practical agnosticism. Daily pressures and demands are confronted as if Calvary and Pentecost had never happened.

The secret of the renewal of our churches lies in liberating religious people who don't know Christ personally. All that we long to have happen to our churches in new life, mission and evangelism, and courageous stewardship is dependent upon enabling these people to discover how to live the adventure of the abundant life.

How shall we communicate the difference between the prevalent brand of self-help religion and the abundant life? What can we say that will dramatize what happens when grace replaces humanly induced goodness and the Spirit fills the emptiness of dull churchmanship? The answers to these questions are to be found in the next powerful passage from Acts.

This passage from Acts focuses the deep need in the church in America. It also gives us a basis for speaking to it. A sensitive, empathetical exposition of what happened to Apollos and, later, to the disciples of John on the road to Ephesus enables us to affirm the qualities of religious people and then alert them to the fact that something . . . Someone . . . may be missing. This is one of the most effective vehicles for communicating to church members the power available to live the Christian life with joy and excitement.

William Penn said, "That religion cannot be right that a man is worse for having." The danger of a religion of self-effort is that it makes a person defensive against finding the authentic life in Christ which is liberated by forgiveness, motivated by His Spirit, and enabled by His power. William James was aware of this danger when he stated: "Religion is a monumental chapter in the history of human egotism." Our task is to expose the inadequacy of religion and lead people beyond its limitations. Aquila and Priscilla did that for Apollos, and Paul did it for the disciples of John. How they accomplished it gives us a marvelous opportunity to do no less for our religious listeners today.

I have taken Acts 18:24—19:7 as a unit because both Apollos and the disciples of John were part of a sect of Judaism which followed the message, teaching, and baptism of repentance of John the Baptist. They believed that Jesus was the Messiah, and they were part of a movement of preparation for the messianic age. Also, they must have known of Jesus' death and Resurrection. What was missing was an experience and realization of the profound personal meaning of His death and Resurrection, as well as His return in the power of Pentecost. These religious, ascetic followers of John the Baptist were in the same spiritual condition as the disciples of Jesus before Pentecost. Their willingness to receive new truth is commendable. The lack of defensiveness and the openness to growth are the qualities we want to emphasize as we reach out to people like them today.

WHAT APOLLOS HAD

24 Now a certain Jew named Apollos, born at Alexandria, an eloquent man and mighty in the Scriptures, came to Ephesus. 25 This man had been instructed in the way of the

Lord; and being fervent in spirit, he spoke and taught accurately the things of the Lord, though he knew only the baptism of John. [26] So he began to speak boldly in the synagogue.

—Acts 18:24–26a

Luke gives us Apollos's *vita* in a way that introduces us to a paragon of religious accomplishment. Our commendation of these qualities will diffuse the defensiveness of religious people we want to reach. Luke paints a vivid picture of a very well-qualified man who seemed to have it all together, except what was most important—an experience of the grace and power of the indwelling Lord. Note carefully the dimensions of his dossier.

1. *An educated man.* Apollos was a Jew from Alexandria. Alexander the Great had founded the city in 332 B.C. and had placed a colony of Jews there. The Hebrews had flourished and their population was one-third of the city at Apollos's time. That means that he was a Hellenist whose mind had been cultivated by the finest of Hebrew and Greek culture and thought. Alexandria was one of the three great centers of learning in the world at that time. The university and its extensive library contained the resources of Greek, Latin, and Hebrew rhetoric, philosophy, medicine, mathematics, geography, and history. It was there that the Hebrew interpretation of Scripture came under the influence of Philo and the disciplines of Platonism. The wisdom of Plato and Moses converged and flowed together.

2. *Eloquent in speech.* Apollos is described as an eloquent man. The Greek word is *lógios*, meaning both learned and eloquent in expression of that knowledge. He had a special capacity of being able to lucidly explain his thoughts in a way that captured the intellect and swayed the emotions of his listeners.

3. *Versed in Scripture.* Apollos was mighty, *dunatós*, in the use of Scripture. The Greek word is the verbal of *dúnamai*, from the same root as *dúnamis*, meaning power; thus Apollos was dynamic in his preaching of the Scriptures. He was not only versed, but vital in the way he utilized his knowledge of years of training in the intellectual atmosphere of Alexandria. He probably actualized Philo's method of allegorical interpretation, lifting from each historical account the hidden and deeper meaning. He interpreted what happened and explained the exciting implications. This, plus his impelling rhetoric, won him a hearing and following in Ephesus.

4. *Accomplished in religion.* Added to all the above, Apollos was one of the very religious disciples of John the Baptist. *"The way of the Lord"* (v. 25) suggests this. I think he was a leader of a band of John's followers in Ephesus. The thrust of the movement was preparation for the ministry of the Messiah. The baptism of repentance was in response to John's clear preaching of Isaiah, "Repent ye: for the kingdom of heaven is at hand. . . . Prepare ye the way of the Lord." In keeping with this, the followers of the Baptist observed strict rules and regulations for living. The misconception was that their impeccable asceticism would earn the blessing of the coming of the Messiah. The water baptism of John had symbolized the death to self and a new beginning of religious vigilance. John clearly had identified Jesus as the Lamb of God, and like the disciples of the Lord, Apollos had committed himself to loyalty and allegiance to Him. The scholar's learning in the Old Testament had prepared him to understand and teach the prophecies about the Messiah.

5. *Enthusiastic in Spirit.* We are told that Apollos was also fervent in Spirit. The Greek *zéōn tōi pneúmati* means that his enthusiasm boiled with excitement. *Zéōn* is from *zéō,* to boil as in water or yeast. But the enthusiasm was humanly induced from learning and training. Religious enthusiasm does not last when it is based on principles rather than the Person of the Lord. Apollos knew about Christ, but was not in personal contact with Him.

6. *An accurate teacher.* So far as he went, Apollos was accurate about the life and ministry of Jesus. However, the true meaning of Jesus' death, Resurrection, and Spirit baptism of His followers at Pentecost had not reached Alexandria and, therefore, was not a part of Apollos's experience or teaching. He knew the water baptism of repentance, but not the Spirit baptism of regeneration. Human effort, not the effusion of the Spirit of Christ, brought him close, and yet he was still so far from the abundant life.

7. *A bold man.* Luke tops off all the religious qualities of Apollos by telling us that he spoke boldly in the synagogue of Ephesus. The Greek word *parrēsía,* meaning confidence or boldness, you will remember, is a compound of words meaning to tell all. Boldness meant freedom of speech exercised without restraint. As it is used here, it means that Apollos told all that he knew and he told it with daring and fearlessness.

We can see that Apollos was a personification of religious virtues to the people around him. He was like many in our churches who believe in Christ, try to live His message, and faithfully celebrate His death and Resurrection without an intimate union with Him. It is possible to be a follower of Jesus without His enabling power. We can religiously extol His death and still justify ourselves with our own goodness and performance. And it's equally possible to enjoy Easter without the liberation that comes from death to self and personal resurrection to a new life. But most crucial of all, it is possible to be religious without Pentecost. Thousands of Christians in our churches are trying to pull it off. The way to get through to them about what they are missing is not to tell them the inadequacy of their religion, but to put the emphasis on the triumphant adequacy of the indwelling Lord as the source of power to live the Christian life with more than human effort. I am convinced that this is what Aquila and Priscilla communicated to Apollos.

WHAT APOLLOS NEEDED AND RECEIVED

When Aquila and Priscilla heard him, they took him aside and explained to him the way of God more accurately. [27] And when he desired to cross to Achaia, the brethren wrote, exhorting the disciples to receive him; and when he arrived, he greatly helped those who had believed through grace; [28] for he vigorously refuted the Jews publicly, showing from the Scriptures that Jesus is the Christ.

—*Acts 18:26b–28*

Picture the scene. Apollos has just finished a very successful preaching engagement. We can identify by thinking of one of those times when we were effective in our communication and received the applause and adulation of our listeners. We can also remember those times when an experience of triumph was followed by constructive criticism which tended to dampen our triumph. Most of us do not handle that very well. Our experience heightens our appreciation of Apollos. He was able to receive what Aquilla and Priscilla had to say. It is crucial to underline this strongly in our exposition of this passage. Our religious listeners will be given a new perception of the fact that whatever they know or however faithful they have been, there always is more to learn. The sure sign of spiritual maturity is the undefensive willingness to grow. When we extol that quality, we prepare a new benchmark for our listeners to appropriate what happened to Apollos.

After swaying the crowd, the mighty Apollos was willing to listen to two tentmakers! They approached him in such a way that he could receive what they had to say. We are sure that they affirmed his eloquence and knowledge of the Scriptures. That established the trust in which they could help him press on to what and Who was missing in his life and teaching.

We are told that Priscilla and Aquila *"took him aside"* (v. 26). I think they took him to their lodging. They did not need the recognition of the synagogue for being able to instruct the preacher nor did they wish to embarrass him in front of his enthusiastic followers. When they were alone, they shared from their own experience that the same Jesus whom Apollos had preached was alive. Surely they explained the profound fulfillment of the atonement of Calvary, the victory of Easter morning, *and* the infilling of the Spirit of the Lord at Pentecost. Jesus Christ was alive! He was not a dead hero or even a resurrected but departed Savior. He was present, and the power of His presence was not around but within the minds and hearts of His people. Apollos needed what all religious people desperately need—an experience of the substitutionary sacrifice of Calvary as the only basis of righteousness with the Lord, and an infusion of His Spirit as the only source of power to live life as He meant it to be lived. A further Pentecost happened as Apollos heard their good news. He was baptized in the power of the Spirit. Now what he had taught about Jesus became enlightened with the true meaning, and he began to live in a Spirit-gifted abundance beyond the limited level of talent.

We are left with the question, "What does it mean to explain the way of God more accurately so that religious people are free to respond?" The two tentmakers had helped Apollos to see that his ministry was self-induced and self-propelled. Their own sharing of what life was like in the flow of the Spirit's power gave him a viable example of what could happen to him. There is nothing more powerful than our own before-and-after experience of the indwelling Spirit. That, coupled with the stories of real people who have received Christ's Spirit, paints a vivid picture of what can happen to our listeners. And be sure of this: the Spirit will be working as you teach or preach. He will give the gift of readiness and openness.

What happened to Apollos when he arrived at Achaia gives us a springboard. We learn from Paul's letter to the Corinthians that

Apollos became a leader of the church there. It is significant that Luke tells us that Apollos helped those in Corinth *"who had believed through grace"* (v. 27). His own fresh experience of grace through the Spirit's enlightenment of the meaning of the Cross had cut at tap root his religious self-justification. Renewed experiences of the Lord's unmerited favor put us in touch with people's deepest needs. We become sensitive, caring, and forgiving of human inadequacy. The spirit of religious judgmentalism is replaced by acceptance and love. We don't have to establish how bad people are, but rather, how great is the Lord's transforming love.

Because the living Spirit of Christ indwelt Apollos, his impelling preaching of the gospel contained all the elements of the Lord's life, death, Resurrection, and Pentecost power. Apollos had no need to build up Apollos any longer; instead, he built up the church. He encouraged Paul's converts, watering the seed the apostle had planted, and he won new people to the Lord and the joy of the Spirit-filled life. Paul, therefore, could write, "I planted, Apollos watered, but God gave the increase" (1 Cor. 3:6).

WHAT DID YOU RECEIVE WHEN YOU BELIEVED?

19:1 And it happened, while Apollos was at Corinth, that Paul, having passed through the upper regions, came to Ephesus. And finding some disciples ² he said to them, "Did you receive the Holy Spirit when you believed?"

So they said to him, "We have not so much as heard whether there is a Holy Spirit."

³ And he said to them, "Into what then were you baptized?"

So they said, "Into John's baptism."

⁴ Then Paul said, "John indeed baptized with a baptism of repentance, saying to the people that they should believe on Him who would come after him, that is, on Christ Jesus."

⁵ When they heard this, they were baptized in the name of the Lord Jesus. ⁶ And when Paul had laid hands on them, the Holy Spirit came upon them, and they spoke with tongues and prophesied. ⁷ Now the men were about twelve in all.

—Acts 19:1–7

In this passage Luke returns to his main story-line of the ministry of the apostle Paul. He picks up his account of the apostle's third missionary journey by giving us a resume of Acts 18:23. Paul has come through Galatia and Phrygia along the higher and faster direct route, rather than the customary trade route through the Lycus and Meander valleys. A sense of urgency is implied. The apostle wanted to resume the ministry in Ephesus.

What happened in Paul's encounter with the disciples of John is essentially the same as occurred with Apollos. They were cut from the same narrow cloth. They too were followers of the Baptist's teaching about the "Coming One." But they knew only what John had taught about Jesus. He had preached Him as the Messiah and called people to repent and be baptized. What these followers of John had missed was one of the key thrusts of his teaching about what the Messiah would do. "I indeed baptize you with water; but One mightier than I is coming, whose sandal strap I am not worthy to loose. He will baptize you with the Holy Spirit and fire" (Luke 3:16). Like Apollos, these disciples did not know the meaning of the Cross and the Resurrection, or the gift of Pentecost.

Luke exposes Paul's dynamic gifts as a communicator. The apostle begins with the subject of baptism. The religious disciples of John were proud of their allegiance to John and their baptism of repentance.

Paul's question took a known idea and introduced an unknown. It was as if he said, "You are disciples of John. Your baptism of repentance is very important to you. Now allow me to ask, What happened to you when you were baptized? Did you receive the Holy Spirit when you confessed your belief in the Messiah and repented with a water baptism?"

The response to Paul's question was a confession that they had not heard of the Holy Spirit. This crucial part of John's teaching had not reached them. They had joined a religion of preparation for the Messiah but knew nothing of His return to empower those who believed in Him. By affirming his knowledge of John's life and message, Paul quickly established his credentials as one who could help them move on to further truth. He did not negate what had happened to them thus far. Rather, he pressed on to share the fulfillment of what John had really taught. The conversation is capsulized by Luke. We imagine that there was a much more complete exchange between Paul and these earnest, religious people. Again Luke shows us the same remarkable lack of defensiveness and openness to receive he cited in Apollos. As soon as they learned about the living Christ and His presence in the Holy Spirit, they wanted to be baptized anew.

The impact of this incident in Acts for our ministry to religious people is that many of them could honestly say that they have not heard whether there is a Holy Spirit, a living, present Christ. We can be sympathetic with that. Many of us had heard but did not hear; that is, we heard words about the Spirit but were either not ready or were resistant. Also, others of us did not have the advantage of having preaching and teaching that included the clear explanation of the need for, and the availability of, the indwelling Spirit. Still others may have had such an alarming explanation of the Spirit's ministry that they fear the eccentric behavior manifested in some who emphasize Him. Our task is to communicate the continuing ministry of our Lord and Savior in the Spirit in a way that will create a longing for a life filled with His strength, wisdom, fruit and gifts.

In this particular outpouring of the Spirit on the disciples of John, once again there is an outward manifestation of praise, expressed in tongues and prophecy. The faithful disciples now had reason to rejoice with uncontainable adoration. The Lord they had been taught to expect was alive and in them. Their enkindled emotions were set ablaze with expressions of thanksgiving and their enlightened intelligence spoke truth about the Lord and their new life in Him. The gift of tongues was given for adoration; the gift of prophecy for explanation. Praise and witness are sure signs of the indwelling of the Spirit.

The Apolloses and disciples of John are waiting in our congregations and classes. We cannot lead them any further than we have grown ourselves. Academic knowledge is not enough. Apollos shows us that. As communicators we need to experience "the way of God more accurately." Then we can teach and preach the whole gospel of all that Christ did and does as indwelling Lord. The result will be that religious people will experience both grace and power.

That will have a profound result in our churches. Pray for your Apolloses. Spend time with him or her or them. They are the key to renaissance. When the Lord sets them free of a religion of self-sufficiency, they will radiate a new quality of joy. Then ask them to tell their story. As they witness to the difference the indwelling Spirit has made, others will desire the quality of new life they observe. The revival of the parish will have begun!

CHAPTER SEVENTEEN—CLAIMING A CITY FOR CHRIST

ACTS 19:8—20:38

Scripture Outline

The Test of a Great Ministry (19:8–10)

The Power of the Name (19:11–20)

A Long–Range Purpose and Short–Range Goals (19:21–22)

A Victorious Gospel Meets Vested Interests (19:23–41)

Love for the Churches (20:1–16)

Realizing Our Full Potential (20:17–38)

A thoughtful exposition of Paul's ministry in Ephesus is a recall to personal evangelism and social responsibility in the cities where the Lord has deployed us. We cannot preach and teach Christ with any authenticity without also confronting the social and economic problems that debilitate people in our cities. Paul did both in Ephesus. We can do no less where we live.

When we study the background on the city of Ephesus where Paul spent three years (Acts 20:31), we are denied the luxury of thinking that the problems of our city are unique or that preaching Christ where we are is more difficult than at any other time or place in history. Paul's faithfulness to Christ in Ephesus reminds me of the Lord's challenge through Jeremiah to the exiled Israelites in Babylonia. "But seek the welfare of the city where I have sent you into exile, and pray to the Lord on its behalf, for in its welfare you will find your welfare" (Jer. 29:7, RSV). That's exactly what Paul did in Ephesus under trying circumstances and humanly impossible odds. And yet, three years of teaching, preaching, working miracles, and building up a strong church of thoroughly converted, Christ-filled believers, resulted in Ephesus becoming a Christian stronghold and a strategic center for the future expansion of Christianity.

Ephesus was called the "treasure house of Asia." It was located at the mouth of the Cayster River and commanded the trade into the river valley of the rich province of Asia Minor. Known as the marketplace of the area, it became a prosperous center of commerce, trade, and political power. Ephesus became an "assize town" because the Roman governor tried cases there. He also introduced the grandeur and pageantry of Rome. The Roman theater there seated 25,000 people and hosted the Pan-Ionian Games.

I have visited the ruins of the ancient city of Ephesus in my travels in what is now modern Turkey. Walking around the excavated remains of the architectural glory of the city, I felt the magnificent grandeur of the human accomplishment that once flourished there. But a closer look also reveals the voluptuous sensuality that dominated the city. For example, centuries have not totally eroded the carving of an arrow on one of the stone blocks of the street to show the way to one of the many brothels in the metropolis. Ephesus was filled with superstition, sorcery, spiritualism, and sophistry.

The ancient city was very proud of the opulent Temple of Artemis, one of the seven wonders of the then-known world. One hundred and twenty-seven Parian marble pillars inlaid with precious jewels and gold surrounded its exterior. It was 425 feet long, 220 feet wide and 60 feet high. The pride of Ephesus was kept inside. Placed on an altar carved by the famous Greek sculptor Praxiteles was a black, multi-breasted image of Artemis which was supposed to have fallen from the heavens. It was the symbol of fertility and prosperity for the Ephesians. Ritual prostitution flourished in the temple.

The silversmiths of Ephesus capitalized on the worship of Artemis by making miniature silver shrines of the image for sale in the city and around the world. This became one of the leading trades and a source of great wealth for the city.

Ephesus was also a gathering place for merchants, magic workers, and astrologers, as well as criminals of all types. Every imaginable sort of social misfit made his way there. There was a strange custom—if such persons could reach the precincts of the Temple of Artemis, they were given asylum in the city.

THE TEST OF A GREAT MINISTRY

8 And he went into the synagogue and spoke boldly for three months, reasoning and persuading concerning the things of the kingdom of God. 9 But when some were hardened and

did not believe, but spoke evil of the Way before the multitude, he departed from them and withdrew the disciples, reasoning daily in the school of Tyrannus. [10] And this continued for two years, so that all who dwelt in Asia heard the word of the Lord Jesus, both Jews and Greeks.

—Acts 19:8–10

The test of any ministry is what happens through the people to whom we minister. Luke tells us that as a result of Paul's proclamation of the kingdom of God, all who dwelt in Asia heard the word of the Lord Jesus Christ, both Jews and Greeks. That's quite an accolade for a short time of teaching in the synagogue and two years of daily meetings in the lecture hall of the philosopher Tyrannus. Research reveals that Paul probably was given use of the hall when it was not being used by the philosopher, the hours of 11:00 A.M. to 4:00 P.M. These are the hours of rest when all work in the city stopped—five hours a day when most people would be free to listen leisurely. These few hours each day for two years produced a movement that reached the entire province of Asia Minor!

We are sure that Paul was disappointed once again when he was put out of the synagogue because of the hardness of the hearts of the Jews. But the closed door again led to an open door of opportunity. The hall of Tyrannus was a perfectly suited, natural place to reach the inquiring Greeks who would be interested in a new philosophy. But Paul gave them more than a new set of ideas. He preached Christ and the kingdom of God. Inherent in the proclamation of the kingdom was the Lord's rule over all of life. The theme of the kingdom of God, coupled with the lordship of Christ, produces a responsibility in those who respond. It makes them aware that they have the obligation to claim the realm for the true King—Jesus.

The joy of the new converts must have been contagious. Wherever they went they told about what had happened to them. Paul could not have reached the whole province in two years even if he had walked the length and breadth of the area talking to everyone he met. Instead he preached daily, and those who were won to Christ multiplied his ministry. The people who became Christians did the rest. They could not stop talking about what had happened to them. All of Asia Minor heard about Christ through them. The successful communicator can judge his or her effectiveness not only in what happens to those who listen, but through them in the reproduction of their faith in others. There is no greater joy than to meet our spiritual grandchildren—those who have met the Savior through those whom we've introduced to Him.

THE POWER OF THE NAME

[11] Now God worked unusual miracles by the hands of Paul, [12] so that even handkerchiefs or aprons were brought from his body to the sick, and the diseases left them and the evil spirits went out of them. [13] Then some of the itinerant Jewish exorcists took it upon themselves to call the name of the Lord Jesus over those who had evil spirits, saying, "We exorcise you by the Jesus whom Paul preaches." [14] Also there were seven sons of Sceva, a Jewish chief priest, who did so.

[15] And the evil spirit answered and said, "Jesus I know, and Paul I know; but who are you?"

[16] Then the man in whom the evil spirit was leaped on them, overpowered them, and prevailed against them, so that they fled out of that house naked and wounded. [17] This became known both to all Jews and Greeks dwelling in Ephesus; and fear fell on them all, and the name of the Lord Jesus was magnified. [18] And many who had believed came confessing and telling their deeds. [19] Also, many of those who had practiced magic brought their books together and burned them in the sight of all. And they counted up the value of them, and it totaled fifty thousand pieces of silver. [20] So the word of the Lord grew mightily and prevailed.

—Acts 19:11–20

There is no limit to what can happen when we base our entire ministry on the power of the name of Jesus. The "name" carries with it the authority, power, and will of the person designated. When we minister, preach, pray, and confront the forces of evil in the name of Jesus, we are assured that He will be present to release the same wonders we witness in the Gospels during His incarnate ministry.

Paul's ministry in Ephesus was marked by many miracles done through the name of Jesus. The power at work through the apostle was so great that the Ephesians actually believed that the handkerchiefs and aprons he wore working at a trade would have his power. Superstition? Perhaps. But the Lord condescended to meet people's need because of Paul's clear preaching of the power of the name of Jesus. Paul's sweatbands and artisan apron were not powerful in themselves. It was because people had heard the apostle's message and witnessed the Lord's miracles through him they they believed an article from him would be efficacious. The evil spirits could not resist the name of Jesus and the simple faith of those who trusted, however primitive their method was. The point is that the Holy Spirit was moving mightily in Ephesus, confronting the entrenched evil of the city. When the power of the Name is proclaimed He does miracles.

This shows us how the Lord takes people where they are. At this time there was a belief in the spiritual power of articles fashioned in the image of a god or blessed in its shrine. These were called *grammata.* The Lord blessed the prayers of people who held articles of Paul's clothing because He knew of the apostle's faithfulness to point away from himself to the source of his power in the name of Jesus Christ.

But the demonstration of that kind of power usually attracts the counterfeit. Itinerant Jewish exorcists roamed the world at the time offering to rid people of evil spirits. Sadly, the profession had become a source of revenue for the exorcists. Superstitious Ephesians attracted many of these would-be liberators of possessed people. When they saw the miracles of Paul's ministry, they tried to emulate his power by using the name of Jesus. The seven sons of a priest named Sceva sought to use Jesus' name without personal belief in Him. They tried to exorcise evil spirits by saying, *"We adjure you by the Jesus whom Paul preaches."* To that secondhand pretense of power the evil spirit responded, *"Jesus I know, and Paul I know; but who are you?"* Evil cannot cast out evil. The evil spirit recognized the self-serving exploitation engaged in by the sons of Sceva. Only a person in whom Jesus lives has the power to use His name in prayer and healing.

Confronting evil without the only name which is greater than it, is dangerous. What happened to the sons of Sceva is evidence of that. A possessed man with whom they had tried to use their counterfeited formula for exorcism turned on them and beat them badly. They fled naked and wounded.

The exposure of the difference between magic and miracles had a profound impact on the entire city. It caused a moral reform. A creative awe and wonder came upon those who had believed in Christ. They *"came confessing and telling their deeds"* (v. 20). That's fascinating. Those who had become Christians now confessed their false dependence on magic. They brought their magic books, horoscopes, cult manuals, and occult literature and burned them in a public display of their total dependence on the name of Jesus. The clear preaching of the Name brings confession, repentance, and a radical change of lifestyle.

We are challenged to think about what that means for our contemporary ministry. What are the things in which our people put their trust even after conversion to Christ? Money, possessions, persons, human capabilities. But note that it was those who believed in Christ through Paul's ministry who participated in the moral reform. Often we preach reform before we have helped people begin the new life in Christ. We become moralistic without introducing people to the power to make the necessary changes. Often our standards of required behavior are heard so loudly that people can't hear what we are saying about Christ. They are put off and miss the only power that can help them change. Behavior change follows belief in Christ.

That was Paul's method in Ephesus. He introduced people to Christ knowing that once He took up residence in a new believer, His reform would begin in them and continue throughout their lifetime.

We can depend on the Lord to augment our communication with an outward sign of its source of power. The changed lives of the people we've introduced to Him will alarm others with their own need. We will be given a hearing not because of our learning or eloquence, but because of what's happened to people around us.

A visitor made a telling comment after a worship service recently. "I came here this morning because of what I see happening in the life of a good friend of mine who is a member of your church. He's been one of the most negative, angry people I've ever known. But something's going on in his life. He's changed completely. He's become a caring, generous man. He tells me the difference is in receiving Christ's indwelling Spirit. I just had to come see what was going on in his church that caused this transformation." This visitor eventually became a Christian and joined the church.

Lifestyle speaks as loudly as our words. A congregation has a corporate thrust of evangelism that either affirms or negates its message. The quality of inclusive love in a congregation must also be expressed in tangible programs of ministry to the social ills in a community. There is nothing more powerful than a local church that preaches and teaches the power of Christ and is also involved in a ministry to the poor, the troubled, and the socially disadvantaged.

Ephesus had its own brand of belief in magic; we have ours today. The magic of money dominates many of us. When people receive Christ's Spirit, He confronts this false god in our lives. In the context of His love we are able to grapple with the biblical guide of the tithe in our giving. Money is released for the work of ministry through the mission of the congregation. A new congruity of message and mission gives authenticity to the total life of the congregation.

This happened in the life of a man who watched our television ministry and was attracted to our church in Holywood. Through attending the worship services, he committed his life to Christ and received His Spirit. Eventually his love of money as the meaning of his life was brought into sharp focus. He began to grow as a believer when he started tithing his immense income. In the past few years, his giving has won him the privilege of sharing his faith with other believers. Not only has his giving made possible a great advance in the work of the church, it has also confronted others with their need to admit their false loyalty to money as their source of security.

Preaching and teaching in the power of the name of Christ will produce results. People will be changed. Then we can introduce them to the adventure of the kingdom of God. Allowing Christ to rule in all areas of life will expose attitudes and values that contradict the gospel. Then changed people can band together to claim the power of the name to change their homes, places of work, and communities.

A LONG-RANGE PURPOSE AND SHORT-RANGE GOALS

21 When these things were accomplished, Paul purposed in the Spirit, when he had passed through Macedonia and Achaia, to go to Jerusalem, saying, "After I have been there, I must also see Rome." 22 So he sent into Macedonia two of those who ministered to him, Timothy and Erastus, but he himself stayed in Asia for a time.

—Acts 19:21–22

Luke's description of the ministry in Ephesus is interrupted briefly to set the stage for the final chapters of Paul's life. At the height of the success of the ministry in Ephesus, Paul's mind is guided by the Spirit to grasp a conviction which was to become the driving compulsion of his life. "I must see Rome!" The apostle longed to communicate the gospel in the center of military might and political power. He had observed the far-flung Roman roads which reached like fingers around the then-known world. They provided Roman legions and merchantmen routes of travel to the frontiers of civilization. Rome had to be captured for Christ!

This passage changes us to think about what great convictions are gripping us. What is our long-range goal, and what short-range goals will move us forward toward it? Our purpose is communicating Christ. The Lord will make clear where and when He wants us to do that. We are not meant to drift from one challenge to another without a clear destination. Life passes quickly. Without Spirit-inspired goals we tend to luxuriate in the progress we have made. Paul could have spent the rest of his ministry in Ephesus thinking that the blessing of the Spirit on his efforts there was confirmation of the Spirit for him to live out all his days in that city.

Our exposition of this portion of Luke's chronology of Paul's life provides an excellent basis for helping people seek the Spirit's guidance in their personal goals. The Spirit transforms our wants to desire what He has planned for us. Our obedience, multiplied by the guidance of the Spirit, will equal our particular Rome.

When we know where we are going, we can endure what seem to be delays along the way. They are all part of the Lord's strategy. Paul knew that Rome was his destination. Since the Lord Himself had made that clear, he felt urgency but he was not rushed. He remained in Ephesus for a time. During that period he wrote his epistles to the Corinthians and was on hand to help the church face the attack of the silversmiths. Often the Lord clarifies the next step and then we must wait for clear orders about when to take it.

Our ultimate destination is heaven. And on the way there is a special assignment each of us is singled out to do. For us it may be in our Ephesus or in some clearly assigned Rome. When we accept an essential calling to be communicators of the Lord's grace and power, He will deploy us in that particular place which no one else can fill. If we ask Him, He will make the where and when perfectly clear.

A VICTORIOUS GOSPEL MEETS VESTED INTERESTS

23 And about that time there arose a great commotion about the Way. 24 For a certain man named Demetrius, a silversmith, who made silver shrines of Diana, brought no small profit to the craftsmen. 25 He called them together with the workers of similar occupation, and said: "Men, you know that we have our prosperity by this trade. 26 Moreover you see and hear that not only at Ephesus, but throughout almost all Asia, this Paul has persuaded and turned away many people, saying that they are not gods which are made with hands. 27 So not only is this trade of ours in danger of falling into disrepute,

but also the temple of the great goddess Diana may be despised and her magnificence destroyed, whom all Asia and the world worship."

[28] Now when they heard this, they were full of wrath and cried out, saying, "Great is Diana of the Ephesians!" [29] So the whole city was filled with confusion, and rushed into the theater with one accord, having seized Gaius and Aristarchus, Macedonians, Paul's travel companions. [30] And when Paul wanted to go in to the people, the disciples would not allow him. [31] Then some of the officials of Asia, who were his friends, sent to him pleading that he would not venture into the theater. [32] Some therefore cried one thing and some another, for the assembly was confused, and most of them did not know why they had come together. [33] And they drew Alexander out of the multitude, the Jews putting him forward. And Alexander motioned with his hand, and wanted to make his defense to the people. [34] But when they found out that he was a Jew, all with one voice cried out for about two hours, "Great is Diana of the Ephesians!"

[35] And when the city clerk had quieted the crowd, he said: "Men of Ephesus, what man is there who does not know that the city of the Ephesians is temple guardian of the great goddess Diana, and of the image which fell down from Zeus? [36] Therefore, since these things cannot be denied, you ought to be quiet and do nothing rashly. [37] For you have brought these men here who are neither robbers of temples nor blasphemers of your goddess. [38] Therefore, if Demetrius and his fellow craftsmen have a case against anyone, the courts are open and there are proconsuls. Let them bring charges against one another. [39] But if you have any other inquiry to make, it shall be determined in the lawful assembly. [40] For we are in danger of being called in question for today's uproar, there being no reason which we may give to account for this disorderly gathering." [41] And when he had said these things, he dismissed the assembly.

—*Acts 19:23–41*

It is significant that Luke uses the name "the Way" when he describes the confrontation of the Christians with the vested interests of the silversmiths. Christianity *is* a way of life. Following Christ, the Way, frees us of dependence on false, diminutive gods of our culture and provides us with an ethical resoluteness that disturbs practices that contradict the kingdom of God.

That's exactly what happened in Ephesus. The moral reformation of the Way cut to the core of the silver shrine business. Believing in Christ and being filled with His Spirit made silver shrines of Artemis totally unnecessary. These diminutive images of Artemis were carefully crafted by the silversmiths and sold at great profit. The more Ephesians who became followers of the Way, the less shrines were sold. But added to that, each May there was a great gathering of people from all over Asia Minor. They came to Ephesus for a month-long religious celebration in honor of Artemis. I suspect that it was during that time that the silversmiths realized the threat the followers of the Way were to their business. Sales fell off. Their pocketbooks were pinched and they cried out in angry protest. A "trial" was arranged against the Way in the great Roman theater. Two of Paul's associates, Gaius and Aristarchus, were dragged before the assembly of irate silversmiths.

Demetrius was the spokesman of the silversmiths. His charges against the Christians were inflammatory. He incited the silversmiths with the dangers of economic disaster and the eventual demise of the worship of Artemis (also called Diana). The content of his accusations reveals the content of Paul's preaching. Paul had flatly told people of the impotence of the false god and any image that represented it. Reminding the silversmiths of this agitated them into an angry mob.

Paul wanted to go to the assistance of his friends but was dissuaded by two groups. The disciples of Christ in the Ephesian church saw that the apostle's life was in jeopardy. The second group concerned for his safety was called *officials of Asia*. This tells us a great deal about the extent of the success of Paul's preaching. These officials were called "Asiarchs," a title given to leading citizens who were elected annually by Rome to oversee the perpetuation of the cult of emperor worship throughout the cities of the province of Asia.

Once again, Luke astounds us with an understatement and provides the expositor with fertile ground to plow. Paul undoubtedly had reached these officials with the power of the gospel. Why else would they be concerned about the life of an itinerant preacher? If, on the other hand, we reason that they were simply cautioning a Roman citizen of the danger because it was their duty as representatives of Rome, we still have the evidence that they were impressed with Paul and his message. Don't forget that his preaching against false gods also would have threatened emperor worship. The weight of the evidence is that these officials had either been won to Christ or were sympathetic. The Lord had prepared them to step in to warn Paul at just the right moment.

The fervor of the disgruntled silversmiths continued to grow in the theater. A man named Alexander was pushed forward by the Jews. The plot thickens. Who was this Alexander and why would the Jews want to make him the target of the silversmith's rage? That Luke knew his name may indicate that he was a Jewish convert to Christianity. Perhaps the Jews wanted to punish him for his defection and thereby keep the blame on the Christians rather than on the Jewish community, which also stubbornly held to monotheism and was equally opposed to the worship of Artemis. The tactic didn't work. When Alexander was recognized as a Jew, the crowd would not listen to him. Instead the silversmiths began chanting, *"Great is Artemis of the Ephesians!"* which they prolonged for two hours.

The town clerk was the Lord's agent to quiet the crowd. This man, who would have been the Roman proconsul of Asia Minor, ruled that the mob had no power to try the Christians. He reasoned with the crowd with the cool discernment of an uninvolved Roman official. Note the progression of his thought. There was no reason to chant about Diana-Artemis; everyone in Ephesus knew about the goddess and her origins. And those being accused had not committed any crime. They had neither robbed nor blasphemed the temple—the only charges that could legally have been leveled. But most important, there were courts for such trials. If Demetrius and the silversmiths had a legitimate charge, they should follow the due process established by Rome. With that the proconsul dismissed the assembly. He had performed the same function for the Christians at Ephesus that Gallio had performed for Paul in Corinth.

A further word about Demetrius. The apostle John, in his third epistle to the Christians in Asia Minor, mentions a Demetrius. Could it have been the same Demetrius? Knowing the prominent place Demetrius had held as leader of the silversmiths, if John meant another man by the same name, would it not be likely that he would have distinguished him? My supposition is that John is commending Demetrius for his witness because of lingering questions about his conversion. "Demetrius has a *good* testimony from all, and from the truth itself" (3 John 12). It is not beyond possibility that after that day of defeat in the Roman theater Demetrius came in contact with Paul and became a Christian.

Paul was kept out of the theater, but I doubt that he would have been kept from sharing Christ's love with Demetrius.

The gospel had captured a city. The strategic center was penetrated with the Spirit of Christ. Superstition, sorcery, and sophistry were exposed as inadequate sources of confidence. The preaching of Christ crucified, risen, and present in power had made inroads into a city gripped by materialism and cults of every imaginable kind. The "treasure house of Asia" now had real treasure for the first time. And the treasure of Christ's Spirit resided in the earthen vessels of very unlikely people called the followers of the Way!

LOVE FOR THE CHURCHES

20:1 After the uproar had ceased, Paul called the disciples to himself, embraced them, and departed to go to Macedonia. [2] Now when he had gone over that region and encouraged them with many words, he came to Greece [3] and stayed three months. And when the Jews plotted against him as he was about to sail to Syria, he decided to return through Macedonia. [4] And Sopater of Berea accompanied him to Asia—also Aristarchus and Secundus of the Thessalonians, and Gaius of Derbe, and Timothy, and Tychicus and Trophimus of Asia. [5] These men, going ahead, waited for us at Troas. [6] But we sailed away from Philippi after the Days of Unleavened Bread, and in five days joined them at Troas, where we stayed seven days.

[7] Now on the first day of the week, when the disciples came together to break bread, Paul, ready to depart the next day, spoke to them and continued his message until midnight. [8] There were many lamps in the upper room where they were gathered together. [9] And in a window sat a certain young man named Eutychus, who was sinking into a deep sleep. He was overcome by sleep; and as Paul continued speaking, he fell down from the third story and was taken up dead. [10] But Paul went down, fell on him, and embracing him said, "Do not trouble yourselves, for his life is in him." [11] Now when he had come up, had broken bread and eaten, and talked a long while, even till daybreak, he departed. [12] And they brought the young man in alive, and they were not a little comforted.

[13] Then we went ahead to the ship and sailed to Assos, there intending to take Paul on board; for so he had given orders, intending himself to go on foot. [14] And when he met us at Assos, we took him on board and came to Mitylene. [15] We sailed from there, and the next day came opposite

Chios. The following day we arrived at Samos and stayed at Trogyllium. The next day we came to Miletus. [16] For Paul had decided to sail past Ephesus, so that he would not have to spend time in Asia; for he was hurrying to be at Jerusalem, if possible, on the Day of Pentecost.

—Acts 20:1–16

We are tempted to skip over this next section of chapter 20. Looking ahead, we know that Paul completed his ministry in building a strong church in Ephesus with his parting message to the elders at the meeting at Miletus (Acts 20:17–38). No exposition of the Ephesian ministry is complete without that as a conclusion.

However, Acts 20:1–16 maintains the chronology of Paul's third missionary journey. This was also a very important and productive time in his ministry. Checking corollary references in the epistles, we discover that some of his most refined theological dissertations which have blessed Christians through the ages were written during this period.

Acts 20:1 sets the theme for this brief passage. It shows us the profound love Paul had for his newly won converts to Christ. He called the disciples to him before departing for Macedonia. The scene is a tender one, dramatizing the love they shared together in the bond of Christ.

The rest of this section is so much more than a travelogue. The same love Paul felt for his new friends in Ephesus pressed him on to strengthen believers in churches he had started. His route took him to Macedonia. There he wrote Second Corinthians (2 Cor. 8:1; 9:2–4). The energetic mind of the apostle was focused on the needs of new Christians who needed encouragement, affirmation, and loving correction. Amazing—while visiting the Macedonian churches of Philippi, Thessalonica, and Berea, his concern pressed on ahead to Corinth. When he arrived there, he encouraged the church and found time to write the Epistle to the Romans, his most comprehensive statement of the gospel. How fortunate we are that he was given the vision to go to Rome and that his letter to the Christians there has been preserved as part of sacred Scripture.

When Paul planned to return to Jerusalem by way of the sea, a plot against his life was discovered. This prompted a change in plans to go overland back through Macedonia.

Verses 4 through 6 seem to have little to offer the expositor. But a further look unearths some pure gold. The list of names not only shows the growth of a band of strong leaders around the apostle, but also indicates the mutual caring of the churches represented by them. It has been suggested that the reason Luke listed them here is that these men were all delegates from their churches to bring monetary and spiritual help to the distressed church in Jerusalem. They were carrying the offering! We are impressed with the fact of their unity. And we are also challenged by the fact that in each place Paul preached and ministered, he developed strong leaders whom he discipled.

The account of the healing of Eutychus in verses 7–12 shows Luke the physician reporting on still another evidence of the power of Christ over sickness and death. The account also has a touch of the beloved physician's humor. We wish we could assure our listeners of the same prognosis when they fall asleep during our preaching or teaching. Our concern is that they may fall out of the fellowship, not a window!

As we read this account of Eutychus, we are reminded of the humanness of the early Christians. We are tempted to imagine that no one could have fallen asleep while the apostle Paul was preaching. This sensitive, human touch by Luke provided the vehicle for revealing that the same Lord who had brought Paul back to life after the stoning at Lystra was now at work in him. Luke could not resist the opportunity to add that miracle to his account.

Paul's band of followers went on from Troas to Assos. The sea voyage took longer so the apostle took the shorter route on foot. This gave him more time with the believers at Troas. Why else would Luke go into the details of how Paul and his friends proceeded to Assos differently? Luke paints a picture of a mighty missionary pulled on to new challenges, but always reluctant to leave his beloved friends in Christ behind. At Assos Paul joined the others on ship and sailed to Mitylene on the island of Lesbos. From there they proceeded to Chios and then on to Samos where they stayed at Trogyllium. The next day brought them to Miletus, thirty miles from Ephesus.

Again we feel Paul's deep love and concern for people. He had planned to sail past Ephesus in order to reach Jerusalem by Pentecost. His longing for his friends at Ephesus and his desire to further build up the church there prompted his pastor's heart to overcome his schedule. He called for the elders of the church for still another affirmation of Christ's power in their lives and leadership. Paul knew two realities: the danger the church faced and the sufficiency of the living Christ to meet those dangers.

REALIZING OUR FULL POTENTIAL

[17] From Miletus he sent to Ephesus and called for the elders of the church. [18] And when they had come to him, he said to them: "You know, from the first day that I came to Asia, in what manner I always lived among you, [19] serving the Lord with all humility, with many tears and trials which happened to me by the plotting of the Jews; [20] how I kept back nothing that was helpful, but proclaimed it to you, and taught you publicly and from house to house, [21] testifying to Jews, and also to Greeks, repentance toward God and faith toward our Lord Jesus Christ. [22] And see, now I go bound in the spirit to Jerusalem, not knowing the things that will happen to me there, [23] except that the Holy Spirit testifies in every city, saying that chains and tribulations await me. [24] But none of these things move me; nor do I count my life dear to myself, so that I may finish my race with joy, and the ministry which I received from the Lord Jesus, to testify to the gospel of the grace of God.

[25] "And indeed, now I know that you all, among whom I have gone preaching the kingdom of God, will see my face no more. [26] Therefore I testify to you this day that I am innocent of the blood of all men. [27] For I have not shunned to declare to you the whole counsel of God. [28] Therefore take heed to yourselves and to all the flock, among which the Holy Spirit has made you overseers, to shepherd the church of God which He purchased with His own blood. [29] For I know this, that after my departure savage wolves will come in among you, not sparing the flock. [30] Also from among yourselves men will rise up, speaking perverse things, to draw away the disciples after themselves. [31] Therefore watch, and remember that for three years I did not cease to warn everyone night and day with tears.

[32] "So now, brethren, I commend you to God and to the word of His grace, which is able to build you up and give you an inheritance among all those who are sanctified. [33] I have coveted no one's silver or gold or apparel. [34] Yes, you yourselves know that these hands have provided for my necessities, and for those who were with me. [35] I have shown you in every way, by laboring like this, that you must support the weak. And remember the words of the Lord Jesus, that He said, 'It is more blessed to give than to receive.'"

36 And when he had said these things, he knelt down and prayed with them all. 37 Then they all wept freely, and fell on Paul's neck and kissed him, 38 sorrowing most of all for the words which he spoke, that they would see his face no more. And they accompanied him to the ship.

—Acts 20:17–38

The Lord's will is that we become all that He intended us to be. His grace is for our growth. We have been programmed for greatness. Sanctification means growth in holiness. That's a word we use far too little, and it needs to be reclaimed. Holiness is belonging to the Lord and being remade in His image. The word "saint" also has its root in the word "holy." It means to be set apart, called, chosen, belonging to the Lord. His purpose for us is that we grow intellectually, emotionally, and volitionally. We are meant to be grown-up saints!

A boy in our Sunday school in Hollywood had learned the true definition of the word "saint" and pondered what that meant. During lunch he asked his dad, "Pop, what's it like to be a grown-up saint?" Good question. One we all need to answer. We should be able to say, "I'm not what I used to be; I'm not what I ought to be; but praise the Lord, I'm on my way to becoming all that I was intended to be."

Paul's parting talk to the elders of the Ephesian church was focused in his desire for their sanctification. After reviewing how the Lord had blessed them together during his ministry in their city and the difficulties they had endured together, the apostle turned his attention to their future as persons and leaders. *"So now, brethren, I commend you to God and to the word of His grace, which is able to build you up and give you an inheritance among all those who are sanctified"* (v. 32).

This verse, in the context of the whole passage, provides a basis for communicating the adventure of growth. Paul longed for his friends to grow up in Christ, to be sanctified. Imagine the urgency he felt as he looked into the faces of his converts. Among those elders there must have been some of the disciples of John who had received the Holy Spirit. Perhaps one of the itinerant exorcists had received Christ's power and was there. Surely a transformed silversmith was there. And what about some of the converted Jews? Leaders of the city who had received Christ were certainly among them. And what of the broken people who had been given peace in exchange for the broken pieces of their lives?—transformed criminals, liberated leaders of the cults, and Roman officials who had made Christ king of their lives. We picture all these among the new humanity in Christ now entrusted with the leadership of the church. And Paul knew that what the Lord had begun in them, He would continue.

It is significant that *"the word of His grace"* is noted as the secret of sanctification. The unmerited, unchanging, forgiving love of the Lord enables us to own the failures of the past, disown them in the Lord's tender mercy, and move on to the next step of growing up in the full stature of Christ. That's what Paul wanted for the Ephesian elders and what we long for for ourselves and our listeners.

Paul's final admonition is the key to sanctification. He quoted the Lord Jesus, *"It is more blessed to give than to receive"* (v. 35). Growth in Christ takes place as we give Him away to others. That always involves giving ourselves and what we have to help them discover what we have found. In actuality, it is blessed both to receive and to give. In fact, we cannot give away what we have been unwilling to receive. Sanctification is a continuing process of being filled with the Lord's Spirit. The more we receive of Him, the more we have to give of what people really need—love, forgiveness, and lasting care.

The final scene with Paul and the elders praying together on the seashore is an example of what the Lord wants to provide us with the people we seek to lead. Paul had been a dynamic teacher and preacher, but he had also been a caring friend. When he had to leave for the ship, tears of love flowed freely and the elders tenderly kissed the apostle on the neck. The Lord is gracious in offering us the same possibility of love and loyalty from the people to whom we teach and preach.

CHAPTER EIGHTEEN—BOUND IN THE SPIRIT
ACTS 21:1–14

Scripture Outline
>   A Testing at Tyre (21:1–7)
>   The Lord's Will Be Done (21:8–14)

Paul's spiritual commitment to go to Jerusalem and then on to Rome had come from the guidance of the Holy Spirit. Acts 19:21 records that guidance: "Paul purposed in the Spirit, when he had passed through Macedonia and Achaia, to go to Jerusalem, saying, 'After I have been there, I must also see Rome.'" That guidance had been confirmed repeatedly so that the apostle could reaffirm it to the Ephesian elders before leaving them. "And see, now I go bound in the Spirit to Jerusalem, not knowing the things that will happen to me there, except that the Holy Spirit testifies in every city, saying that chains and tribulations await me" (Acts 20:22–23). Note that the Spirit guided him to go, and then alerted him to the trials which were ahead. The clarification of the difficulties did not contradict the initial guidance, but clarified the nature of it.

It is crucial to catch the relationship of "bound in the Spirit," and "the Holy Spirit testifies." Paul's own spirit was under the control of the Holy Spirit. A short time earlier he had written the Christians at Rome from Corinth explaining this and expressing autobiographically what he knew was ahead of him. "The Spirit Himself bears witness with our spirit that we are children of God, and if children, then heirs—heirs of God and joint heirs with Christ, if indeed we suffer with Him, that we may also be glorified together" (Rom. 8:16–17). In a real sense, the apostle was bound by the Holy Spirit. The physical chains that awaited him could be endured because of the bond of love which bound him to the Lord.

Understanding this gives us a handle to grasp in our exposition of this transitional section in Acts, which describes in detail the route to Jerusalem and the stops along the way. Paul was repeatedly warned about the dangers ahead. Some of his Christian friends even asserted the authority of the Holy Spirit for their advice. Unless he had been bonded to the Spirit in his own spirit, he could have been confused and missed what he was intended to do. This passage gives us an opportunity to consider how the Spirit guides and how we can deal with conflicting guidance from well-meaning friends who love us and want what they think is best for us. The danger is the possibility of missing the Spirit's best.

A TESTING AT TYRE

21:1 Now it came to pass, that when we had departed from them and set sail, running a straight course we came to Cos, the following day to Rhodes, and from there to Patara. ² And finding a ship sailing over to Phoenicia, we went aboard and set sail. ³ When we had sighted Cyprus, we passed it on the left, sailed to Syria, and landed at Tyre; for there the ship was to unload her cargo. ⁴ And finding disciples, we stayed there seven days. They told Paul through the Spirit not to go up to Jerusalem. ⁵ When we had come to the end of those days, we departed and went on our way; and they all accompanied us, with wives and children, till we were out of the city. And we knelt down on the shore and prayed. ⁶ When we had taken our leave of one another, we boarded the ship, and they returned home.

⁷ And when we had finished our voyage from Tyre, we came to Ptolemais, greeted the brethren, and stayed with them one day.

—Acts 21:1–7

When Paul and his companions reached the mainland at the port of Tyre, they sought out the disciples of Christ there. The Greek verb used here, the second aorist active participle of *aneurískō,* means that they found them by searching. They did not *happen* to meet them; they made an effort to be with them. Perhaps the Christians at Tyre had fled from Jerusalem. Paul knew that they were there and sought them out for fellowship and mutual encouragement. What happened when they were together may make us wonder how much encouragement they were to Paul.

Luke tells us they stayed at Tyre seven days. At the end of the time, the Tyrean Christians told Paul *"through the Spirit"* (v. 4) not to go to Jerusalem. The words "through the Spirit" imply that they had a word of knowledge from the Spirit that the apostle was not to go to Jerusalem. Conflicting guidance? Hardly, if He was the same Spirit. Allow me to offer a possibility of what happened. I think the Spirit revealed the dangers ahead for Paul. The people interpreted this as a prohibition and told Paul that he should not go. But Paul had received orders from the Spirit to go and also had been given a clear picture of what going would mean. "Bound in the Spirit," he pressed on. He did not argue or spend a long time discussing guidance. He simply followed what he knew he had been told to do.

Often loved ones and friends get the same guidance as we do but it is channeled to us through the grid of their own fears of their concern for our safety. Also, sometimes there is a kind of sloppy sentimentalism about the Spirit's guidance. We can't imagine that trials and difficulties could ever be the Lord's will for people we love. Success, ease, and peace without conflict have become the false signs of the Spirit's blessing. He often wills these, but they can never become the sure signs that His will is being done. Success is doing what the Lord wills, ease is living in the flow of His Spirit, and peace is often discovered in outwardly turbulent circumstances. It is equally dangerous to think that we are doing the will of the Lord only if we are suffering or facing trouble. Circumstances cannot be trusted to give us a final assurance that we are in the Lord's will. Paul's guidance was to go to Rome by way of Jerusalem. With raw courage and determination, he forged ahead, kindly accepting his friends' counsel, but not veering from his clearly set course.

THE LORD'S WILL BE DONE

[8] On the next day we who were Paul's companions departed and came to Caesarea, and entered the house of Philip the evangelist, who was one of the seven, and stayed with him. [9] Now this man had four virgin daughters who prophesied. [10] And as we stayed many days, a certain prophet named Agabus came down from Judea. [11] When he had come to us, he took Paul's belt, bound his own hands and feet, and said, "Thus says the Holy Spirit, 'So shall the Jews at Jerusalem bind the man who owns this belt, and deliver him into the hands of the Gentiles.'"

[12] Now when we heard these things, both we and those from that place pleaded with him not to go up to Jerusalem.

13 Then Paul answered, "What do you mean by weeping and breaking my heart? For I am ready not only to be bound, but also to die at Jerusalem for the name of the Lord Jesus."

14 So when he would not be persuaded, we ceased, saying, "The will of the Lord be done."

—*Acts 21:8–14*

We wish Paul's friends at Caesarea had begun where they ended. Only after pleading with Paul and breaking his heart with their insistence that he not go to Jerusalem did they say with resignation, *"The will of the Lord be done."*

After a short journey from Tyre by way of Ptolemais, Paul stopped for a visit at the home of Philip in Caesarea. Philip was one of the deacons elected by the church (Acts 6:5) who had been sent down to Samaria to preach the gospel (Acts 8:4–24) and had introduced the Ethiopian eunuch to Christ (Acts 8:26–39). In Acts 8:40 we are told that he went to Caesarea. He settled there and continued the ministry of an evangelist. His four daughters had the gift of prophecy.

While Paul was there, a prophet named Agabus came down to Caesarea from Jerusalem and dramatized his prophecy for Paul in a very vivid way. He took Paul's belt, or girdle, which gathered his outer tunic about his waist, and bound his own hands and feet. Like an Old Testament prophet, he acted out his prophecy: *"Thus says the Holy Spirit, 'So shall the Jews at Jerusalem bind the man who owns this belt, and deliver him into the hands of the Gentiles'"* (v. 11). This was nothing that Paul did not know already, except that his own Hebrew people would be the conspirators in his arrest and persecution.

Paul could have handled that clarification of his own guidance. What troubled him was the combined restraint imposed by Philip, his prophetic daughters, his companions, and even Luke. Note the "we" in verse 12. Together they all pleaded with him not to go to Jerusalem. The Spirit's prophetic word through Agabus did not forbid Paul from going to Jerusalem; He simply made it clear what would happen when he went.

The difficulty for Paul was that he had to digest the information about what the Jews would do to him and at the same time deal with his grief-stricken friends who wanted to keep him out of danger. It is not easy to fly in the face of a host of friends, all of whom believe your decision or direction is wrong. They had all prayed their prayers and Paul stood alone in the guidance he received. How can we account for these counterconvictions? The Spirit had not given different guidance; Paul and his friends interpreted the guidance differently. It is what the friends and Paul added to the guidance that made the difference. Paul added the resoluteness of previous clarity; his friends added the reserve of tender affection for the apostle.

Through Luke's eyes, we are given an inside look at the warm and caring relationship between Paul and his friends. They really cared about the apostle. He was not only the spiritual and intellectual giant we meet on the pages of Acts and in the epistles; he was also a man capable of receiving and giving deep affection. Christ in him had softened his rigid, cold Pharisee's heart and made him able to share in profound friendships in the family of faith.

It was this openness to his friends that nearly closed him to the Spirit's guidance. He felt the full impact of his friends' anxiety for him. It began to wear on him, troubling his own spirit, and clouding his vision. All the physical exhaustion of the days of travel, the persistent questioning of his guidance, and the internalization of the panic of his friends burst in an explosion of emotion. *"What do you mean by weeping and breaking my heart?"* (v. 13). It was as if he had said, "Why are you doing this to me? I need your encouragement to follow the Spirit's leading. Instead you are crippling me with your grief over what is going to happen to me in Jerusalem!"

The Greek word used here for "to break" is a form of *sunthrúptō,* from *apothrúptō,* meaning to crush together. The implication is that Paul's friends were trying to crush his guidance from the Lord. Perhaps it also meant that they were crushing their will for his safety into the Lord's will for his obedience. The reason for Paul's outburst of emotion was that his weeping friends were making him question his own heart's desire to obey the Lord.

When he had regained his emotional equilibrium, he went on to explain why his friends should not persist further in crushing his spirit: *"For I am ready not only to be bound, but also to die at Jerusalem for the name of the Lord Jesus."* Paul did not fear death if it would glorify his Master. He was so sure of the Lord that he did not fear rejection, persecution, or even death. He knew he was alive forever. The only concern for however long he lived was to obey the Lord's guidance and to honor Him in all he did and said. We are not free to live the abundant life until we have been brought to this unreserved commitment and trust.

Only after this courageous statement were Paul's friends able to say what they should have said all along. Verse 14 is very telling: *"So when he would not be persuaded, we ceased, saying, 'The will of the Lord be done.'"* Does this suggest that they had tried to dissuade the apostle from doing the will of God? Or was it just resignation? Or, what's worse, did they echo the oft-repeated idea that the only explanation of tragic eventualities is that they must be, or have been, the will of God? None of these alternatives is very commendable. What is tragic is that no one stepped forward to say, "Paul, I'm for you. You have received guidance from the Lord to go to Jerusalem. I know that will mean arrest, persecution, and imprisonment. But I praise God that He will be with you and will use what you will go through for His ultimate purposes. Do what you must do!"

We are left to wonder about Paul's friends. And then our criticism of them turns back on us. What would we have done? What do we do in similar situations today? Some reflective thoughts prepare us to communicate the meaning of the passage to others.

Do we have a clear guidance from the Lord about what he wants us to do in obedience to Him? Have we ever been dissuaded from following the Lord because of conflicting guidance from others? Has our own or others' concern for safety or popularity or success ever kept us from pressing ahead to follow guidance in difficult circumstances? Do we tend to equate being in the Lord's will with everything working out happily? Has our own fear of radical obedience ever prompted us to crush someone else's determination to do the Lord's will? Has tender affection ever been substituted for courageous love in wanting God's best for someone else?

These questions bridge this passage and our lives today. We all want to know and do God's will in our lives. We need friends who do not twist His guidance for us with protective sentiment. And we all long to be the quality of adventures in the will of God who can spur others on in faithfulness to Him, regardless of the cost.

CHAPTER NINETEEN—AN ANATOMY OF COURAGE

ACTS 21:15—26:32

Scripture Outline

Luke's dramatic account of Paul's arrest, imprisonment, and repeated trials in Jerusalem and Caesarea on the way to Rome, provides us with a magnificent description of Christian courage. I have found it helpful to deal with Acts 21:15 through chapter 26 as a whole. Taking one of the meanings of the word "anatomy"— separating into parts for detailed study—we find that this portion of Acts affords us the opportunity to dissect the aspects of Paul's courage in the midst of conflict. He had an amazing resiliency under impossible strain because of the indwelling power of the resurrected Lord, the Holy Spirit. Luke gives us a series of vivid illustrations of how the Spirit sustains in the pressures and stresses of life. The apostle's faith was tested under fire.

A few months before his arrival in Jerusalem, Paul had written the church at Rome about the stabilizing power of the Lord in the stresses of life. He told them, "I long to see you, that I may impart to you some spiritual gift, so that you may be established—that is, that I may be encouraged together with you by the mutual faith both of you and me" (Rom. 1:11–12). Then, after describing the source of that stability in Christ, he closed his letter with, "Now to Him who is able to establish you according to my gospel and the preaching of Jesus Christ. . ." (Rom. 16:25). The Greek word translated as "establish" in the NKJV is from *stērizō,* to make stable. The stability Paul longed to impart to the Christians at Rome is what he displayed in Jerusalem and Caesarea during the months of excruciating conflict. Luke gives us the privilege of living with the apostle each step of the way. The same courage he received from the Lord is available to us today.

That's what the people for whom we will preach or teach this passage need to know. Life for them, or us, is not easy. It has its own turbulent brew of challenges, difficulties, and conflicts. As expositors we have the responsibility to follow Luke's story line through Paul's ordeal. But we can do that in a way that will be immeasurably encouraging to our listeners. We can be faithful in an explanation of the history in a way that provides hope for living today. By following the theme of Christ-implanted courage we will cover the biblical material and at the same time be sensitive and empathetical about the implication of each event in exposing the stability available to us now.

A concern an expositor faces in carrying his or her listener along through these five and one-half chapters is that the various phases of Paul's trial and his defense often are repetitious. His witness before various judges covers much of the same autobiographical material. However, by emphasizing the theme of courage as the central thread in Luke's account, we are able to build a message or a class session around that theme. If we choose to do a longer series on this section, it will be helpful to tie it together as a study of the nature of true courage.

Recently, I had a long lunch with one of America's leading market research analysts. He spends his life polling what people are thinking and feeling today. His closing comment has lingered in my mind: "Don't forget the needs of people. They are living with tremendous stress and they need courage. Just know this: when

you help them to live courageously, you will always be on target."
This portion of Acts gives us the guide to do that.

COURAGE IN THE MIDST OF CRITICISM

[15] And after those days we packed and went up to
Jerusalem. [16] Also some of the disciples from Caesarea went
with us and brought with them a certain Mnason of Cyprus,
an early disciple, with whom we were to lodge.

[17] And when we had come to Jerusalem, the brethren
received us gladly. [18] On the following day Paul went in with
us to James, and all the elders were present. [19] When he had
greeted them, he told in detail those things which God had
done among the Gentiles through his ministry. [20] And when
they heard it, they glorified the Lord. And they said to him,
"You see, brother, how many myriads of Jews there are who
have believed, and they are all zealous for the law; [21] but they
have been informed about you that you teach all the Jews who
are among the Gentiles to forsake Moses, saying that they
ought not to circumcise their children nor to walk according
to the customs. [22] What then? The assembly must certainly
meet, for they will hear that you have come. [23] Therefore do
what we tell you: We have four men who have taken a vow.
[24] Take them and be purified with them, and pay their
expenses so that they may shave their heads, and that all may
know that those things of which they were informed concerning you are nothing, but that you yourself also walk orderly
and keep the law. [25] But concerning the Gentiles who believe,
we have written and decided that they should observe no such
thing, except that they should keep themselves from things
offered to idols, from blood, from things strangled, and from
sexual immorality."

[26] Then Paul took the men, and the next day, having
been purified with them, entered the temple to announce the
expiration of the days of purification, at which time an offering should be made for each one of them.

[27] Now when the seven days were almost ended, the Jews
from Asia, seeing him in the temple, stirred up the whole
crowd and laid hands on him, [28] crying out, "Men of Israel,
help! This is the man who teaches all men everywhere against
the people, the law, and this place; and furthermore he also
brought Greeks into the temple and has defiled this holy
place." [29] (For they had previously seen Trophimus the

Ephesian with him in the city, whom they supposed that Paul had brought into the temple.)

30 And all the city was disturbed; and the people ran together, seized Paul, and dragged him out of the temple; and immediately the doors were shut. 31 Now as they were seeking to kill him, news came to the commander of the garrison that all Jerusalem was in an uproar. 32 He immediately took soldiers and centurions, and ran down to them. And when they saw the commander and the soldiers, they stopped beating Paul. 33 Then the commander came near and took him, and commanded him to be bound with two chains; and he asked who he was and what he had done. 34 And some among the multitude cried one thing and some another.

So when he could not ascertain the truth because of the tumult, he commanded him to be taken into the barracks. 35 When he reached the stairs, he had to be carried by the soldiers because of the violence of the mob. 36 For the multitude of the people followed after, crying out, "Away with him!"

37 Then as Paul was about to be led into the barracks, he said to the commander, "May I speak to you?"

He replied, "Can you speak Greek? 38 Are you not the Egyptian who some time ago stirred up a rebellion and led the four thousand assassins out into the wilderness?"

39 But Paul said, "I am a Jew from Tarsus, in Cilicia, a citizen of no mean city; and I implore you, permit me to speak to the people."

40 So when he had given him permission, Paul stood on the stairs and motioned with his hand to the people. And when there was a great silence, he spoke to them in the Hebrew language, saying,

—Acts 21:15–40

The first illustration of Paul's courage is shown when he met with the leaders of the church in Jerusalem. He was greeted warmly and given an opportunity to share *"in detail those things which God had done among the Gentiles through his ministry"* (v. 19). The report was received with enthusiasm. The church leaders glorified God for all that He had done through Paul. But the time of praise was quickly followed by the sharing of a problem. The apostle's presence in Jerusalem presented the leaders with a dilemma. He was under heavy criticism, not only from the officialdom of Israel, but from fellow Christians. Hostility from the

Hebrew leaders was one thing, but criticism from believers was more difficult to take.

The problem was with the converted Jews who had become disciples, and had swelled the ranks of the Jerusalem church. They believed in Christ, but were still *"zealous for the law"* (v. 20). An old problem reared its ugly head. Rumors had reached the Hebrew Christians that Paul was telling Jews among the Gentiles to forsake the Law of Moses, encouraging them not to circumcise their children and not to keep the customs of Israel. The very people who should have rejoiced with Paul over the success of his ministry were the source of negative criticism that was raging in the church at Jerusalem.

Most of us are able to withstand criticism from our protagonists or enemies. It is when fellow Christians criticize us that it hurts deeply. When the very people who should be the first to understand and side with us become our negative critics, we require a special quality of courage from the Lord. Imagine how Paul must have felt. He was bursting with the joy of the victories of the Lord in Asia Minor, Macedonia, and Greece. His homecoming was denied the triumph because of the criticism of those who had chosen to believe, and pass on, the rumors about his ministry.

What probably hurt the most was that the church leaders had not silenced the criticism. They knew what Paul had been doing. Many of them had shared the responsibility with him of making the historic decision about Gentile converts in the Jerusalem council. Why hadn't James or some of the others squelched the rumors and criticism long before the apostle arrived back in Jerusalem? Had no one said, "That's enough! We believe in our brother Paul and know that these rumors are false. There will be no further criticism of his ministry. We trust that the apostle has faithfully kept what we all agreed upon together." Could it have been that the leaders were not sure? Often we allow criticism around us when we are secretly suspicious ourselves.

Whatever the case, the leaders chose not to make a defense for Paul among the believers, but asked him to do it for himself. He would have to solve the problem. We wonder why the leadership of the Jerusalem church was not as decisive with the critics as they were with Paul when they told him what to do to diffuse the criticism. *"Therefore do what we tell you"* (v. 23) is not exactly a permissive suggestion but a command! Paul was told to participate in a compromise for unity. Again we wonder: did Paul groan inside at the necessity of proving his integrity? We do not know. After all he'd faced out on the frontiers, the test of his loyalty to the Law of Moses and customs of Israel must have seemed absurd, if not an affront. But the courage of the Lord stabilized him. Christ was his security, not people; not even fellow believers. Whatever would free him to get on with his true calling, with however much support from the church he could muster, should be done.

Paul was asked to be the sponsor of four Jewish Christians who were taking the Nazarite vow in the temple. Remember that the apostle himself took that vow when returning to Jerusalem from the second missionary journey (Acts 18:18). You will recall that the vow involved abstention from eating meat, drinking wine, and also required the shaving of one's head as an outward sign of inner commitment to God and the Law. The concluding seven days were to be spent in the temple courts. A lamb was given as a sin offering, and a ram as a peace offering. There was a meat and drink offering, as well as a basket of unleavened bread and cakes. Paul's participation as a sponsor required that he pay for the offerings and reimburse the men for their pay lost during the time away from their work. By having him fulfill the customary role of sponsor, the leaders of the church in Jerusalem hoped to quiet the criticism and give a final assurance of Paul's allegiance to the Law of Moses. The apostle's ready compliance revealed to his critics what they should have known all along: he had never departed from loyalty to the Law and customs of Israel in his preaching of the gospel. Sponsoring the four men took a special kind of greatness—and courage. Paul was able to compromise for unity without sacrificing his union with Christ. Secondary things did not matter because of his ultimate commitment to Christ.

The strategy of reconciliation by the leaders of the church boomeranged. It may have helped alleviate the criticism of the Jewish Christians within the church, but it placed Paul in direct line for the fire of some Jews from Asia Minor who were pilgrims in the Holy City for Pentecost. They were not just critics of the apostle, but vigilantes determined to destroy him. We assume that they were Jews from the synagogue of Ephesus who were among those who rejected Paul's preaching and hassled his ministry all during his time in Asia.

Luke's parenthesis in verse 20 explains what caused the uproar. Paul had been seen in Jerusalem with a young Greek named Trophimos from Ephesus. We met this Greek convert in Acts 20:4 as the representative of the churches of Asia in bringing the offering to the Jerusalem church. Paul had not brought the Greek Christian into the temple. The Asian Jews obviously confused him with one of the four Hebrew Christians Paul was sponsoring. Or, perhaps, having seen the apostle with Trophimos in the city, they assumed he had brought him to the temple. Whatever the assumed data, the angry Jews needed some charge against Paul. In reality, they built a case against him based on no concrete evidence at all. The fanaticism of their charge didn't need facts to inflame the Jews who were present in the temple courts. Mobs are stirred up by prejudice and exclusivism, not by reason and just charges. Religious fervor is as dangerous as political hatred.

All the pent-up emotion of the Jerusalem Jews and pilgrims from around the then-known world was turned on Paul. They seized him, dragged him out of the temple, and began beating him with the intent of killing him. Note how fanaticism fired by hatred breaks laws to take the law into its own hands. If Paul were a blasphemer of the temple, there were orderly procedures for charging and trying him.

News of the uproar reached the Roman barracks. The word for news in verse 31 is *phásis,* from *phaínō,* a verb used for the act of giving unauthorized information or for the exposing of a secret crime. Who informed the Romans? Surely some fellow Christians. During special festivals in Jerusalem, the Roman soldiers were stationed in the Tower of Antonia at the northwest corner of the temple area. The fact that there was a commander present means that a cohort, or a thousand men, were billeted there. The Romans knew that the Pentecost feast was fraught with potential dangers in Jerusalem. When the commander heard of Paul's beating, he rushed to the scene outside the court of the temple. Luke tells us that there were centurions and soldiers. Each had charge of a hundred men. So we can picture hundreds of Roman soldiers rushing into the mob of blood-thirsty Jews. To bring order the commander immediately put Paul in chains, as much for protection from the mob as for arrest. When he had the apostle separated from the mob, he then asked who he was and what the charge was against him.

The frenzied accusers, not Paul, shouted the charges. Some charged one thing; others, another. The cries were so muddled that the commander decided to take Paul to the barracks. But the mob was so violent that it resisted the Roman authority, trying to pull Paul away from the soldiers. The apostle was in such danger that the legionnaires had to pick him up and carry him, the mob following with angry cries, *"Away with him!"* (v. 36). These are the very words, *"Aîre autōn,"* used by Luke to translate the cry of the mob to Pilate when they chose Barabbas in preference to Jesus in the final hours before the Crucifixion (Luke 23:18).

But Paul was not ready to be dismissed by his accusers even in the safety of the Roman hands that held him aloft away from the murderous clutching of the mob. Instead, he asked to speak to the commander. Don't miss the calm courtesy of Paul's request. In Greek he said, *"May I speak to you?"* No panic, no frenzied cry. The fact that he spoke in Greek astounded the commander. *"Can you speak Greek?"* he asked, startled. What the commander went on to say indicated that he had assumed he knew whom he had put in chains. He thought he had in custody an Egyptian revolutionary who had stirred up an insurrection and was still at large.

A quick check of Josephus[1] and other corollary history accounts, reveals that there was an uprising of insurrectionists during the reign of Felix, the Roman governor at that time. Josephus says that there were not four thousand, but thirty thousand assassins in the Egyptians' movement. The insurrection was crushed by the Romans, who killed or imprisoned the rebels. The Egyptian had somehow escaped the purge and was high on the Romans' "wanted" list. The commander just assumed that Paul was this dangerous political criminal.

That explains why the Roman was astounded when Paul spoke in Greek and explained his racial and geographic background. In the pressure of the moment the commander did not catch the full impact of what Paul said. He asserted that he was a Jew, but also a citizen of Tarsus. What the commander should have discerned then, he discovered only later: he was dealing with a Roman. Paul was not only a citizen; he had been born in a Roman province with all the rights and privileges of a Roman. At this point, however, Paul's credentials, as the commander understood them, were enough for the commander to use his authority to hold back the crowd and permit his mysterious prisoner to speak.

This portion of Paul's time in Jerusalem shows us courage in his reaction to the confluence of criticism. He took the criticism of fellow Christians with ready magnanimity and the criticism of the Asian Jews with calm determination. There on the steps, facing the mob, Paul, and not the commander, was in charge. The apostle had nothing to lose; He belonged to Christ. Preaching the gospel, even to his self-appointed enemies, was more important than his safety. He belonged to Christ for eternity. That's the first aspect of our dissection of courage.

THE COURAGE OF PERSONAL EXPERIENCE

22:1 "Brethren and fathers, hear my defense before you now." [2] And when they heard that he spoke to them in the Hebrew language, they kept all the more silent.

Then he said: [3] "I am indeed a Jew, born in Tarsus of Cilicia, but brought up in this city at the feet of Gamaliel, taught according to the strictness of our fathers'law, and was zealous toward God as you all are today. [4] I persecuted this Way to the death, binding and delivering into prisons both men and women, [5] as also the high priest bears me witness, and all the council of the elders, from whom I also received letters to the brethren, and went to Damascus to bring in chains even those who were there to Jerusalem to be punished.

[6] "Now it happened, as I journeyed and came near Damascus at about noon, suddenly a great light from heaven shone around me. [7] And I fell to the ground and heard a voice saying to me, 'Saul, Saul, why are you persecuting Me?' [8] So I answered, 'Who are You, Lord?'And He said to me, 'I am Jesus of Nazareth, whom you are persecuting.'

[9] "And those who were with me indeed saw the light and were afraid, but they did not hear the voice of Him who spoke to me. [10] So I said, 'What shall I do, Lord?'And the Lord said to me, 'Arise and go into Damascus, and there you will be told all things which are appointed for you to do.' [11] And since I could not see for the glory of that light, being led by the hand of those who were with me, I came into Damascus.

[12] "Then a certain Ananias, a devout man according to the law, having a good testimony with all the Jews who dwelt there, [13] came to me; and he stood and said to me, 'Brother Saul, receive your sight.'And at that same hour I looked up at him. [14] Then he said, 'The God of our fathers has chosen you that you should know His will, and see the Just One, and hear the voice of His mouth. [15] For you will be His witness to all men of what you have seen and heard. [16] And now why are you waiting? Arise and be baptized, and wash away your sins, calling on the name of the Lord.'

[17] "Now it happened, when I returned to Jerusalem and was praying in the temple, that I was in a trance [18] and saw Him saying to me, 'Make haste and get out of Jerusalem

quickly, for they will not receive your testimony concerning Me.' [19] So I said, 'Lord, they know that in every synagogue I imprisoned and beat those who believe on You. [20] And when the blood of Your martyr Stephen was shed, I also was standing by consenting to his death, and guarding the clothes of those who were killing him.' [21] Then He said to me, 'Depart, for I will send you far from here to the Gentiles.'"

[22] And they listened to him until this word, and then they raised their voices and said, "Away with such a fellow from the earth, for he is not fit to live!" [23] Then, as they cried out and tore off their clothes and threw dust into the air, [24] the commander ordered him to be brought into the barracks, and said that he should be examined under scourging, so that he might know why they shouted so against him.

—Acts 22:1–24

Paul told his story in a way that glorified Christ and dignified the Christian movement. Here is a dramatic "before-and-after" account of the transformation of a human being. It is witnessing at its very best. Paul described the man he was and the man Christ had enabled him to be. At each stage of his evolving witness he clarified that it was Christ who had changed him. The careful recounting of his conversations with the Lord established the truth. Jesus Christ was alive, and He was the guiding Lord of Paul's life.

This section of Luke's account is firsthand validation of the narrative passages we've studied about the same events. We have seen what happened through Luke's eyes and now see these same events through the apostle Paul's own words. For the expositor who is leading a group through all of Acts, this portion is repetitious, but when it is used as the biblical basis of a message on the transformation of human personality, it has progression and force. The descriptive exposition we did together on Acts 9:1–29 can be utilized here.

What is significant for us in our progressive exposition of Acts as a whole is to note that the Jews heard Paul until he touched the raw nerve of their predetermined prejudice. The same thing happens today in our own personal study of the gospel and in our efforts to communicate. Paul pushed his hearers too far when he told them that the Lord had sent him to preach to the Gentiles. They could listen to his own story until it involved inclusive love for the Gentiles.

A man said to his pastor, "You've gone from preaching to meddling!" Preaching is meddling, sooner or later. We all have areas in our lives we want to reserve away from the searching eye and remedial penetration of the Savior. There are times that relationships, expenditures, and unhealed memories, as well as values, customs, and ways of reacting, are excluded from the Master's reformation.

Accounts of mass baptisms of conscripted crusaders tell us that some of the knights were marched through rivers as their baptism into Christ. Some however, held their swords and dueling arms high out of the waters, excluding that portion from Christ's control. We wonder: what have we held out of the commitment of our lives to Christ?

Note verse 22: *"They listened to him until this word."* The word "Gentiles" did it. What would that word be for you? Or for the people to whom you teach or preach? Paul knew his audience. He did not sidestep the issue. The tragic thing was that he was not able to go on to show the undeniable proof of the blessing of the Lord in his ministry to the Gentile world. Some prejudices could have been changed, but they stopped listening before Paul stopped preaching.

Commenting on this, Halford E. Luccock says,

> The word "Gentiles" has no such effect today. But we have other words which cause the same paralysis of mind and hearing, for most of us have some prejudice, some cherished aversion, some forbidden subject which, when touched, acts an an immediate stop to reason.
> . . . When they are pronounced there is a rush of blood to the head, the doors of the ears bang shut and the mind is darkened.
> . . . It creates a blind mob spirit which substitutes violence for reason, or a granite-like imperiousness to new truth.   To all of us there comes an old question, "Lovest thou Me more than these?"—more than these beloved hatreds of yours, more than your pet aversions, more than your fixed ideas?[2]

Our concern is to discover how to approach these subjects to which our listeners close their ears. The only way is to discuss the subject of "click words" that trigger the closing of our minds. Acts 22:21–23 provides an opportunity to raise the question with our listeners about what in them would correspond to the word "Gentiles" here. We can raise some possibilities as illustrations and allow the Spirit to send the arrow of conviction to the various targets in people's hearts.

That has to be done in an attitude of sharing rather than accusation. Telling our own story as Paul does in this passage is the secret. Also the illustrations of real people who have allowed the Lord to heal the raw nerves of prejudice or resistance packs a wallop. By far the most effective way to get at the closets of untouchable subjects is to discuss the problem in a way that people can define what it is in them that needs Christ's healing. Then we are in position to follow our teaching and preaching with a deep time of prayer in which they can talk to the Lord in confession of what is their sword held out of the water of baptism.

THE COURAGE OF THE LORD OF CIRCUMSTANCES

25 And as they bound him with thongs, Paul said to the centurion who stood by, "Is it lawful for you to scourge a man who is a Roman, and uncondemned?"

26 When the centurion heard that, he went and told the commander, saying, "Take care what you do, for this man is a Roman."

27 Then the commander came and said to him, "Tell me, are you a Roman?"

He said, "Yes."

28 The commander answered, "With a large sum I obtained this citizenship."

And Paul said, "But I was born a citizen."

29 Then immediately those who were about to examine him withdrew from him; and the commander was also afraid after he found out that he was a Roman, and because he had bound him.

30 The next day, because he wanted to know for certain why he was accused by the Jews, he released him from his bonds, and commanded the chief priests and all their council to appear, and brought Paul down and set him before them.

—*Acts 22:25–30*

It is interesting to note that Paul did not press the subject of his Roman citizenship when he was before the angry mob of his fellow Jews. That would have been cowardice and not courage. Before the Jews, he wanted to communicate that as a Hebrew he had believed in Jesus Christ and had become His loyal and obedient apostle. Now about to be scourged, he used the powerful weapon of his Roman citizenship.

The commander of the Roman legions in Jerusalem had obviously decided that he would get to the bottom of the truth about his prisoner. The implication is that he ordered this severe treatment not as a punishment for a crime, for he still did not know what charge was being leveled against Paul, but as an effort to get Paul to confess whatever it was that he had done or been to cause such violent anger and hostility from the mob. Torture for truth seemed to be his method. And the means was to be a beating with the Roman flagellum, a much more cruel instrument than a whip or rods. In the flagellum, the leather strips of the lash were intertwined with pieces of sharp bone or metal. Crippling, or even death, could result. For this reason, scourging of Roman citizens was strictly forbidden, positively when there had been no trial.

Paul was not afraid of death, but he was not about to be permanently maimed or even killed in a Roman barracks and miss the real reason he had come to Jerusalem, and his further destination of Rome.

The richness of the Greek language describes the picture vividly. *"And as they bound him with thongs"* (v. 25) actually means they stretched him forward, *hos dè proèteinan autòn.* Paul was stretched or bent forward and tied to a post. His back was then arched and exposed to the scourges. He was being terrorized as well as prepared for torture. Just as the flagellum was raised by the centurion, Paul asked the incisive question that terrorized the torturer. *"Is it lawful for you to scourge a man who is a Roman, and uncondemned?"* The upraised arm of the centurion dropped immediately. He ran to tell the commander what he had heard. No wonder: the penalty for scourging a Roman citizen was death!

The commander shared the centurion's dismay over what they had almost done. His alarmed question to Paul is really, "You a Roman?" expressed with emphatic consternation, *sù Romaîos eî?* The "you" is in the emphatic position. The commander was shaken with astonishment . . . and fear. Feel the thudding impact of Paul's sledgehammer "Yes!" With that the commander's astonishment turned to awe. He had purchased his citizenship with a large sum of money. In Acts 23:26 Luke tells us that the commander's name was Claudius Lysias, a fact that explains the purchase of his citizenship. During the reign of Claudius, Roman citizenship was sold for great sums. It was customary for these new citizens to adopt the name of the reigning emperor. Now we can understand why the commander exclaimed, in essence, "I know how much it cost me to buy my citizenship!"

In response Paul simply says, "I was born one." Being born in Tarsus did not make Paul a Roman citizen. Tarsus, a free city, was not a Roman colony like Philippi. His father must have been awarded citizenship because of some service to the emperor. Jerome, in his *On Famous Men,* suggests that Paul's father had come from Gishala. Lake and Cadbury, in *Beginnings of Christianity* IV, reason that citizenship might have been awarded for a service done for Mark Antony in Palestine. The fact is that we do not know. What we do know is that Paul was a Roman citizen because his father, though a Hebrew, was a citizen and the apostle had inherited the status he now used so strategically.

At this point there is a strange twist in Luke's account. Paul's appeal to his rights as a citizen should have prompted Claudius Lysias to refer his case to a higher Roman authority. Instead, he commanded the Sanhedrin to meet and had Paul appear before the chief priests and the Sadducees and Pharisees. Reading between the lines, we can speculate that Lysias was probably intrigued by his mysterious prisoner and wanted to know what charge the Jews had against him. Paul may even have suggested that alternative, hoping for a further opportunity to witness to the leaders of Israel. Lysias, still unsettled by what he had almost done to a Roman citizen, might have complied. We are left to wonder why a Roman commander called a meeting of a Hebrew court to try a Roman citizen. What is evident is that Paul was not a helpless victim. He had come to Jerusalem to preach Christ and he was willing to use every means to be heard. The Lord, not a Roman commander, or even the Sanhedrin, was calling the shots.

There is an indomitable courage that comes from knowing that Christ is the Lord of circumstances. He controls coincidences. It was not by chance that Paul's father bequeathed him Roman citizenship. Nor was it a fluke that the commander was one who would have respect for a fellow citizen because of his own purchased status. The picture we get of the apostle through all the changing circumstances is of a man who is ready to grasp opportunities to reach the center of religious and political power with his witness to Christ.

THE COURAGE OF THE RESURRECTION

23:1 Then Paul, looking earnestly at the council, said, "Men and brethren, I have lived in all good conscience before

God until this day." ² And the high priest Ananias commanded those who stood by him to strike him on the mouth. ³ Then Paul said to him, "God will strike you, you whitewashed wall! For you sit to judge me according to the law, and do you command me to be struck contrary to the law?"

⁴ And those who stood by said, "Do you revile God's high priest?"

⁵ Then Paul said, "I did not know, brethren, that he was the high priest; for it is written, 'You shall not speak evil of a ruler of your people.'"

⁶ But when Paul perceived that one part were Sadducees and the other Pharisees, he cried out in the council, "Men and brethren, I am a Pharisee, the son of a Pharisee; concerning the hope and resurrection of the dead I am being judged!"

⁷ And when he had said this, a dissension arose between the Pharisees and the Sadducees; and the assembly was divided. ⁸ For Sadducees say that there is no resurrection—and no angel or spirit; but the Pharisees confess both. ⁹ Then there arose a loud outcry. And the scribes of the Pharisees'party arose and protested, saying, "We find no evil in this man; but if a spirit or an angel has spoken to him, let us not fight against God."

¹⁰ Now when there arose a great dissension, the commander, fearing lest Paul might be pulled to pieces by them, commanded the soldiers to go down and take him by force from among them, and bring him into the barracks.

—Acts 23:1–10

Paul's argument before the Sanhedrin is vital for our study of the anatomy of courage because it brings into sharp focus the cause of his conflict with the leaders of Israel and the source of his courage in those pressured days in Jerusalem.

Many commentators have felt that this section of Acts is a non sequitur that detracts, rather than follows Luke's story line. Not so. It shows us Paul's humanity, humility, and hope—all because of the courage of the Resurrection.

1. *Paul's humanity.* Luke has never been reluctant to expose the human frailties of the apostle. In Paul's heated exchange with the high priest, his genuine anger is evident. Paul's opening statement about his integrity in verse 23:1 brought forth a charge of blasphemy. He used the name of God and asserted that he had lived in good conscience. Also,

we wonder if his salutation was what enraged the high priest. Paul had been a highly respected Pharisee who had been commissioned by that very body years before to purge Jerusalem of the Way. Did *"Men and brethren"* presume on that previous association? The statement may have been Luke's summary of a longer dissertation by Paul of his life before and after conversion. What he claimed was that he had done his work as a Pharisee and then as an apostle in good conscience. The Greek word used here for conscience is a form of *suneídēsis,* meaning joint knowledge, from *súnoida,* to know together. Paul distinguished himself as a man by energetically living in the truth he had. Truth was known because it was obeyed, and obeyed because it was known. As a Pharisee he was vigilant in his impassioned defense of the Law and traditions of Israel; as a man in Christ, he lived and preached the Lord with zeal. His conscience was the servant of a congealed thought and action. The claim before the Sanhedrin was that he had been faithful at each stage to the highest truth he knew and had experienced.

The punishment Ananias inflicted hardly fit the "crime." He had those who were standing beside Paul strike him across the mouth. This was a particularly offensive, but also illegal, act. Paul had not been charged officially. The smiting irritated the apostle. He responded with an angry retort. In substance he said, "Do you smite me, you hypocrite?! You sit as my judge and yet you break the law by having me smitten without charge." A true statement, but not very tactful under the circumstances. But then, Paul was not trying to win a popularity contest. And Ananias was exactly what Paul charged him to be.

We should not try to defend Paul's retort any more than he did. The fact is that he did respond in anger, didn't turn the other cheek as Jesus had taught, and didn't live out the potent admonitions about patience he had written in his epistles to the churches. Confronted by that evidence of humanity, we are then challenged by Paul's expression of humility.

2. *Paul's humility.* It is not our mistakes that do us in; it's our pride that keeps us from admitting them. Paul had overstepped the boundaries of Christ-centered attitudinal control. Exodus 22:28 clearly dictates, "You shall not revile God, nor curse a ruler of your people." Ananias had broken a rule by having Paul struck across the mouth without an official charge of blasphemy. The apostle had broken another regulation imposing respect for the high priest. They were both wrong. But Christ in Paul made him willing to admit his mistake. Some expositors have reasoned that he had poor eyesight and did

not recognize the high priest. That's simplistic. Paul failed and was ready to admit it.

The sure sign of pride is that we defend our mistakes with protestations of our purity or goodness. Think of how many failures we have willfully refused to admit because of our need to be right. Pride controls us and keeps us from confessing an imperfection. We back people into the corner of their own failures when we won't admit our own. Humility is admitting that we are people in process. Christ's perfection and not our own is our security.

3. *Paul's hope.* The reason Paul could courageously stand before the awesome assembly of the rulers of Israel and make his bold claim of integrity and then admit a mistake was the risen Christ. Verse 6 gives us the secret of the resources of his resiliency: *"Concerning the hope and resurrection of the dead I am being judged!"*

The apostle crystallized the issue. The charges against him were that he was teaching disobedience to the Law and customs of Moses. Beneath that was a deeper contention. He believed Jesus was the Messiah, that He had risen from the dead, and that He was the present, reigning Lord of Israel. All the old hatred about Jesus was being focused on Paul and sublimated in disputation about his irreverence for the law and traditions. Paul forced the issue out into the open.

Belief in Christ's Resurrection and the promise of our own is the source of lasting courage. Christ was not only vindicated by the Resurrection, but clearly taught that through Him we too will be resurrected. Death has no power over us. We are alive forever. But our realization of the Resurrection does not have to wait until the moment of our physical death. When we surrender our lives to Christ, our self-control is crucified, and we are raised to a new level of intimate companionship with Him. Hope results. It is a hope that out of our impossibilities the Lord will raise up possibilities of which we never dreamed. And with fear of death expunged from our souls, we become fearless in our discipleship. The same power that raised Jesus from the dead can be the driving, uplifting, encouraging force within us.

Paul's focusing of the issue of the Resurrection divided the Sanhedrin. The Pharisees did believe in a resurrection, but the Sadducees did not. Paul's fellow Pharisees rose up in a defense of him, not so much in affirmation of his ministry, but in contention against their rivals, the Sadducees. The hearing ended in confusion and argument, not with Paul, but between the rival factions in the high priest's court. The apostle again won the day. He had made his point about the Resurrection, had drawn the fire away from himself, and was able to get on with his plan to confront Rome with the claim of Christ. The risen Christ had given him sublime wisdom. That too is courage.

THE ULTIMATE SOURCE OF COURAGE

¹¹ But the following night the Lord stood by him and said, "Be of good cheer, Paul; for as you have testified for Me in Jerusalem, so you must also bear witness at Rome."
—*Acts 23:11*

The Lord is the initiator of the courage we need. His interventions provide us with the stability for the strains of life. We come to Him because He first comes to us. He knows our hurts and hopes. The desire to seek Him in prayer is ours because He has created the desire.

Verse 23:11 is so crucial for our understanding of courage that I have taken it for a separate section of discussion. It explains the reason for Paul's determination and vision. The Lord's personal appearance to the apostle, and what He said to him, reveals the ultimate source of our courage. What the Lord said to Paul, He says to us in our times of difficulty and pressure.

"The Lord stood by him." If that had been all He did for the apostle, it would have been enough. To know that the Lord is with us is a magnificent source of courage. He promised that He would never leave or forsake us (Heb. 13:5). And He always makes the first move toward us. We seek Him because He has found us.

What He says to us gets us moving in the next step of His strategy for us. The thing He desires us to have, He provides. The admonition He gave Paul was coupled with the assurance of provision. *"Be of good cheer"* can also be translated as "Be of good courage." The Greek word is *thársei*, from *thársos*, courage. The RSV renders the Lord's admonition as "Take courage." Courage is a gift offered by the Lord. The psalmist realized that. The Lord said to him, "Be strong, and let your heart *take courage*" (Ps. 31:24, italics added). On the night before His crucifixion, the Christ said, "These things I have spoken to you, that in Me you may have peace. In the world you have tribulation, but *take courage;* I have overcome the world" (John 16:33, NASB, italics added).

The Lord knows when we need the gift of courage and comes to us to offer it for the challenges He has given us. Our only responsibility is to take what He has offered.

That's exactly what Paul needed to do that lonely night in the Roman barracks in the Tower of Antonia in Jerusalem. But he also needed a reaffirmation of the Lord's guidance. That was given with incisive clarity. *"For as you have testified for Me in Jerusalem, so you must bear witness also at Rome."* The witness to the leaders of Israel was completed. Rome was now to be his focus and destination. When he needed reconfirmation of the Lord's strategy the most, the Lord provided it in full measure.

This vital verse of Acts tells us that success in the ministry is not the only sign of the Lord's blessing. Paul was faced with discord and turmoil. That did not mean he was out of the Lord's will, but that he was following the Lord's guidance. And in times of uncertainty in our lives, the Lord will get through to us with an assurance that we are following His guidance for us. He will use all means available to communicate with us. We may not hear a voice as Paul did, but the Lord will speak to us through Scripture, and through an inner voice of conviction that is more powerful than an audio message. The reassurance will come so powerfully within that there will be no question. And it will not be simplistic or false piety to say, "The Lord spoke to me!"

THE COURAGE OF THE LORD'S INTERVENTION

12 And when it was day, some of the Jews banded together and bound themselves under an oath, saying that they would neither eat nor drink till they had killed Paul.
13 Now there were more than forty who had formed this conspiracy. 14 They came to the chief priests and elders, and said, "We have bound ourselves under a great oath that we will eat nothing until we have killed Paul. 15 Now you, therefore, together with the council, suggest to the commander that he be brought down to you tomorrow, as though you were going to make further inquiries concerning him; but we are ready to kill him before he comes near."
16 So when Paul's sister's son heard of their ambush, he went and entered the barracks and told Paul. 17 Then Paul called one of the centurions to him and said, "Take this young man to the commander, for he has something to tell him."
18 So he took him and brought him to the commander and said, "Paul the prisoner called me to him and asked me to bring this young man to you. He has something to say to you."

¹⁹ Then the commander took him by the hand, went aside, and asked privately, "What is it that you have to tell me?"

²⁰ And he said, "The Jews have agreed to ask that you bring Paul down to the council tomorrow, as though they were going to inquire more fully about him. ²¹ But do not yield to them, for more than forty of them lie in wait for him, men who have bound themselves by an oath that they will neither eat nor drink till they have killed him; and now they are ready, waiting for the promise from you."

²² So the commander let the young man depart, and commanded him, "Tell no one that you have revealed these things to me."

²³ And he called for two centurions, saying, "Prepare two hundred soldiers, seventy horsemen, and two hundred spearmen to go to Caesarea at the third hour of the night; ²⁴ and provide mounts to set Paul on, and bring him safely to Felix the governor." ²⁵ He wrote a letter in the following manner:

²⁶ Claudius Lysias,

To the most excellent governor Felix:

Greetings.

²⁷ This man was seized by the Jews and was about to be killed by them. Coming with the troops I rescued him, having learned that he was a Roman. ²⁸ And when I wanted to know the reason they accused him, I brought him before their council. ²⁹ I found out that he was accused concerning questions of their law, but had nothing charged against him deserving of death or chains. ³⁰ And when it was told me that the Jews lay in wait for the man, I sent him immediately to you, and also commanded his accusers to state before you the charges against him.

Farewell.

³¹ Then the soldiers, as they were commanded, took Paul and brought him by night to Antipatris. ³² The next day they left the horsemen to go on with him, and returned to the barracks. ³³ When they came to Caesarea and had delivered the letter to the governor, they also presented Paul to him. ³⁴ And when the governor had read it, he asked what province he was from. And when he understood that he was from Cilicia, ³⁵ he said, "I will hear you when your accusers also have come." And he commanded him to be kept in Herod's Praetorium.

—Acts 23:12–35

The Lord not only gave Paul a reaffirmation of His will that he should witness in Rome, He intervened in a very dramatic way to make sure that nothing got in the way. Luke's description of the plot against the apostle's life shows the depth of the hatred for him by the Jews. Undoubtedly those who took an oath for a hunger strike until they saw Paul dead were the Jews from Asia who had begun the riot outside the temple a few days before. This shocked the leaders of Israel in the Sanhedrin out of their internal squabbling. They realized that their arguments with each other had distracted them momentarily from their purpose of trying Paul. This made them open to a devious plot to get the Roman commander to bring the apostle back before them. The purpose, however, was not for further questioning, but so that the fanatical Asians could kill him on his way to the Sanhedrin. They had to get Paul out into the open where he could be seized and murdered.

But the Lord was capable of a much more ingenious plot. Paul's sister was in Jerusalem with her son. Luke does not tell us much about the apostle's family other than that his father was a Pharisee and a Roman citizen. This is the first and only mention of relatives in Jerusalem, and it gives us the opportunity for some thoughtful conjecture. If Paul's family did not share his belief in Christ, probably they had followed the custom of disowning and disinheriting him after his conversion. Converts to Christ were considered as dead by orthodox Jewish families. If that were the case, then Paul's sister may have been a pilgrim to the Holy City for the celebration of Pentecost. Some have suggested that perhaps his nephew was a student there, much as Paul had been years before, and that his mother had come to visit him. This might explain her inside knowledge of the planned ambush. In that event, her filial love for her brother overcame her family's rejection of him, and she encouraged her son to inform him of the impending danger.

A much better possibility is that Paul's nephew was also a Christian. Remember that the apostle went back home to Tarsus after his conversion. We wonder if he led his family to Christ. If so, his sister's son would have been influenced in becoming a follower of the Way. Or consider that perhaps Paul influenced his nephew personally and now the young man had an opportunity to express his gratitude. One other possibility was that the nephew was indeed a student of Pharisaism and had come to know Christ through the Jerusalem church. Some Greek scholars explain that the aorist participle *paragenómenos*, translated in verse 16 in the NKJV as "went," may also be translated as "having been present." This would suggest that Paul's nephew might have been present at the meeting of the Jewish vigilantes as they plotted the demise of the apostle. He may have been a spy placed there by the church. All the alternatives are fascinating to contemplate. The truth is that we don't know for sure.

What we do know is that the Lord intervened and arranged the details of informing Paul of the plot to ambush him and take his life. Behind the scenes the Lord was protecting His apostle for the purpose He intended. His nephew was either a member of the Sanhedrin, informed by someone who was, or had picked up intelligence about the plot from rumors. I think the Lord had sympathizers in high places. Our experience of the way He works would lead us to suspect that, long before this crisis, He had deployed the right person to be available to help. His plans for His beloved cannot be thwarted.

That too gives us courage. Beneath the surface of our human analysis of the impossibilities we face, the Lord is arranging things to press us forward to accomplish His will. Luke delights to imply that in his accounts.

Whenever we get involved in the adventure of doing the Lord's will, we are amazed by the people He has ready to help us. They step in at the right moment. We are amazed, and then filled with adoration, by the serendipities the Lord stages.

The Lord had a network of believers in Jerusalem. As the hatred against Paul intensified, the church became all the more alive to protect their brother in Christ. My own conviction is that Paul's nephew was dispatched by the church to inform him and subsequently the commander.

Lysias was not about to have the Jews outwit him. He understood now how vicious and determined they were. He had no other alternative than to arrange for Paul to be arraigned before Felix. The forty Jews plotting to kill the apostle were not a formidable threat to the commander and the Roman procedures for protecting a prisoner.

We smile with amusement at the precautions Lysias took to assure that Paul arrived safely in Caesarea for a hearing before the Roman governor. He assigned two hundred soldiers, seventy horsemen, and two hundred spearmen as guards to be sure nothing went wrong. That's four hundred and seventy men to protect a single prisoner! Actually, there were four hundred and seventy-one. The Savior of the world was keeping watch over His own. Surely Paul chuckled inside as he rode from Jerusalem to Caesarea. His real safety was not in the Roman soldiers, but in the never-forsaking, everlasting arms of his Master. The Lord had used Paul's nephew and now He used Rome's legionnaires. All circumstances and very unlikely people are at His disposal.

This prompts us to look beneath what is happening around us to recognize what the Lord is doing for us. This gives us calm assurance and vibrant expectancy. Nothing can happen without His permission, and what happens cannot be understood until, with retrospective wisdom, we can see that He was in charge.

THE COURAGE OF IMPELLING TRUTH

24:1 Now after five days Ananias the high priest came down with the elders and a certain orator named Tertullus. These gave evidence to the governor against Paul.

² And when he was called upon, Tertullus began his accusation, saying: "Seeing that through you we enjoy great peace, and prosperity is being brought to this nation by your foresight, ³ we accept it always and in all places, most noble Felix, with all thankfulness. ⁴ Nevertheless, not to be tedious to you any further, I beg you to hear, by your courtesy, a few words from us. ⁵ For we have found this man a plague, a creator of dissension among all the Jews throughout the world, and a ringleader of the sect of the Nazarenes. ⁶ He even tried to profane the temple, and we seized him, and wanted to judge him according to our law. ⁷ But the commander Lysias came by and with great violence took him out of our hands, ⁸ commanding his accusers to come to you. By examining him yourself you may ascertain all these things of which we accuse him." ⁹ And the Jews also assented, maintaining that these things were so.

¹⁰ Then Paul, after the governor had nodded to him to speak, answered: "Inasmuch as I know that you have been for many years a judge of this nation, I do the more cheerfully answer for myself, ¹¹ because you may ascertain that it is no more than twelve days since I went up to Jerusalem to worship. ¹² And they neither found me in the temple disputing with anyone nor inciting the crowd, either in the synagogues or in the city. ¹³ Nor can they prove the things of which they now accuse me. ¹⁴ But this I confess to you, that according to the Way which they call a sect, so I worship the God of my fathers, believing all things which are written in the Law and in the Prophets. ¹⁵ I have hope in God, which they themselves also accept, that there will be a resurrection of the dead, both of the just and the unjust. ¹⁶ This being so, I myself always strive to have a conscience without offense toward God and men.

[17] "Now after many years I came to bring alms and offerings to my nation, [18] in the midst of which some Jews from Asia found me purified in the temple, neither with a mob nor with tumult. [19] They ought to have been here before you to object if they had anything against me. [20] Or else let those who are here themselves say if they found any wrongdoing in me while I stood before the council, [21] unless it is for this one statement which I cried out, standing among them, 'Concerning the resurrection of the dead I am being judged by you this day.'"

[22] But when Felix heard these things, having more accurate knowledge of the Way, he adjourned the proceedings and said, "When Lysias the commander comes down, I will make a decision on your case." [23] So he commanded the centurion to keep Paul and to let him have liberty, and told him not to forbid any of his friends to provide for or visit him.

[24] And after some days, when Felix came with his wife Drusilla, who was Jewish, he sent for Paul and heard him concerning the faith in Christ. [25] Now as he reasoned about righteousness, self-control, and the judgment to come, Felix was afraid and answered, "Go away for now; when I have a convenient time I will call for you." [26] Meanwhile he also hoped that money would be given him by Paul, that he might release him. Therefore he sent for him more often and conversed with him.

[27] But after two years Porcius Festus succeeded Felix; and Felix, wanting to do the Jews a favor, left Paul bound.

—Acts 24:1–27

Paul's encounter with Felix gives us further evidence of the courage of the resurrected Lord. The apostle makes his bold witness to the governor and is sustained both by his own message and the impact it had on the Roman leader.

Some background on Felix is helpful. He was a complicated, strange mixture of Roman training and spiritual inquisitiveness. His brother Pallos was a favorite of Nero. Through his family influence, Felix had risen from being a slave to becoming a Roman governor. He never outgrew his humble beginning, however. Tacitus, the Roman historian, paints a strange word portrait of him: "He exercised the prerogatives of a king with the spirit of a slave." His quest for power was never completely satisfied. It had propelled him through three social and political-climbing marriages. At the time of his encounter with Paul, he was married to Drusilla, the daughter of Herod Agrippa I. Intrigue, greed, and unscrupulous lust for advancement had made him a feared and formidable foe of any who got in his way.

Luke presents us with several conflicting dimensions of Felix's character. We feel an almost imperious control of his affairs. He was not manipulated by the Jews nor swayed by solicitous compliments. Felix obviously was taken with what Paul said. In verse 22 Luke tells us that he had a *"more accurate knowledge of the Way."* He probably had encountered the followers of Jesus before. What is implied is that he knew more about Christianity than the Jews had supposed. But Luke also displays him true to his greedy nature when he tells us that he had hoped to get money from Paul in exchange for his release (v. 26). Later in his Palestinian career, Felix was recalled to Rome by Nero because of the complaints of the Jews that he encouraged bandits and raked off personal profit from their plunder. Felix was a hard, conniving man. In Paul he met a courageous man whose belief in the power of Christ made him unafraid and bold. The account of these two men who drew their strength from very different sources is fascinating to consider.

The Jews came to Caesarea well prepared to make their charges against the apostle Paul. They brought with them an eloquent and clever trial lawyer from Jerusalem named Tertullus. He began his case against Paul by trying to win Felix's favor with flattery. Knowing the disdain the Jews had for the governor, the lawyer's compliments were hypocritical and flagrantly false. His solicitous salutation was as untrue as the charges he proceeded to make against Paul. He called the apostle a "plague" (v. 5). The Greek word, *loimós,* means pestilence, plague, or pest. It was a demeaning charge. But that was not enough of a charge to alarm Felix.

The lawyer went on to make a further charge that he knew would disturb the Roman. Paul was charged as an insurrectionist. That was an offense against Roman law. *"A creator of dissension"* (v. 5) also means a mover of insurrections. The accuser offered no specific proof but was sweeping in his inclusive *"among all the Jews throughout the world."* What he wanted to imply was the reaches of the Roman world. Paul was charged as *"a ringleader of the sect of the Nazarenes."* Ringleader, *prōtostátēn,* means head, leader, champion, or instigator of action. Jesus often was referred to as the Nazarene. Apparently His followers had been given this name. Here it is used in a derogatory way. The further charges, that Paul had profaned the temple, dealt with matters that would not concern Felix. But the lawyer kept his attention by a criticism of Lysias for seizing Paul out of their hands *"with great violence"*

(v. 7). Every possible inflammatory and emotional trick was employed to turn Felix against Paul.

When the apostle was given an opportunity to speak, his defense was brilliant. He established all that he had in common with his accusers and his love for his nation of Israel. Then he carefully pointed out that he worshiped the God of their fathers, *"believing all things which are written in the Law and in the Prophets"* (v. 14). He believed only what had been clearly predicted. The thrust, however, was that the promises had been fulfilled. The Resurrection did happen. Paul flatly stated his case: it was concerning the resurrection of the dead that he was being tried. Note what Paul had done. He shifted the emphasis off the charges of insurrection and focused the issue on a difference of theology. That matter did not concern the Roman court. By sticking to his central message of the risen Lord he won the day.

Felix was obviously impressed with Paul. He showed his partiality by allowing the apostle's friends to visit him. If he had sided with the Jews, Felix would have been much more severe with Paul. He put off a decision, saying he would rule on the case when Lysias came down to Caesarea. The governor was bargaining for more time. In the interval, he and his wife listened intently to Paul *"concerning the faith in Christ"* (v. 24). The apostle shared the essentials of the faith: righteousness in Christ, the new person created in those who trust Him (self-control), and the urgency of making a response because of the judgment of those who hear but reject the gospel (v. 25).

Felix and Drusilla had thought hearing Paul would be an entertaining encounter. What they had not anticipated was that moral implications and the cutting edge of judgment would follow the glorious explanation of righteousness in Christ. The governor and his wife were alarmed by the penetrating power of the gospel Paul preached. Like so many who trifle with Christianity as one more set of ideas or philosophic musings, they suddenly saw the personal cost of commitment to Christ. Felix did not want his morals meddled with or his motives questioned. But the real issue was that his lust for money was more urgent than the pull within him to respond to Paul's message. He wanted an under-the-table exchange of money from Paul for his release. The tragedy was that the Roman and his wife missed the opportunity to come alive and live forever. The irony was that two years later Felix was deposed and transferred. He left Caesarea devoid of political power, and, because he rejected Christ, devoid of any meaning or hope in his life.

Felix's words in verse 25, *"Go away for now; when I have a convenient time I will call for you,"* are expressed in a multiplicity of different ways by people outside and inside the church. It is the old "don't-call-me, I'll-call-you" attitude to the communicator—really to God. Felix called for Paul, not in order to hear more of the gospel, but to make a deal for money.

Consider the ways we say "go away for now" to the call of Christ or the claims of the gospel. A character study of what prompted Felix to say that leads into an honest inventory of the ways we put off the Lord. F. W. Boreham, the great Australian preacher, said, "We make our decisions, and then our decisions turn around and make us." But I would say—we refuse to choose and our indecisiveness shapes us. There's always a next step in growth in fellowship with Christ. Some obedience is demanded, some restitution required, some reconciliation mandated, some area of life awaiting commitment. Joel described life as a valley of decision. "Multitudes, multitudes in the valley of decision! For the day of the Lord is near in the valley of decision" (Joel 3:14). The Lord is pressing some of us to become more contagious in communicating love; others He is challenging to be more bold in sharing our faith; some He is disturbing with the biblical admonition to tithe; still others He has on the edge of responding to an opportunity of leadership. "Go away, Lord! Later . . . Lord."

Augustine put the Lord off for a long time. "I could give no reply except a lazy and drowsy, 'Yes, Lord, yes, I'll get around to it right away; just don't bother me for a little while.' But 'right away' didn't happen right away; and a 'little while' turned out to be a very long while." The frightening thing is that we can express that not only before becoming a Christian, but at each new frontier of discipleship. One of my favorite sayings has been attributed to Etienne de Grellet. "I shall pass through this world but once. If, therefore, there be any kindness I can show, or any good thing I can do, let me do it now; let me not defer it or neglect it, for I shall not pass this way again."

Felix is a classic study in procrastination. The result of his indecision was that he missed his opportunity to allow the Lord to fill the emptiness of his things-oriented, power-hungry, money-grasping heart. He could not decide about Paul, Christ, or himself. The exposition of this passage about this dissolute Roman governor gives both communicator and listeners a walk through the valley of decision.

THE COURAGE TO FACE THE FUTURE

25:1 Now when Festus had come to the province, after three days he went up from Caesarea to Jerusalem. ² Then the high priest and the chief men of the Jews informed him against Paul; and they petitioned him, ³ asking a favor against him, that he would summon him to Jerusalem— while they lay in ambush along the road to kill him. ⁴ But Festus answered that Paul should be kept at Caesarea, and that he himself was going there shortly. ⁵ "Therefore," he said, "let those who have authority among you go down with me and accuse this man, to see if there is any fault in him."

⁶ And when he had remained among them more than ten days, he went down to Caesarea. And the next day, sitting on the judgment seat, he commanded Paul to be brought. ⁷ When he had come, the Jews who had come down from Jerusalem stood about and laid many serious complaints against Paul, which they could not prove, ⁸ while he answered for himself, "Neither against the law of the Jews, nor against the temple, nor against Caesar have I offended in anything at all."

⁹ But Festus, wanting to do the Jews a favor, answered Paul and said, "Are you willing to go up to Jerusalem and there be judged before me concerning these things?"

¹⁰ So Paul said, "I stand at Caesar's judgment seat, where I ought to be judged. To the Jews I have done no wrong, as you very well know. ¹¹ For if I am an offender, or have committed anything deserving of death, I do not object to dying; but if there is nothing in these things of which these men accuse me, no one can deliver me to them. I appeal to Caesar."

¹² Then Festus, when he had conferred with the council, answered, "You have appealed to Caesar? To Caesar you shall go!"

—Acts 25:1–12

Festus, the new governor, did no better at untangling the charges against Paul by the Jews than his predecessor. He had barely arrived to take up his duties before he was confronted with the sticky issue. He began his responsibilities as Roman governor by trying to establish good relations with the Jewish leaders in Jerusalem. They had one thing on their minds: getting rid of Saul of Tarsus! The chief priests were indefatigable. Once again they tried to arrange an ambush assassination by getting the governor to have Paul moved from Caesarea to Jerusalem. Festus saw through that and insisted on a further trial in Caesarea. After the first hearing, the governor reconsidered the possibility of a Jerusalem trial. The best that we can say about Festus was that he was an honest and just man. But he was also weak. He wanted to succeed with the volatile Jews and gain their favor. His lack of fiber as a leader is indicated by the fact that he asked Paul if he were willing to be tried in Jerusalem. That was Festus's decision, not his prisoner's!

The dialogue about the place of the protracted trial is used by Luke to prepare us for one of Paul's most courageous statements, one that sealed his destiny. We feel a growing impatience in Paul to get on with the Lord's guidance as he refused to be tried in Jerusalem on fallacious and fictitious charges. Then he said the deciding words: *"I appeal to Caesar"* (v. 11). All Roman citizens had the right to appeal their case to the higher court in Rome. Paul knew the law. But more than that, he knew his Master and what He wanted him to do. The one thing Festus could not refuse was the appeal to Caesar. *"You have appealed to Caesar?"* he asked in astonished relief. *"To Caesar you shall go!"*

The secret of this expression of Paul's courage was that he had nothing to fear. Neither life nor death held fearsome restrictions on him. Remember his confession of faith to the Philippians: "For to me, to live is Christ, and to die is gain" (Phil. 1:21). That's not masochism. We can't really live until we are free of the fear of dying. Our culture has sandbagged us into a tenacious grasp on this life as if it were all we had. Often we face sickness and danger with little more courage than people who have no faith. The assurance, not only of Christ's Resurrection, but our own, diffuses that anxiety. We want to live physically however long the Lord has planned for us. Until that is settled in our minds, every sickness, problem, crisis, and disappointment will be a little death.

Anxiety is really fear of losing some aspect of life. We can't say, "For to me to live is Christ" until we really believe that "to die is gain." Surely, it is part of our stewardship of the gift of life to take care of our bodies. The Lord does not want us to contribute to the shortness of life. Nor does He want us to live so cautiously in our spiritual life that we miss the adventure of living while we are alive.

Some time ago, I led my congregation in worship in grateful memory of one of the truly great women of our fellowship. Together we dared to consider Paul's words "to die is gain." It forced us to work through our grief in the context of eternal life. The woman had lived a courageous life right up to the moment of her death. During the last two years she knew she had a virulent, terminal cancer. That didn't make her resentful or cautious. Rather, she lived with greater gusto than ever. After her memorial service her husband came up to me and said, "You really put me through a wringer, but thanks. I came to this service feeling sorry for my wife—that she didn't live longer. As you shared Paul's words, I realized that I have thought about this part of eternity as best and death as tragic. The Spirit spoke to me and revealed how earth-bound I've been. That's why I have been so afraid of death. I feel ready now, and however long I'm to live, I want to grasp the joy and live it with abandonment, the way my wife did."

That was Paul's courage. He was not afraid of Rome, or Caesar, or death. He could make his appeal to Caesar because his ultimate appeal had been made years before to Christ. He had been acquitted by grace. After that, there was nothing left for him to fear, and there was everything to anticipate.

THE COURAGE OF CHRIST'S POWER BEFORE EARTHLY POWERS

¹³ And after some days King Agrippa and Bernice came to Caesarea to greet Festus. ¹⁴ When they had been there many days, Festus laid Paul's case before the king, saying: "There is a certain man left a prisoner by Felix, ¹⁵ about whom the chief priests and the elders of the Jews informed me, when I was in Jerusalem, asking for a judgment against him. ¹⁶ To them I answered, 'It is not the custom of the Romans to deliver any man to destruction before the accused meets the accusers face to face, and has opportunity to answer for himself concerning the charge against him.'¹⁷ Therefore when they had come together, without any delay, the next day I sat on the judgment seat and commanded the man to be brought in. ¹⁸ When the accusers stood up, they brought no accusation against him of such things as I supposed, ¹⁹ but had some questions against him about their own religion and about a certain Jesus, who had died, whom Paul affirmed to be alive. ²⁰ And because I was uncertain of such questions, I asked whether he was willing to go to Jerusalem and there be judged concerning these matters. ²¹ But when Paul appealed to be reserved for the decision of Augustus, I commanded him to be kept till I could send him to Caesar."

[22] Then Agrippa said to Festus, "I also would like to hear the man myself."

"Tomorrow," he said, "you shall hear him."

[23] So the next day, when Agrippa and Bernice had come with great pomp, and had entered the auditorium with the commanders and the prominent men of the city, at Festus'command Paul was brought in. [24] And Festus said: "King Agrippa and all the men who are here present with us, you see this man about whom the whole assembly of the Jews petitioned me, both at Jerusalem and here, crying out that he was not fit to live any longer. [25] But when I found that he had committed nothing deserving of death, and that he himself had appealed to Augustus, I decided to send him. [26] I have nothing certain to write to my lord concerning him. Therefore I have brought him out before you, and especially before you, King Agrippa, so that after the examination has taken place I may have something to write. [27] For it seems to me unreasonable to send a prisoner and not to specify the charges against him."

26:1 Then Agrippa said to Paul, "You are permitted to speak for yourself."

So Paul stretched out his hand and answered for himself: [2] "I think myself happy, King Agrippa, because today I shall answer for myself before you concerning all the things of which I am accused by the Jews, [3] especially because you are expert in all customs and questions which have to do with the Jews. Therefore I beg you to hear me patiently.

[4] "My manner of life from my youth, which was spent from the beginning among my own nation at Jerusalem, all the Jews know. [5] They knew me from the first, if they were willing to testify, that according to the strictest sect of our religion I lived a Pharisee. [6] And now I stand and am judged for the hope of the promise made by God to our fathers. [7] To this promise our twelve tribes, earnestly serving God night and day, hope to attain. For this hope's sake, King Agrippa, I am accused by the Jews. [8] Why should it be thought incredible by you that God raises the dead?

[9] "Indeed, I myself thought I must do many things contrary to the name of Jesus of Nazareth. [10] This I also did in Jerusalem, and many of the saints I shut up in prison, having received authority from the chief priests; and when they were put to death, I cast my vote against them. [11] And I punished

them often in every synagogue and compelled them to blaspheme; and being exceedingly enraged against them, I persecuted them even to foreign cities.

[12] "While thus occupied, as I journeyed to Damascus with authority and commission from the chief priests, [13] at midday, O king, along the road I saw a light from heaven, brighter than the sun, shining around me and those who journeyed with me. [14] And when we all had fallen to the ground, I heard a voice speaking to me and saying in the Hebrew language, 'Saul, Saul, why are you persecuting Me? It is hard for you to kick against the goads.' [15] So I said, 'Who are You, Lord?' And He said, 'I am Jesus, whom you are persecuting. [16] But rise and stand on your feet; for I have appeared to you for this purpose, to make you a minister and a witness both of the things which you have seen and of the things which I will yet reveal to you. [17] I will deliver you from the Jewish people, as well as from the Gentiles, to whom I now send you, [18] to open their eyes, in order to turn them from darkness to light, and from the power of Satan to God, that they may receive forgiveness of sins and an inheritance among those who are sanctified by faith in Me.'

[19] "Therefore, King Agrippa, I was not disobedient to the heavenly vision, [20] but declared first to those in Damascus and in Jerusalem, and throughout all the region of Judea, and then to the Gentiles, that they should repent, turn to God, and do works befitting repentance. [21] For these reasons the Jews seized me in the temple and tried to kill me. [22] Therefore, having obtained help from God, to this day I stand, witnessing both to small and great, saying no other things than those which the prophets and Moses said would come— [23] that the Christ would suffer, that He would be the first to rise from the dead, and would proclaim light to the Jewish people and to the Gentiles."

—Acts 25:13—26:23

King Herod Agrippa would have been alarmed if he had realized that his official visit to Festus in Caesarea to welcome the new governor was in fulfillment of a prophecy of Jesus of Nazareth. The Lord had predicted that His followers would witness before kings in His name. "Beware of men," He said, "for they will deliver you up to councils and scourge you in their synagogues. And you will be brought before governors and kings for My sake, as a testimony to them and to the Gentiles. But when they deliver you up, do not worry about how or what you will speak. But it will be given to you in that hour what you will speak . . ." (Matt. 10:17–19). The apostle Paul had been before councils and synagogues, governors and officials, and now Luke sets the stage for him to appear before a king. Enter King Agrippa II.

This section of Luke's account obviously was to introduce Agrippa and to allow us to listen in on Festus's recapitulation of the conflict between Paul and the chief priests. We hear the case from the Roman's point of view and are amazed at Agrippa's strange interest in meeting Paul and hearing his testimony. Since there is no new information about the trial presented here by Luke, it gives us an opportunity to look carefully at Agrippa and review the mysterious way the Herods had been intertwined in the life and followers of Jesus of Nazareth.

King Herod, Agrippa II's grandfather, had been the king who feared the birth of Jesus when told about Him by the wise men. His panic over the threat to his power prompted him to murder the male children in the vicinity of Bethlehem. Jesus and His family escaped to Egypt and later became a threat to subsequent Herods. John the Baptist was murdered by Herod Antipas, the son of Herod the Great by Maithace. He was also present in Jerusalem at the time of Jesus' trial and Crucifixion, and Jesus was sent to him by Pilate. Luke portrays him as having a great interest in Jesus and His miracle-working power. When the Lord refused to answer his questioning or do a miracle for his amusement, his soldiers mocked Him and arrayed Him in a purple robe (Luke 23:6–12). Herod Agrippa I had executed James, imprisoned Peter, and subsequently was eaten with worms as punishment for allowing people to worship him as a god (Acts 12:20–23). The very Hall of Audience in which Agrippa II would meet Paul had been built by Herod the Great. The history of the Herods and the movement of the Messiah were mysteriously woven together.

Agrippa II was born in A.D. 27. Coins of his era record his full name as Marcus Julius Agrippa. He was in Rome at the time of his father's ignominious death in Caesarea in A.D. 44. Claudius made Judea a Roman province under a procurator at that time. In A.D. 50 he gave Agrippa II the kingdom of Chalcis, the northeast portion of Palestine, and the right to appoint the Jewish high priest. Then in A.D. 53 Chalcis was exchanged for the larger territory of Batanea, Gaulonitis, Trachonitis, and Abila. In A.D. 56 Nero was emperor and gave Agrippa II the regions of Tiberias, Tarichaea, and Julius in Perea. In response Agrippa, named his capital Neronias, changing it from Caesarea Philippi as a compliment to Nero.

Now a word about Bernice. She was actually Agrippa II's sister. She married Agrippa I's brother who was then King of Chalcis. When he died in A.D. 48, Bernice came to live with her brother. Together they ruled over Chalcis during Agrippa II's brief appointment there. When Polemon was appointed King of Chalcis and Agrippa was given greater territory to rule, Bernice and Polemon were married. It didn't last and Bernice returned again to live with her brother.

The Herod family tree was an infested one. Murder, maneuvers for power, incest, and moral dissoluteness marked its many branches preceding and during the incarnate and risen ministry of Jesus Christ.

Luke is very careful to show us the keen desire of Herod Agrippa II to learn more about Paul and his faith in Jesus of Nazareth. He also captures the pageantry of Paul's appearance. The king and his sister appeared in their royal splendor dressed in purple robes. We imagine that Festus probably wore his scarlet governor's robe. The pretentious elegance of the Hall of Audience was further adorned with decorations befitting the king's presence. Captains, commanders, centurions, and legionnaires were deployed inside and around the hall for safety. It was an imposing setting in which the apostle was to witness for Christ. We picture Paul, chains dangling about his stooped, physically unimposing stature. What a moving study in contrasts!

After Festus stated the case against Paul, Agrippa gave his permission for the apostle to speak. The man in Christ was neither impressed by the pageantry of Agrippa's court nor frightened by Roman power. He grasped the occasion, and his words soared. Paul cut through the pretentious ambience and into King Agrippa's mind.

The context in which Paul put his witness is crucial to note. He affirmed the king's knowledge and understanding of the customs and affairs of the Jews. In substance he was saying, "If anyone, can understand how false are the charges against me, you can." Then he forcefully established the reason he was on trial—that he believed that the hope for which he and the Hebrew people had hoped so long, had been fulfilled. *"For this hope's sake, King Agrippa, I am accused by the Jews."* Then Paul clearly identified that hope with the Resurrection. Again, as in earlier defenses of his ministry, the apostle reviewed how vigorously he had opposed and persecuted the Way, and how that had prepared for the mighty metamorphosis that happened in his life when he met the risen Christ. Verses 12–18 repeat the now-familiar account. It is interesting how often Luke had repeated these same words. They are new each time because we hear them through the ears of different listeners.

The triumphant transition in Paul's life is etched in Agrippa's mind by the apostle. The result of meeting the risen Christ personally made Paul a new man with a new purpose. What he had persecuted he now proclaimed. And it was nothing other than the hope he and the Hebrew people had waited for so long: *"no other things than those which the prophets and Moses said would come—"* (v. 22). Then Paul gave the essence of the gospel as the fulfillment of Israel's hope: Christ's life as the Messiah, His suffering, Resurrection, and His living presence as the Light of the World—for Jews and Gentiles alike.

The hymn "I Love To Tell the Story" rings in my mind when I read this passage. The account of "Jesus and His glory" has transforming power. Those who have heard and believed rejoice to hear it again and again. And those who have never heard it, like Agrippa, are moved and stirred by its impelling power.

The gospel of Christ's atoning death, liberating Resurrection and empowering, indwelling presence is our old, old story that never grows old. Wherever we begin, with whatever text or topic, our destination is Calvary, an open tomb, and Pentecost. The secret of living whatever we preach or teach is in the healing and releasing impact of the gospel. No one can begin the Christian life without accepting the unqualified grace of the Lord Jesus. Growing in that grace produces dynamic Christ-esteem.

THE COURAGE OF CHRIST-ESTEEM

24 Now as he thus made his defense, Festus said with a loud voice, "Paul, you are beside yourself! Much learning is driving you mad!"

25 But he said, "I am not mad, most noble Festus, but speak the words of truth and reason. 26 For the king, before whom I also speak freely, knows these things; for I am convinced that none of these things escapes his attention, since this thing was not done in a corner. 27 King Agrippa, do you believe the prophets? I know that you do believe."

28 Then Agrippa said to Paul, "You almost persuade me to become a Christian."

29 And Paul said, "I would to God that not only you, but also all who hear me today, might become both almost and altogether such as I am, except for these chains."

³⁰ When he had said these things, the king stood up, as well as the governor and Bernice and those who sat with them; ³¹ and when they had gone aside, they talked among themselves, saying, "This man is doing nothing deserving of death or chains."

³² Then Agrippa said to Festus, "This man might have been set free if he had not appealed to Caesar."

—Acts 26:24–32

There is a great difference between self-esteem and Christ-esteem. The second makes possible the first, but the first without the second is misplaced pride. The joy of loving ourselves as accepted, valued,and cherished people comes from Christ. He is the source of lasting delight in being the unique, never-to-be-repeated miracle each of us is.

Christ-esteem is being able to say with Paul, "I would to God that you might become such as I am." A good test of the extent Christ has liberated us from self-condemnation and guilt is the degree to which we want everyone to become as we are. This is the liberating motivation of great communication. The communicator who is excited about the new person Christ has made her or him to be, will be an effective, life-changing agent.

So many Christians are down on themselves. They find it difficult to communicate acceptance and affirmation to anyone else. The result is that negative vibrations exude from their words and countenances. It is an observable rule of life that the more joy we feel about what Christ is doing in our own lives, the greater esteem we will be able to communicate to others.

This passage gives the communicator an opportunity to talk about Christ-centered self-esteem. Paul's delight in Christ filled him with confident, courageous enthusiasm. Apparently he became so excited about the gospel he proclaimed that both Festus and Agrippa had to make some response. The issue of the charges against Paul were forgotten temporarily as both were drawn by the magnetism of what the apostle said and how he said it. Luke tells us that Festus used a loud voice when he resisted Paul's preaching and suggested Paul was mad. The governor was obviously stirred up by the apostle.

His accusations gave Paul an opportunity to draw the net around Agrippa, for the king had been the target of his message all along. With Christ-inspired boldness, he turned to the king for validation of what he had said and the freedom with which he had said it. Paul discounted the charge of his being mad. The word Festus had used was *maínēi*, from *mania*, meaning manic or frenzied. Festus had made the wrong diagnosis. Paul's enthusiasm and excitement was not a manic high but authentic joy. In his own defense Paul retorted that Agrippa had given him encouragement to speak freely. And he had granted that, the apostle asserts, because he knew not only the prophets but also knew about Christ and the Christian movement.

Paul's full attention was now on Agrippa as he maneuvered the king into making a response. When he asked him if he believed in the prophets, he knew that if he said "no" his credibility with the listening chief priests would be lost. If he said "yes," then Paul could have asked if he was ready to accept the Messiah who had come in fulfillment of the prophets. We can be sure that the leaders of Israel leaned forward to listen intently to his response.

The English translation of Agrippa's response falls short of the mark in most versions. *"You almost persuade me to become a Christian"* (v. 28) implies that the king was on the edge of conversion. The Greek translated as "almost," *en oligōi*, means in little time, briefly or in small measure. Whatever shading of meaning we choose must be congruent with Paul's play on the king's words in verse 29 when he said that he wanted all present to become *"almost and altogether such as I am."* Here the Greek phrase *kaí en olígōi kaí en megáloi*, deals with comparisons of quantity—with little or with much. Putting Agrippa's statement with Paul's response, we discern that what the king meant was, "In a short time you want to make me a Christian," or "In small measure, you are persuading me to become a Christian." Paul's use of "little or much" in response implies either length of time or extent of belief.

Whether it took a short or long time, or whether it was a small or great beginning, Paul wanted Agrippa and all present to experience both an initial conversion through rebirth and full growth in Christ. He wanted everyone to know the fullness of the love and joy which Christ had given to him.

Agrippa was not ready for that. When he stood up, it was the signal to the governor and Bernice that the trial was over. The king's analysis of the case to Festus when they were alone reveals the extent to which Paul had penetrated the barriers around his mind. He flatly said that the Jews' charge against Paul was not worthy of death. Festus picked up on his conciliatory mood with the assertion that they could have set the apostle free if he had not appealed to Caesar. The king and the governor had been moved by Paul. We conjecture about what might have happened with further encounters. But that was not the Lord's first priority for Paul at that moment. He had the apostle scheduled for Rome.

We pause to reflect on the meaning of these long and often repetitive chapters of Acts that cover the Jerusalem and Caesarea trials. We ask what Luke was trying to help us grasp about the apostle and his dynamic faith. The beloved physician has used his favorite method, telling stories, to paint a portrait of courage. The unifying theme is the Resurrection and what belief in the victorious Lord can do to make us strong and bold in the most excruciating pressures of life. Paul's Christ-esteem made him fearless and joyous in spite of what happened to or around him.

When our basic purpose in living is to help others find the grace which has set us free, we become courageous communicators. All the aspects of the anatomy of courage Luke has shown us in these chapters of Acts are available to us. We can say with Paul, "If God is for us, who can be against us?" (Rom. 8:31).

NOTES

1. *Jewish War* II. 13. 5.

2. Luccock, Halford E., *The Acts of the Apostles in Present-Day Preaching*, 1-vol. ed. (New York: Harper & Brothers, 1942), pp. 151–52.

Chapter Twenty—The Gift of Calmness in the Storm

Acts 27:1—28:16

Scripture Outline

Friends for the Voyage (27:1–8)

Care in Spite of Carelessness (27:9–12)

Trust in the Tempest (27:13–26)

Anchors and Prayer for the Night (27:27–38)

The Malta Ministry of Healing (27:39—28:10)

A Brother's Welcome (28:11–16)

Paul's sea voyage to Rome was filled with high adventure, danger, disasters, and interventions of the Lord. Luke uses twice as many words describing the voyage to Rome as he does explaining what happened when Paul got there. He wants us to see his hero in still another set of difficult circumstances. And behind that, the beloved physician wants to reveal the power of the Holy Spirit, the risen Christ, to give calmness in the calamities of life, on land or sea. In this section we witness Paul, a passenger become the commanding captain of a ship—all because the Pilot of his life was the Lord of all creation.

Portions of these passages read like a ship's log. The nautical detail is impeccable. Luke's knowledge of the sea, ships, and sailing is vividly shown. But in each section of the account there are powerful insights about living in the Spirit. Careful exposition reveals these to the communicator and makes this portion of Acts exciting to preach or teach.

FRIENDS FOR THE VOYAGE

27:1 And when it was decided that we should sail to Italy, they delivered Paul and some other prisoners to one named

335

Julius, a centurion of the Augustan Regiment. [2] So, entering a ship of Adramyttium, we put to sea, meaning to sail along the coasts of Asia. Aristarchus, a Macedonian of Thessalonica, was with us. [3] And the next day we landed at Sidon. And Julius treated Paul kindly and gave him liberty to go to his friends and receive care. [4] When we had put to sea from there, we sailed under the shelter of Cyprus, because the winds were contrary. [5] And when we had sailed over the sea which is off Cilicia and Pamphylia, we came to Myra, a city of Lycia. [6] There the centurion found an Alexandrian ship sailing to Italy, and he put us on board.

[7] When we had sailed slowly many days, and arrived with difficulty off Cnidus, the wind not permitting us to proceed, we sailed under the shelter of Crete off Salmone. [8] Passing it with difficulty, we came to a place called Fair Havens, near the city of Lasea.

—Acts 27:1–8

In addition to giving us the details of the beginning of the voyage to Rome, in this passage Luke shows us the provision of the Lord in the friends He gives us to help us. Paul was not left alone without encouraging and strengthening friends at any point in his ministry. One of the transforming results of his conversion to Christ was that he became a loyal friend to others and had a host of friends who cared deeply for him. The lonely, friendless Pharisee had been changed into a man who could give and receive profound love expressed in faithful friendships. Wherever he went he established deep bonds of love with people who became life-long friends.

Aristarchus is a good example. He was among the converts during Paul's ministry at Thessalonica. He was with Paul through the disputation with the silversmiths in Ephesus and was arrested during that conflict. That indicates that he had come from Macedonia to assist Paul while he was in Ephesus. Aristarchus accompanied the apostle to Jerusalem and was with him for the two and a half years of turbulence there and in Caesarea during the protracted trial. When it was time to sail for Rome, the loyal Thessalonian was permitted to accompany the apostle as his servant. He was with him in Rome at the end of his life.

Luke also was with Paul. The pointed "us" in verse 2 underlines this. The beloved physician had been a consistent and encouraging friend in Christ each step of the way. His admiration and loving esteem for Paul flashes throughout his account of the apostle's ministry. He too was with Paul until his death. Read the closing lines of most of Paul's epistles and feel the warmth of friendship he had for the gift of friendships in the Lord.

But Paul also won friends among the most unlikely candidates. Reading between the lines, we observe that he boarded the ship for Rome as no ordinary prisoner. The orders from Festus must have contained instructions for preferential treatment. Luke uses a term which may point up this fact. The use of *hetérous* for "other" in verse 1, *"Paul and some other prisoners,"* suggests a difference in category. Perhaps Festus was a secret admirer of Paul's courage. Whatever the case, Julius, the centurion put in charge of delivering the apostle to Rome, treated him with respect and gave him privileges not accorded to the other prisoners.

The nautical account of the first stages of the voyage is punctuated by the visit of Paul to friends in Sidon. Note the words Luke uses in verse 3: *"And Julius treated Paul kindly and gave him liberty to go to his friends and receive care."* There's a gem for exposition. Paul had never been to Sidon, and yet he had friends there. During his visit to nearby Tyre (Acts 21:3), perhaps he had met some of them. He knew that there were Christians there and that meant immediate friendship, for the love of Christ gave them instant rapport. Luke gives us the secret of Paul's ability to make and keep lasting friends, indicating that he went into Sidon to receive as well as give. Some have suggested that the care the apostle needed was medical. That's questionable, with Luke the physician at his side.

Paul needed the uplifting boost of fellowship. Visiting the Christians in Sidon gave the apostle further assurance that the Christian movement not only would survive, but flourish. Paul established great friendships because he allowed people to love him and meet his needs. Lonely Christians are those who have confused strength with independence and self-reliance. Doing things for people makes friends; allowing them to do something for us as well, forges lasting friendship. And behind all truly great Christian friendships is the One who said, "No longer do I call you servants . . . but friends" (John 15:15). Paul was on his way to Rome, but he was not alone or lonely. Christ and his friends were with him.

Luke traces the first leg of the journey. From Caesarea, the ship stayed alongside the coast of the Mediterranean to Sidon. After the brief stop we mentioned, a west wind carried them along the coast of Cilicia, under the protection of the Island of Cyprus. At Myra, a port on the coast of Lycia, Paul and his companions, along with the prisoners, were transferred by the centurion to a grain vessel bound for Italy.

CARE IN SPITE OF CARELESSNESS

9 Now when much time had been spent, and sailing was now dangerous because the Fast was already over, Paul advised them, 10 saying, "Men, I perceive that this voyage will end with disaster and much loss, not only of the cargo and ship, but also our lives." 11 Nevertheless the centurion was more persuaded by the helmsman and the owner of the ship than by the things spoken by Paul. 12 And because the harbor was not suitable to winter in, the majority advised to set sail from there also, if by any means they could reach Phoenix, a harbor of Crete opening toward the southwest and northwest, and winter there.

—Acts 27:9–12

There is a profound theological truth beneath the account of the decision to proceed in spite of the time of the year and the treacherous sailing conditions. Paul did not allow the urgency he felt about getting to Rome cause him to push the captain of the ship and the centurion to proceed. In fact, he warned against it and urged that they winter at Fair Havens on Crete before moving on. A straight course across the Aegean was impossible at that time of the year. Luke tells us that the Feast of Atonement was over, indicating that it was sometime early in October. In A.D. 59 the feast was held on October 5.

In those days, people seldom sailed after September, and by November, it was considered foolhardy. Between fall and early spring, the waters were dangerous not only because of the winds and the turbulent sea, but because the cloudy weather made navigation difficult without the sun by day and the stars by night. Paul predicted that a voyage at that time would end with disaster in the loss of the ship and many lives. The centurion did not take his advice. The helmsman and the owner of the ship wanted to strike out for another harbor on Crete to winter there. It was a disastrous decision, as we shall see.

The point for our exposition is that Paul did not make rash decisions on the basis of his expectation of the Lord's protection. So many of our difficulties occur when we make foolhardy decisions and expect the Lord to get us out of our self-made problems. But also, often we find ourselves in difficulties caused by the wrong choices of others.

We may ask, if the Lord was so anxious to get Paul to Rome, why all the disasters during the sea voyage? Why didn't He calm the seas and change the direction of the winds? Instead, He guided Paul to warn the centurion and the owner of the ship not to proceed.

The Lord gives us intelligence and experience, as well as specific guidance. The problems Paul and the others had at sea were because the centurion denied all three. As we will see, Paul was right in not wanting to leave Fair Havens. And, as we shall also observe, the Lord intervened to help them in spite of the careless choice.

The Lord obviously had planned for the ship to stay where it was until spring. If it had, the rest of Acts 27 would not have been written, and Luke's only account would have been of a smooth sailing from Crete to Italy. So many of our problems are brought on by foolish or unguided decisions. And when trouble results, we blame God. The impact of the next section is that He helps us even then.

TRUST IN THE TEMPEST

13 When the south wind blew softly, supposing that they had obtained their desire, putting out to sea, they sailed close by Crete. 14 But not long after, a tempestuous head wind arose, called Euroclydon. 15 So when the ship was caught, and could not head into the wind, we let her drive. 16 And running under the shelter of an island called Clauda, we secured the skiff with difficulty. 17 When they had taken it on board, they used cables to undergird the ship; and fearing lest they should run aground on the Syrtis Sands, they struck sail and so were driven. 18 And because we were exceedingly tempest-tossed, the next day they lightened the ship. 19 On the third day we threw the ship's tackle overboard with our own hands. 20 Now when neither sun nor stars appeared for many days, and no small tempest beat on us, all hope that we would be saved was finally given up.

21 But after long abstinence from food, then Paul stood in the midst of them and said, "Men, you should have listened to me, and not have sailed from Crete and incurred this disaster and loss. 22 And now I urge you to take heart, for there will be

no loss of life among you, but only of the ship. [23] For there stood by me this night an angel of the God to whom I belong and whom I serve, [24] saying, 'Do not be afraid, Paul; you must be brought before Caesar; and indeed God has granted you all those who sail with you.' [25] Therefore take heart, men, for I believe God that it will be just as it was told me. [26] However, we must run aground on a certain island."

—Acts 27:13–26

A soft southerly wind gave the sailors false confidence as they sailed out of Fair Havens bound for Phoenix, coasting along the shores of Crete. Then the fierce winds Paul had predicted hit them. It was a northeaster called the Euroclydon, well known and feared by sailors. The ship was driven off course as the winds tossed it to and fro in the high, frothy, angry waves of the sea. In an effort to save the ship, cargo was thrown overboard. Cables were drawn under the hull of the ship and tightened to keep the vessel from breaking under the tempestuous winds and waves. The great fear was that they surely would be carried into the Syrtis Sands, off the coast of North Africa. That had been the fate of many ships caught by the Euroclydon. Terror gripped all on board the ship. All hope was abandoned.

But not by Paul. He remained calm in the calamity. His trust was not in the ship or its crew, but in the resurrected Lord. The apostle had been through every imaginable kind of danger and difficulty. And the Lord had come to him at just the right moment. This crisis at sea was no exception. After a long fast, a messenger of the Lord came to him and assured him. The message was unmistakable: *"Do not be afraid, Paul; you must be brought before Caesar; and indeed God has granted you all those who sail with you"* (v. 24).

When Paul relayed the good news to the centurion, owner, and sailors of the ship, he was in command of the ship. He was calm and confident. We picture his radiant face in contrast to the seasick and panic-stricken passengers and crew. His voice rang above the howling winds, communicating new hope. They would all be saved, even though they would have to run aground on an island. Awe and wonder filled the hearts of all aboard. This was no ordinary man who exuded such a vibrant hope. But the prisoner in chains pointed away from himself to the source of his discernment and bright promise: *"Therefore take heart, men, for I believe God that it will be just as it was told me"* (v. 25).

ANCHORS AND PRAYER FOR THE NIGHT

27 Now when the fourteenth night had come, as we were driven up and down in the Adriatic Sea, about midnight the sailors sensed that they were drawing near some land. 28 And they took soundings and found it to be twenty fathoms; and when they had gone a little farther, they took soundings again and found it to be fifteen fathoms. 29 Then, fearing lest we should run aground on the rocks, they dropped four anchors from the stern, and prayed for day to come. 30 And as the sailors were seeking to escape from the ship, when they had let down the skiff into the sea, under pretense of putting out anchors from the prow, 31 Paul said to the centurion and the soldiers, "Unless these men stay in the ship, you cannot be saved." 32 Then the soldiers cut away the ropes of the skiff and let it fall off.

33 And as day was about to dawn, Paul implored them all to take food, saying, "Today is the fourteenth day you have waited and continued without food, and eaten nothing. 34 Therefore I urge you to take nourishment, for this is for your survival, since not a hair will fall from the head of any of you." 35 And when he had said these things, he took bread and gave thanks to God in the presence of them all; and when he had broken it he began to eat. 36 Then they were all encouraged, and also took food themselves. 37 And in all we were two hundred and seventy-six persons on the ship. 38 So when they had eaten enough, they lightened the ship and threw out the wheat into the sea.

—Acts 27:27–38

Often, making it through the night is not easy. In the night hours worry and fear stalk their prey. We've all known restless nights when sleep eludes us and our minds multiply our problems, conjuring them into larger and more grotesque monsters than they are. What can we do to make it through the night?

What Paul and the sailors did on the fourteenth night at sea provides a good parabolic image for what we can do to make it through the night. When they sensed they were drawing near to some land, they sounded the depth. First twenty fathoms, and then fifteen. The fear of going on the rocks was real. To slow the drift until morning, they let out four anchors and prayed for day to come.

Verse 29 provides an excellent basis for communicating what to do during the dark night of the soul as well as during any night of sleepless anxiety. Night is not only determined by the revolving of the earth around the sun. The very word "night" is symbolic of those times when all seems dark and foreboding for us. Like those on the ship, we pray, but for us that prayer is also our time in which we let down our anchors. What are they for you? What keeps the ship of your life off the rocks of despair and doubt that God will use what you are going through? Allow me to share my anchors.

The first anchor for me is faith. In the darkness, I repeat all the names of the Lord that describe His nature. One of my professors at the University of Edinburgh was the late John Baillie. Listening to him pray before and after his lectures taught me how to pray with power. I was impressed with the introduction to his communion with the Lord. Before intercessions or supplications, he would address the Lord with His biblical names. God didn't need to be reminded of who He was, but the great Baillie did. It reestablished in his mind the magnificence of God and in his heart, the grace and acceptance of God. Only then would he pray about needs and concerns. Renewed faith in God results from this kind of meditation. Stating who God is and what He had done for us in Christ, and what He does for us through His present, intervening power, engenders a faith for the night. Our essential faith in the Cross, the Resurrection, and the Pentecost miracle is reaffirmed. Then the Holy Spirit gift of specific faith is released for problems. We move from the faith that has reconciled us to the faith that releases us.

The second anchor is closely related to the first. It is the surrender of the need or concern of the night. So often our night of the soul is prolonged because we insist on holding onto a problem with one hand while we reach out for God's help with the other. Freedom comes only when we completely release our needs.

A third anchor is hope. Emil Brunner said, "What oxygen is to the lungs, such is hope for the meaning of life." Hope is a combination of trust in the faithfulness of the Lord and the perfectly timed invasion of His Spirit into our affairs. As we have seen all through our study of Acts, He has people to deploy for our aid, and He has power over the rearrangement of circumstances. Our hope is that He will act—on time and in time.

The last anchor is thanksgiving. Thanking the Lord for the problem of the night gives perspective and inner strength. I am never free until I thank Him for what I will learn through the complexity. Thanking the Lord in advance of a solution breaks the bind of worry. It expresses our willingness to cooperate with Him in the solution. Often after thanking the Lord, a specific step becomes clear.

Just before dawn, Paul led the people on board the ship in eating and thanksgiving. They had been on a fast seeking the blessing of the Lord. Undoubtedly Paul had called for the fast as an expression of unreserved dependence on the Lord for survival. Now it was time to eat and give thanks. The Lord had spoken and given assurance that they would be saved.

A thanksgiving celebration during the night of the soul is a way of breaking the tension and reaffirming our conviction that the Lord has been and will be in charge.

The four anchors can vary. Perhaps you have your own set to keep you off the rocks. In the exposition of this passage and the parable it provides for the dark times of life, it is crucial to list the four which have worked for you. Encourage people to identify their anchors. Those in a dark night will be kept off the rocks and others will become prepared for the future.

THE MALTA MINISTRY OF HEALING

[39] When it was day, they did not recognize the land; but they observed a bay with a beach, onto which they planned to run the ship if possible. [40] And they let go the anchors and left them in the sea, meanwhile loosing the rudder ropes; and they hoisted the mainsail to the wind and made for shore. [41] But striking a place where two seas met, they ran the ship aground; and the prow stuck fast and remained immovable, but the stern was being broken up by the violence of the waves.

[42] And the soldiers'plan was to kill the prisoners, lest any of them should swim away and escape. [43] But the centurion, wanting to save Paul, kept them from their purpose, and commanded that those who could swim should jump overboard first and get to land, [44] and the rest, some on boards and some on parts of the ship. And so it was that they all escaped safely to land.

28:1 Now when they had escaped, they then found out that the island was called Malta. [2] And the natives showed us unusual kindness; for they kindled a fire and made us all welcome, because of the rain that was falling and because of the cold. [3] But when Paul had gathered a bundle of sticks and laid them on the fire, a viper came out because of the heat, and fastened on his hand. 4 So when the natives saw the creature hanging from his hand, they said to one another, "No doubt this man is a murderer, whom, though he has escaped the sea, yet justice does not allow to live." 5 But he shook off the creature into the fire and suffered no harm. 6 However, they were expecting that he would swell up or suddenly fall down dead. But after they had looked for a long time and saw no harm come to him, they changed their minds and said that he was a god.

7 In that region there was an estate of the leading citizen of the island, whose name was Publius, who received us and entertained us courteously for three days. 8 And it happened that the father of Publius lay sick of a fever and dysentery. Paul went in to him and prayed, and he laid his hands on him and healed him. 9 So when this was done, the rest of those on the island who had diseases also came and were healed. 10 They also honored us in many ways; and when we departed, they provided such things as were necessary.

—Acts 27:39—28:10

Dawn brought sight of land for Paul and his shipmates, They did not know that it was Malta. A beach on the land looked like a safe place to ground the ship. What they didn't know was that beneath the waters was a treacherous reef. They cut the four anchors, loosed the rudder ropes, and hoisted the mainsail. Then it happened. The prow of the ship stuck fast in the shoal and the stern was battered to pieces by the surging waves. There was nothing to do but abandon ship and grasp anything afloat to aid in swimming ashore.

Paul and the other prisoners barely escaped execution. The soldiers wanted to kill them, fearing they would swim away and, once on land, would slip out of their grasp. Julius, the centurion, stepped in. Luke tells us that he wanted to save Paul. Was this allegiance to his duty to deliver the apostle to Rome, or in gratitude for what he had done to save their lives? I think the latter. He knew that they would not have made it if it had not been for Paul's leadership, prayers, and the blessing of his Lord. The apostle had made another friend.

The account of what happened on Malta is further evidence of how the Lord will use everything for His glory and our effectiveness. Paul could have been disgruntled because of this further

344

delay in reaching Rome. Instead he took the disaster in stride. He didn't sit on the beach grumbling with the survivors about why this difficulty had happened.

Note the human dimension of active helpfulness shown us as the great apostle gathers firewood to help warm and dry the soaked and weary travelers. He could have ordered Aristarchus to do that, or held back waiting for others to serve him. Life presents us with a splendid succession of opportunities to put our faith into practical action. Often our best opportunities to share our faith result from involvement and caring in unspectacular ways for the people we long to introduce to the Savior. We earn the right to be heard.

But something happened to Paul while building the fire that was even more convincing than his practical helpfulness. A viper was forced out of a crevice in one of the pieces of wood by the heat of the fire. It fastened itself to Paul's hand. This was a vivid picture: a leaping fire, the apostle in chains, a serpent dangling from his hand, and the natives of the island, as well as Paul's shipmates, looking on in horrified fright. The natives who had kindly greeted the survivors now expressed the superstition of their culture. The viper's attack was surely the just punishment of one they perceived to be a murderer on the way to his execution.

Paul, with customary calmness, shook the viper off his hand and went about his duties of helping others. The natives watched, waiting for his hand to swell and death to come. After a long time, when Paul was still joyously alive and active, the natives decided that this was no murderer but a god!

We are interested to note that in the rest of the Malta ministry Paul did not preach—at least, not in a sermon to an assembled group. His sermons on Malta were enacted healing miracles. He laid hands on the father of Publius, a leading citizen of the island. We can be sure that as he prayed for the old man's fever and dysentery, he also shared with him the power of the One to whom he prayed. The result of the man's healing was that other islanders came to Paul and were healed of their diseases.

Luke has given us further bright splashes of color on the canvas of his portrait of Paul. The living Lord Jesus was continuing His ministry through the apostle—serving, revealing authority over a poisonous viper (He had promised that—Mark 16:18), healing, and caring profoundly for people.

Preaching the gospel and the ministry of healing are inseparable. When healing is understood in the deeper context of salvation, wholeness, health, and ultimate well-being, we can practice both preaching and healing prayer as a part of Christ's ministry through us.

The ministry of healing has been a vital part of the care of people in my church in Hollywood. In addition to individual times for healing in the privacy of the study, a person's home, or a hospital room, the Lord has led the pastors and elders of our church to hold healing services for prayer for the spiritual, emotional, and relational illnesses of people.

As a result of a thorough study of worship, the elders on the Session's Worship Department began to pray about a way to bring the healing ministry into our Sunday morning worship where the Lord brings the largest crowds. As I mentioned earlier, the elders gather on the chancel steps after each service to meet with people who have responded to the invitation to confess Christ. But now, in addition, the elders wanted to try having a portion of a particular Sunday's services set aside for prayer and the laying on of hands for healing. The exciting possibility of the experiment in faith was received with enthusiasm by the rest of the elders in the church. A particular Sunday was set and a message on Christ's power to heal all of life was prepared. The order of worship was altered, leaving fifteen minutes for prayer, quiet singing of hymns, and the opportunity for people to come forward to kneel for the laying on of hands by the elders. This invitation was printed in the bulletin and reinforced verbally: "This time of quiet is for all of us to reflect on what the Lord has said to us in this time of worship and to receive His Spirit for the healing of our spiritual, emotional, and physical needs. Pray for yourself and those around you. The Elders are available in the front of the sanctuary to help you claim the healing power of the Lord in your life. They are also ready to talk and pray with those who wish to confess Christ and those who wish to become members of this church. We care about what concerns you!"

The response was overwhelming. People came streaming to the chancel to pray for themselves and others. The results have been gratifying. The church as a worshiping congregation and an equipping center, was also a healing community. By having a time for healing in addition to the preaching in the Sunday morning hours of worship, the congregation as a whole was able to reaffirm the threefold calling to preach, teach, and heal.

The experience of that Sunday changed the way we end all of our services on Sunday morning. After the exposition and a hymn there is a time for quiet prayer during which people are encouraged to pray for themselves and others and the elders are available to pray with those who come forward. People look forward to having an opportunity to claim what Christ is continuing to do in our age.

In this portion of our exposition of Acts we have witnessed the Lord's power in dangerous circumstances. Life is a voyage. It has its winds, angry seas, and crises we barely survive. The Lord helps us by trying to keep us out of danger, and He steps in when our own or other's choices are foolish or careless. The gift of calmness in the turbulent seas of life is given by the Lord who never panics. Why should He? He knows the outcome and the destination. And so do we. Our Rome . . . and beyond that an eternal city called heaven.

A BROTHER'S WELCOME

¹¹ After three months we sailed in an Alexandrian ship whose figurehead was the Twin Brothers, which had wintered at the island. ¹² And landing at Syracuse, we stayed three days. ¹³ From there we circled round and reached Rhegium. And after one day the south wind blew; and the next day we came to Puteoli, ¹⁴ where we found brethren, and were invited to stay with them seven days. And so we went toward Rome. ¹⁵ And from there, when the brethren heard about us, they came to meet us as far as Appii Forum and Three Inns. When Paul saw them, he thanked God and took courage.

¹⁶ Now when we came to Rome, the centurion delivered the prisoners to the captain of the guard; but Paul was permitted to dwell by himself with the soldier who guarded him.

—Acts 28:11–16

I have included this passage in our consideration of Paul's voyage to Rome for two reasons. It completes the last leg of the trip, but also gives us a further evidence of the growing fellowship of the "brethren," the fellowship of the believers in Christ. We have seen the influence of friends on Paul's life and his inclusive capacity to make deep friendships in Christ. This section adds two more examples of that, first in the visit of the "brethren" in Puteoli (v. 13) and then in the welcome of the church at Rome through emissaries sent to meet Paul at the Appii Forum (v. 15). In that light, Acts 28:11–16 is more than a travelogue. It is another sign of the way the Lord cared for His apostle through the new family of brothers and sisters who were committed to Christ and to each other. With that in mind we can pick up and appreciate the stunning story Luke is trying to communicate.

When the three months of waiting on Malta for the winter to pass were completed, the shipwrecked survivors boarded another Alexandrian ship headed for Italy. We assume the ship sailed from Valetta, the main harbor of Malta at that time. Luke's attention to detail gives us another interesting insight for our exposition. He tells us that the figurehead on the bow of the ship was the Twin Brothers. Sailors at that time put great trust in two mythological characters called Castor and Pollux, of the astrological sign of Gemini. They were purported to give protection in storms, and were adopted as mascot heroes of the sailors. We are sure that Paul, Luke, and Aristarchus, and perhaps even Julius the centurion, smiled as they boarded the ship and examined the wood carving protruding from the bow. The Lord alone had saved them from death at sea, and He, not the Twin Brothers, would bring them safely to Italy. Their hope was not in the stars or their astrological signs, but the Savior of the world.

From Valetta the ship made the eighty-mile voyage to Syracuse on the island of Sicily for a three-day layover. From there it sailed a further seventy miles to Rhegium, a port on the toe of the Italian mainland. A south wind filled the sails of the ship for a straight course to Puteoli, in the Bay of Naples.

Julius's kindness and respect for Paul was expressed again when he allowed the apostle to visit a fellowship of Christians who lived there. We are taken by the fact that Paul and his companions stayed seven days. Now that the apostle was on the Italian mainland and a few miles from Rome, there seemed to be no hurry—another evidence of Paul's calmness in Christ to live to the fullest each step of the way. People were more important than plans or scheduled programs.

The "brethren" at Rome had received word of Paul's arrival at Puteoli and could not wait to welcome him. A deputation of believers was sent to greet him and express their joy. It is significant that Luke uses the Greek word *apántēsin* from *apántēsis*, which, according to F. F. Bruce, was "sort of a technical term for the official welcome of a newly arrived dignitary by a deputation which went out to greet him and escort him there." There is deep significance in the use of this word to describe the welcome received by Paul from the Roman church. Paul had written the Christians at Rome about his fondest expectations for his visit. "For I hope to see you on my journey, and to be helped on my way there by you, if first I may enjoy your company for a while. . . . And I am sure that when I come to you, I shall come in the fullness of the blessing of the gospel of Christ" (Rom. 15:24b, 29).

He had not anticipated coming as a prisoner. Surely he had told the church at Puteoli what he had been through in Jerusalem, Caesarea, and the sea voyage. Perhaps news had been carried by a Puteolian Christian or word from Caesarea had reached Rome about Paul's arrest, trial, and appeal to Caesar. Whatever the source, the Christians in Rome knew of Paul's circumstances and wanted to give him the hero's welcome he deserved. This, too, must have startled and further amazed Julius, the centurion. Who was this prisoner he was delivering to Caesar? If he had interfered with the jubilant reception, Luke would have told us. It could not have happened without his approval.

Two groups of welcoming disciples met the apostle, one at the Appii Forum, forty miles from Rome, and the other at the Three Inns, thirty miles away. These stops along the Appian Way meant a great deal to Paul. When he saw them, he thanked God. All the good things which happened to him were maximized by recognizing them as gifts of God and expressing his thanksgiving.

The church at Rome had looked forward to Paul's visit. They needed his encouragement as much as he needed theirs. The church had grown from a small nucleus of Jews who had been in Jerusalem at Pentecost when the church was born. The fellowship grew as Hebrew-Christian merchants and travelers settled in the Roman capital. A significant portion of the church was made up of the Liberti, slaves who had purchased their freedom. And then there were converts from among the population of Jews. Added to all these were Romans, many of whom were secret followers of Christ, some in fact, from Caesar's household. Christianity was alive and well in Rome. And now the apostle Paul had come to them. We can imagine the sheer delight and exuberance expressed that day along the Appian Way to Rome.

CHAPTER TWENTY–ONE—THE END OF THE BEGINNING

ACTS 28:17–31

Scripture Outline

The Three D's of Dullness (28:17–29)

The Dynamics of Great Communication (28:30–31)

We have come to the long-awaited arrival of Paul in Rome. Some may be disappointed by the fifteen verses that cover what happened there. There are no appearances before Caesar or stirring sermons in the Roman courts as we witnessed in Caesarea. Luke records only that Paul was delivered to the captain of the guard and was given the privilege of a private residence with a soldier to guard him, that he met with the leaders of the Jews in Rome, and that for two years he encouraged the church and received all who came to him.

Our author ends his account abruptly. The reason for this, I believe, is that he probably wrote Acts during the two years he was with Paul in Rome. That supports the dating of Acts around A.D. 63. He wrote as much as he knew of at that time. Further, it is believed that Paul was acquitted and released after this first of two arraignments in Rome. Later, after about four years of further ministry, he was again arrested and brought back to Rome where he was tried and executed. Second Timothy was written by Paul during those final days before his death.

Luke has accomplished his goal and purpose. He has told us what Jesus Christ, the risen Lord, in the power of the Holy Spirit, continued to do. He ends his account with the last observations he had made of Christ's magnificent and mighty ministry in the Holy Spirit. If he had completed Acts at a later time, it would have included subsequent events.

The abrupt ending leaves us with the challenge and opportunity to allow the Spirit to write the next chapter in the Book of Acts today in and through us! And that's exactly what the last verses in Luke's account enable us to do. I am convinced that he wanted to give us one final descriptive contrast between the old and the new Israel. We are shown the negative, cautious, and restrictive religion of the Jews at Rome in contrast with the dynamic, inclusive, and loving fellowship of the church gathered around Paul in his quarters. The passage gives us a concluding opportunity to expose the difference between sterile religion of rules and regulations and the vibrant new life in Christ.

Here is a summary of what Jesus continued to do and continues to do today.

THE THREE "D'S" OF DULLNESS

¹⁷ And it came to pass after three days that Paul called the leaders of the Jews together. So when they had come together, he said to them: "Men and brethren, though I have done nothing against our people or the customs of our fathers, yet I was delivered as a prisoner from Jerusalem into the hands of the Romans, ¹⁸ who, when they had examined me, wanted to let me go, because there was no cause for putting me to death. ¹⁹ But when the Jews spoke against it, I was compelled to appeal to Caesar, not that I had anything of which to accuse my nation. ²⁰ For this reason therefore I have called for you, to see you and speak with you, because for the hope of Israel I am bound with this chain."

²¹ Then they said to him, "We neither received letters from Judea concerning you, nor have any of the brethren who came reported or spoken any evil of you. ²² But we desire to hear from you what you think; for concerning this sect, we know that it is spoken against everywhere."

²³ So when they had appointed him a day, many came to him at his lodging, to whom he explained and solemnly testified of the kingdom of God, persuading them concerning Jesus from both the Law of Moses and the Prophets, from morning till evening. ²⁴ And some were persuaded by the things which were spoken, and some disbelieved. ²⁵ So when they did not agree among themselves, they departed after Paul had said one word: "The Holy Spirit spoke rightly through Isaiah the prophet to our fathers, ²⁶ saying,

'Go to this people and say:

352

"Hearing you will hear, and shall not understand;
And seeing you will see, and not perceive;
²⁷ *For the hearts of this people have grown dull.*
Their ears are hard of hearing,
And their eyes they have closed,
Lest they should see with their eyes and hear with their
ears,
Lest they should understand with their hearts and turn,
So that I should heal them." '
²⁸ "Therefore let it be known to you that the salvation of
God has been sent to the Gentiles, and they will hear it!"
²⁹ And when he had said these words, the Jews departed and
had a great dispute among themselves.
—Acts 28:17–29

An alliteration of "d's" summarizes the response of the leaders of the synagogue at Rome. They disbelieved, departed, and disputed among themselves—all because of their spiritual dullness. That gives us an outline of the passage for our exposition.

Paul never gave up on his fellow Jews. No more than three days after he arrived in Rome he called the leaders of the Jews together. After all that he had been through on his missionary journeys and then in Jerusalem and Caesarea, meeting hostility, rejection, and persecution from his countrymen everywhere, we would assume that he would not have wanted to meet with more of them. But this was not the case with Paul; he had to share the gospel. The hope of Israel was Jesus Christ, the Messiah. Because of that hope he was in chains. He had done no wrong worthy of death. The first meeting with the leaders was concluded with their expression of willingness to hear what he had to say. That was couched in the reserve they had about *"this sect"* (v. 22), which they said was spoken against everywhere.

When the second visit began, Paul got down to essentials. All day long, *"from morning till evening,"* (v. 23), he explained and testified to the true meaning of the kingdom of God and the fulfillment of the prophets and Moses in Jesus as Messiah. Luke uses the verb *exetítheto,* "expanded," to indicate the exhaustive detail and care Paul used in explaining the Scriptures. Note that he began with the kingdom of God, His rule and reign over all history. Then he told them about Christ, the Messiah, King of that kingdom. All we have to do is read Colossians and Philippians to imagine the words Paul may have used to describe Jesus Christ—

"the fullness of the Godhead bodily" (Col. 2:9) and "the righteousness . . . which is through faith in Christ" (Phil. 3:9). It is likely that these magnificent words when Paul subsequently wrote during this first imprisonment in Rome, were on his mind and tongue as he spoke that day to the leaders.

Verse 24 tells us of the mixed response. Some were persuaded, and *"some disbelieved."* Before they departed, Paul, grieved by their disbelief, repeated a passage from Isaiah 6:9-10, quoting the Lord's words to the prophet about Israel. The implication was that Paul believed that the passage described his listeners. It had also been used by Jesus in response to the disbelief of the Jews (John 12:40).

Paul's point was to show the leaders that they had come to the dreadful stage of religious dullness. They heard words but did not understand; they saw truth but would not respond; their emotions were insensitive; and their ears were weary of great ideas which they had not lived. The tragic result of their faithless familiarity was that they were no longer able to receive truth and order their lives around it. Most of all, traditions and customs, rules and regulations had been substituted for God. They had resisted so long, they could not receive. There was no longer a desire or a need for God's healing love and forgiveness. Status as the people of God had excluded God!

The Isaiah passage was startling and stinging enough. But added to it, Paul asserted that the salvation of God offered to the Jews was now sent to the Gentiles. That did it. When the leaders heard that, they *"departed."* But the matter did not end with leaving Paul. A great dispute ensued among them. That means that some had been convinced by Paul's preaching. We wonder how many returned to listen further and, through the gift of faith from the Holy Spirit, joined the growing church in Rome.

THE DYNAMICS OF GREAT COMMUNICATION

30 Then Paul dwelt two whole years in his own rented house, and received all who came to him, 31 preaching the kingdom of God and teaching the things which concern the Lord Jesus Christ with all confidence, no one forbidding him.
—*Acts 28:30-31*

The closing two verses of Acts describe the essential elements of powerful communication and of a great church. Paul was receptive to all inquirers, preached the kingdom of God, proclaimed the

Lord Jesus Christ with confidence, and was given freedom. These two concluding verses help us summarize what we've learned about being communicators and about the results we desire in the people to whom we communicate. Luke shows us the communicator's message, method, and magnanimity.

1. *The Christian communicator's message.* Picture the apostle Paul in his house-arrest quarters in Rome. Hebrew and Gentile inquirers from every level of the capital's society crowded in around him. They listened for hours with rapt attention. With one hand the apostle was chained to the Roman guard; with the other he gestured emphatically as he communicated his impelling message. The deepest needs and most urgent questions of the people were being met. Their intellectual and spiritual hungers were being fed.

Luke tells us that Paul's central theme was the kingdom and the King. For the apostle, the kingdom provided the sublime context for the communication of the gospel and the introduction of men and women to the King of kings. With customary thoroughness, he traced the royal theme with incisive exposition revealing the kingdom as the purpose, plan, and power of God. We imagine that he began with Exodus 19:6 and declared God's purpose to create a people who would be faithful and obedient to Him as sovereign king of their lives. They were to be a special people in whom His reign and rule on earth would be accomplished and shared with all people: "You shall be to Me a kingdom of priests and a holy nation." Then surely Paul reminded his listeners of David's clear proclamation of Jehovah as King of Israel and the unique destiny of His people to be a true theocracy under His guidance and care.

We wonder if Paul's exposition included David's words in 1 Chronicles 29:10–11: "Blessed are You, LORD God of Israel, our Father, forever and ever. Yours, O Lord, is the greatness, the power and the glory, the victory and the majesty; for all that is in heaven and earth is Yours; Yours is the kingdom, O Lord, and You are exalted as head over all." Perhaps that doxology was followed by Paul with quotations from Psalms 103 and 145, revealing the psalmist's growing perception of God as King of all creation. "The Lord has established His throne in heaven, and His kingdom rules over all" (Ps. 103:19); and, "They shall speak of the glory of Your kingdom, and talk of Your power, to make known to the sons of men His mighty acts, and the glorious majesty of His kingdom. Your kingdom is an everlasting kingdom, and your dominion endures throughout all generations" (Ps. 145:11–13).

Having established the essential conviction of the Lord as King over all creation and His chosen people, we suppose Paul went on to show what happened in Israel's departure from that magnificent truth. We can hear his voice filled with passion and pathos as he recounted the sad tale of Israel's effort to be like other nations in dependence on military might and human glory. Probably he led his listeners through a disturbing but honest reflection on the painful memories of the divided kingdom, the demise of political and military power, and eventually the excruciating events of the Exile.

That would have prepared Paul's listeners for the message of the prophets about the coming of the Messiah and the establishment of a distinctly different quality of kingdom. With the apostle we leaf back to Isaiah 9:6–7 and feel the expectant hope for the "Wonderful, Counselor, Mighty God, Everlasting Father, Prince of Peace," who was to come to establish a new kingdom with "judgment and justice." Then we hear Paul move in rapid-fire through the prophetic hope of Micah, Obadiah, the vision of Daniel and the longing for the kingdom of God. It was to come when Israel least expected or deserved it. The kingdom rule of God would be established in the life and message of Immanuel. He would be the reign and rule of the Lord on earth, and His realm would be the minds and hearts of those who would recognize Him and make Him king of their lives.

With that background of exposition of Scripture, Paul had set the stage to proclaim Jesus of Nazareth as Messiah and King of the kingdom. We are sure that the apostle declared that the kingdom of God was the central theme of the Messiah's message and life. For Paul, the kingdom was not a concept alone, but the surging power of God released in and through Christ. The Master had begun His ministry declaring that the kingdom was at hand: it was the keynote of His preaching; His parables taught the secrets of accepting it and entering into the flow of its power; His systematic discourses were centered on its true meaning; and the purpose of His passion, Resurrection, and return in power was to establish His reign in the lives of His disciples. All that must have been a part of Paul's teaching there in Rome.

But we are confident that the apostle did not end there. The study of his epistles indicates that Paul used the term "kingdom of God" as the metonym for the continued ministry of the resurrected Christ. During this period he wrote the Philippian epistle in which he declared that Christ had been given a name above every name, "that every tongue should confess that Jesus Christ is Lord, to the glory of God the Father" (Phil. 2:11).

What name is above every name? Yahweh! The name was so sacred to the Hebrews that it was not spoken. *Adonai* became a respectful synonym. To say that Jesus is Lord is to acknowledge that He is God. Thus for Paul all that Jesus did as Jesus of Nazareth was now possible in the believers who accepted His kingly rule as Lord of their lives. The person in whom the Lord lived was to be made like Him in both disposition and attitude. The same healing, miraculous power unleashed in the incarnation was to be the resource and resiliency of the indwelt believer.

And all through Paul's teaching of the kingdom and teaching of Jesus Christ as Lord there in Rome, we assume that he punctuated his exposition and witness with his own story and the countless case histories of people whom he had seen enter the kingdom through rebirth and surrender of their lives to Christ.

In summary, Paul's message of the kingdom was Christ the Lord. As he had written the Corinthians, "For the kingdom of God is not in word but in power" (1 Cor. 4:20). And to the Colossians he asserted that we had been delivered "from the power of darkness and translated into the kingdom of the Son" (Col. 1:13). When the Lord reigns supreme in us, we become the realm of the kingdom. Then, under His guidance, we become "fellow workers for the kingdom" (Col. 4:11) by seeking to know and do His will in every relationship and responsibility.

Entering the kingdom of God by rebirth and living in the dynamic of the King's power are the bases of authentic evangelism, mission, and social action. A kingdom person sees every person and every facet of society as potential realms to be won for the kingdom. We cannot rest easily with injustices or debilitating social conditions.

The servant is not above his Master. We cannot enjoy the kingdom without being engaged in meeting the King's goals. Remember when John the Baptist was put into prison and he sent his disciples to inquire of Jesus as to whether He was the One or whether he should look for another? The Lord replied, "Go and tell John the things you hear and see: The blind receive their sight and the lame walk, the lepers are cleansed and the deaf hear, the dead are raised up and the poor have the gospel preached to them" (Matt. 11:4–5). In effect, Jesus was saying, "Go tell John that these things I am doing are the things of the kingdom. I am doing the works of the kingdom and manifesting the power of the kingdom."

As they departed He said a mysterious thing: "And from the days of John the Baptist until now the kingdom of heaven suffers violence, and the violent take it by force" (v. 12). The meaning is that up to that time the kingdom purposes of God had suffered neglect, but now through the Messiah, those who do violence to their own anarchy, self-will and prejudice, enter the kingdom, adopt its goals, and receive the power of the King. Isaiah 61:1–2 was Jesus' charter. Our work in the kingdom is to do nothing less. We are anointed by His Spirit to bring the gospel to the physically and spiritually poor, heal the brokenhearted, liberate people from the psychological and social captivity, and unbind the self-incarcerated and those who are caught in the sick structures of our society. The acceptable year of the Lord meant that Jubilee Year when debts were cancelled and persons set free. As kingdom people we live in the Jubilee dispensation. We are free to set others free.

As communicators, we wonder if Paul's message of the kingdom will work today. Should the preaching of the kingdom of God be our central message? We live in a country where talk of kings and kingdoms may need amplification. But there is no theme which presses nearer the biblical truth about what it means to make Christ Lord of our lives and realize the unlimited power He offers us. An exposition of the Scriptures explaining the kingdom of God brings people to the crisis of deciding who is ruling and running their lives. But more than that, when we explain the kingdom in terms of the power of the risen Christ in the Holy Spirit, then we can invite our listeners and readers to accept their status as beloved recipients of present and eternal glory. Proclamation of the kingdom unlocks the secret of Christ's message, gives us an opportunity to explain the wonder of being born again as the first step of entering the kingdom, and provides a basis for expanding the amazing resources available to us for adventuresome, obedient service.

2. *The Christian communicator's method.* Luke tells us that Paul was preaching—*kērússōn*—the kingdom of God and teaching—*didáskōn*—the Lord Jesus Christ. Is there a difference? In one sense, no. All great preaching is the communication of dynamic truth, and all creative teaching leads to forceful witness and persuasion. I suggest that the reason Luke used two different words to describe Paul's method was to indicate the way he presented the kingdom and the way he instructed people about the continuing ministry of the risen Lord.

For Paul, the kingdom was a manifestation of grace. It could not be bought or wrought by human effort. With prophetic preaching he declared the new age, the new dispensation of grace instead of law, and he called for people to become new creatures in Christ. He preached what Christ had done. Then he taught the implication for new believers about what Christ continues to do in the receptive mind and heart of a kingdom person. He preached powerfully that the long-awaited Messiah was none other than Jesus Christ the Lord, and then he taught how the new life of walking in the Light should be lived.

The method of proclamation followed by teaching is evident in all of Paul's epistles. In Galatians, for example, Paul declares the new Christians as free and then spells out how to walk in freedom. A Christian preacher also teaches and the Christian teacher is obligated to do more than disseminate information. People are the focus of both. The communication of truth is relational. It is done in the context of caring profoundly. We are not Greeks in our orientation, thinking of truth as ideas or principles. We are followers of the Master Teacher for whom truth was understood in the Hebrew context of "walking in the way of righteousness." Christian truth can never be theoretical. It is inseparably related to the One who said, "I am the truth." In Him the ultimate reality is present. He is God unveiled and undistorted for us to see and respond to. No theory, idea, or ethical mandate can ever be understood or lived apart from living in Him and having Him live in us.

So, as communicators, we are constantly moving back and forth between proclamation of what Christ did and instruction about what He does. We are to incite and instruct, excite and explain, dramatize and delineate. And all are part of any great sermon or teaching. Truth in Christ is known if it is done and done if it is known. Changed lives are the final test of both preaching and teaching.

Our study of Acts has called us to the urgent task of proclamation and instruction about the kingdom and age of the Holy Spirit. That gives us a lifetime assignment to communicate the biblical truth about who the Holy Spirit is as the risen Lord continuing His ministry today and about the unlimited power available through His indwelling presence in us and His intervening strength for our struggles.

3. *The Christian communicator's magnanimity.* Paul's message and method were maximized by a magnanimous attitude. He *"received all who came to him"* (Acts 28:30). He was open and receptive because he knew that all who came had been liberated to come by the Holy Spirit. The desire was His gift. Paul was not running a popularity contest, constantly measuring his own effectiveness. All of life was a free gift of grace. By grace, he had been set free, by grace he had become a new

man, by grace he was used magnificently as an agent of reconciliation, by grace he was called into the kingdom and given an intimate relationship with the King. He knew that the people in his quarters there in Rome were being given the capacity to hear and the gift of faith to respond. No wonder he preached and taught with confidence.

Luke's final phrase in Acts provides us a striking conclusion to our exposition—*"no one forbidding him."* The Greek word *akōlútōs* is from *kōlúō,* to hinder. What Luke means is that no one forbade Paul from preaching and teaching with boldness. There are several reasons for this. By the Lord's grace and intervention, the apostle was permitted a private dwelling. Festus's interpretation of the charges against Paul and centurion Julius's experience with him on the voyage to Rome may have convinced the captain of the guard in Rome that Paul had done nothing deserving solitary confinement. Added to that, the guards to whom Paul was chained did not stop him from receiving visitors and communicating the gospel to them. Tradition has it that many of the guards had to be relieved of the duty because they were becoming Christians. That idea is validated by what Paul wrote to the Philippians about the way the Lord used his imprisonment.

We picture what it might have been like to be chained to the apostle Paul! Those guards did not hinder him because many of them came to realize that he was bonded to Someone else. As the rotating guards did their duty, they were forced to listen to Paul and watch the results in the lives of people. They could not resist the impelling exposure to the living Christ. And the Lord Himself had created the permissive attitude of those guards.

Most important of all, Paul was not hindered by Paul! He set no limits on what Christ could do. It was from that same dwelling in Rome, while chained to a guard, that he wrote, "I can do all things through Christ who strengthens me" (Phil 4:13). And so can we, regardless of the circumstances in which we are called to be communicators.

The Lord is the author of authentic revival. He creates the receptivity and opens the way for response. Our calling is to pray and then communicate with boldness. He will deal with the problems of resistance and make them opportunities for even greater effectiveness. The church in America has never been more ready for the preaching and teaching of Acts. A magnanimous communicator is one who has experienced what is preached or taught. That releases him or her to reach out with love to people. And when people are loved, they are conditioned to receive what we communicate.

The propitious, powerful age of the kingdom is now. Christ in the power of the Spirit is doing what He did as Jesus of Nazareth. The Acts of the Holy Spirit continue in our churches, pulpits, and classrooms. Nothing or no one can ultimately hinder Him. He is the divine Logos, the Creator and Recreator, the Healer, the Liberator, the indwelling fullness of the Godhead. He is the Lord! We can confidently expect miracles, changed lives, and churches on fire with joy and power. And why not?

BIBLIOGRAPHY

Bruce, F. F. *The Acts of the Apostles.* The Greek Text with Introduction and Commentary. 1951. Reprint. Grand Rapids: Wm. B. Eerdmans Publishing Co., 1968.

Cadbury, H. J. *The Book of Acts in History.* New York: Harper & Bros., 1955.

Dodd, C. H. *The Apostolic Preaching and Its Development.* New York: Harper & Bros., 1937.

Foakes-Jackson, F. J. *The Acts of the Apostles.* In The Moffatt New Testament Commentary. London: Hodder and Stoughton, 1960.

_____. and Lake, Kirsopp. *The Acts of the Apostles.* Part 1 of *The Beginnings of Christianity,* vols. 4 and 5. Reprint. Grand Rapids: Baker Book House, 1965.

Hobart, W. K. *The Medical Language of St. Luke.* Dublin: n.p., 1882.

Josephus. *Jewish Antiquities.* Loeb Classical Library. 1957.

_____. *The Jewish War.* Loeb Classical Library. 1956.

Kallas, James. *The Story of Paul.* Minneapolis: Augsburg Publishing House, 1966.

Kent, Homer A., Jr. *Jerusalem to Rome: Studies in Acts.* Winona Lake, Ind.: BMH Books, 1976.

Kittel, Gerhard, and Friedrich, Gerhard, eds. *Theological Dictionary of the New Testament.* 10 vols. Grand Rapids: Eerdmans Publishing Co., 1964–1976.

Luccock, Halford E. *The Acts of the Apostles in Present Day Preaching.* New York: Harper & Bros., 1938.

Maclaren, Alexander. *The Acts of the Apostles.* London: Hodder and Stoughton, 1907.

Morgan, G. Campbell. *The Acts of the Apostles.* 13th ed. New York: Fleming H. Revell Co., 1924.

Novum Testamentum Graece. Ed. Eberhard Nestle, Edwin Nestle, and Kurt Aland. 20th printing. Stuttgart: Wurttembergische Biblanstalt, 1950.

Ramsay, William M. *The Cities of St. Paul.* Reprint. Grand Rapids: Baker Book House, 1949.

_____. *St. Paul the Traveler and the Roman Citizen.* Reprint. Grand Rapids: Baker Book House, 1949.

Robertson, A. T. *The Acts of the Apostles.* In *Word Pictures of the New Testament.* New York: Harper & Bros., 1931.

Stagg, Frank. *The Book of Acts.* Nashville: Broadman Press, 1955.

Stewart, James S. *A Man in Christ: The Vital Elements of St. Paul's Religion.* New York: Harper & Bros., 1935.

Studies in the Acts of the Apostles. London: Student Christian Movement, 1956.

Vine, W. E. *Expositor's Dictionary of Bible Words.* 1940. Reprint. London: Marshall Morgan and Scott, 1979.